THE BIG
THAW

SUNY series in Environmental Governance:
Local-Regional-Global Interactions

Peter Stoett and Owen Temby, editors

THE BIG THAW

POLICY, GOVERNANCE, AND CLIMATE CHANGE IN THE CIRCUMPOLAR NORTH

Edited by

Ezra B. W. Zubrow, Errol Meidinger, and Kim Diana Connolly

SUNY
PRESS

Published by State University of New York Press, Albany

For information, contact State University of New York Press, Albany, NY
www.sunypress.edu

Library of Congress Cataloging-in-Publication Data

Names: Zubrow, Ezra B. W., editor. | Meidinger, Errol, editor. | Connolly, Kim Diana, editor.
Title: The big thaw : policy, governance, and climate change in the circumpolar north / edited by Ezra Zubrow, Errol Meidinger, Kim Diana Connolly.
Description: Albany : State University of New York Press, [2019] | Series: SUNY series in environmental governance | Includes bibliographical references and index.
Identifiers: LCCN 2018043675 | ISBN 9781438475639 (hardcover) | ISBN 9781438475646 (pbk.) | ISBN 9781438475653 (ebook) Subjects: LCSH: Global warming. | Climatic changes. | Arctic regions—Climate. | Arctic regions—Environmental conditions.
Classification: LCC QC981.8.G56 B45945 2019 | DDC 363.738/74609113—dc23
LC record available at https://lccn.loc.gov/2018043675

10 9 8 7 6 5 4 3 2 1

*The editors wish to dedicate this volume
to our families and to the
inspirational peoples of the Arctic.*

Contents

PART 1

PART 2

Illustrations

Tables

Figures

Foreword

OWEN TEMBY AND PETER STOETT

Ezra Zubrow, Errol Meidinger, and Kim Diana Connolly have edited what they refer to in their conclusion as an elegy, defined as "a piece of writing . . . imbued with a sense of mourning or melancholy affection for something." That "something" is the vast expanse known as the Arctic, and it is changing at a rapid pace before our eyes.

Based initially on the proceedings from a conference held at the Baldy Center for Law and Social Policy at the University at Buffalo in 2013 with funding from the Baldy Center and the National Science Foundation Polar Program's Social Science Division, the text has evolved since the conference to reflect other developments in the climate change science and policy landscape, but its essential thrust remains: the Arctic is changing as the global climate changes. It is changing faster than other areas, and we are just beginning to understand the implications of this shift not only for circumpolar states but for the indigenous peoples living in Arctic regions and, indeed, the rest of the world. Few books have taken on this complexity, and The Big Thaw is one of them.

Once considered a mysterious region, the Arctic is now subject to intense scrutiny by academics, industrialists, governments, environmentalists, and many others. This volume reflects the breadth of interest in the future of the Arctic as climate change manifests with numerous geophysical changes. The threats to biodiversity are well known; the impact of melting ice sheets on global sea levels is alarming; the cultural threats to Arctic civilizations are perhaps less popularized in the media but are slowly raising serious concern.

This SUNY series focuses on the links between local and global environmental governance issues and policy. The Arctic is a firm example of how important these linkages are, and many of the chapters in this well-referenced and varied volume capture this complexity. We trust it will add to the growing literature on the impact of climate change in the Arctic and inspire readers to learn more and take commensurate action to limit climate change before the elegy presented here is even more mournful and irreversible.

1

In the Vortex of the Thaw

General Introduction

EZRA B. W. ZUBROW, ERROL MEIDINGER,
AND KIM DIANA CONNOLLY

[I]n almost every case, even down to the level of specific communities, there are likely to be winners and losers almost living next
door to one another. The issue is to understand how the downside
and upside is distributed across the Arctic from natural ecologies
to human activities.

—Professor David Vaughan, Director of Science
at the British Antarctic Survey

The captain had been telling how, in one of his Arctic voyages, it
was so cold that the mate's shadow froze fast to the deck and had
to be ripped loose by main strength. And even then he got only
about two-thirds of it back.

—Samuel Clemens, *Following the Equator*

Climate Change is Real, and It Is Impacting the Arctic

Climate change is one of the drivers of global change. Some aspects of
causation and control are controversial. But experts agree on one thing:

climate change is real.[1] And those who have looked at how climate change is impacting the Arctic region agree that it is catalyzing change across systems in multiple and profound ways.

Many experts in various disciplines have explored climate change issues in the Arctic in recent years. This book has been written to add a unique transdisplinary perspective, bringing together diverse expert contemplations of climate change across various Arctic systems and offering complementary perspectives. It aims to provide readers with further insight into information they may already have while also offering new information delivered from unique perspectives that may suggest new ways to contemplate our thawing world.

What proof is there that climate change is real? The United States National Aeronautics and Space Administration (NASA) presents monthly updates of the planet's vital signs. In 2016, NASA reported that carbon dioxide in the atmosphere reached 404.48 parts per million—the highest in 650,000 years.[2] The worldwide average global temperature has risen 1.4 degrees Fahrenheit—the highest since 1880. Arctic ice has been shrinking at a rate of 13.4 percent per decade. The land ice is decreasing about 281 gigatonnes per year. Greenland's land ice loss doubled between 1995 and 2005. Global average sea level has risen nearly seven inches over the last 100 years. Together, these proxies indicate substantial climate change.

Moreover, the United Nation's Intergovernmental Panel on Climate Change (IPCC) has released multiple installments of detailed expert assessments over the years.[3] It is in its sixth assessment cycle and has offered proof again and again, with increasing specificity, that climate change is undeniable. As one set of experts participating in the IPCC work remarked several years ago, "Dramatic changes to the lives and livelihoods of Arctic-living communities are being forecast unless urgent action is taken to reduce greenhouse gases, according to the Intergovernmental Panel on Climate Change (IPCC)."[4]

This very real climate change is of central importance today for individuals, communities, states, nations, and the world. Foretelling what he now calls "climate reality," former vice president Al Gore was part of an early call to action by telling the world about the "inconvenient truth" of climate change and starting a "crusade"[5] Gore stated in his book entitled *Earth in the Balance* that "[w]e can believe in the future and work to achieve it and preserve it, or we can whirl blindly on, behaving as if one day there will be no children to inherit our legacy. The choice is ours; the earth is in balance."[6] A quick Google search reveals many hundreds of thousands of reports, books, websites, conferences, etc. since 1992 talking about climate change and this balance. Yet to paraphrase a saying attributed to Samuel Clemens, everyone is talking about climate change, but only a few are doing something about it.

Is this surprising? Coping with the challenges of climate change is a daunting enterprise for all of us. From natural scientists and engineers to social scientists, from economists, artists, and musicians to individuals—all are called upon to comprehend alternative futures and plan to adapt or otherwise cope. Yet it is not easy.

Policymakers and politicians will be increasingly called upon not only to understand, but also to make hard choices in our thawing world. They must decide on both short-term responses and dedication of resources and long-term strategies to balance risks and costs. In doing so, they will be forced to reconcile and stabilize many difficult and tense relationships among communities, interest groups, and governments. The regular IPCC Conferences of the Parties attempt to bring world leaders together regularly.[7] Yet politics in various powerful nations[8] and among various organizations[9] can create barriers to meaningful progress. Moreover, the unique nature of the Arctic itself, with its multiple nations and various laws governing the environment, adds even more of a challenge to crafting a meaningful and achievable response.[10]

This edited volume draws together writings from acute observers with different perspectives. It considers pressing issues of how climate change in the Arctic is affecting, and will continue to affect, environments, cultures, societies, and economies throughout the world. It explores how these sectors are actually responding, are capable of responding, and, in many cases, it makes suggestions as to how they should respond going forward.

The Arctic Is Special,
and It Is Threatened by Climate Change

Long ago, scientists who studied the Arctic discovered that climate change transpires in that region between two to four times faster than elsewhere on this planet.[11] Experts believe Arctic climate change is a forerunner and a predictor of forthcoming ecological transformation that will sweep the planet.

Some have come to view the Arctic as the earth's "environmental canary." In days gone by, when a caged canary taken into mines stopped singing, coal miners knew that the carbon monoxide gas level was so high that they had to escape the chamber. The thawing Arctic may be the earth's early warning system.[12]

Few who know the Arctic will dispute that temperatures are "a-rising," the sea and land ice is "a-melting," the permafrost is "a-thawing," and the natural and human ecosystems are "a-changing." While these realities are increasingly accepted—they are also increasingly alarming. As one recent popular online magazine termed it, "The melting arctic has become this decade's Amazon deforestation crisis. There's no Sting album or fair trade coffee fundraiser, but the world's attention turns north with each piece of distressing news of the catastrophic polar melt."[13]

Yet, the scientific realities underlying these realities beg for more. Increased carbon dioxide absorbed into the ocean creates carbonic acid. The colder Arctic Ocean then absorbs more carbon dioxide, making it extra acidic. At the same time, patchy permafrost (which is particularly conducive to thawing) encounters ground temperatures within 1 to 2 degrees of thawing, catalyzing even more disappearing ice across the Arctic.[14]

The changing ecology means life and culture must shift. The Arctic's human population is approximately 4 million people in eight countries who live in a wide range of situations. Some live in modern industrial cities, some in pastoral and hunting and gathering settlements, and others in entirely different situations. For all, melting permafrost, reduced ice, and warming temperatures undermine necessary conditions for human survival. The people who live in the Arctic depend on reliable roads and buildings, stable hunting, and sufficient and safe pastoral ranges. At the same time, increasing sea levels destroy coastal towns and change fishing patterns.[15] However, some parts of the complex interaction may not always be detrimental.[16]

Rising temperatures have increased the growing season in the Arctic. The result is changed ecosystems with increased diversity. NASA has observed a 7–10 percent increase in vegetation, resulting in a ring of greening by trees and shrubs around what was previously tundra in the far northern latitudes. This is complemented and augmented by melting sea ice that opens many thousands of square miles of ocean, providing homes for large, new populations of phytoplankton.[17]

In considering why the Arctic is just a bit different than other areas in the era of climate change, recall that the earth depends on two worldwide environmental systems. The first, which covers the entire globe, is the atmospheric system. The second, which covers approximately 71 percent of the world, is the oceanic system. Each system is a connected whole—what happens in one part will impact other parts. And the interplay between the two is played out intensely in the Arctic Region.[18] A number of chapter authors help bring this to light. And climate change's impact on the culture in the Arctic is unique, a story that is explored by other chapter authors. Yet more authors explore another reality: it is more than the physical and cultural environment that must be considered when talking about climate change in the Arctic—the political environment comes into play as well. Some developments as this book was coming into being help illustrate this fact.

Modern Politics and the Arctic:
The Polar Code, President Obama, The Paris Agreement,
President Trump, and Other Actors

This book took several years to get to press. A number of events have occurred since the conference that initially brought the authors together, and a brief discussion of them highlights some relevant context for the political and policy-based discourse in the coming chapters.

First, in light of the impact on shipping of the thawing Arctic, shortly after The Big Thaw conference, new safety-related requirements addressing operating ships in polar waters were adopted by the 94th session of the Maritime Safety Committee in November 2014. Thereafter, at the 68th session of the Marine Environment Protection Committee of the International Maritime Organization from 11–15 May 2015, updated environmental provisions of the International Code for Ships Operating in Polar Waters (Polar Code) were formally adopted, completing the creation of the Polar Code. One scholar praises the safety aspects of the code but raises concerns about the environmental protections as follows: "The adoption of a mandatory Polar Code is no doubt good news for the Arctic. The Polar Code provides improved and uniform safety and environmental standards for shipping in the Arctic. The International Maritime Organization has responded to international community concerns regarding increased shipping activities in an ice-free Arctic relatively quickly. One should not, however, overestimate the role of the Polar Code for the prevention of vessel-source pollution in the Arctic. The Polar Code has left several issues of vessel-source pollution for another day."[19] The passage of the Polar Code, regardless of its eventual impact, is a strong signal of the changing views of ship traffic and commerce in Arctic waters.

Second, in 2015 Barack Obama became the first sitting U.S. president to visit the Arctic.[20] His speech upon his departure lamented the damage that climate change had already brought to this region, and he urged action, noting that "a very serious reality lies within those breathtaking sights. And that's the fact that this state's climate is changing before our eyes. A couple of days ago, I stood on rock where, just 10 years ago, there was a glacier. Yesterday, I flew over Kivalina Island, an Arctic town that's already losing land to the sea from erosion and further threatened by sea-level rise. I've seen shores that have been left battered by storm surges that used to be contained by ice. And now, that ice is gone."[21] This commitment to Arctic protection was cemented in the closing months of his administration, when President Obama's Department of the Interior announced an energy plan precluding drilling in the Arctic that stated, "Considering the fragile and unique Arctic ecosystem and the recent demonstrated decline in industry interest, the Proposed Final Program does not include any lease sales in the Chukchi or Beaufort Seas. Based on consideration of the best available science and significant public input, the Department's analysis identified significant risks to sensitive marine resources and communities from potential new leasing in the Arctic. Moreover, due to the high costs associated with exploration and development in the Arctic and the foreseeable low projected oil prices environment, demonstrated industry interest in new leasing currently is low."[22] President Obama faced critics in his work regarding the Arctic and climate change, and the final upshot of his legacy will continue to unfold over time.

Third, this book was being edited when a pivotal worldwide event took place in 2015 addressing climate change: The Paris Agreement was negotiated and came into force. This agreement was made within the United Nations Framework Convention on Climate Change (UNFCCC) and addresses greenhouse gases emissions, mitigation, adaptation, and finance starting in the year 2020. Representatives from 197 nations negotiated the language of the agreement at the 21st Conference of the Parties of the UNFCCC in Paris, adopting it by consensus on December 12, 2015. Formally opened for signature on April 22, 2016 (Earth Day) at a ceremony in New York, the European Union's ratification in

October 2016 meant that it entered into force shortly thereafter. At its heart, this agreement committed the global community to limiting the temperature increase to below 2 degrees Celsius and involves myriad and complex commitments.[23]

Fourth, the United States elected Donald Trump as its 45th president. President Trump has vowed to remove the United States from the Paris Agreement, and he recommitted to recent views that he held as a private citizen to deny the reality of climate change. For example, in 2012 Mr. Trump posted on Twitter that "the concept of global warming was created by and for the Chinese in order to make U.S. manufacturing non-competitive." After his election, Mr. Trump reiterated this belief as well as campaign promises to pull the United States from the Paris Agreement. He has also indicated support for drilling in the Arctic National Wildlife Refuge. A shift in U.S. policy began during the last part of the United States holding the chair position at the Arctic Council (through 2017).[24] President Trump actively tweets climate denial, and experts respond, including one Arctic expert, who noted, "The top of the world is now warming at twice the average global rate. . . . Since 1979, peak sea-ice coverage has fallen from about 6.5 million to 5.5 million square miles. At the dawn of the 20th century, it took the great polar explorer Roald Amundsen three years and three icebound winters to sail the fabled Northwest Passage at the top of the continent. Today ships steam right through, and forecasters predict that the entire Arctic Ocean may be ice-free in summer 2050."[25]

Fifth and finally, the youth of the planet are raising their voices. There has been intense attention to the youth climate lawsuit filed in 2015, *Juliana v. United States*, which asserts that affirmative U.S. government actions causing climate change violate the youngest generation's constitutional rights to life, liberty, and property, as well as fail to protect essential public trust resources.[26] Likewise, young political activists are getting attention, such as Greta Thunberg, the 15-year-old from Sweden who captured the hearts of people in 2018 with statements such as, "We cannot solve a crisis without treating it as a crisis."[27] Simultaneously, organizations such as the United Nations are highlighting youth action on climate change as "helping all of us change the way we live and do business."[28] It is the voices of Arctic youth who often appear in campaigns to warn of the impacts of Arctic climate change that they have been witnessing all their lives, and to urge action.[29] Readers may notice that the urgent messages of these youth efforts are mirrored in some content woven through various chapters of this book.

Readers should remain aware that some of the chapters in this book reflect data and developments that are several years old. This is inevitable, as the many changes that are happening in the Arctic on all levels are moving swiftly, and the political landscapes are ever shifting. As the next section explains, the contributions compiled here nevertheless contain a tapestry of insights that will contribute to considerations and debate about Arctic climate change going forward.

What This Book Is Designed to Do

This Book Presents Findings from a 2013 Conference

This book, *The Big Thaw: Policy, Governance, and Climate Change in the Circumpolar North*, is the result of an international conference held at the Baldy Center for Law & Social Policy at the University at Buffalo on April18–19, 2013. The conference was financed in part by a grant from the Baldy Center and additionally from the National Science Foundation's Polar Program's Social Science Division. There was further sponsorship from the University at Buffalo Anthropology Department, the School of Law, and other university departments. The event brought together academics, lawyers, and policy planners as well as Arctic fishing boat sea captains and representatives of indigenous hunting and trapping organizations. There was rousing conversation and an interest in building on the transdisciplinary conversation going forward.

This Book Collects Ideas to Inspire Further Thinking

The Big Thaw was created to bring together the learning that grew out of the original conference papers, nurtured by the conference discussions and reflected in two sets of revisions of each of the chapters. Together, these chapters provide a set of collected ideas that allow readers to think through these profoundly complicated and multicausal issues. To help guide the reader, the book is divided into three themes.

The first theme focuses on actual physical changes in the Arctic. That section offers evidence-based commentary on what has been and is actually happening in the Arctic, from a variety of disciplines. The second theme considers Arctic policy and governance at all scales: international, national, community, and individual. It helps connect the physical to the political and provides insights into what makes the issues so complex. The third theme concentrates on culture and community. It acknowledges the mosaic of indigenous and nonindigenous populations with a diversity of economies, ideologies, and religions as well as dissimilar agendas that makes for a very complex set of interrelationships.

The current climate situation leading to the conference and this book has come to be known as *The Big Thaw* for a variety of reasons. First, although there have been previous periods of global cooling and warming, this time is turning out to be a considerably more serious period of global warming than anticipated by anyone. The rate of climate change and associated ecosystem shifts are occurring at a faster pace than predicted by scientists, policymakers, and politicians. It is "big" in many ways. It is large quantitatively, it is vast geographically, it is enormous in its environmental and cultural impact, and it is immense in the effort necessary to address and ameliorate.

Second, the book is titled *The Big Thaw* because it really is a thaw. The word *thaw* is both a verb (process) and a noun (event). As a verb, this thawing involves icecaps, glaciers, snow, hail, and other frozen substances, such as permafrost, to dramatically change: They unfreeze, dissolve, melt, liquefy, and change their state into other forms. As an event, this thawing is a period—a period of time characterized by heightened temperatures that have environmental and human consequences.

Third, the current climate is not only a change in what had occurred before: it is now and going forward as well. The Big Thaw is neither binary (thawing or not thawing), nor episodic. It is continuously incremental. Climate change is continuing to warm the atmosphere and the oceans. It is melting ice caps as well as large amounts of snow and glacier ice. It is changing the boundaries between environmental zones— and consequently changing the boundaries of the cultural and political world. Climate change is changing the Arctic (and other environments on our planet) into a new world. The new world of the Arctic will be where the Northwest Passage is open, Franklin's ships are found, oil and fishing are possible near the pole, and nations send fighter planes and naval ships to defend frozen wilderness.

Fourth, if globally incremental, climate change is locally far more variable. Across the planet, extreme climate and its consequent extreme weather events are becoming more frequent, less predictable, and considerably more intense. Monsoon seasons have changed and tsunamis such as the one that devastated Ache, Indonesia, and large parts of the Asian Pacific shoreline have created an apprehensive mentality not seen since the early-nineteenth-century influenza epidemics or the

Cold War. This mentality is reflected in decision makers wringing their collective hands, populations living in fear, and profit-making popular culture such as major motion pictures using climate change as a plot. Some examples of such movies include *The Thaw* (in which the melting polar ice cap has released a deadly prehistoric parasite), *The Steam Experiment* (in which a deranged scientist threatens to kill six hostages if the local paper does not publish his story about global warming), and *The Day After Tomorrow* (a father seeking to rescue his son from catastrophic climatic effects following the disruption of the North Atlantic Ocean circulation that ushers in a new ice age).

Climate change creates a potential conundrum in terms of the planet's population. On one hand, the global population is increasing—it is now well over seven billion. Prior to the twentieth century, no person had lived through a doubling of world population, but there are people now who have seen a tripling during their lifetimes. On the other hand, if climate change is, as expected, sufficient to melt the polar icecap, the Greenland ice sheet, and the Antarctica ice sheet, the world's coastal populations could diminish drastically. A 40-centemeter rise stands to impact at least 100 million people. Some posit that unchecked climate change would not only stabilize the population but also cause it to decrease.[30]

Yet this Big Thaw should not be a surprise. Humans have been warned about it for more than a decade. The IPCC issued its first assessment report in 1990.[31] Now it seems that these projections were underestimations. The projected global rise in temperature by the end of the century thought to be 2 degrees Celsius has been doubled to 4 degrees Celsius. Sea level is rising 60 percent faster than predicted, and the Greenland ice sheet is shrinking twice as fast—and even more importantly, the mass lost is five times what was thought in 1990.[32]

Table 1.1. Number of people impacted by type of climate disasters worldwide from 1975 to 2001[33]

	Drought	Flood	Windstorm
	1,100,000,000	2,100,000,000	416,000,000
Africa	222,000,000	29,000,000	9,000,000
Latin America	48,000,000	40,000,000	22,000,000
Oceania	9,000,000	500,000	6,000,000
Europe	6,000,000	8,000,000	8,000,000
North America	30,000	800,000	300,0000

It is vital to keep in mind that the Big Thaw affects politics, economics, security, and community. A sea-level change impacts the mega-deltas and food production. Population displacement will create potential conflict from the recipient developed countries. Examples of the impact of climate migrations are easily found. For instance, consider Bangladesh. Given land loss, land degradation, and increasing violent storms, agricultural scarcity has resulted in 12 to 17 million Bangladeshis moving to India and at least a half-million moving internally.

Table 1.2. Climate-induced migration, comparing the number of people moving and the intensity of resulting conflicts

Origin	Number moving	Conflict intensity
1. Bangladesh, 1970s–1990s	600,000	High
2. Ethiopia: (a) central/northern; (b) Awash river basin/Afar, 1984–1985	600,000	Medium
3. Rwanda, rural south, center, early 1990s	1.7 million	Very high
4. Mexico, Southern Guatemala, 1960s–1990s	280,000	High
5. Bangladesh, various regions 1950s–present	12–17 million	High
6. El Salvador, 1950s–1980s	300,000 to Honduras, 500,000 to United States	Very high
7. Ethiopia/Eritrea, 1960s–1980s	1.1 million	Medium
8. Mauritania, 1980s–1990s	69,000	High
9. Somalia, late 1970s	400,000	Medium
10. Haiti, north, 1970s–1990s	1.3 million	Medium
11. Philippines, lowlands, 1970s–1990s	4.3 million	High
12. South Africa, black areas 1970s–1980s	Up to 750,000 per year	Medium
13. Sahel, rural areas, late 1960s–1980s	10 million	Medium
14. Brazil, northeast, 1960s–present	8 million	Medium
15. Sudan, north, south, west, 1970s–1980s	3.5–4 million by early 1990	High
16. United States, Great Plains, 1930s	2.5 million	Medium
17. Ethiopia, late 1970s	450,000	Very high
18. Nigeria, Jos Plateau, 1970s–1990s	n/a	Medium
19. Pakistan, 1980s–1990s	n/a	Medium

Was the Big Thaw a historical surprise? Perhaps. Until recently, many held a conceptual fixity about the climate. Even if it was variable, all but a few believed changes were ephemeral and not incremental until the end of the last century.[34]

Moreover, the Arctic of old was marginal—colonially, demographically, and economically. It was (generously speaking) a place of mystery, adventure, and obscurity, occupied by the Tungus, Sami, Yakuts, Chukchee, Inuit, and others. In reality, the Arctic was largely ignored by most for many centuries because it had few people, few resources, and even its geography was generally unknown. It was considered by some to be the last frontier for a time. While Stanley was exploring Africa in the 1870s, Peary and Cook were trying to reach the North Pole in the first decade of the twentieth century.

More recently, fairly rapid demarginalization of the Arctic took place because of what was there. As the need for resources changed the shape of the earth, nonnative people ventured forth into that last frontier. Sequentially, outsiders have sought access in the Arctic to fur, gold, and oil. Shipping lanes will be next.

The now-changing Arctic may be seen as a precursor for what could happen to the rest of the earth in the era of climate change. Although originally a surprise to most, in retrospect one understands how the cultural and environmental Arctic of today is a long-term result of the evolutionary dynamics of both the environment and the humans who adapted to it.

Science has shown a coherent structure in the turbulent flows of climate change. While complex, the Big Thaw has understandable causes. Likewise, the degree of incompressibility at its core is nevertheless intuitively clear. The Big Thaw creates change and then communicates and exports change to other systems. Change impacts civilization on all scales: international, national, state, municipality, and even smaller communities.

Thank you for reading this book and joining a journey that began in 2013 at The Big Thaw conference at the University at Buffalo, State University of New York. A thaw is really happening. It is big. It will impact many people and systems. So, interested minds must come together to learn, understand, and plan. As editors, the three of us hope that you will find this book interesting, useful, and motivating.

Notes

1. See Robert Sweeney, "Analysis: The Most 'Cited' Climate Change Papers," Carbon Brief, July 2015; https://www.carbonbrief.org/analysis-the-most-cited-climate-change-papers.

2. See generally http://climate.nasa.gov/.

3. See generally IPCC's website, https://www.ipcc.ch/.

4. United Nations Environment Programme, Science Daily, "IPCC Report—The Arctic: Thawing Permafrost, Melting Sea Ice And More Significant Changes," April 11, 2007; https://www.sciencedaily.com/releases/2007/04/070410140922.htm. See also R. A. Black, J. P. Bruce, and I. D. M. Egener, "Managing the Risks of Climate Change: A Guide for Arctic and Northern Communities"; http://ccrm-cier.redrockconsulting.com/2019.

5. See *The Climate Reality Project*, https://www.algore.com/project/the-climate-reality-project.

6. Al Gore, *Earth in the Balance: Ecology and the Human Spirit* (Boston: Houghton Mifflin 1992), 393.

7. For a list of IPCC meetings related to climate change, see United Nations Framework Convention on Climate Change, Meetings, http://unfccc.int/meetings/items/6240.php.

8. S. Childress, "Timeline: The Politics of Climate Change," PBS, Oct. 23, 2012; http://www.pbs.org/wgbh/frontline/article/timeline-the-politics-of-climate-change/.

9. See J. Light, "Five Groups Fighting Climate Change," *Moyers and Company*, Feb. 7, 2014; http://billmoyers.com/2014/02/07/five-groups-leading-the-charge-to-halt-climate-change/.

10. J. F. DiMento, "Environmental Governance of the Arctic: Law, Effect, Now Implementation," *UC Irvine Law Review* 2016; https://papers.ssrn.com/sol3/papers.cfm?abstract_id=2853673.

11. See, e.g., I. Krupnik and D. Jolly, eds., "The Earth Is Faster Now: Indigenous Observations of Arctic Environmental Change" (Fairbanks, AK: *Arctic Research Consortium of the United States*, 2002).

12. S. Duyck, "Which Canary in the Coalmine? The Arctic in the International Climate Change Regime," *The Yearbook of Polar Law, Volume 4*, 2012.

13. E. Niiler, "The Arctic Is Melting, and Fast. But Maybe Data Can Save It," *Wired*, Sept. 28, 2016; https://www.wired.com/2016/09/arctic-melting-fast-maybe-data-can-save/.

14. National Snow and Ice Data Center, University of Colorado, Boulder, "Arctic Sea Ice News and Analysis," 2016; http://nsidc.org/arcticseaicenews/.

15. F. Duerden, "Translating Climate Change Impacts at the Community Level," *Arctic* 57, no. 2 (June 2004); http://www.jstor.org/stable/40512620.

16. For example, Patrick Charupata has shown that climate change has had no impact on the stress or reproductive status of the Prudhoe walrus. P. Charupata "Back to the Future: The Stress and Reproductive Status of the Picabe Walrus"; Scholar Works at University of Alaska.

17. NASA, "NASA Studies Details of a Greening Arctic," June 2, 2016; https://www.nasa.gov/feature/goddard/2016/nasa-studies-details-of-a-greening-arctic.

18. W. Perrie, Z. Long, H. Hung, A. Cole, A. Steffen, A. Dastoor, D. Durnford, J. Ma, J. W. Bottenheim, S. Netcheva, R. Staebler, J. R. Drummond, and N. T. O'Neill, "Selected Topics in Arctic Atmosphere and Climate," *Climatic Change* (Springer) 115, Issue 1 (Nov. 2012).

19. N. Liu, "Can the Polar Code Save the Arctic?" American Society of International Law (ASIL) *Insights* 20, Issue 7, March 22, 2106; https://www.asil.org/insights/volume/20/issue/7/can-polar-code-save-arctic.

20. President Obama's Trip to Alaska, The White House, Aug. 31, 2015; https://www.whitehouse.gov/2015-alaska-trip.

21. Ibid.

22. Office of the Secretary, Department of the Interior, "Secretary Jewell Announces Offshore Oil and Gas Leasing Plan for 2017–2022: Plan Offers 70 Percent of Economically Recoverable Resources While Ensuring Protection of Critical Areas, Including the Arctic," Nov. 18, 2016; https://www.doi.gov/pressreleases/secretary-jewell-announces-offshore-oil-and-gas-leasing-plan-2017-2022.

23. UNFCCC, "The Paris Agreement"; http://unfccc.int/paris_agreement/items/9485.php.

24. Arctic Council, "U.S. Chairmanship 2015–2017," Secretary of State John Kerry, chair of the Arctic Counsel under President Obama, listed three focus areas, the last of which was "Addressing the Impacts of Climate Change."

25. E. Scigliano, "LETTER FROM THE ARCTIC: Trump Says Climate Change Isn't Real. My Trip to the Top of the World Proved Otherwise," Politico, Nov. 27, 2018: www.politico.com/magazine/story/2018/11/27/trump-says-climate-change-isnt-real-my-trip-to-the-top-of-the-world-proved-otherwise-222691.

26. "JULIANA v. UNITED STATES: Youth Climate Lawsuit," Our Childrens Trust; www.ourchildrenstrust.org/juliana-v-us.

27. "Greta Thunberg," Wikipedia; https://en.wikipedia.org/wiki/Greta_Thunberg. For more about Thunberg and other youth activists, see also E. Bloch, "15-Year-Old Activist Greta Thunberg Schooled World Leaders on Climate Change at a United Nations Summit," Teen Vogue, Dec. 5, 2018; www.teenvogue.com/story/15-year-old-activist-greta-thunberg-schooled-world-leaders-climate-change-united-nations-summit.

28. United Nations, "Youth for Climate Action"; https://unfccc.int/topics/education-and-outreach/workstreams/youth-engagement.

29. B. Hill and S. Fayne Wood, "ARCTIC YOUTH WITNESS TO CLIMATE CHANGE: Profiling Alaskan Youth to Tell the Story of Direct Impacts of Climate Change in the Arctic," Survival Media Agency, May 2016; http://survivalmediaagency.com/project/arctic-youth-witness-to-climate-change/.

30. National Center for Science Education, "How Will Climate Change Affect the World and Society?"; https://ncse.com/library-resource/how-will-climate-change-affect-world-society.

31. IPCC, "Climate Change: The IPCC Scientific Assessment," 1990; www.ipcc.ch/publications_and_data/publications_ipcc_first_assessment_1990_wg1.shtml.

32. NASA, "Climate Change: How Do We Know?"; http://climate.nasa.gov/evidence/.

33. R. Reuveny, "Climate Change–induced Migration and Violent Conflict," Political Geography 26, Issue 6 (Aug. 2007).

34. S. Weart, American Institute of Physics, 2016, "The Discovery of Global Warming"; http://history.aip.org/history/climate/timeline.htm.

PART 1

2

Red Sky in Morning, Sailors Take Warning

Forewarnings from a Thawing Arctic

Ezra B. W. Zubrow, Errol Meidinger,
and Kim Diana Connolly

Yes, Virginia, there really is a "big thaw." It exists and it is changing the Arctic (and the Antarctic)—as the ice sheets are diminishing and the glaciers are retreating, they herald a new era of climate transformation worldwide.

Climate can be viewed as a dialogue between the decades. One generation's actions impact not only the next generation, but all the following as well. And our generation has created a chain reaction having a domino impact over time.

The first chapters of the book involve the scientific and observational characteristics of climate change. The next section will emphasize the political-legal framework, and the last section will address advocacy and the humanities.

There are several aspects of climate change that are noted in the next scientific chapters that we wish to emphasize. First, climate change is systemically globally important and locally incredibly relevant. Second, it is causally complicated. Thus, there do not seem to be any workarounds for climate change. But there do seem to be numerous test cases that range from the jungles of the Amazon to the Arctic tundra of Chukota. Third, there is a paradox to climate change. Too little protection creates the situation in which we find ourselves; too much protection leads to unexpected impacts and secondary effects derived from the protections themselves. Fourth, for climate change, it is easy to be the game player, but it is hard to be a game changer. Fifth, when we consider climate change, we cannot miss a single year, month, week, or day—for any one of these may be a local or even a global transition point. Sixth, climate change is both scientific and political. To solve the issues created by the Big Thaw, one needs both a strong analytical and policymaking background.

The Big Thaw is taking place far more rapidly in the Arctic than anywhere else in the world—approximately four times more alacritously. For most people, the Arctic is an unknown region. It is a great wasteland of ice, snow, and desolate environs. However, the Arctic presently is having a Lehman Brothers moment. It is called by some the canary for the coalmine of global warming. Like that ill-fated bird carried by the pitman into the twentieth century, the Arctic is sensitive to changes that otherwise might not be obvious. Canaries expired in contact with such gases as carbon monoxide and methane, warning miners to leave the area. The Arctic and its sea ice are similarly expiring as the Earth warms. It is attracting new species and industry to previously uninhabitable areas. For example, in November 2011, an American icebreaker set off for the Chukchi Sea. The expectation was that life would be sparse and in hibernation; instead, they found a bubbling caldron of active creatures (*The Economist*, Feb. 14, 2015, 69).

Scientific

The scientific history of the Big Thaw is the history of many fits and starts. It has not been a unified theory of global warming nor a unified science of climate change. Rather, it has been numerous studies of particular areas or particular time periods. For these particularities, the science has tried to find out how global warming worked or how it presently works locally. There have been two decades of stagnation and research and then a burst of innovation in this decade. But even this last decade has been a palindrome with default, recovery, opening up, and rising expectations, only to have slow reversals. Yet, if one steps back and looks from afar, most of the effective innovations with regard to climate change have been with regard to personal climate. When it comes to environmental control, the great innovations of the furnace and air conditioner have impacted the human condition far more than any change that we have been able to do on a more systemic environmental level.

If we try to make generalizations, most researchers agree. First, there is significant global warming in the Arctic—as previously noted, four times the worldwide average. Second, there is a significant increase in the lack of predictability. Third, there is an increasing amount of volatility in the weather patterns. In terms of Arctic weather, there seems to be an inversion perversion. There are bigger droughts, bigger storms, smaller respites, increased precipitation, and so on and on.

It also is clear that the impact of global warming on the physical domain and the biological domain in the Arctic is quite different. Physically, the ice sheets are shrinking and the glaciers are melting. The sea level is starting to climb. The temperatures on land and in water are rising.

There are several feedback and snowball loops that are operating in the physical domain. First, with the reduction of ice, there is less white reflecting the solar energy. With more solar energy being absorbed by the black and darker hues of the water, further increased heating results in an increasing snowball effect. Second, there is an equilibrium loop between the amount of seawater and the amount of salt within the seawater. The saltier the saltwater, the lower the freezing point and thus, there is less ice formed and more water in the Arctic Ocean. However, as more water occurs, the proportion of salt diminishes and more ice forms. We clearly are in the former part of this loop. Similarly, there is another equilibrium loop regarding the reduction of multiyear ice related to first-year ice. The two have different properties. Multiyear ice is eroded by wind and rain. It is pressured from below. When multiyear ice thaws, melt water goes to the margins. Thus, reflection is high. But the formations of new ice are usually at the margins, and since they are frequently covered by melt waters, there is less reflection.

For the biological domain in the Arctic, the Big Thaw is an expanding arrangement. The number and types of biological organisms are significantly increasing in the Arctic as global warming occurs. For example, the cod, as are many species, are moving north and today can be found between 80° and 81° North. Furthermore, the seabed under the North Pole is now becoming green from photosynthesis, resulting in significantly increased primary production. One might ask what will be the size of the nutrient base in an "Ice Free" North. There have been many estimates ranging as high as a 300 percent increase. Some oceans do not take place in the Far North.

Finally, for those watching the Arctic, the "age of experience" has arrived. We have had plenty of forewarning. We have passed the fine line between laudable perseverance and a stubborn refusal to admit reality.

The articles in this section tackle a wide range of subjects.

Roberts shows that some climate change inhibitors are not only more effective than others but are also more easily implemented. In particular, the immediate and aggressive action with regard to short-term climate pollutants will not only help reduce climate change but will also provide more time for implementing CO_2 remedies.

Stroud uses bird migration as a biological remote sensor of changes in Arctic environments, allowing monitoring at a distance and informing policies for species conservation. The impacts of the Big Thaw include changes to migration schedules, enhanced predation levels, habitat loss, changes to the availability of food resources, and enhanced risk from diseases, parasitic infections, and ice-free marine pollution. Birds give added political and policy emphasis to the need to sustain, manage, and restore existing habitats for the benefit of migratory water birds.

Cuciurean presented a compilation of Cree qualitative observations of inland ice conditions and compared them with long-term measurements (> 25 years) of air temperature, precipitation, and snow depth from three meteorological stations in Cree territory. Cree hunters observed a weakening of lake ice cover (e.g., change in ice composition and structure, increased rain in winter). They conclude that Cree and scientific knowledge are complementary. This presentation was the basis of a co-authored paper appearing in a scientific journal and thus is not republished.

Price argues that to successfully conserve the natural environment and allow for economic development, comprehensive baseline data are required, including the status and trends of Arctic species, habitats, and ecosystem health. When collected, these data show that biodiversity is being reduced, climate change threatens numerous species, migratory species are overharvested, pollution is increasing, invaders are increasing, knowledge is fragmentary, and the challenges are biologically interconnected and require all levels of governmental solutions and international cooperation.

Nuñez maintains that Fennoscandia has had a long history of experiencing the effects of climate warming. In fact, the contemporary Big Thaw is not big, or unique, or surprising. Rather, it is a weak resurgence of climatic processes that have been in Finland for more than 10 thousand years.

Zubrow examines how climate change in one area of the world impacts climate change in other areas and how societies have adapted to these changes. Climate changes are disseminated (teleconnected) by both the atmospheric and marine circulation systems and are related to the North Atlantic Oscillation and the Eurasian Oscillation patterns. The areas considered are northern Russia (Siberian Kamchatka), northern North America (Canada), northern Scandinavia (Finland), Bay of Bengal (Sri Lanka), and Mexico (Yucatan). Considering that the large-scale climate change in the Arctic is roughly four times greater and four times more rapid than in the more temperate zones, Zubrow demonstrates that these same changes are teleconnected with a calculable time lag to the more temperate areas.

Our euphoria about every small success concerning global warming is dangerous and makes us overbearingly blind to what still needs to be done. You may remember that the *Bulletin of Atomic Scientists* created a doomsday clock that hangs on the wall of the Bulletin Office at the University of Chicago. This symbolic clock represents the countdown to global nuclear catastrophe. The closer the clock is set to midnight, the closer the scientists believe the world is to global disaster. In 2007, they added climate change and global warming to the developments in nuclear technology and the life sciences that could inflict irrevocable harm to humanity. As of 2017, it is reading 2½ minutes to midnight and ticking. Even if we are able to relieve global warming in the Arctic and diminish the present climate change there, the result actually will only be a decisive stopgap and a leap sideways. We will have revived the canary but the worldwide systemic problem will continue to exist.

3

Will Action on Short-Lived Climate Forcers Give the Arctic Time to Adapt?

Mark W. Roberts

There are risks and costs to action. But they are far less than the long-range risks of comfortable inaction.

—John F. Kennedy

Climate Change Is Already Affecting the Arctic

Temperatures in the Arctic have increased more than twice the global average in the last one hundred years, and average temperatures are two to three degrees Celsius warmer in summer and up to four degrees Celsius warmer in some parts of the Arctic in the winter.[1] The five hottest years have occurred in the last five years.[2] The impacts of climate change also can be seen in long-term trends in declining terrestrial snow cover, increasing river flows, increasing temperatures, increasing precipitation, rising sea levels, increasing summertime Arctic river discharges, the greening of Arctic tundra vegetation, and the melting of the Greenland ice sheet and Arctic lake ice.[3]

In March 2018, the extent of sea ice (14.48 million square kilometers or 5.59 million square miles) was the second lowest sea ice maximum extent in the 39 years of satellite surveillance, just behind

2017, which suffered the greatest sea ice losses in record history.[4] All 12 of the lowest extents of Arctic sea ice have occurred in the last 12 years.[5] Additionally, in 2015 new record high temperatures at 20-meter depths occurred at most permafrost observations on the North Slope of Alaska, and melting on Greenland's ice sheet lasted about two months longer than average.[6]

There have been dramatic changes throughout the Arctic's ecosystem, with shifts in vegetation, increases in wildfires, invasion of plants and insects that never used to exist in the Arctic, and increases in risks to traditional species of land and marine animals.[7] For example, changes in the terrestrial ecosystem of the Arctic, specifically higher water temperatures, is causing seabirds to change their foraging behavior, their diet, and even their physiology, which is greatly affecting survival rates.[7] The combination of climate pollutants and ozone-depleting substances created the first ozone hole over the Arctic in 2012, causing ultraviolet concerns both for plants and humans.[8] Ultraviolet rays can cause glaucoma and skin cancer in humans and dramatically affect the development of animal and plant life.[9]

NOAA also has documented toxic algae blooms in the ever-warmer Arctic oceans. These algae blooms are increasingly widespread and greater in size, impacting the entire marine ecosystem.[10] The algae toxins are having particularly adverse impacts on marine mammals, which are at the top of the food chain, and also are causing significant illnesses and fatalities all along the food chain.[11]

A recent study in the journal *Nature* showed that because the region is pivotal to the functioning of earth systems such as oceans and the climate, changes in the Arctic have huge future financial costs. For example, the release of methane (CH_4) from the thawing permafrost beneath the East Siberian Sea alone will have (absent any mitigation) an average annual global price tag of $60 trillion. This figure is "comparable to the size of the world economy in 2012." The total cost of Arctic change will be much higher.[12]

Experts predict that the Arctic is going to get dramatically warmer by the end of this century if no action is taken, as there are many feedback loops that could cause nonlinear climate change to occur.[13] For example, a massive amount of CH_4 is trapped both in the permafrost and in the seabed, and if released, this CH_4 will substantially exacerbate climate change not only in the Arctic but also worldwide.[14] Permafrost soils are warming even faster than Arctic air temperatures—as much as 2.7 to 4.5 degrees Fahrenheit (1.5 to 2.5 degrees Celsius) in just the past 30 years.[15] Likewise, as sea ice and snow melt earlier and form later in the season, increased warming both of the land and seabed will further accelerate changes in the Arctic ecosystem.[16]

Reducing Emissions of Carbon Dioxide Is Not Enough

Reducing emissions of carbon dioxide (CO_2) gets substantial attention; it is responsible for 55–60 percent of climate forcing[17] and accounts for approximately 80 percent of the overall increase in radiative forcing since 1990.[18] However, CO_2 stays in the environment for an extremely long period of time, hundreds if not thousands of years,[19] so even if CO_2 emissions stopped tomorrow, only 50 percent would exit the atmosphere over the next hundred years;[20] 20 to 40 percent would remain for millennia.[21]

Accordingly, if we want to have action that actually arrests climate change in the near term, we have to address short-lived climate pollutants (SLCPs)—pollutants with relatively short lifetimes in the atmosphere, from days to decades.[22] Additionally, many SLCPs have significant detrimental health and environmental impacts[23] because they include hydrofluorocarbons (HFCs), black carbon, methane (CH_4), and tropospheric ozone.[24] These pollutants are the other half of climate change, but addressing these climate forcers is not the primary focus of the United Nations Framework Convention on Climate Change (UNFCCC).[25] Recently, increased interest in addressing SLCPs has received attention in an effort to gain time to address the larger issue of CO_2 emissions.[26] The Climate and Clean Air Coalition (CCAC)—with 50 countries, 16 international organizations and 43 NGOs—was created in 2012 with just 6 partners that began to highlight the need for action on SLCP.[27] Likewise, the Arctic Council[28] is beginning to evaluate the impact of SLCPs on climate change in the Arctic.[29]

The increased interest in SLCPs stems from the realization that reducing these climate agents aggressively now can actually slow the rate of climate change, sea level rise, and temperature increase in the first half of this century.[30] Actions to reduce SLCPs has the potential to slow the warming expected by 2050 by as much as 0.6 degrees Celsius and more than 1 degree Celsius by 2100.[31] Addressing SLCPs is not a replacement for dramatically reducing emissions of CO_2; in fact, only simultaneous reduction of both CO_2 and SLCPs will keep anthropogenic temperature rise below the 2-degree warming threshold[32] and create any hope of achieving the 1.5 degree aspirational goal in the 2015 UNFCCC agreement in Paris.[33]

Addressing SLCPs is particularly important for the Arctic because the pollutants actually impact the Arctic climate more than the rest of the world.[34] The United States Environmental Protection Agency (EPA) has calculated that SLCPs are responsible for about 0.8 degrees Celsius in increase of current global warming, but in the Arctic, SLCPs have caused 1.2 degrees of warming (see Figure 3.1). In an article on SLCPs in the Arctic, Quinn et al.[35] calculated that the contribution of short-lived climate forcers (i.e., CH_4, tropospheric ozone, and tropospheric aerosols, including black carbon) to Arctic warming is about 80 percent that of CO_2.[36]

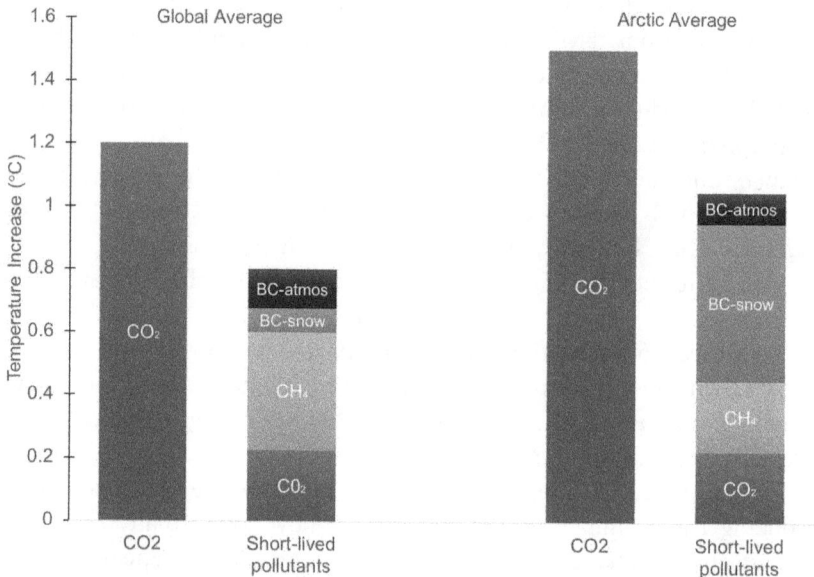

Figure 3.1. Impact of short-lived climate forcers (sans HFCs) on temperature globally and in the Arctic.

In addition to contributing to climate change and related impacts, SLCPs directly impact public health, food, water, and economic security. More than three million people die prematurely due to indoor and outdoor air pollution caused primarily by SLCPs. Taking immediate action to reduce SLCPs, including wide-scale uptake of clean cook stoves and fuels, could prevent more than two million premature deaths annually. Likewise, SLCPs cause significant crop losses: 7–12 percent for wheat, 6–16 percent for soybeans, 3–4 percent for rice, and 3–5 percent for corn. Black carbon also negatively impacts photosynthesis, reducing crop yields. Further, the collection of CH_4 from landfills and coalmines could prevent 50 million tons of crop loss annually.[37] Clearly, there are multiple reasons for reducing these climate forcers.

What Exactly Are the Short-Lived Climate Pollutants?

Hydrofluorocarbons

Hydrofluorocarbons are human-made fluorinated gases used primarily in refrigeration, air conditioning, foam blowing, aerosols, fire protection, and solvents.[38] They were commercialized as replacements for ozone-depleting substances being phased out under the Montreal Protocol.[39] The weighted average for HFCs is only 15 years, meaning phasing down HFCs could have a demonstrable effect by 2050 and an even greater effect by 2100.[40] According to predictions, a phase-down of HFCs would result in a 0.1 degree reduction in warming by 2050[41] and a reduction of 0.5 degree in warming by 2100.[42]

Under the Montreal Protocol, the countries of the world came together to phase out ozone-depleting gases, starting with chlorofluorocarbons and then their replacements, hydrochlorofluorocarbons (HCFCs).[43] Unfortunately, developed countries chose HFCs as a primary replacement for HCFCs. Although not ozone depleting, HFCs are super greenhouse gases with global warming potentials hundreds or thousands of times that of CO_2.[44] Not marketed commercially at any significant scale before 1990, HFCs have rapidly become commercialized since, and in 1995, HFC emissions constituted approximately 1 percent of the existing "basket" of covered UNFCCC greenhouse gases for the United States (weighted by global warming potential [GWP]). By 2009, HFC emissions had grown to nearly 2 percent of the basket. If left unaddressed, HFC consumption is projected to roughly double by 2020 relative to 2014, which (assuming emissions of other greenhouse gases remain about constant) would result in HFCs constituting 3 to 4 percent of the basket by 2020.[45]

Currently, HFC emissions globally are growing at 10–15 percent per year and are expected to double by 2020.[46] Climate was not a major political focal point when developed countries undertook the majority of their HCFC phase out, and as a result, by 2009, 77 percent of all conversions in developed countries were from HCFCs to HFCs.[47] Developing countries are still undergoing their HCFC phase-out, and if they follow a similar path—with the increasing gross domestic product throughout many developing nations and demands for air conditioning, refrigeration, and automobiles increasing exponentially—by 2050, HFC emissions could amount to 9–19 percent of all greenhouse gas emissions, more than offsetting current CO_2 mitigation pledges under the UNFCCC's Paris Agreement and the Kyoto Protocol.[48]

On October 15, 2016, after eight years of negotiation, the 197 countries of the Montreal Protocol adopted an amendment to phase down the consumption and production of HFCs in Kigali, Rwanda.[49] The countries unanimously committed that over the next 30 years, they will cut the production and consumption of HFCs by more than 80 percent. The phase-down of HFCs will avoid 70 to 100 billion tonnes of carbon dioxide equivalent emissions by 2050—avoiding between 0.5° Celsius

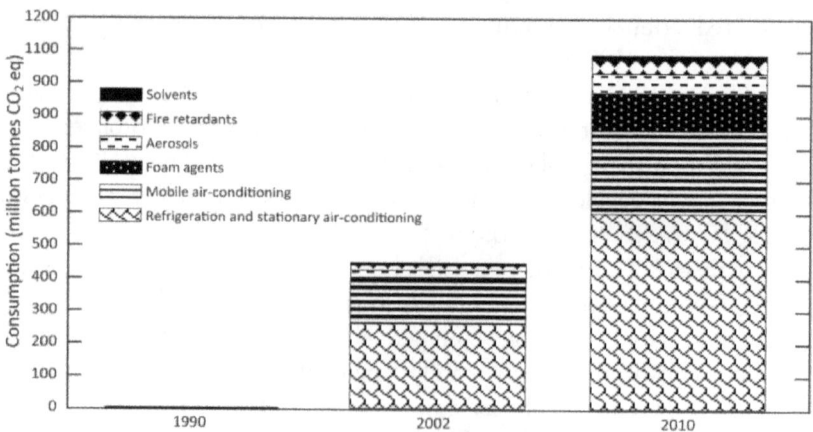

Figure 3.2. Increase in global consumption of HFCs.

warming by 2100.[50] Most developed countries have to reduce HFC consumption beginning in 2019, while most developing countries will have until 2024 to begin reducing their consumption. The Amendment also provides financing and technology transfers to developing countries to facilitate the transition to climate-friendly alternatives.[51] The institutions and procedures created by the Montreal Protocol for the phaseout of ozone-depleting substances are well suited to implement the HFC phasedown. By addressing HFCs, the Montreal Protocol will be able to restore the ozone layer without exacerbating the global climate.

The Kigali Amendment includes:

1. Enforceable commitments by all parties;

2. Common but differentiated phasedown schedules and obligations;

3. A flexible and innovative structure;

4. Ambitious phasedown schedules for most countries;

5. Financial and other incentives for actions by developing countries in advance of the proscribed schedules;

6. Provisions to enforce obligations and to hold all countries accountable; and

7. Clear opportunities for increased ambition.[52]

The phasedown of HFCs has incentivized an explosion of zero and low-GWP (global warming potential) alternatives in almost all industrial sectors.[53] Unfortunately, there is no one obvious perfect alternative to replace HFCs as there was to replace CFCs and HCFCs. There are two very distinct visions of the path forward for phasing out HFCs. The first vision promoted by the same companies that brought the world CFCs and HCFCs and HFCs is to transition to new fluorinated gases, called HFOs, to lower-GWP HFCs and HFC/HFO blends.[54] Many HFO/HFC blends have GWPs hundreds or even thousands of times higher than CO_2.[55] These HFO/HFC blends will need to be phased out in 10 or 20 years to meet the phaseout reductions mandated by the Montreal Protocol and the EU fluorinated gas regulations.[56] The second vision is to transition HFCs directly to natural refrigerants (including hydrocarbons, ammonia, CO_2, air, and water), and not-in-kind technologies, which will be the final transition.[57] New natural refrigerants have already been proven and commercialized and these alternatives are safe for use and protective of human health and the environment.[58] Since natural alternatives have different characteristics than fluorinated gases, they require different equipment with a higher upfront costs but reduced operation and maintenance costs.[59] However, if all costs are considered, transitions to lower-GWP HFCs and HFC/HFO blends will only be "cost effective" when there are no truly low-GWP alternatives in a particular sector, as the HFCs and HFO/HFC blends will require two transitions—first to lower-GWP HFCs and HFC/HFO blends, and then to zero- or low-GWP alternatives.[60] In order to maximize the climate benefits of the phasedown, the Montreal Protocol Multilateral Fund will need to incentivize transitions to final low-GWP, energy-efficient natural refrigerants and HFOs. Actions taken during the implementation of the HFC phasedown could double the climate benefits, reduce total costs, and provide more short-term relief to the Arctic.

The world has recognized the need for immediate action to phase down HFCs, which is the largest, fastest, and most cost-effective climate change mitigation option currently available. It will deliver climate benefits to the Arctic beginning in 2030 and huge beneficial impacts by 2100. The Arctic desperately needs a fast reduction of HFCs as their short atmospheric lifetimes mean that climate benefits will be delivered in the next few decades; the Arctic cannot wait longer.

Black Carbon

Black carbon, also known as soot, is formed by the incomplete combustion of fossil fuels, biofuels, and biomass. It is a significant contributor to sea ice melt and overall warming in the Arctic.[61] Black carbon has a substantial impact on warming in the Arctic, as it is estimated to be second only to CO_2 in its atmospheric heat-trapping power.[62] Major emission sources of black carbon in Arctic nations stem from agricultural burning, wildfires, and on-road diesel vehicles as well as residential burning (brick kilns, cook stoves), off-road diesel vehicles, and industrial combustion such as gas flaring.[63] Figure 3.3 summarizes the global emission sources of black carbon; however, it is important to note that black carbon emissions in Arctic nations have the greatest impact due to their proximity.[64] Emissions of black carbon impacting the Arctic are largely the responsibility of Russia and the former Soviet Union, European countries, countries

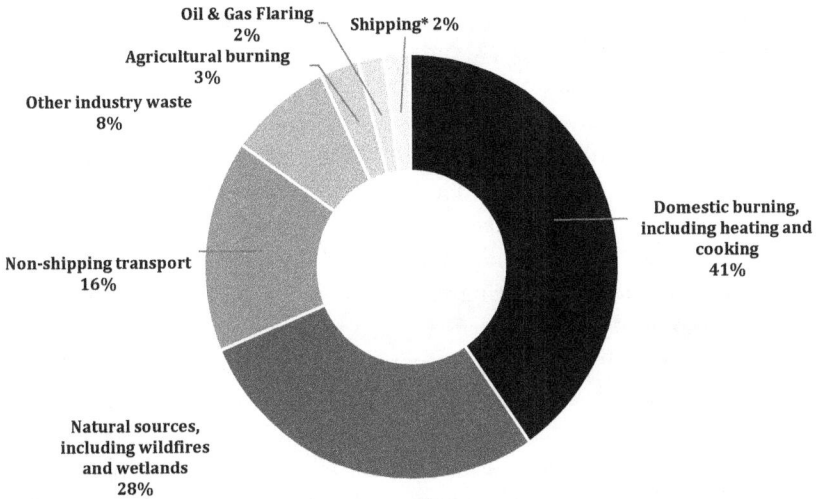

Figure 3.3. 2010 Sources of Global Black Carbon Emissions.

throughout East Asia, and the United States and Canada.[65] Additionally, there is concern that as the Arctic sea ice retreats, shipping in the Arctic, which currently contributes minimally at around 5 percent of black carbon emissions in the Arctic, could double by 2030 and quadruple by 2050 under various projections of Arctic shipping traffic.[66]

Black carbon is disproportionately affecting the Arctic, with close to 50 percent of warming observed to date attributable to black carbon.[67] The Arctic is affected by black carbon in two major ways: the snow/albedo affect and suspended particles of black carbon in the atmosphere. As black carbon is deposited on snow and ice, it changes the albedo (reflectivity) of the surface. This change from a white surface to a darker surface leads to an increase in absorption of solar radiation, promoting snow and ice melt. The change in the albedo is a significant cause of climate change in the Arctic.[68] In addition to the changes the Arctic is already experiencing due to melting snow and ice, the melting of arctic sea ice could lead to a climate tipping point by disrupting or slowing down the ocean's thermohaline circulation (global conveyor belt),[69] which brings warm water from the tropics toward the northern hemisphere and sends cool water south.[70] A disruption in the thermohaline circulation would cause significant shifts in climate throughout the Arctic, Europe, and eastern North America.[71]

Black carbon also has significant impacts on the climate when in the atmosphere. When black carbon particles are in the atmosphere, they absorb solar radiation and produce heat, which affects cloud formation and rain patterns.[72] In fact, black carbon is the most efficient atmospheric particulate species at absorbing visible light.[73] Unlike most greenhouse gases, black carbon not only absorbs outgoing solar radiation but also incoming radiation, greatly contributing to warming of the atmosphere.[74] Additionally, black carbon changes the properties and distribution of clouds, affecting cloud reflectivity and lifetime, stability, and precipitation.[75]

Black carbon is a significant contributor to warming in the Arctic and the globe, with as much as 50 percent of Arctic warming and 40 percent of current warming of the planet coming from black carbon. Decreasing emissions of black carbon is critical to mitigating climate change in the Arctic and the globe, particularly since black carbon has a very short atmospheric life of just days to weeks, making major reductions in emissions capable of immediate impact.[76] Black carbon's strong warming potential and its short lifetime are why targeted strategies to decrease emission sources will provide significant climate benefits in the near future in the Arctic region.

Methane

Methane is a greenhouse gas with a 100-year GWP 28 times that of CO_2.[77] However, given the short atmospheric life of CH_4, a 20-year GWP reflects actual climate forcing, making it 72 times as damaging to the climate as CO_2.[78]

Methane stays in the atmosphere for approximately 12 years.[79] Produced from a variety of human-caused activities—for example, coal mining; oil and gas production and distribution; biomass burning; and municipal waste landfills, agricultural operations including rice cultivation, and the keeping of ruminant livestock—mitigation of CH_4 takes a complex effort.[80] Methane is the primary component of natural gas, emitted during natural gas production, processing, storage, transmission, and distribution. Hydraulic fracturing, also known as fracking, is greatly increasing CH_4 emissions in the Arctic and elsewhere, as demonstrated by one fracking natural gas well blowout in California that caused a quarter of California's greenhouse gas emissions for months—work is still ongoing to cap the well.[81] About 60 percent of global CH_4 emissions are due to human activities.[82] Without additional mitigation efforts, anthropogenic CH_4 emissions will increase by approximately 25 percent by 2030.[83]

Controlling anthropogenic CH_4 emissions is critical, given its high GWP and large volume. Fracking to obtain natural gas is a new and increasing source of CH_4 emissions. A mid-April 2014 report from the EPA stated that tighter pollution controls instituted by the natural gas industry resulted in an average annual decrease of 41.6 million metric tons of CH_4 emissions from 1990 through 2010, or more than 850 million metric tons overall.[84] However, fracking is still a significant source of CH_4 emissions and is expected to increase.

Another new source of CH_4 emissions is due to anthropogenic-caused climate change in the Arctic that is thawing the permafrost and clathrates under the seabed, leading to massive long-term CH_4 releases. Shakhova et al.[85] estimate that not less than 1,400 gigatons of carbon is currently locked up as CH_4 and methane hydrates under the Arctic submarine permafrost, and 5–10 percent of that area is subject to puncturing by open taliks.[86] Shakhova et al. conclude that "release of up to 50 gigatonnes of predicted amount of hydrate storage [is] highly possible for abrupt release at any time."[87] This could increase the CH_4 content of the planet's atmosphere by a factor of 12.[88] According to the Arctic Methane Emergency Group,

> Emissions threaten to break through the gigaton-per-year level within 20 years. AMEG has been continuing its research into the situation. A recent paper, co-authored by Peter Wadhams, a founder member of AMEG, has used the Stern Review economic model to show that the economic cost of a 50 megaton release of methane from the Arctic Ocean seabed will cost $60 trillion. Research in the East Siberian Arctic Shelf has suggested that such a vast release of methane was possible, and continued exponential increase of methane could, within 20 years, reach a level where methane dominated over CO2 in global warming. Some researchers warn of a 50 gigaton burst being possible "at any time."[89]

Methane is both a direct greenhouse gas and a precursor gas of tropospheric ozone that damages both the climate and human health. Increased CH_4 emissions has caused approximately one-half of the increase in tropospheric ozone levels worldwide.[90] It also is locked in the Arctic permafrost and sea bed and will be released with increasing temperature. Recent studies of thermokarst lakes, lakes which form when ice within permafrost melts and creates voids that then fill with water found that the continuing growth of these lakes—many of which have already formed in the tundra—could more than double the methane emissions coming from the Arctic's soils by 2100.[91]

Given that CH_4 is 28 times as powerful a climate forcer as CO_2 but with a short atmospheric life, controlling emissions of CH_4 can have real short-term impacts and slow or eliminate the feedback loop caused by the emissions of additional CH_4 from the Arctic subsurface.

Tropospheric Ozone

Tropospheric ozone is formed from a series of chemical reactions between precursor gases in the presence of sunlight, including nitrogen oxides, carbon monoxide, CH_4, and non-methane volatile organic compounds (see Figure 3.4).[92] These gases stem largely from emissions from industrial facilities and electric fossil fuel–based utilities, motor vehicle exhaust, gasoline vapors, and chemical solvents.[93] Agricultural and forest fires also play a role in Arctic tropospheric ozone.[94] The United States, East Asia, and Southeast Asia are the primary contributors to atmospheric ozone and have the largest effect on ozone levels in the Arctic.[95] Some evidence indicates that ozone levels are steadily increasing in the Arctic and that increased shipping would result in more local ozone production.

Tropospheric ozone reacts differently than the ozone in the stratosphere—the same chemical in two different places can cause vastly different effects.[96] The ozone layer in the stratosphere protects the Earth from dangerous ultraviolet light that can cause cancer, cataracts, and adversely impact plant growth and animal development,[97] whereas tropospheric ozone causes positive radiative forcing of climate—meaning it absorbs long-wave radiation and shortwave solar radiation. Additionally, tropospheric ozone causes a variety of health problems and has harmful effects on sensitive vegetation and ecosystems such as in the Arctic. High levels of tropospheric ozone show visible leaf injuries, growth and yield reductions, and altered sensitivity to biotic and abiotic stresses.[98] Tropospheric ozone's impacts also affect regional temperature and precipitation.[99]

Tropospheric ozone is the third most important factor in human-induced climate forcing[100] and has significantly contributed to accelerated warming.[101] Over the past 100 years, tropospheric ozone concentrations

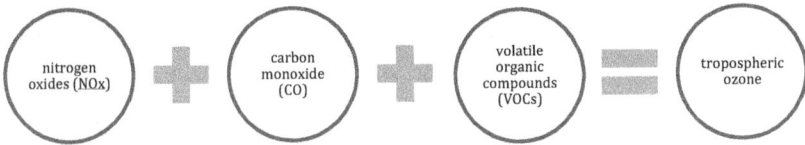

Figure 3.4. Creation of tropospheric ozone.

have increased threefold.[102] Further, during the boreal summer, tropospheric ozone causes enhanced warming (more than 0.5 degrees Celsius) over polluted northern continental regions.[103] Climate models indicate that tropospheric ozone has contributed about 0.3 degree Celsius annual average and about 0.4–0.5 degree Celsius during winter and spring to Arctic warming.[104] However, while tropospheric ozone has significantly contributed to warmer temperatures in the Arctic to date, due to its short atmospheric lifetime of only 20 to 24 days,[105] mitigating emissions would have an immediate impact on protecting the arctic climate.

Tackling Short-lived Climate Pollutants Can Have a Significant Short-term Effect on Climate Change in the Arctic

Short-lived climate pollutants are attracting the attention of governments around the world. As discussed above, the CCAC was formed in 2011 specifically to address SLCP.[106] Short- and long-term strategies are being created to address each SLCP in a concerted effort to impact climate change in the near term. Specifically, actions are underway to reduce black carbon emissions from heavy-duty diesel vehicles, cook stoves, and in brick production.[107] The CCAC is also taking the lead to reduce CH_4 and black carbon through solid waste and oil and natural gas production initiatives. The European Union, United States, and China have taken domestic actions to reduce HFCs, and the Montreal Protocol is working to adopt a global phase down of HFCs. By raising the profile of SLCP and encouraging national, bilateral, and international actions, real reductions in these potent greenhouse gases are possible.

In addition to CCAC, the UNFCCC is attempting to catalyze action on SLCPs in response to the United Nations Environment Programme's *Emissions Gap Report 2012*.[108] That report showed a gap of between 8 and

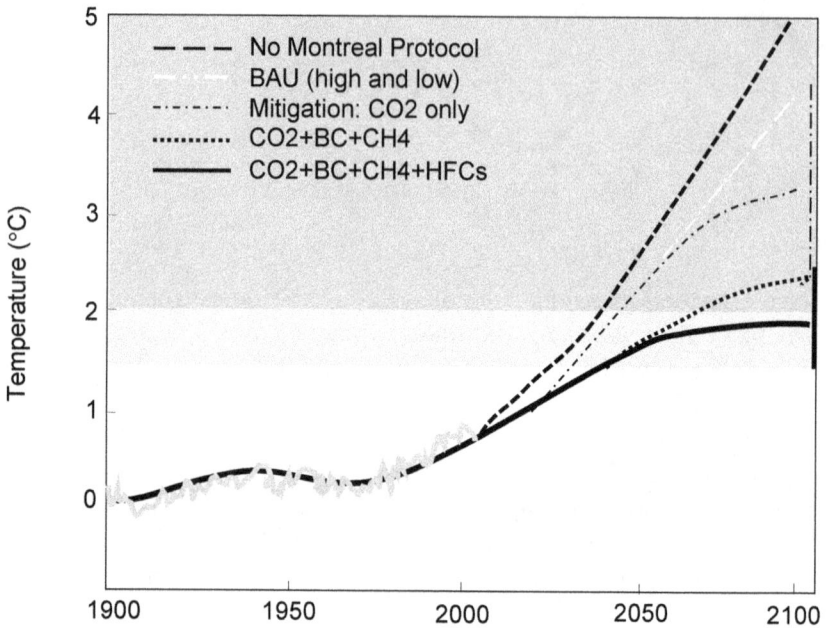

Figure 3.5. Impacts of mitigation of CO_2 and SLCPs.

13 gigatons of CO_2-equivalent emissions ($GtCO_2e$) between the emissions reductions required to limit global temperature rise to 2 degrees Celsius by 2020 and UNCCC parties' current pledges.[109] The global climate discussion has metamorphosed from an almost unilateral focus on CO_2 to discussions of disaggregated climate actions to address all agents of climate change, including SLCP to give time for the agreement finalized at the Paris UNFCCC Conference of the Parties in November 2015 to be adopted, implemented, and strengthened.

Conclusion

Climate change will be solved only by fast action addressing emissions of CO_2, the other UNFCCC-identified greenhouse gases, and SLCPs collectively. It is important to remember that global warming does not occur evenly and that a 2 degrees Celsius increase would see the annual hottest daytime temperature in the Arctic increase by around 3 degrees Celsius and the annual coldest nighttime temperature will rise by close to 6 degrees Celsius.[110] A changing Arctic could lead to significant alterations in the global climate as climate tipping points pose significant threats, such as changes to the thermohaline circulation, CH_4 emissions from the tundra permafrost and the Arctic Ocean seabed, and a rise in the number of fires leading to increased black carbon emissions in the Arctic. Near-term slowing of climate change in the Arctic will occur only if SLCPs are immediately and aggressively addressed. The Arctic's future depends on it. Real mitigation actions must occur, or climate impacts will irreversibly alter the people and ecosystems of the Arctic.

Notes

1. S. Hassol, *Arctic Climate Impact Assessment: Impacts of a Warming Arctic*, ed. Carolyn Symon (Cambridge: Cambridge University Press, 2004), 8.

2. NOAA Climate.gov Staff, 2018 Arctic Report Card: Visual highlights, Dec. 11, 2018; https://www.climate.gov/news-features/understanding-climate/2018-arctic-report-card-visual-highlights.

3. Ibid.; Arctic Monitoring and Assessment Programme (AMAP), *Summary for Policy-makers: Arctic Climate Issues 2015*; http://www.amap.no/documents/doc/summary-for-policy-makers-arctic-climate-issues-2015/1196.

4. National Ice and Snow Data Center, "Arctic Sea Ice News & Analysis"; http://nsidc.org/arcticseaicenews/.

5. Supra, note 3.

6. Ibid.

7. Arctic Climate Impact Assessment Scientific Report, *Arctic Climate Impact Assessment. ACIA Overview report* (Cambridge: Cambridge University Press, 2005), 1020.

8. Ibid., 513.

9. Ibid., 5.

10. Ibid.

11. Ibid.

12. G. Whiteman et al., "Vast Costs of Arctic Change: Methane Released by Melting Permafrost Will Have Global Impacts That Must Be Better Modeled," *Nature Magazine* 299 (2013): 401–403; C. Hope and K. Schafer, "Economic Impacts of Carbon Dioxide and Methane Released from Thawing Permafrost," *Nature Climate Change* 6 (2016): 56–59.

13. Ibid., 1; see also, "East Siberian Heat Wave Begins; 98.78 Temperature Recorded well within the Arctic Circle," *The Old Speak Journal* (2015); https://

theoldspeakjournal.wordpress.com/2015/07/04/east-siberian-heatwave-begins-98-78-degree-temperature-recorded-well-within-arctic-circle/.

14. A. Gaskill, "DOE Meeting Summary: Catastrophic Methane Hydrate Release Mitigation"; http://www.physics.rutgers.edu/~karin/140/articles/Methane-Hydrates.pdf.

15. J. Romm, "NASA Finds 'Amazing' Levels Of Arctic Methane And CO2, Asks 'Is a Sleeping Climate Giant Stirring in the Arctic?'" *Think Process* (2013); http://thinkprogress.org/climate/2013/06/13/2138531/nasa-finds-amazing-levels-of-arctic-methane-and-co2-asks-is-a-sleeping-climate-giant-stirring-in-the-arctic/.

16. Ibid.

17. P. Forster et al., "Changes in Atmospheric Constituents and in Radiative Forcing," *Climate Change 2007: Physical Science Basis, Contribution of Working Group I to the Fourth Assessment Report of the Intergovernmental Panel on Climate Change*, ed. S. Solomon et al. (Cambridge: Cambridge University Press, 2007), Figure 2.21.

18. U.S. EPA, "Climate Change Indicators in the US"; https://www3.epa.gov/climatechange/science/indicators/ghg/climate-forcing.html.

19. USEPA, Climate Change Indicators: Gases Greenhouse; www.epa.gov/climate-indicators/greenhouse-gases.

20. G. Meehl et al., "Global Climate Projections," *Climate Change 2007: The Physical Science Basis. Contribution of Working Group I to the Fourth Assessment Report of the Intergovernmental Panel on Climate Change*, ed. S. Solomon et al. (Cambridge: Cambridge University Press, 2007).

21. Ibid.

22. J. Kuylenstierna et al., *Near-term Climate Protection and Clean Air Benefits: Actions for Controlling Short-Lived Climate Forcers* (New York: United Nations, 2011); http://www.unep.org/publications/ebooks/slcf/.

23. Ibid.

24. Ibid.

25. See, e.g., *The United Nations Framework Convention on Climate Change* (New York: United Nations, 1992); http://unfccc.int/essential_background/convention/items/6036.php.

26. See, e.g., "The Climate and Clean Air Coalition"; http://www.unep.org/ccac/.

27. Ibid.

28. The Arctic Council is the leading intergovernmental forum promoting cooperation, coordination, and interaction among the Arctic states, Arctic Indigenous communities, and other Arctic inhabitants on common Arctic issues, in particular on issues of sustainable development and environmental protection in the Arctic. More information available at http://www.arctic-council.org/.

29. Ibid.

30. Supra, note 17.

31. Climate and Clean Air Coalition, "Short-lived Climate Pollutants: Science & Resources"; http://www.ccacoalition.org/en/science-resources.

32. UNEP and World Meteorological Organization, "Integrated Assessment of Black Carbon and Tropospheric Ozone: Summary for Decision Makers"; http://www.unep.org/dewa/Portals/67/pdf/Black_Carbon.pdf.

33. United Nations Framework Convention on Climate Change, "COP 21: Adoption of the Paris Agreement," https://unfccc.int/resource/docs/2015/cop21/eng/l09r01.pdf.

34. Supra, note 32; A. Stohl et al., "Evaluating the Climate and Air Quality Impacts of Short-lived Pollutants," *Atmospheric Chemistry and Physics* 15 (2015): 10529–66.

35. P. Quinn et al., "Short-lived Pollutants in the Arctic: Their Climate Impact and Possible Migration Strategies," *Atmospheric Chemistry and Physics* 8 (2008): 1723–35.

36. N. Domodaran and J. Donahue, *Report to Congress on Black Carbon*, ed. E. Sasser et al. (U.S. EPA, 2012): 51.

37. Supra, note 32.

38. A. Ravishankara et al., *HFCs: A Critical Link in Protecting Climate and the Ozone Layer* (UNEP, 2011).

39. Ibid.

40. Y. Xu et al., "The Role of HFCs in Mitigating 21st Century Climate Change," *Atmospheric Chemistry and Physics* 13 (2013): 6083–89.

41. Supra, note 32.

42. Supra, note 38.

43. Ibid.

44. J. Guus, M. Velders et al., "The Large Contribution of Projected HFC Emissions to Future Climate Forcing, "*Proceedings of the National Academy of Sciences* (2009): 106.

45. U.S. EPA, "Benefits of Phasing Down HFCs under the Montreal Protocol"; http://www.epa.gov/ozone/downloads/HFCBenefits.pdf.

46. Supra, note 41.

47. Supra, note 45.

48. United Nations Climate Change Newsroom, "Historical Agreement on Climate Change"; http://newsroom.unfccc.int/unfccc-newsroom/finale-cop21/; See, J. Guus, M. Velders et al., "The Importance of the Montreal Protocol in Protecting Climate," Proceedings of the National Academy of Sciences 104 (2007): 4814; http://www.pnas.org/content/104/12/4814.full.pdf.

49. Kigali Amendment to the Montreal Protocol on Substances that Deplete the Ozone Layer (adopted Oct. 15, 2016, not yet in force); https://treaties.un.org/doc/Publication/CN/2016/CN.872.2016-Eng.pdf.

50. Ministry of Natural Resources, Republic of Rwanda, "Historic Amendment to the Montreal Protocol adopted in Kigali, giving Renewed Hope in Fight against Climate Change," Oct. 17, 2016; http://www.minirena.gov.rw/index.

php?id=61&tx_ttnews%5Btt_news%5D=451&cHash=d5f244e04d3f9408b021da
f6e00d74a5>; L. Del Bello, "UN Agrees Historic Deal to Cut HFC Greenhouse
Gases," *Climate Change News*, Oct. 15, 2016.

51. UNEP, "The Kigali Amendment to the Montreal Protocol: HFC
Phase-Down"; http://multimedia.3m.com/mws/media/1365924O/unep-fact-sheet-
kigali-amendment-to-mp.pdf.

52. Ibid.

53. See, e.g., Environmental Investigation Agency (EIA), "Putting the
Freeze on HFCs: A Global Digest of Climate-Friendly Refrigeration and Air
Conditioning" (EIA 2014), and the 2015 and 2016 updates of this report at
https://eia-global.org/reports/putting-the-freeze-on-hfcs.

54. See, e.g., Chemours, "New Opteon HFO Refrigerants Are Transforming
the Industry"; https://www.chemours.com/businesses-and-products/fluoroproducts/
opteon-refrigerant; and "The OpteonTM Portfolio of Low GWP Refrigerants for Stationary Applications"; https://www.chemours.com/Refrigerants/en_
US/products/Opteon/Stationary_Refrigeration/assets/downloads/news/new-
generation-hfo-refrigerants.pdf; and http://refrigeranthq.com/hfo-refrigerants-
need-know/.

55. Ibid.

56. The European Commission estimates that to achieve a 79 percent
reduction in HFC use the all refrigerants will need to be reduced to average
GWP of 400. To achieve the 80–85 percent reductions required under the
Kigali Amendment An even lower average will be needed. The phasedown
steps required for developed countries will require refrigerants with zero or
low-GWP alternatives where they have been proven in order to allow higher-
GWP alternatives to be used in sectors where low-GWP alternatives do not
exist, such as flood fire suppression and unitary air conditioning. See Area, "Area
F-Gas Guide: A Practical Guide on the Application of the New F-Gas Regulation to Refrigeration, Air Conditioning, and Heat Pump Contractors" (2016);
www.refcom.org.uk/media/1183/area-guidelines-fgas-master-3-final-_updated.
pdf.

57. See, e.g., cooltechnologies.org and www.shecco.com.

58. Ibid.

59. The Greens/European Free Alliance in the European Parliament and
Shecco, "F-Gas Regulation Shaking Up the HVAC&R Industry" (2016); http://
publication.shecco.com/upload/file/org/57fe03c438c881476264900fdfko.pdf.

60. Multilateral Fund for the Implementation of the Montreal Protocol,
"Annex IX.2: Guidelines for Technical Review" http://www.multilateralfund.org/
Our%20Work/Policy-searchfor%2066/index.html?n=AnneIX2GuidForTechRevi.
html.

61. U.S. EPA, "Black Carbon: Basic Information."

62. T. Bond et al., "Bounding the Role of Black Carbon in the Climate System: A Scientific Assessment," *Journal of Geophysical Research: Atmospheres* 118 (2013): 5380–552.

63. National Oceanic and Atmospheric Administration (NOAA), "Equivalent Black Carbon in the Arctic," http://www.esrl.noaa.gov/psd/iasoa/sites/default/files/Equivalent%20Black%20Carbon%20in%20the%20Arctic_ver03.pdf; U.S. EPA, *Report to Congress on Black Carbon, Chapter 12, Key Black Carbon Mitigation Opportunities and Areas for Further Research.*

64. U.S. EPA, "Summary for Policy-Makers: Arctic Climate Issues 2015"; http://www.amap.no/documents/doc/summary-for-policy-makers-arctic-climate-issues-2015/1196.

65. Ibid.

66. Ibid.

67. M. Jacobson, "Short-Term Effects of Controlling Fossil-Fuel Soot, Biofuel Soot and Gases, and Methane on Climate, Arctic Ice, and Air Pollution Health," *Journal Geophysical Research* 11 (2010): D14209.

68. NOAA, "Arctic Report Card: Update for 2013: Black Carbon in the Arctic."

69. National Center for Atmospheric Research, "Melting Arctic Sea Ice and Ocean Circulation," (2011); http://scied.ucar.edu/longcontent/melting-arctic-sea-ice-and-ocean-circulation.

70. Ibid.

71. Ibid.

72. NOAA, "Black Carbon," *Ocean Today*; http://oceantoday.noaa.gov/blackcarbon/.

73. AMAP, "Assessment 2015: Black Carbon and Ozone as Arctic Climate Forcers"; http://www.amap.no/documents/doc/amap-assessment-2015-black-carbon-and-ozone-as-arctic-climate-forcers/1299.

74. U.S. EPA, *Report to Congress on Black Carbon, Chapter 2: Black Carbon and Its Effects on Climate.*

75. Ibid.

76. Ibid.

77. G. Myhre et al., "Chapter 8: Anthropogenic and Natural Radiative Forcing," in *Climate Change 2013: The Physical Science Basis, Working Group I Contribution to the Fifth Assessment Report of the Intergovernmental Panel on Climate Change* (Cambridge, UK, and New York: 2013), Table 8.A.

78. Supra, note 15.

79. U.S. EPA, "Overview of Greenhouse Gases," http://www3.epa.gov/climatechange/ghgemissions/gases/ch4.html.

80. U.S. EPA, "Methane Emissions," http://epa.gov/climatechange/ghgemissions/gases/ch4.html.

81. S. Goldenberg, "A Single Gas Well Leak is California's Biggest Contributor to Climate Change," *The Guardian*, Jan. 5, 2016.

82. Ibid.

83. S. Anenberg et al., "Global Air Quality and Health Co-benefits of Mitigating Near-Term Climate Change through Methane and Black Carbon Emission Controls," *Environmental Health Perspectives* 120, no. 6: 831–39.

84. Ibid.; U.S. EPA, "Inventory of U.S. Greenhouse Gas Emissions and Sinks: 1990–2011"; http://www.epa.gov/climatechange/ghgemissions/usinventoryreport.html.

85. N. Shakhova et al., "Anomalies of Methane in the Atmosphere over the East Siberian Shelf: Is There Any Sign of Methane Leakage from Shallow Shelf Hydrates?" *Geophysical Research Abstracts*, 10 (2008): EGU2008-A-01526; http://www.cosis.net/abstracts/EGU2008/01526/EGU2008-A-01526.pdf.

86. Ibid.

87. Ibid.

88. Ibid.

89. Arctic Methane Emergency Group, "Press Conference Announcement," Dec. 4, 2014; http://ameg.me/.

90. UNEP, Nairobi, Kenya, "Opportunities to Limit Near-Term Climate Change: An Integrated Assessment of Black Carbon and Tropospheric Ozone and Its Precursors;" UNEP, Nairobi, Kenya, "Near-term Climate Protection and Clean Air Benefits: Actions for Controlling Short-lived Climate Forcers"; UNEP, Nairobi, Kenya "Near-term Climate Protection and Clean Air Benefits: Actions for Controlling Short-Lived Climate Forcers."

91. Chris Mooney et al. "Arctic Cauldron," Washington Post, Sept. 22, 2018; https://www.washingtonpost.com/graphics/2018/national/arctic-lakes-are-bubbling-and-hissing-with-dangerous-greenhouse-gases/?utm_term=.c30d8bfbc3da.

92. Supra, note 83.

93. U.S. EPA, "Ground Level Ozone"; https://www.epa.gov/ozone-pollution.

94. Supra, note 83.

95. Supra, note 64.

96. Supra, note 15.

97. Ibid.

98. R. Bobbink, "Impacts of Tropospheric Ozone and Airborne Nitrogenous Pollutants on Natural and Semi-natural Ecosystems: A Commentary," *New Phytologist* (1998): 139, 161–68; http://onlinelibrary.wiley.com/doi/10.1046/j.1469-8137.1998.00175.x/epdf.

99. S. Anenberg et al., *Impacts of Black Carbon and Tropospheric Ozone*, UNEP.

100. D. Shindell et al., "Role of Tropospheric Ozone Increases in 20th-Century Climate Change," *Journal of Geophysical Research* 111 (2006); http://meteo.lcd.lu/globalwarming/Shindell/role_of_tropospheric_ozone_increases.pdf.

101. Ibid.

102. UNEP, "Integrated Assessment of Black Carbon and Tropospheric Ozone: Summary for Decision Makers," (2011).

103. Ibid.

104. Ibid.

105. O. Cooper, *Tropospheric Ozone: Global Distribution and Radiative Forcing* (University of Colorado and NOAA ESRL), http://www.esrl.noaa.gov/research/themes/forcing/TroposphericOzone.pdf.

106. Climate and Clean Air Coalition, "The History of the CCAC"; http://www.ccacoalition.org/en/content/about-us.

107. Climate and Clean Air Coalition, "Reducing Black Carbon Emissions from Heavy Duty Diesel Vehicles and Engines"; http://www.ccacoalition.org/ru/initiatives/diesel.

108. M. den Elzen et al., "The Emissions Gap Report 2010," UNEP.

109. Ibid.

110. S. Seneviratne et al., "Allowable CO2 Emissions Based on Regional and Impact-Related Climate Targets," *Nature* 529 (2016): 477–83; http://www.nature.com/nature/journal/vaop/ncurrent/full/nature16542.html.

4

Sustaining Arctic Breeding Waterbirds

Policy Implications for Temperate Countries Resulting from Arctic Climate Change

DAVID A. STROUD

Introduction

One of the distinctive ecological features of nearly all Arctic environments is the presence in summer months of breeding terrestrial waterbirds—ducks, geese, and swans (*Anatidae*) as well as shorebirds (*Charadrii*) (Table 4.1). The Arctic is much less species diverse than tropical areas; however, total numbers of Arctic-breeding waterbirds can be considerable. Many species are of significance not only as a source of food for human populations, but also as important elements of local culture.[1] In the northern summer, waterbirds occur in both the low and high Arctic. They use a wide range of wetland habitats, but also in some cases nest in non-wetland areas such as cliffs (Barnacle Geese *Branta leucopsis*) or dry barrens (Brent Geese *Branta bernicla* and Red Knot *Calidris canutus*).

Other than a few species of geese that breed colonially, densities of most breeding waterbirds on their Arctic nesting areas are low as a consequence of various forms of territoriality and nest-site and/or food limitation. Thus, the Red Knot—a typical shorebird of the high

48 / David A. Stroud

Table 4.1. The distribution of breeding terrestrial waterbird species in different arctic regions. Information from Ganter & Gaston 2013

	Alaska	North West Territories	Nunavut, Quebec & Labrador	Greenland	Iceland	Lapland	Svalbard	European Russia	W Siberia	C Siberia	E Siberia	Eastern Russia incl. Wrangel
Waterfowl												
Anatidae: ducks, geese & swans	22	20	16	14	15	13	6	18	15	15	17	20
Shorebirds												
Haematopodidae: oystercatchers					1	1		1				
Charadriidae: plovers	4	3	4	2	2	3	1	4	5	5	4	7
Scolopacidae: sandpipers & Snipes	30	24	20	11	10	18	7	24	25	27	25	39

Arctic—breeds at densities of just 0.1–1.7 pairs/km2 in East Greenland[2] and 1.2–1.3 pairs/km2 in Northeast Greenland.[3]

After the breeding season, Arctic waterbirds migrate to temperate or even tropical nonbreeding areas, thus ecologically linking the Arctic to all other continents.[4] For example, the coasts and wetlands of the United Kingdom and Ireland are visited by waterbirds that migrate from as far as 122° W in high Arctic Canada (Light-bellied Brent Geese *Branta bernicla hrota*) and from 122° E in high Arctic Russia and Canada (Dark-bellied Brent Geese *Branta b. bernicla*)—an entire hemisphere (Table 4.2). In contrast to the summer, however, some waterbirds aggregate at huge densities during the nonbreeding season. Just one site in the UK holds an average of 147,600 Red Knot from Greenland and eastern Canada—crudely, the breeding birds from roughly 115,000 km² of high Arctic tundra. Individual sites hold enormous numbers: 10 UK wetlands

Table 4.2. Some migratory waterbird linkages between Britain and Ireland and breeding areas in the Arctic

	Canada	Greenland	Iceland	Svalbard	Scandinavia	Russia
Whooper Swan *Cygnus cygnus*			✓			✓
Bewick's Swan *Cygnus bewickii*						✓
Pink-footed Goose *Anser brachyrhynchus*			✓	✓		
Greylag Goose *Anser anser*			✓			
White-fronted Goose *Anser albifrons*		✓				✓
Barnacle Goose *Branta leucopsis*		✓		✓		✓
Brent Goose *Branta bernicla*	✓			✓		✓
Wigeon *Anas penelope*			✓		✓	✓
Northern Pintail *Anas acuta*			✓			✓
Greater Scaup *Aythya marila*			✓			✓
Eurasian Golden Plover *Pluvialis apricaria*			✓		✓	✓
Grey Plover *Pluvialis squatarola*		✓				✓
Ringed Plover *Charadrius hiaticula*		✓				✓
Red Knot *Calidris canutus*	✓	✓		✓		✓
Sanderling *Calidris alba*	✓					✓
Purple Sandpiper *Calidris maritima*	✓	✓	✓		✓	✓
Dunlin *Calidris alpina*		✓	✓		✓	✓
Black-tailed Godwit *Limosa limosa*			✓		✓	
Bar-tailed Godwit *Limosa lapponica*					✓	✓
Common Redshank *Tringa totanus*			✓		✓	
Ruddy Turnstone *Arenaria interpres*		✓			✓	✓

hold more than 100,000 waterbirds in winter, mainly from northern breeding areas. Most of these sites are monitored on a monthly basis.[5]

Lindström and Piersma described migratory shorebirds as "integrative sentinels of global environmental change" in that the breeding success of individual birds (and thus the size and trends of overall populations) is determined by multiple linked factors that impact on individuals throughout their annual cycle.[6] Actual or potential impacts of climatic change on Arctic waterbirds include:

- Changes to migration schedules leading to "phenological mismatch."[7]

- Enhanced predation levels arising from the spread of new predators such as red foxes *Vulpes vulpes* into the Arctic.

- Habitat loss or change including consequences of loss of intertidal habitats resulting from rising sea level.[8]

- Changes to the availability of food resources.[9]

- Enhanced risk from diseases and parasitic infections.[10]

- Especially for birds of coastal and marine areas, enhanced risk from oil and other forms of marine pollution following opening of seas to oil exploration and/or increased transportation in ice-free Arctic waters.[11]

Climatic Influences on Breeding Waterbirds

Weather, and thus climate, has both direct and indirect influences on potentially breeding Arctic waterbirds. Patterns of winter snowfall and spring snow melt are particularly important and have multiple effects. For ground-nesting birds, snow can affect the ability for, and thus timing of, nesting as well as influencing availability of food and the exposure of nests to predation. For example, where snow continues to lie long after the arrival of birds, nests on a few snow-free "islands" are easily found by terrestrial predators such as Arctic foxes (*Alopex lagopus*).[12]

Earlier onset of spring melt has been shown to give population-scale effects on some geese through releasing earlier constraints on breeding.[13] Snow can also constrain feeding opportunities and thus potential reproductive success by restricting access to food. For example, among other waterbirds, many geese are critically dependent on feeding on arrival at breeding areas to acquire necessary nutrient resources for clutch initiation.[14]

The detailed implications of weather for Arctic waterbirds will vary according to species and ecological strategies adopted, but the ultimate effects can be measured far away, on nonbreeding areas. In many countries, annual surveillance programs assess both waterbird number and breeding success. These data are collated internationally and have for many years been reported by Wetlands International's International Waterbird Census to provide an overview of the changing status of these populations across their migratory flyways.

Population Level Impacts of Arctic Change Assessed through Waterbird Monitoring—an Example

Our knowledge of the population dynamics of the Greenland White-fronted Goose (*Anser albifrons flavirostris*), an Arctic bird showing major population change, depends entirely on monitoring on the nonbreeding areas. These geese are thinly distributed across their low Arctic breeding areas in West Greenland, with an average nesting density of just 0.25 pairs/km².[15] In the nonbreeding season however, these birds occur at a small number of traditionally used sites in the United Kingdom and Ireland. Just 80 sites hold the entire world population, and annual monitoring at these sites has allowed the fortunes of this population to be tracked over the last 30 years in a way that would be simply impossible by assessments on the breeding grounds.[16]

Greenland White-front annual productivity is assessed by measuring the ratio of adult to young geese on their arrival back on wintering areas. Young of the year have a distinctive plumage, and each year more than half the population (56 percent in Fall 2014) is aged this way. Of course, this statistic relates to numbers of young arriving on wintering areas and gives no information on losses at earlier stages of the breeding period—for example, nest failures prior to hatching, post-hatch losses of young in Greenland, or losses on migration. However, it is a consistent measure of reproductive output for a larger proportion of the population than would ever be possible from survey on the nesting areas, where nests are highly dispersed with an average distance between nests of about 2 km.[17]

Results show significant changes in reproductive output during the last decades (Figure 4.1). Since the mid-1990s, there has been a significant decline in reproductive output—statistically significant at the main Irish haunt of Wexford and near significant at the main Scottish haunt of Islay.[18] With persistently depressed reproduction, a decline in population could be anticipated, and the global population has indeed been in decline since 1999. With adult mortality calculated as approximately 15 percent per annum and productivity at approximately 5 percent per annum, simply not enough young are being produced to replace the adults that are dying.

The population declined from a rate of −3.9 percent per annum from 1999 to 2005, when shooting on autumn migration was prohibited. Since then, the population has continued to decline more slowly at −0.9 percent per annum (Figure 4.2).

Fox et al.[19] explored the reasons for the lower productivity and concluded that it was highly probable that this was the consequence of female geese being unable to "refuel" after arrival on the breeding grounds as a consequence of: (1) changed late-spring snow conditions in West Greenland since the mid-1990s[20] and/or (2) competition with Canada Geese *Branta canadensis interior*, newly established in West Greenland since the early 1990s.[21]

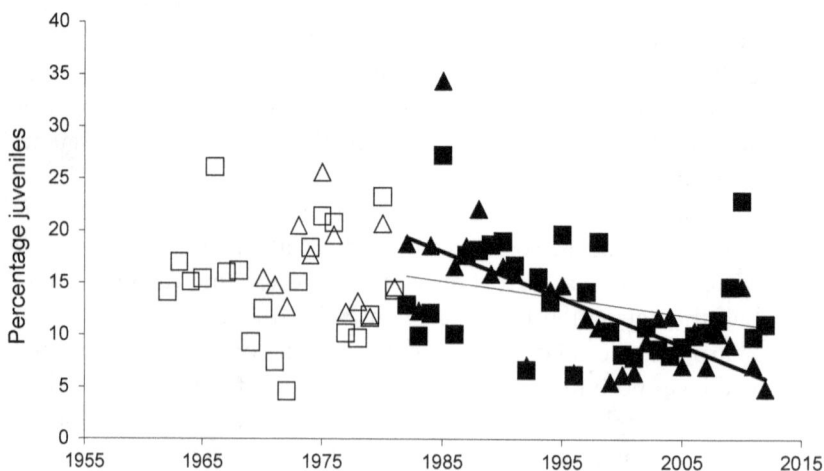

Figure 4.1. Proportion of first year Greenland White-fronted Geese at their main wintering haunts at Wexford, Ireland (triangles) and Islay, Scotland (squares). Open symbols indicate breeding years 1970–1981; closed symbols 1982–2012. Data from Stroud et al. 2012.

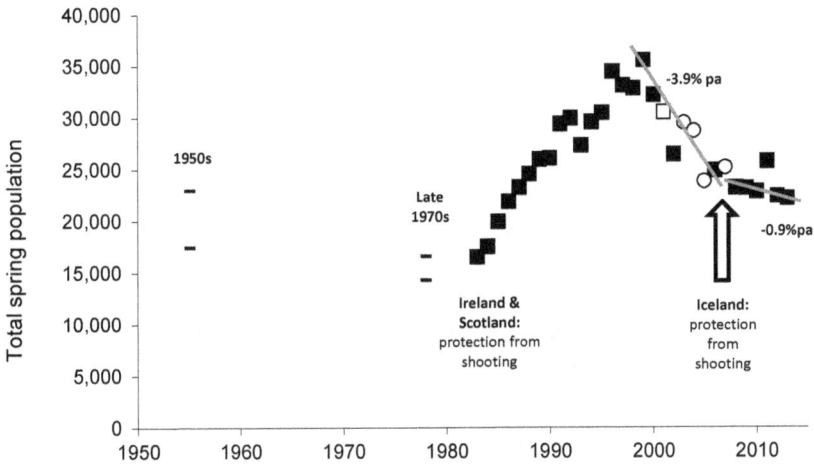

Figure 4.2. Trend in global population of Greenland White-fronted Geese. Data from Stroud et al. 2012.

The change of the Atlantic Multidecadal Oscillation from a negative to a positive phase in 1995 bought dramatically increased levels of snowfall in late April and early May—exactly the period when clutch initiation occurs.[22] If the geese do manage to locate snow-free lowland areas for feeding, it seems likely that larger bodied Canada Geese are now also occurring—with consequent competition for available resources.

An international action plan has now been developed for Greenland White-fronts that seeks to reverse this negative trend.[23] However, for conservation managers in Ireland and the United Kingdom, both the probable drivers of change in the Arctic are beyond their influence, putting particular emphasis on the need for international collaboration bilaterally as well as through multilateral environmental agreements such as the Ramsar Convention on Wetlands and the Agreement on the Conservation on African Eurasian Migratory Waterbirds (AEWA).

Conserving Arctic Waterbirds:
Policy Implications for Temperate Countries

Many countries have assumed treaty obligations to conserve migratory (Arctic) birds and/or the (wetland) habitats on which they depend. Principle among these are the requirement of the Convention on Migratory

Species (CMS) to seek to maintain the favorable conservation status of migratory species, with a similar requirement for EU Member States under the EU Directive on the conservation of wild birds. The Ramsar Convention urges its Contracting Parties to identify and designate wetlands of international importance and then to maintain the ecological character of those sites, which in turn means sustaining the population levels of those species for which those sites have been designated.

For some countries, these international obligations are transposed into national legislation. Thus, in the UK, the statutory nature conservation agencies have legal responsibility to maintain the "favorable condition" of EU Natura 2000 sites, the ecological character of Ramsar sites, and the favorable conservation of Sites of Special Scientific Interest. Typically, this is through the maintenance of the status of the species for which the site is designated, using numbers at the point of designation as the baseline for assessment.

Table 4.3 summarizes the status of Greenland White-fronted Geese at twelve UK Ramsar sites and EU Special Protection Areas (SPAs—classified under Article 4 of the Birds Directive). Since their designation, there have been long-term population declines at all but one of these sites, ranging from –26 percent to –84 percent. As we know that the causes of the declines at sites lie on the breeding grounds, the ability of a temperate country to sustain population levels of Greenland White-fronts at designated sites of international importance—in principle—requires actions in Greenland to enhance population productivity.

Engaging Non-Arctic Countries with the Ecological Consequences of Arctic Climate Change: Policy Options

A range of policy mechanisms exist to facilitate the engagement of non-Arctic countries with Arctic countries to address the consequences of climate change—in the current instance as expressed though impacts on migratory waterbirds and their habitats (Table 4.4 on page 56). Principal formal/legal opportunities arise through CMS (and its daughter agreements such as AEWA) and the Ramsar Convention. A wide range of less formal mechanisms exists notably through the work of the Arctic Council and CAFF's Working Group international flyway action plans and strategies such as, notably, the East Asia–Australasia Flyway Partnership.

Table 4.3. Designated sites of international importance for Greenland white-fronted geese in the UK and population trends at these sites since legal designation. Data from Greenland White-fronted Goose Study annual reports

	Ramsar Site	SPA	At designation	Current status (March 2015)	Change
Caithness Lochs	✓	✓	440	244	–45%
Coll	✓	✓	789	126	–84%
Dyfi Estuary	✓	✓	139	25	–82%
Eilean na Muice Duibhe/Duich Moss, Islay	✓	✓	600	223	–63%
Gruinart Flats, Islay	✓	✓	1,000	414	–59%
Kintyre Goose Roosts	✓	✓	2,323	1,711	–26%
Laggan, Islay		✓	300	300	0%
Loch of Inch and Torrs Warren	✓	✓	534	206	–31%
Loch Ken and River Dee Marshes	✓	✓	350	163	–53%
Loch Lomond	✓	✓	221	193	–45%
Rinns of Islay	✓	✓	1,600	868	–46%
Sleibhtean agus Cladach Thiriodh (Tiree Wetlands and Coast)	✓	✓	1,419	748	–53%

The Convention on Biological Diversity recently reflected (in Decision XI.6) on a range of issues related to Arctic biodiversity, stressing inter alia:

- The global ecological repercussions of changes in Arctic biodiversity.

- The need for cooperation between non-Arctic and Arctic countries for the effective conservation of migratory Arctic species.

- The relevance of data held by non-Arctic contracting parties and other governments for Arctic assessment processes.

Table 4.4. Main multilateral policy mechanisms linking Arctic and non-Arctic countries in issues of biodiversity conservation—especially as related to migratory birds

Treaty/initiative	Instrument	Opportunities for non-Arctic countries
Convention on the Conservation of Migratory Species of wild animals	Article II	Binding multilateral convention providing for the strict protection of species listed in Appendix 1 and urges conclusion of further specific Agreements. Also Parties "should promote, co-operate in and support research relating to migratory species."
Agreement on the conservation of African-Eurasian migratory waterbirds www.unep-aewa.org	Agreement Action Plan	Binding multilateral Agreement that encourages cooperative research and conservation related to migratory waterbirds in the African-Eurasian region
	Single Species Action Plans	Nonbinding action plans for particular species or populations of highly threatened waterbirds for implementation by Range States. Seven of AEWA's 25 action plans relate to Arctic or sub-Arctic species[1]—mostly populations of geese.
"Ramsar" Convention on wetlands of international importance www.Ramsar.org	Article 5	Binding multilateral convention providing for designation of wetlands of international importance. One of the three "pillars" of the convention is international cooperation, not just for transboundary wetlands but also as related to migrant, wetland-dependent fauna.
Conservation of Arctic Flora and Fauna www.caff.is		Nonbinding programme of the Arctic Council focused on the monitoring and assessment of Arctic fauna including development of species action plans
	Arctic Biodiversity Assessment http://www.arctic biodiversity.is/#	Regular assessment of the state of the Arctic environment as the basis for policy responses from the Arctic Council and other decision makers

Arctic Bird Monitoring habitat Initiative www.caff.is/arctic-migratory-birds-initiative-ambi		Collation of knowledge on population status, key sites, and requirements of a selection of Arctic breeding birds as the basis for conservation management
East Asia-Australasia Flyway Partnership www.eaaflyway.net		Formal, though legally nonbinding, Partnership aimed at the conservation of migratory waterbirds and their habitats. Partners include national governments, intergovernmental organizations, International nongovernmental organizations, and international private enterprise.
Convention on Biological Diversity www.cbd.int		Overarching binding multilateral convention related to biodiversity conservation. Recent decisions related to Arctic conservation issues
UN General Assembly https://sustainabledevelopment.un.org/post2015/transformingourworld	Transforming our world: the 2030 Agenda for Sustainable Development	AEWA Resolution 5.15 showed that delivery of implementation of AEWA actions will also contribute to the delivery of many of the Sustainable Development Goals
UN Framework Convention on Climate Change https://unfccc.int/resource/docs/2015/cop21/eng/l09r01.pdf	Paris Agreement	Delivery of objectives of Paris Agreement will directly benefit the conservation of arctic species and their habitats, including relevant adaptation and mitigation measures

1. Bewick's Swan *Cygnus columbarius bewickii*, Pink-footed Goose *Anser brachyrhynchus*, Greenland White-fronted Goose *Anser albifrons flavirostris*, Taiga Bean Goose *Anser fabalis fabalis*, Canadian Light-bellied Brent Goose *Branta bernicla hrota*, Red-breasted Goose *Branta ruficollis*, and Long-tailed Duck (Old Squaw) *Clangula hyemalis*.

The Convention on Biological Diversity recently reflected (in Decision XI.6) on a range of issues related to Arctic biodiversity, stressing *inter alia:*

- The global ecological repercussions of changes in Arctic biodiversity.

- The need for co-operation between non-Arctic and Arctic countries for the effective conservation of migratory Arctic species.

- The relevance of data held by non-Arctic contracting parties and other governments for Arctic assessment processes.

It is clear from Table 4.4 that there are many policy mechanisms that allow the engagement of non-Arctic countries in Arctic conservation issues—as will increasingly be the consequence of climatic change. The reality of making actions happen can be more challenging, however.

Using the Greenland White-fronted Goose as an example, the international action plan highlighted that "[t]he top priority action is to investigate the factors acting on geese on the breeding grounds responsible for currently reducing the annual production of young." However, as of January 2016, no funding had been found to implement this action. This is because, typically, conservation funding mechanisms in the resource-rich wintering Range States are constrained for use nationally rather than internationally. Accordingly, the reality of funding research and/or conservation actions in Arctic countries from sources in non-Arctic countries will likely remain a challenge.

Enhancing Uses of Non-Arctic Monitoring Data for Arctic Assessments

Very considerable data on Arctic breeding waterbirds are collected annually on their nonbreeding areas. There is significant scope to enhance the uses of these data to inform future assessment of Arctic biodiversity.[24] These include:

- The production and update of waterbird flyway atlases to provide summarized information on distributions, migration routes, and key sites for decision makers.[25]

- The development of multispecies indices of population change for different regions of the Arctic compiled from annual assessments of those species breeding in these areas.[26]

- To inform the development of multispecies indices, undertake systematic analysis of recoveries of ringed waterbirds to provide better information on distributional limits of biogeographical populations, and migratory linkages between breeding and wintering areas.

- Application of new technologies to help refine knowledge of waterbird biogeographical populations, especially in remote areas where conventional fieldwork is difficult.

Arctic Benefits from Non-Arctic Actions

The continued survival of Arctic migratory breeding birds depends not only on actions on the breeding areas but also on their nonbreeding grounds, and there is increasing international focus on relevant policies to this end (see Table 4.4). Notably, CAFF's Arctic Migratory Bird Initiative aims to make more explicit to decision makers the critical role that non-Arctic countries have in sustaining Arctic migratory birds.

In November 2015, the fifth Meeting of Parties to AEWA concluded:

[T]he full implementation of the Agreement, at all scales and by both Contracting Parties and other actors, has the potential to directly contribute to the attainment of the [UN General Assembly's] Sustainable Development Goals (SDGs) *inter alia* through actions related to the reduction of biodiversity loss; protection and restoration of habitats; climate change adaptation measures; education and awareness building; capacity development; contributing to food security and poverty reduction through the sustainable harvesting of waterbirds and the wise-use use of wetlands; and actions to address illegally taking, killing and trade.

Of course, the reverse is also true: policies and actions to deliver relevant SDGs will also benefit waterbirds, including those breeding in the Arctic. Even more critical for waterbird conservation is the full implementation of the UN Framework Convention on Climate Change 2015 Paris Agreement, not just in curbing global "headline" temperatures, but also through the consequences of actions that will bring this about, including wetland-based adaptation and mitigation measures. These will give added political and policy emphasis to the need to sustain and manage existing habitats and restore lost or degraded habitats not just for carbon sequestration motivations, but also to the benefit of migratory waterbirds.

Notes

1. F. Berkes, *Sacred Ecology: Traditional Ecological Knowledge and Resource Management* (Philadelphia: Taylor and Francis, 1999); A. J. Green and J. Elmberg, "Ecosystem Services Provided by Waterbirds," *Biological Reviews* 89 (2014): 105–22.

2. C. E. Mortensen, "Population Densities of Breeding Birds in Jameson Land, East Greenland, 1984–88," *Dansk Ornitologisk Forenings Tidsskrift* 94 (2000): 29–41.

3. T. Piersma et al., "A Single-Year Comparison of Two Methods of Censusing Breeding Red Knot and Sanderling in High Arctic Greenland," *Wader Study Group Bulletin* 109 (2006): 83–87.

4. A. Lindström and T. Piersma, "Migrating Shorebirds as Integrative Sentinels of Global Environmental Change," *Ibis* 146 (2004, Supplement 1): 61–69; K. D. Wohl, "The Arctic—Origin of Flyways," in *Waterbirds Around the World*, ed. G. C. Boere, C. A. Galbraith, and D. A. Stroud (Edinburgh: The Stationery Office, 2006), 120–23.

5. C. A. Holt et al., *Waterbirds in the UK 2013/14: The Wetland Bird Survey* (BTO, RSPB and JNCC, in association with WWT, British Trust for Ornithology, Thetford 2014).

6. Lindström and Piersma, 61–69.

7. H. Boyd and J. Madsen, "Impacts of Global Change on Arctic-Breeding Bird Populations and Migration," *Global Change and Arctic Terrestrial Ecosystems, Ecological Studies* 124 (1997): 201–17; M. H. Dickey, G. Gauthier, G. and M. C. Cadieux, "Climatic Effects on the Breeding Phenology and Reproductive Success of an Arctic-Nesting Goose Species," *Global Change Biology* 14 (2008): 1973–85; A. D. Fox, *The Greenland White-fronted Goose, Anser albifrons flavirostris. The Annual Cycle of a Migratory Herbivore on the European Continental Fringe"* (PhD diss., National Environmental Research Institute, Denmark, 2003).

8. A. Lindström and J. Agrell, "Global Change and Possible Effects on the Migration and Reproduction of Arctic-Breeding Waders," *Ecological Bulletins* 47 (1999): 145–59; C. Zöckler and I. Lysenko, *Water Birds on the Edge: First Circumpolar Assessment of Climate Change Impact on Arctic Water Birds*, World Conservation Monitoring Centre Biodiversity Series 1 (2000): 1–20.

9. B. Ganter and A. J. Gaston, "Birds," in *Arctic Biodiversity Assessment: Status and Trends in Arctic Biodiversity*, ed. H. Meltofte (Conservation of Arctic Flora and Fauna, Arctic Council): 143–80.

10. Lindström and Agrell, "Global Change," 145–59.

11. Ibid., note 9.

12. G. H. Green, J. J. D. Greenwood, and C. S. Lloyd, "The Influence of Snow Conditions on the Date of Breeding of Wading Birds in North-East Greenland," *Journal of Zoology* 183 (1999): 311–28.

13. G. H. Jensen et al., "Snow Conditions as an Estimator of the Breeding Output in High-Arctic Pink-footed Geese *Anser brachyrhynchus*," *Polar Biology* 37 (2003): 1–14.

14. V. G. Thomas, "Spring Migration, the Prelude to Goose Reproduction and a Review of its Implications," in Proc. IWRB Symposium, Edmonton 1982, ed. H. Boyd (1983): 73–81; T. Meijer and R. Drent, "Re-examination of the Capital and Income Dichotomy in Breeding Birds," *Ibis* 141 (1999): 399–414; A. D. Fox et al., "Potential Factors Influencing Increasing Numbers of Canada Geese *Branta canadensis* in West Greenland," *Wildfowl* 61 (2011): 30–44.

15. R. A. Malecki, A. D. Fox, and B. A. Batt, "An Aerial Survey of Nesting Greenland White-fronted and Canada Geese in West Greenland," *Wildfowl* 51 (2011): 49–58.

16. Stroud et al. (compilers), "International Single Species Action Plan for the conservation of the Greenland White-fronted Goose (*Anser albifrons flavirostris*," AEWA Technical Series No. 45. Bonn, Germany, 2012.

17. A. D. Fox and D. A. Stroud, "The Breeding Biology of the Greenland White-fronted Goose *Anser albifrons flavirostris*," *Meddelelser om Grønland, Bioscience* 27 (1988): 1–16.

18. Stroud et al., 2012.

19. Fox et al., "Potential Factors," 30–44.

20. H. Boyd, and A. D. Fox, "Effects of Climate Change on the Breeding Success of White-fronted Geese *Anser albifrons flavirostris* in West Greenland." *Wildfowl* 58 (2008): 55–70.

21. Fox et al., 30–44.

22. H. Boyd, and A. D. Fox, "Effects of Climate Change on the Breeding Success of White-fronted Geese *Anser albifrons flavirostris* in West Greenland." *Wildfowl* 58 (2008): 55–70.

23. Fox et al., note 16.

24. Ganter and Gaston, *Arctic Biodiversity Assessment*, 142–80.

25. D. A. Scott and D. A. Rose, *Atlas of Anatidae Populations in Africa and Western Eurasia*, Wetlands International Publication No. 41. Wageningen, The Netherlands, 1998; S. Delany et al., eds., *An Atlas of Wader Populations in Africa and Western Eurasia*, Wetlands International, Wageningen, The Netherlands, 2009.

26. Holt et al., 2015.

5

Arctic Biodiversity

Conservation of Arctic Flora and Fauna with Excerpts Taken from the Arctic Biodiversity Assessment

Courtney Price et al.

(Synthesized from the
Arctic Biodiversity Assessment lead authors' work)

Background

This document summarizes a report submitted by the executive secretary of the Conservation of Arctic Flora and Fauna (CAFF)[1] to the Convention on Biological Diversity (CBD) in 2010.[2] It provides information from a report that presents an overview of CAFF activities, and highlights current and planned work within CAFF that will contribute to the objectives of the process conserving Arctic biodiversity.

As the biodiversity working group of the Arctic Council,[3] CAFF consists of national representatives assigned by each of the eight Arctic Council Member States,[4] representatives of Indigenous Peoples' organizations that are Permanent Participants to the Council,[5] and Arctic Council observer countries[6] and organizations.[7] CAFF serves as a vehicle to cooperate on species and habitat management and utilization, to share information on management techniques and regulatory regimes, and to facilitate more knowledgeable decision making. It provides a mechanism to develop common responses on issues of importance for the Arctic ecosystem, such as development and economic pressures, conservation opportunities, and political commitments.

CAFF operates at the interface between science and policy. It works to ensure that science is communicated in as effective a way as possible to facilitate the development of well-informed policymaking. CAFF's mandate is to address the conservation of Arctic biodiversity and to communicate its findings to the governments and residents of the Arctic, helping to promote practices that ensure the sustainability of the Arctic's living resources. It does so through various monitoring, assessment, and expert group activities.

CAFF's projects provide data for informed decision making to resolve challenges arising from trying to conserve the natural environment and permit regional growth. This work is based on cooperation among all Arctic countries, Permanent Participant organizations, non-Arctic observer countries' international conventions, and observer organizations. It is guided by the CAFF Strategic Plan for the Conservation of Arctic Biological Diversity[8] and biennial Work Plans. To successfully conserve the natural environment and allow for economic development, comprehensive baseline data are required, including the status and trends of Arctic species, habitats, and ecosystem health. CAFF is developing the framework and tools necessary to create a baseline of current knowledge and to provide dynamic assessments over time. This evolving, flexible, and responsive approach can produce more regular, timely, and informed analyses.

Why Is the Arctic of Global Importance?

The Arctic holds some of the most extreme habitats on Earth, with species and peoples that have adapted through biological and cultural evolution to its unique conditions. A homeland to some, and a harsh if not hostile environment to others, the Arctic is home to iconic animals such as polar bears (*Ursus maritimus*), narwhals (*Monodon monoceros*), caribou/reindeer (*Rangifer tarandus*), muskoxen (*Ovibos moschatus*), Arctic fox (*Alopex lagopus*), ivory gull (*Pagophila eburnean*), and snowy owls (*Bubo scandiaca*), as well as numerous microbes and invertebrates capable of living in extreme cold and large intact landscapes and seascapes with little or no obvious sign of direct degradation from human activity. In addition to flora and fauna, the Arctic is known for the knowledge and ingenuity of Arctic peoples, who thanks to great adaptability have thrived amid ice, snow, and winter darkness.[9] The Arctic plays host to a vast array of biodiversity, including many globally significant populations.[10] Included among these are more than half of the world's shorebirds,[11] 80 percent of the global goose populations,[12] several million reindeer and caribou, and many unique mammals. During the short summer breeding season, 279 species of birds arrive from as far away as South Africa, Australia, New Zealand, and South America to take advantage of the long days and intense period of productivity. Several species of marine mammals, including grey and humpback whales and harp and hooded seals, also migrate annually to the Arctic.

The Circumpolar Arctic, as defined by CAFF, covers 32 million kilometers^2. The Arctic is made up of the world's smallest ocean, which is surrounded by a relatively narrow fringe of island and continental tundra. Extreme seasonality and permafrost, together with an abundance of freshwater habitats ranging from shallow tundra ponds fed by small streams to large deep lakes and rivers, determine the hydrology, biodiversity, and general features of the Arctic's terrestrial ecosystems. Seasonal and permanent sea ice are the defining features of the Arctic's marine ecosystems. These vast wilderness areas, where ecosystem processes continue to function in a largely natural state, play a key role in the physical, chemical, and biological balance of the planet.[13]

The Arctic tundra, freshwaters, and seas support more than 21,000 species of plants, fungi, and animals—even when endoparasites and microorganisms are excluded—and tens of thousands of species are not described. Although they are less rich in species than other biomes on Earth, Arctic terrestrial and marine ecosystems provide room for a range of highly adapted and particularly cold-resistant species as well as species that fill multiple ecological niches.[14]

Among the 10 largest remaining wilderness areas on Earth, seven are located in the Arctic region. One of them, the Northeast National Park in Greenland,[2] is the largest national park in the world at 972,000 kilometers. Together with the Antarctic, the Arctic contains the largest freshwater resources on Earth. Some of the richest fisheries are found in northern marine waters, particularly along the Subarctic fringes. These commercial fisheries harvest millions of tons annually, including more than 10 percent of global marine fish catches by weight and 5.3 percent of crustacean catches—for an economic value in billions of dollars.[15] The Arctic is estimated to contain a quarter of the world's remaining oil and gas reserves, and development is expected to increase. Already, 10 percent of the world's oil and 25 percent of the world's natural gas is produced in the Arctic and Subarctic regions, with the majority coming from the Russian Federation.[16] Such information emphasizes that the Arctic is a region of global significance, and what happens there will have an effect felt far beyond its confines.

Not least, the Arctic is home to diverse, vibrant, and unique societies whose Indigenous cultures depend on and maintain close ties to the land, water, and ocean and speak many distinct languages.

What Is Happening with Arctic Biodiversity?

Change in the Arctic comes in many forms and from a variety of sources. Several of these stressors have been the subject of intense research and assessments that document the effects and impacts of human activity both regionally and globally and seek ways to conserve the biological and cultural wealth of the Arctic in the face of considerable pressures to develop its resources. These assessments have focused primarily on effects and impacts from a range of present and future stressors, such as global warming,[17] oil and gas activities,[18] social change,[19] marine shipping,[20] and environmental contaminants.[21]

In 2001, CAFF published *Arctic Flora and Fauna: Status and Conservation*,[22] the first truly circumpolar overview of Arctic biodiversity. The report provided "a clear understanding of the importance of the Earth's largest ecoregion and its status in the face of a rapidly changing world."[23] The report also observed that while much of the Arctic was in its natural state and that the impacts of human activity were relatively minor, individuals, species, and ecosystems throughout the Arctic faced threats from many causes and that the long-term consequences of human impacts were unknown. It particularly noted that the information necessary to determine status and trends of Arctic fauna was fragmentary—and almost entirely nonexistent for flora.

Since the report's assessment, the Arctic has entered into a period of intensive pressure and change involving a new set of challenges and stressors, with climate change at the forefront. A warming climate in the Arctic is projected to set off many environmental changes, including melting sea ice, increased runoff, and an eventual rise in sea level with immense coastal implications. Some of these changes are already being felt. Increasing temperatures are already showing many effects on Arctic biodiversity, including the northward movement of southern species, shrubbing and greening of the land, changing plant communities and their associated fauna, increases in invasive species displacing native Arctic inhabitants, and the emergence of new diseases. Additionally, fluctuations in the timing of events (phenology) are an aspect of change that may lead to mismatches among related environmental factors. As a result, some local biodiversity may be in imminent danger of extinction.

In the past 100 years, average Arctic temperatures have increased at almost twice the average global rate.[24] Over the past 30 years, seasonal minimal sea ice extent in the Arctic has decreased by 45,000 kilometers^2 per year.[25] Along with earlier breakup and freeze-up, the extent of terrestrial snow cover in the Northern Hemisphere has decreased and is expected to continue to do so. The magnitude of these changes will exert major influences on biological dynamics in the Arctic. Some of the most rapid ecological changes associated with warming have occurred in marine and freshwater environments. Species most affected are those with limited distributions or with specialized feeding habits that depend on ice foraging. Other predicted effects of climate change and other stressors, such as industrial development and resource exploitation on Arctic biodiversity, include:

1. Changes in the distribution, geographical ranges, and abundances of species (including invasive alien species);

2. Changes in habitats for endemic Arctic species;

3. Changes in genetic diversity; and

4. Changes in the behavior of migratory species.

A number of challenges and stressors are envisaged for Arctic biodiversity, with climate change emerging as the most far-reaching and significant. Other stressors are also important and continue to have impacts, for example, contaminants, habitat fragmentation, development, bycatch, and unsustainable harvest levels. Complex interactions between climate change and such factors have the potential to magnify impacts on biodiversity.

With a warming climate, shipping and resource development are likely to increase, and there is potential for increased pollution and disturbance to Arctic biodiversity. More development may lead to different human settlement patterns and changes in resource use. Decreased ice cover may increase the number of areas accessible to fisheries and make new species economically available and so create both opportunities as well as challenges for sustainable use. Many Arctic species also migrate great distances throughout the world and so are subject to environmental changes during their travels, including carrying pollutants back to the north in their bodies. These ongoing and developing changes provide a challenge to determining how best to respond and take into account of these changes when planning for the sustainable and effective management of the Arctic. CAFF operates at the interface between science and policy, and as such is crucial in providing a mechanism to develop common responses on issues of importance.

CAFF and the Arctic Council

The Arctic Council countries have recognized that their shared ecosystem, with its unique flora and fauna, is resilient but fragile, is threatened from a number of causes, and that changes in Arctic biodiversity have global repercussions. In order to encourage the conservation of Arctic flora and fauna, their diversity, and their habitats the CAFF working group was established in 1992 under the Arctic Environmental Protection Strategy. CAFF is one of six working groups within the Arctic Council,[26] and it focuses on biodiversity. CAFF covers a circumpolar range, which is reflected in the composition of its management board. The board members come from the eight Arctic countries, six Indigenous organizations, observer countries, and observers from international organizations.

CAFF's mandate is to address the conservation of Arctic biodiversity and to communicate the findings to the governments and residents of the Arctic, helping to promote practices that ensure the sustainability of the use of Arctic resources. In order to successfully conserve the natural environment and allow for economic development, comprehensive baseline data are required—including status and trend of Arctic biodiversity, habitats, and ecosystem health. CAFF's projects provide data for informed decision making, thereby helping to resolve the dilemma between the desire to both conserve the natural environment and permit regional growth. CAFF is guided by the Arctic Council's Strategic Plan for the Conservation of Arctic Biological Diversity, employs an ecosystem approach, and its activities—where feasible—are linked to clearly identified ecosystem units.

In summary, the objectives and actions assigned to CAFF are:

1. to collaborate for more effective research, sustainable utilization, and conservation;

2. to cooperate to conserve Arctic flora and fauna, their diversity, and their habitats;

3. to protect the Arctic ecosystem from human-caused threats;

4. to seek to develop more effective laws, regulations, and practices for flora, fauna, and habitat management, utilization, and conservation;

5. to work in cooperation with the Indigenous Peoples of the Arctic;

6. to consult and cooperate with appropriate international organizations and seek to develop other forms of cooperation;

7. to regularly compile and disseminate information on Arctic conservation;

8. to contribute to environmental impact assessments of proposed activities; and

9. to provide policy recommendations to facilitate more knowledgeable decision making and sustainable use of the Arctic's living resources.

The common priorities agreed upon in the most recent Norwegian, Danish, and Swedish chairmanship period (2007–2013) of the Arctic Council were concerned with climate change, integrated resource management, the International Polar Year (IPY), Indigenous Peoples, local living conditions, and management issues. Sweden's chairmanship of the Arctic Council (2011–13) added biodiversity to this list. On May 15, 2013, Canada became the chair of the Arctic Council and CAFF at the Kiruna, Sweden, Arctic Council Ministerial meeting. The theme of

Canada's 2013–15 chairmanship was "development for the people of the North," with a focus on responsible Arctic resource development, safe Arctic shipping, and sustainable circumpolar communities.[27] The U.S. chairmanship (2015–17) had three focus areas: improving economic and living conditions for Arctic communities; Arctic Ocean safety, security, and stewardship; and addressing the impacts of climate change. Most recently, the Finnish chairmanship (2017–19) focus areas include environmental protection, connectivity, meteorological cooperation and education.[28]

CAFF's work reflects the emphasis placed on these priorities with a focus on outreach/communication, cooperation, data integration, spatial information, and circumpolar datasets and analyses. CAFF has also placed a focus on the IPY both through benefiting from IPY-generated research and contributing to the IPY legacy. CAFF's Arctic Biodiversity Assessment (ABA),[29] the Circumpolar Biodiversity Monitoring Program (CBMP),[30] and various other activities are important contributions toward understanding the impacts of climate change and other stressors on biodiversity and the sustainable use of living resources in the Arctic.

The Circumpolar Biodiversity Monitoring Program

Arctic warming, with its many and increasing impacts on flora, fauna, and habitats, has heightened the need to identify and fill the knowledge gaps on various aspects of Arctic biodiversity and monitoring. This need was clearly identified in the 2005 Arctic Climate Impact Assessment, which recommended that long-term Arctic biodiversity monitoring be expanded and enhanced. The CAFF working group responded to this recommendation with the implementation of the Circumpolar Biodiversity Monitoring Program (CBMP).[31]

The CBMP is CAFF's cornerstone program and, via CAFF and the Arctic Council, its activities are being channeled into conservation, mitigation, and adaptation policies that promote the sustainability of the Arctic's living resources. The CBMP is an international network of scientists, governments, Indigenous organizations, and conservation groups working to harmonize and integrate efforts to monitor the Arctic's living resources and improve detection, understanding, and reporting of important trends in biodiversity. It also focusses on reporting to, and communicating with, both key decision makers and stakeholders, thereby enabling effective conservation and adaptation responses to changes in

Arctic biodiversity. These measures will facilitate more informed and timely management decisions. The CBMP functions as an international forum of leading scientists and conservation experts from all eight Arctic countries, the Indigenous organizations of the Arctic Council, and major global conservation organizations.

The CBMP is first and foremost a coordinating entity for: (1) existing Arctic biodiversity monitoring programs; (2) addressing gaps in knowledge through the identification of new programs; (3) gathering, integrating, and analyzing data; and (4) communicating results. Through its coordinating function, the CBMP can create a collaborative framework for Arctic biodiversity monitoring and assessment that will yield insights previously unattainable on a circumpolar scale. The end result is a broader understanding of the Arctic environment and how best to conserve its resources and adapt to the changes occurring within it.

The CBMP focuses its efforts on the following five key program areas:

- Data management

- Capacity building

- Reporting

- Coordination and integration of Arctic monitoring

- Communication, education, and outreach

In order to ensure coordination and integration with related global initiatives, the CBMP is strategically linked to other international conservation programs and research and monitoring initiatives, such as CAFF's ABA, the GEO-Biodiversity Observation Network (CBMP is a regional Biodiversity Observation Network ["Arctic-BON"]); the Biodiversity Indicators Partnership; and the Sustaining Arctic Observing Networks initiative. In 2013, the CBMP underwent reorganization and is currently led by Greenland-Denmark and the United States, with the previous Canadian chair taking an advisory role during the transition year.

Expert Monitoring Groups

The CBMP takes an ecosystem-based management approach, operating as a network of networks coordinating existing species, habitat, and site-based networks. A series of Expert Monitoring Groups have been activated (marine,[32] freshwater,[33] terrestrial,[34] and coastal),[35] each dealing with one of the Arctic's major systems. These serve as umbrella mechanisms for coordinating existing biodiversity monitoring activity in the Arctic. Each Expert Monitoring Group is tasked with developing long-term integrated monitoring plans. The *Arctic Marine Biodiversity Monitoring Plan*,[36] the *Arctic Freshwater Monitoring Plan*,[37] and the *Arctic Terrestrial Biodiversity Monitoring Plan*[38] have been completed and endorsed by the Arctic Council and implementation has begun. Work is underway to complete the coastal component.

Monitoring Networks and Plans

In support of the Expert Monitoring Groups and their circumpolar monitoring plans, a series of monitoring frameworks have been developed or are under development. Completed monitoring frameworks include seabirds, marine mammals, shorebirds, reindeer, and human–wild reindeer systems.

Indices and Indicators

Effective monitoring is the foundation of responsive decision making. However, unless the right information is reported in the right formats to the right audiences, the results of such monitoring are effectively lost. In light of this, targeted and consistent reporting is a cornerstone of the CBMP. In order to facilitate effective and consistent reporting, the CBMP has chosen a suite of indices and indicators that provide a comprehensive picture of the state of Arctic biodiversity—from species to habitats to ecosystem processes to ecological services. Indices and indicators are chosen through an expert consultation process and reflect existing monitoring capacity and expertise. Currently, frequent reporting on the suite of Arctic biodiversity indicators and indices include protected areas, linguistics, and the Arctic Species Trend Index (ASTI),[39] while more are under development. They are developed in a hierarchical manner, allowing clients to "drill" down into the data from the high-order indices to more detailed indicators underpinning a particular index and—where the data allow—to specific populations, subpopulations, or regional habitat trend data. This approach will maximize the utility and reach of the information by addressing the varying data needs of end users. The ASTI is a good example of the effectiveness of this approach and the value of such indicators in contributing to the CBD. The implementation of the CBMP's Arctic Biodiversity Monitoring Plans underpins these indicators, and the resulting information will ensure that they will be continually updated to report on the status and trends in Arctic biodiversity. Further information can be found in the CBMP's Strategy for Developing Indices and Indicators to Track Status and Trends in Arctic Biodiversity.[40]

Indicators have been selected because they are scientifically valid (i.e., rigorous methodology and the ability to detect change); easily understandable and therefore more easily communicated; responsive to change (i.e., key Arctic drivers); relevant to the circumpolar region, CAFF's mandate, other biodiversity programs (both regional and global), people within the circumpolar region, people outside of the circumpolar region, and decision and policy makers; ecologically relevant; have long-term commitments to monitor; and are practical (cost effective, reliant on accessible data, technically feasible to measure, and representative of multiple species, ecosystems, and/or habitats).

Communication and Outreach

The CBMP is developing coordinated reporting and outreach tools that adhere to the CAFF Communications Strategy, targeting key audiences in their preferred formats, time lines, and languages. Results from these efforts include various publications, websites, media activities, and partner development as well as a web-based data management tool, the Arctic Biodiversity Data Service (ABDS).[41] A full list of CBMP publications can be accessed on the CAFF website.[42]

Capacity Building

A key program area of the CBMP is to engage and build upon existing and historical monitoring in regions that are currently underrepresented or that might lack the capacity to sustain monitoring activities. The CBMP believes that community-based monitoring (CBM) has significant contributions to make to circumpolar monitoring efforts. As such, all aspects of CBMP development have strong consideration and integration of CBM. Arctic inhabitants spend vast amounts of time on land and at sea. Drawing on personal experience, information shared with others, and knowledge handed down through generations, Arctic residents recognize subtle environmental changes and offer insights into their causes. They are community-based monitors by virtue of their day-to-day activities.

In addition to their inherent CBM capacity, Arctic residents can employ standard scientific monitoring procedures in the practice of citizen science, thereby extending the reach and effectiveness of programs that rely on a limited number of trained scientists to carry out monitoring.

Indigenous and other Arctic peoples wish to impart their environmental understanding to scientific discourse, not only because they have a great deal to offer, but also because this exchange represents an important step toward full participation in resource management activities.

The CBMP has three primary goals with respect to CBM:

- To incorporate data, interpretation, and expertise from CBM in the CBMP's efforts to detect, understand, and report on significant Arctic biodiversity trends

- To make CBMP data, interpretation, and expertise available to CBM efforts

- To promote the extension and/or replication of established CBM approaches and programs to other regions of the Arctic in conjunction with existing monitoring networks.

Future Direction

The CBMP will continue to focus on further development of its biodiversity indicators, of the ABDS, and completion and implementation of its Arctic Biodiversity Monitoring Plans. The technical framework for the CBMP will be further enhanced through the creation of data management platforms (ABDS and Polar Data Catalogue), pan-Arctic biodiversity indicator datasets (e.g., ASTI), and implementation of the CBMP's integrated monitoring plans and frameworks. The CBMP will continue to focus upon strategic partnership, that is, expanding program capacity in key areas. This involves targeting key organizations in Europe, Russia, and North America with the aim of further developing a broad-based consortium for improved Arctic biodiversity monitoring and conservation. In addition, the CBMP is working on better incorporating CBM activities and is developing a circumpolar registry of such efforts.

Assessments

In order to successfully conserve the natural environment and allow for economic development comprehensive baseline data that include the status and trend of Arctic biodiversity, habitats and ecosystem health are required. To fulfil this aspect of its mandate, CAFF conducts an array of assessment activities that focus on synthesizing and assessing the status and trends of biological diversity in the Arctic.[43] These activities provide much-needed descriptions of the current state of the Arctic's ecosystems and biodiversity, creating baselines for use in global and regional assessments of Arctic biodiversity and inform and guide future Arctic Council work. Examples of recent assessment activities include the Arctic Biodiversity Assessment, Life Linked to Ice,[44] an assessment of Arctic sea ice–associated biodiversity, and the ASTI. It should also be noted that aside from these current assessments, the CBMP will issue state of the Arctic environment assessments on a five-year basis.

The Arctic Biodiversity Assessment

The purpose of the ABA[45] is to synthesize and assess the status and trends of biological diversity in the Arctic. It will provide a much-needed description of the current state of the Arctic's ecosystems and biodiversity and create a baseline for use in global and regional assessments of Arctic biodiversity and a basis to inform and guide future Arctic Council work. It will provide up-to-date scientific and traditional ecological knowledge, identify gaps in the data record, identify key mechanisms driving change, and produce recommendations.

The ABA was conducted in three phases:

PHASE 1

Phase 1 was completed with the release of the *Arctic Biodiversity Trends 2010: Selected indicators of change* report[46] in May 2010. The report presents a preliminary assessment of status and trends in Arctic biodiversity and is based on the suite of indicators developed by the CBMP. For this report, 22 indicators were selected to provide a snapshot of the trends being observed in Arctic biodiversity today. The indicators were selected based on their scientific validity to cover major species groups with wide distributions across Arctic ecosystems. Special consideration was given to indicators closely associated with biodiversity use by Indigenous and local communities as well as indicators with relevance to decision makers. Indicators were also selected on the basis of what was achievable in terms of existing data and in the time frame available. Each indicator chapter provides an overview of the status and trends of a given indicator, information on stressors, and concerns for the future.

The report was aimed at a broad audience, including governments and residents of the Arctic. It was the Arctic Council's contribution to:

1. the 2010 Biodiversity Target of achieving a significant reduction in the rate of biodiversity loss;

2. the International Year of Biodiversity in 2010; and

3. the third edition of Global Biodiversity Outlook.

PHASE 2

The *Arctic Biodiversity Assessment: Status and trends in Arctic biodiversity*,[47] the full scientific assessment and accompanying *Arctic Biodiversity Assessment: Synthesis* report,[48] was released in May 2015 at the Arctic Council Ministerial in Iqaluit, Canada. The ABA represents the best available science informed by traditional ecological knowledge on the status and trends of Arctic biodiversity. It has 20 chapters containing detailed scientific information, supplemented with traditional ecological knowledge on the status and trends in Arctic biodiversity. These chapters include species diversity; mammals; birds; amphibians and reptiles; fishes; terrestrial and freshwater invertebrates; marine invertebrates; plants; fungi; microorganisms; terrestrial ecosystems; freshwater ecosystems; marine ecosystems; parasites; invasive species that are human induced; genetics; provisioning and cultural services; disturbance, feedbacks, and conservations; and linguistic diversity.

PHASE 3

To accompany the *Arctic Biodiversity Assessment* report and the *Arctic Biodiversity Assessment Synthesis*, CAFF has prepared a summary of the key findings and developed policy recommendations in an *Arctic Biodiversity*

Assessment: Report for Policy Makers[49] (available in English, Russian, French, Danish, Greenlandic, and Inuktitut). Relevant aspects from that report are excerpted below:

- Key finding 1: Arctic biodiversity is being degraded, but decisive action taken now can help sustain vast, relatively undisturbed ecosystems of tundra, mountains, fresh water, and seas and the valuable services they provide.

- Key finding 2: Climate change is by far the most serious threat to Arctic biodiversity and exacerbates all other threats.

- Key finding 3: Many Arctic migratory species are threatened by overharvest and habitat alteration outside the Arctic, especially birds along the East Asian flyway.

- Key finding 4: Disturbance and habitat degradation can diminish Arctic biodiversity and the opportunities for Arctic residents and visitors to enjoy the benefits of ecosystem services.

- Key finding 5: Pollution from both long-range transport and local sources threatens the health of Arctic species and ecosystems.

- Key finding 6: There are currently few invasive alien species in the Arctic, but more are expected with climate change and increased human activity.

- Key finding 7: Overharvest was historically the primary human impact on many Arctic species, but sound management has successfully addressed this problem in most, but not all, cases.

- Key finding 8: Current knowledge of many Arctic species, ecosystems, and their stressors is fragmentary, making detection and assessment of trends and their implications difficult for many aspects of Arctic biodiversity.

- Key finding 9: The challenges facing Arctic biodiversity are interconnected, requiring comprehensive solutions and international cooperation.[50]

Recommendations that have been developed in response to these key findings are aimed primarily at the Arctic Council, its member states, and Permanent Participants. Success in conserving Arctic biodiversity, however, also depends upon actions by non-Arctic states, regional and local authorities, industry, and all who live, work, and travel in the Arctic. These recommendations may, therefore, also provide a guide for action for states, authorities, and organizations beyond the Arctic Council. Some of the ABA recommendations directly encourage cooperation with those outside the Arctic Council process.

Large tracts of the Arctic remain relatively undisturbed, providing an opportunity for proactive measures that can minimize or even prevent future problems that would be costly, or impossible, to reverse. The key findings of the ABA are interrelated, and responding to them would benefit from a holistic approach. When taken together, the following three cross-cutting themes are evident:

- The significance of climate change as the most serious underlying driver of overall change in biodiversity

- The necessity of taking an ecosystem-based approach to management

- The importance of mainstreaming biodiversity by making it integral to other policy fields, for instance, by ensuring that biodiversity objectives are considered in development standards, plans, and operations

A comprehensive and integrated approach is needed to address the interconnected and complex challenges facing biodiversity and to ensure informed policy decisions in a changing Arctic. In addition to many Arctic Council initiatives underway, there are other conventions and processes addressing these cross-cutting themes and many of the individual stressors acting on biodiversity. This includes many regulatory and nonregulatory measures that are in place or under development to provide consistent standards and/or approaches to development in the Arctic. Many of these can, or do, provide safeguards for biodiversity.

Care was taken in the development of the ABA recommendations to review recommendations from other major Arctic Council initiatives. Many of the recommendations overlap and are mutually supportive, emphasizing the importance of considering all recommendations together. Some of the ABA recommendations reinforce the significance to biodiversity of recommendations or actions already underway, others build upon existing recommendations or processes, and others are more specifically focused on biodiversity issues. All are important to ensure the conservation of Arctic species, ecosystems, and the services they provide.

Climate Change

Actively support international efforts addressing climate change, both reducing stressors and implementing adaptation measures, as an urgent matter. Of specific importance are efforts to reduce greenhouse and methane gas emissions as well as black carbon and tropospheric ozone precursors. Incorporate resilience and adaptation of biodiversity to climate change into plans for development in the Arctic.

Ecosystem-based Management

Advance and advocate ecosystem-based management efforts in the Arctic as a framework for cooperation, planning, and development. This includes an approach to development that proceeds cautiously, with sound short- and long-term environmental risk assessment and management, using the best available scientific and traditional ecological knowledge, following the best environmental practices, considering cumulative effects, and adhering to international standards.

Mainstreaming Biodiversity

Require the incorporation of biodiversity objectives and provisions into all Arctic Council work and encourage the same for ongoing and future international standards, agreements, plans, operations, and/or other tools specific to development in the Arctic. This should include, but not be restricted to, oil and gas development, shipping, fishing, tourism, and mining.

Identifying and Safeguarding Important Areas for Biodiversity

Advance the protection of large areas of ecologically important marine, terrestrial, and freshwater habitats, taking into account ecological resilience in a changing climate.

1. Build upon existing and ongoing domestic and international processes to complete the identification of ecologically and biologically important marine areas and implement appropriate measures for their conservation.

2. Build upon existing networks of terrestrial protected areas, filling geographic gaps, including underrepresented areas, rare or unique habitats, particularly productive areas such as large river deltas, biodiversity hotspots, and areas with large aggregations of animals, such as bird breeding colonies, seal whelping areas, and caribou calving grounds.

3. Promote the active involvement of Indigenous Peoples in the management and sustainable use of protected areas.

Develop guidelines and implement appropriate spatial and temporal measures where necessary to reduce human disturbance to areas critical for sensitive life stages of Arctic species that are outside protected areas, for example, along transportation corridors. Such areas include calving grounds, den sites, feeding grounds, migration routes, and molting areas. This also means safeguarding important habitats such as wetlands and polynyas.

Develop and implement mechanisms that best safeguard Arctic biodiversity under changing environmental conditions, such as loss of sea ice, glaciers, and permafrost.

1. Safeguard areas in the northern parts of the Arctic where high Arctic species have a relatively greater chance to survive for climatic or geographical reasons, such as certain islands and mountainous areas, which can act as a refuge for unique biodiversity.

2. Maintain functional connectivity within and between protected areas in order to protect ecosystem resilience and facilitate adaptation to climate change.

Addressing Individual Stressors on Biodiversity

Reduce stressors on migratory species rangewide, including habitat degradation and overharvesting on wintering and staging areas and along flyways and other migration routes.

1. Pursue or strengthen formal migratory bird cooperation agreements and other specific actions on a flyway level between Arctic and non-Arctic states with first priority given to the East Asian flyway.

2. Collaborate with relevant international commissions, conventions, networks, and other organizations sharing an interest in the conservation of Arctic migratory species to identify and implement appropriate conservation actions.

3. Develop and implement joint management and recovery plans for threatened species with relevant non-Arctic states and entities.

4. Identify and advance the conservation of key wintering and staging habitats for migratory birds, particularly wetlands.

Reduce the threat of invasive alien/nonnative species to the Arctic by developing and implementing common measures for early detection and reporting, identifying and blocking pathways of introduction, and sharing best practices and techniques for monitoring, eradication, and control. This includes supporting international efforts currently underway, for example, those of the International Maritime Organization to effectively treat ballast water to clean and treat ship hulls and drilling rigs.

Promote the sustainable management of the Arctic's living resources and their habitat.

1. Improve circumpolar cooperation in data gathering and assessment of populations and harvest and in the development of improved harvest methods, planning, and management. This includes improving the use and integration of traditional ecological knowledge and science in managing harvests and in improving the development and use of community-based monitoring as an important information source.

2. Develop pan-Arctic conservation and management plans for shared species that are, or will potentially be, harvested

or commercially exploited that incorporate common monitoring objectives, population assessments, harvesting regimes, and guidelines for best practices in harvest methodology; consider maintenance of genetic viability and adaptation to climate change as guiding principles.

3. Support efforts to plan and manage commercial fisheries in international waters under common international objectives that ensure long-term sustainability of species and ecosystems. Encourage precautionary, science-based management of fisheries in areas beyond national jurisdiction in accordance with international law to ensure the long-term sustainability of species and ecosystems.

4. Support efforts to develop, improve, and employ fishing technologies and practices that reduce by-catch of marine mammals, seabirds, and non-target fish and avoid significant adverse impact to the seabed.

5. Develop and implement, in cooperation with reindeer herders, management plans that ensure the sustainability of reindeer herding and the quality of habitat for grazing and calving.

Reduce the threat of pollutants to Arctic biodiversity.

1. Support and enhance international efforts and cooperation to identify, assess, and reduce existing and emerging harmful contaminants.

2. Support the development of appropriate prevention and clean-up measures and technologies that are responsive to oil spills in the Arctic, especially in ice-filled waters, such that they are ready for implementation in advance of major oil and gas developments.

3. Encourage local and national action to implement best practices for local wastes, enhance efforts to clean up legacy contaminated sites, and include contaminant reduction and reclamation plans in development projects.

Improving Knowledge and Public Awareness

Evaluate the range of services provided by Arctic biodiversity in order to determine the costs associated with biodiversity loss and the value of effective conservation in order to assess change and support improved decision making.

Increase and focus on inventory, long-term monitoring, and research efforts to address key gaps in scientific knowledge identified in this assessment to better facilitate the development and implementation of conservation and management strategies. Areas of particular concern identified through the ABA include components critical to ecosystem functions, including important characteristics of invertebrates, microbes, parasites, and pathogens.

Recognize the value of traditional ecological knowledge and work to further integrate it into the assessment, planning, and management of Arctic biodiversity. This includes involving Arctic peoples and their knowledge in the survey, monitoring, and analysis of Arctic biodiversity.

Promote public training, education, and community-based monitoring, where appropriate, as integral elements in conservation and management.

Research and monitor individual and cumulative effects of stressors and drivers of relevance to biodiversity, with a focus on stressors that are expected to have rapid and significant impacts and issues where knowledge is lacking. This should include, but not be limited to, modeling potential future species range changes as a result of these stressors; developing knowledge of and identifying tipping points, thresholds, and cumulative effects for Arctic biodiversity; and developing robust quantitative indicators for stressors through the CBMP.

Develop communication and outreach tools and methodologies to better convey the importance and value of Arctic biodiversity and the changes it is undergoing.[51]

Implementation

The Arctic Council ministers agreed to implement 17 recommendations articulated in the *Arctic Biodiversity Assessment: Report for Policy Makers.* Implementing the ABA recommendations requires a combination of building on existing efforts and embarking in new directions. As such, CAFF has developed *Actions for Biodiversity 2013–2021: Implementing the recommendations of the Arctic Biodiversity Assessment,*[52] the implementation plan for the ABA's 17 recommendations. It is a living document that will be reviewed and updated every two years. The plan is not meant to be exhaustive or to replace working group work plans; rather, it is complementary, emphasizing specific actions that address the ABA recommendations in a phased approach:

PHASE 1: 2013–15

The focus was on the development of the implementation plan and initiating key actions directed toward:

- Short-lived climate forcers (Recommendation 1);

- Ecosystem-based management (Recommendation 3);

- mainstreaming biodiversity (Recommendation 4);

- addressing stressors on biodiversity, in particular, oil spills (Recommendation 11);

- stressors on migratory species (Recommendation 8);

- improving knowledge and public awareness, in particular, improving access to data (Recommendation 13), integrating traditional knowledge (Recommendation 14), evaluating ecosystem services (Recommendation 12), and communication and outreach tools (Recommendation 17); and

- safeguarding important marine areas (Recommendation 6).

PHASE 2: 2015–17

Phase 2 continues focus on:

- mainstreaming biodiversity (Recommendation 4),

- reducing stressors on migratory birds (Recommendation 8),

- ecosystem services evaluation (Recommendation 12), and

- communications and outreach (Recommendation 17).

Additional focus is on:

- adaptation to climate change (Recommendation 2);

- addressing stressors on biodiversity, in particular, migratory species (Recommendation 8), invasive species (Recommendation 9), and pollution (Recommendation 11);

- safeguarding critical areas (Recommendations 5, 6, and 7); and

- improving knowledge and public awareness, in particular, monitoring and traditional and local knowledge (Recommendations 13, 14, and 15) and indicator development (Recommendation 16).

PHASE 3: 2017–19

The added focus will be on:

- safeguarding biodiversity under changing conditions (Recommendation 7);

- cumulative effects (Recommendation 16); and

- improving knowledge and public awareness (Recommendation 17), including by contributing to the CBD assessment on achievement of the United Nations' Aichi Biodiversity Targets and convening the second Arctic Biodiversity Congress.

PHASE 4: 2019–21

The focus for the final implementation period will be on completing projects, implementing strategies and plans developed in early phases, evaluating progress, and designing follow-up.

Life Linked to Ice:
An Assessment of Arctic Sea Ice–associated Biodiversity

This project, led by Canada, Russia, and the United States, is a response to findings from the Arctic Biodiversity Assessment. It aims to

1. provide a summary of the current status and trends of ice-associated biodiversity, including direct effects on marine species and indirect effects on terrestrial species;

2. discuss the expected reaction of these biota to lower occurrences of ice;

3. reflect on the effects of low ice and its impact on species biodiversity to northern peoples; and

4. recommend actions that might mitigate these changes.

Climate models indicate trends toward reductions in the extent and thickness of sea ice in the Arctic. Many species are found in association with this ice and can therefore be expected to be significantly affected by the projected reduction in ice availability. It is also important to recognize that sea ice–associated species are tropically linked directly and indirectly to others in marine and terrestrial ecosystems and must be considered in any analysis of the effects of sea ice loss.

Consideration of the effects of warming oceans on ice-dependent species in the Arctic is well underway. Snow, Water, Ice, and Permafrost in the Arctic (SWIPA) is the Arctic Council's Project on Climate Change and the Arctic cryosphere. This project has reviewed the biological impacts of changes to sea ice in the Arctic and summarizes the role sea ice plays for several key species in the North. This kind of information will prove valuable for the ecosystem-level analysis that will be conducted as part of the project proposed here. This project will build on other initiatives like the Arctic Biodiversity Assessment and SWIPA in synthesizing and assessing the status and trends of biological diversity in the Arctic.

Arctic Species Trend Index

The ASTI,[53] referred to above as a CBMP indicator, uses population-monitoring data to track trends in marine, terrestrial, and freshwater Arctic vertebrate species. The index allows for a composite measure of the overall population trends of Arctic vertebrate populations (between 1970 and 2004). It can also be organized to display trends based on taxonomy, biome, or region. The index tracks almost 1,000 Arctic vertebrate population datasets by biome, taxon, and migratory status.

To facilitate the examination of regional trends, the Arctic was divided into three subregions: Subarctic, Low Arctic, and High Arctic. As well, species population data were classified based on the broad habitats they live in (land, lakes and rivers, or oceans). The latter were also identified by which ocean basin they inhabit, Arctic, Atlantic, or Pacific. The individual populations in the ASTI were further tagged based on migratory status, trophic level, and other relevant categories. The ASTI allows us to track broad trends in the Arctic's living resources and identify potential causes of those trends, whether they are responses to natural phenomena or human-induced stressors.

Most recently, the ASTI has published an Arctic Migratory Bird Index,[54] which describes the broad-scale trends in 129 selected migratory bird species. This examination is necessary for designing and targeting informed conservation strategies at the flyway level to address reported declines.

Strategies

The framework Cooperative Strategy for the Conservation of Arctic Biodiversity serves as the basis for CAFF's conservation strategies and action plans to conserve specific Arctic habitats species groups of common conservation concern within the Arctic countries. In addition, strategies are also developed on issues of relevance to Arctic biodiversity conservation, including capacity building, data management, and community-based monitoring. Strategies include scientific, conservation, and implementation recommendations to ensure the most effective management response. They are developed through intensive international cooperation between countries and scientists across the Arctic region. They contribute to enhancing cooperation among Arctic countries, communities, and organizations to secure the natural productive capacity of Arctic ecosystems and biological diversity at all levels in the Arctic.

CAFF Activities

Expert Groups

CAFF may establish expert groups with specific mandates related to key activities and ensure that scientists, conservationists, and managers with common Arctic interests have a forum to promote, facilitate, and coordinate conservation, management, and research activities of mutual concern. These groups have been invaluable in synthesizing, coordinating, and publishing research.

Supporting Activities

CAFF also has a wide range of supporting activities that focus on various aspects of Arctic biodiversity by helping to understand and discover the status and trends and ways in which Arctic conservation can be improved and helping to promote practices that ensure the sustainability of the Arctic's resources. An example of such work includes participation in projects such as the Arctic Spatial Data Infrastructure (Arctic SDI).[55] The Arctic SDI will allow for the creation of a harmonized map covering the entire Arctic region. This will facilitate more robust handling and manipulation of data for both research and management purposes.

Challenges Facing Arctic Conservation and the Development of a Dynamic Forward-looking Approach

A number of challenges are envisaged for Arctic biodiversity. With a warming climate, shipping and resource development are likely to increase, with a potential for increased pollution and disturbance to Arctic biodiversity. More development may lead to different human settlement patterns and changes in resource use. Decreased ice cover may increase the number of areas accessible to fisheries and make new species economically available and so create opportunities as well as challenges for sustainable use. Many Arctic species also migrate great distances throughout the world and so are subject to environmental changes during their travels, including carrying pollutants back to the North in their bodies.[56]

Because species move through Arctic as well as non-Arctic territories, international cooperation beyond the Arctic is needed for their concerted and sustained conservation. One response to greater human pressures in the Arctic is the creation of protected areas. Although improving, current protected areas are still inadequate in representation of habitats and ecosystems. For instance, it is generally recognized that marine-protected areas are particularly scarce. However, protected areas are only one aspect of biodiversity conservation, as climate change inevitably calls for greater attention to more general conservation measures due to shifts in distributions and new introductions into local flora and fauna.

We do not know enough about the effects of climate change on biodiversity, what these changes mean to local flora and fauna, and what effects they have on natural resources, which are of great importance to local peoples. The *Arctic Climate Impact Assessment* clearly demonstrated a general lack of information on quantified effects of climate change on biodiversity. It is not enough to show that climate change results in changes to the physical environment.

Directly or indirectly, the peoples of the Arctic live off the biological products of land, fresh water, and sea through hunting, fishing, and agriculture. It is vital that we are able to detect changes and how they vary geographically and among species, populations, and biological communities. We need to understand the complex interactions among human communities, climate, and communities of Arctic species. Although this information is beginning to surface, the accumulation of data on biodiversity is still trailing climate modeling and the gathering of information on the abiotic environment.

Aspects of vanishing local knowledge, such as Arctic languages and traditional ecological knowledge, need to be fully recognized and acted upon. Climate change and all the associated issues—be they of the natural environment or human related—pose a new suite of challenges for biodiversity and peoples of the Arctic. Taking care of the environment poses major challenges for the Arctic Council and all other stakeholders interested in the North. CAFF, as the biodiversity arm of the Arctic Council, contributes toward seeking appropriate solutions to those challenges.

In order to respond, plan, and adapt to the changes currently underway, conservation in the Arctic must be dynamic and forward looking. There are a number of actions to be taken, including the scale, availability, and access to information, communication, and funding.

CAFF is establishing a dynamic forward-looking approach to scientific management and policy needs. Addressing the pressures facing Arctic biodiversity requires better and more coordinated information on changes in biodiversity. Within the Arctic Council, attention has been focused on producing assessments that are static and not dynamic. In this approach, there are extensive time gaps between when information is collected, analyzed, and made available to decision makers—and even more time between similar assessments. This means that often the data they contain may not be the most recent, and consequently the analysis built on this information may be out of date. In addition, identifying and responding to emerging trends becomes challenging. Once completed, the work and effort gone into building circumpolar cooperation on the topic of the one-off assessment stops and the process begins anew on some other aspect, often from the ground up. This highlights a primary challenge: to shorten the gap between when data are collected, processed, and analyzed and when they are presented to decision makers. The aim must be to allow for a quicker response time for policy makers to ensure that their management decisions are more nimble, flexible, and fluid. Conservation activities must be dynamic and forward looking and not stuck in the static approach, which has dominated until now.

CAFF has recognized this challenge and in recent years worked toward developing a solution. This approach has focused not just on conducting traditional assessments but also on the creation of a framework to allow for the collection, processing, and analysis of data on a continuous basis. Through the CBMP, CAFF has brought together numerous datasets that indicate changes in biodiversity. This program is an effective response to the many challenges facing management in the wake of climate change and changing human use of the Arctic. Much data already exist on Arctic biodiversity, but one challenge is to bring data together, analyze and identify the gaps in circumpolar monitoring, and put them to use to facilitate better-informed policy decisions. The CBMP will utilize the baseline of knowledge created by the ABA in order to develop an engine to feed information needs allowing the CAFF approach to become a dynamic living tool that can produce regular and more flexible assessments and analyses. This dynamic baseline will supply up-to-date and regular data to aid decision makers in identifying priority actions.

This approach is a definite response to the international commitments that the Arctic countries have undertaken on halting the loss of biodiversity. The results are of practical use for the many questions facing the Arctic countries and the Arctic Council in their deliberations. The current challenge is to use available data in a better and more coordinated way, fill gaps in knowledge, and increase the geographic coverage of Arctic information for the conservation and sustainability of the environment as well as for the benefit of decision makers, Arctic peoples, science, and the global community at large.

Notes

Courtney Price synthesized this article from the report written by CAFF, "Arctic Biodiversity Assessment Status and Trends in Arctic Biodiversity," *Conservation of Arctic Flora and Fauna* (2013); http://www.caff.is/assessment-series/arctic-biodiversity-assessment/233-arctic-biodiversity-assessment-2013.

1. Conservation of Arctic Flora and Fauna (CAFF); www.caff.is.

2. United Nations Environment Program Convention on Biological Diversity, "Ways and Means to Support Ecosystem Restoration" (Aug. 5, 2011); https://www.cbd.int/doc/meetings/sbstta/sbstta-15/official/sbstta-15-04-en.pdf.

3. Arctic Council; www.arctic-council.org.

4. CAFF, "CAFF Management Board"; http://www.caff.is/management-board/national-representatives (Representatives include Canada, Greenland/Faroe Islands/Kingdom of Denmark, Finland, Iceland, Norway, Sweden, the Russian Federation, and the United States of America).

5. Ibid. (Aleut International Association, Arctic Athabaskan Council, Gwich'in Council International, Inuit Circumpolar Council, Russian Association of Indigenous Peoples of the North, and Saami Council).

6. Ibid. (China, France, India, Italy, Germany, Japan, the Netherlands, Poland, Singapore, Spain, Republic of Korea, and the United Kingdom).

7. Ibid. (International Federation of Red Cross & Red Crescent Societies, International Union for the Conservation of Nature, Nordic Council of Ministers, Nordic Environment Finance Corporation, North Atlantic Marine Mammal Commission, Standing Committee of the Parliamentarians of the Arctic Region, United Nations Economic Commission for Europe, United Nations Development Program, United Nations Environment Program, Advisory Committee on Protection of the Seas, Arctic Circumpolar Gateway, Association of World Reindeer Herders, Circumpolar Conservation Union, International Arctic Science Committee, International Arctic Social Sciences Association, International Union for Circumpolar Health, International Work Group for Indigenous Affairs, Northern Forum, University of the Arctic, World Wide Fund for Nature-Global Arctic Program).

8. CAFF International Secretariat, *Strategic Plan for the Conservation of Arctic Biological Diversity* (Akureyri, Iceland, 1998); http://caff.is/strategies-series/28-all-strategies-documents/62-strategic-plan-for-the-conservation-of-arctic-biological-diversity.

9. CAFF, *Conservation of Arctic Flora and Fauna, Arctic Biodiversity Assessment: Synthesis* (Akureyri, Iceland, 2013): 13.

10. Arctic Climate Impact Assessment, *Arctic Climate Impact Assessment* (Cambridge: Cambridge University Press, 2005): 1042.

11. C. Zöckler, S. Delany, and W. Hagemeijer, "Wader Populations Are Declining—How Will We Elucidate the Reasons?" *Wader Study Group Bull* 100 (2003): 202–11.

12. C. Zöckler, "The Role of the Goose Specialist Group in the Circumpolar Biodiversity Monitoring Program (CBMP)," *Vogelwelt* 129 (2008): 127–30.

13. CAFF International Secretariat, *Conservation of Arctic Flora and Fauna, Arctic Biodiversity Assessment: Synthesis* (Akureyri, Iceland, 2013): 21.

14. Ibid.

15. Ibid.

16. Arctic Monitoring and Assessment Programme, *Arctic Oil and Gas* (Oslo, Norway: 2007): 17.

17. Arctic Climate Impact Assessment, *Arctic Climate Impact Assessment* (New York: Cambridge University Press, 2005).

18. Arctic Monitoring and Assessment Programme, *Oil and Gas Activities in the Arctic: Effects and Potential Effects* (Oslo, Norway: 2009).

19. Arctic Human Development Report, *Arctic Human Development Report,* Stefansson Arctic Institute (Akureyri, Iceland: 2004).

20. Arctic Marine Shipping Assessment, *Arctic Marine Shipping Assessment 2009 Report,* Arctic Council.

21. Arctic Monitoring and Assessment Programme (AMAP) 1998, *AMAP Assessment Report: Arctic Pollution Issues* (Oslo, Norway: 1998); https://oaarchive.arctic-council.org/handle/11374/924.

22. CAFF, *Arctic Flora and Fauna: Status and Conservation* (Helsinki: Edita, 2001): 266.

23. Ibid.

24. S. Solomon, ed., et al., "Intergovernmental Panel on Climate Change (IPCC), Summary for Policymakers," *Climate Change 2007: The Physical Science Basis. Contribution of Working Group I to the Fourth Assessment Report of the Intergovernmental Panel on Climate Change.*

25. E. Post et al., "Ecological Dynamics Across the Arctic Associated with Recent Climate Change," *Science* 325 (5946) (2009): 1355–58.

26. Supra at 4 (Arctic Contaminants Action Program, Arctic Monitoring and Assessment Programme, Conservation of Arctic Flora and Fauna, Emergency Prevention, Preparedness and Response, Protection of the Arctic Marine Environment, Sustainable Development Working Group).

27. Government of Canada. *Development for the People of the North: The Arctic Council Program During Canada's Chairmanship 2013–15.* Arctic Council.

28. Finland's Chairmanship Program for the Arctic Council 2017–2019, "Exploring Common Solutions," Ministry for Foreign Affairs of Finland, 2017; http://www.arctic-council.org/images/PDF_attachments/FIN_Chairmanship/Finnish_Chairmanship_Program_Arctic_Council_2017-2019.pdf.

29. Arctic Biodiversity Assessment; www.arcticbiodiversity.is.

30. The Circumpolar Biodiversity Monitoring Programme; www.cbmp.is.

31. The Circumpolar Biodiversity Monitoring Programme, available at https://www.caff.is/monitoring.

32. CAFF, available at www.caff.is/marine.

33. CAFF, available at www.caff.is/freshwater.

34. CAFF, available at www.caff.is/terrestrial.

35. CAFF, available at www.caff.is/coastal.

36. M. J. Gill et al., *Arctic Marine Biodiversity Monitoring Plan (CBMP-MARINE PLAN)*, CAFF Monitoring Series Report No. 3 (Akureyri, Iceland: 2011).

37. J. M. Culp et al., *The Arctic Freshwater Biodiversity Monitoring Plan*, CAFF Monitoring Series Report No. 7 (Akureyri, Iceland: 2012).

38. T. Christensen et al., "The Arctic Terrestrial Biodiversity Monitoring Plan. CAFF Monitoring Series Report No. 7. CAFF International Secretariat. Akureyri, Iceland" (2013).

39. Arctic Species Trend Index; www.asti.is.

40. M. J. Gill and C. Zöckler, *A Strategy for Developing Indices and Indicators to Track Status and Trends in Arctic Biodiversity*, CAFF CBMP Report No. 12 (Akureyri, Iceland: 2008).

41. The Arctic Biodiversity Data Service; www.abds.is.

42. CAFF Publications; www.caff.is/publications.

43. CAFF Search Guide Service, available at http://searchguide.level3.com/search/?q=http%3A//www.caff.s/assessments&r=&t=0.

44. J. Eamer, G. M. Donaldson, A. J. Gaston, K. N. Kosobokova, K. F. Lárusson, I. A. Melnikov, J. D. Reist, E. Richardson, L. Staples, C. H. von Quillfeldt, 2013. *Life Linked to Ice: A Guide to Sea-Ice-Associated Biodiversity in This Time of Rapid Change*. CAFF Assessment Series No. 10. Conservation of Arctic Flora and Fauna, Iceland.

45. Arctic Council, *Welcome to the Arctic Biodiversity Assessment* (2014); https://www.arcticbiodiversity.is/.

46. CAFF, *Arctic Biodiversity Trends 2010—Selected Indicators of Change* (Akureyri, Iceland: 2010); https://www.caff.is/assessment-series/arctic-biodiversity-assessment/162-arctic-biodiversity-trends-2010-selected-indicators-of-change.

47. CAFF. "Arctic Biodiversity Assessment Status and Trends in Arctic Biodiversity," *Conservation of Arctic Flora and Fauna* (2013); http://www.caff.is/assessment-series/arctic-biodiversity-assessment/233-arctic-biodiversity-assessment-2013.

48. Arctic Council, *Synthesis: Implications for conservation*, 2013; https://www.arcticbiodiversity.is/the-report/synthesis.

49. CAFF, *Arctic Biodiversity Assessment: Report for Policy Makers*. CAFF International Secretariat (Akureyri, Iceland); https://www.caff.is/assessment-series/229-arctic-biodiversity-assessment-2013-report-for-policy-makers-english.

50. Ibid., 8–16.

51. Ibid., 17–22.

52. CAFF. 2015. *Actions for Arctic Biodiversity, 2013–2021: Implementing the Recommendations of the Arctic Biodiversity Assessment* (Akureyri, Iceland); http://www.caff.is/actions-for-arctic-biodiversity-2013-2021.

53. CAFF, *Arctic Species Trend Index (ASTI)*, https://www.caff.is/asti/.

54. S. Deinet et al., *The Arctic Species Trend Index: Migratory Birds Index*, CAFF (Akureyri, Iceland, 2015).

55. Arctic Spatial Data Infrastructure; www.arctic-sdi.org.

56. CAFF, *Arctic Biodiversity Assessment: Synthesis* (Akureyri, Iceland, 2013), 14; https://www.caff.is/assessment-series/arctic-biodiversity-assessment/232-arctic-biodiversity-assessment-2013-synthesis.

6

Is the Climatic Optimum
on Its Way Back?

Consequences, Measures, and Attitudes Associated with Climate Change in Finland

MILTON NÚÑEZ

Fennoscandia's Last Major Thawing

One possible explanation for Finland's calm attitude toward global warming may be the knowledge that this is not the first time the territory that is now the country of Finland has undergone such processes. In point of fact, there have been dozens of "big thaws" connected with past interstadials and interglacials. Some 20,000 years ago, Fennoscandia lay under a 2–3 kilometers of thick ice sheet, and the weight of more than 1,000 cubic kilometers of ice had pressed down the bedrock by hundreds of meters.[1] Based on current data from Greenland, mean temperatures were probably around –30°C, possibly colder. Then, as world climates became increasingly warmer in the last 18,000 years, the ice sheet gradually melted and Fennoscandia became once again ice free. This last major thawing event took place during the years 10,500–8,500 years calibrated before the present era (hereinafter "cal BP").

Finland then became a dynamically changing world. As the ice sheet receded, water from melt and the ice-dammed Baltic basin flooded the still ice-depressed bedrock, which was at the same time reacting with powerful isostatic rebound (up to 50 centimeters per year). The Baltic basin went from being an ice-dammed lake to a glacial sea and then to another huge lake. The latter lasted until around 9,000 cal BP, when the rising ocean breached the Danish sound, gradually turning the Baltic basin into a true sea. By then, the isostatic uplift had declined to less than three centimeters per year and mean temperatures were 2–3° Celsius higher than today—this was the so-called Climatic Optimum. After 4,000 cal BP, both temperature and Baltic basin conditions gradually evolved into those of modern times. The same applies to the isostatic rebound which, though considerably slower, continues at the impressive rate of 8–2 millimeters per year (Figure 6.1). This uplift phenomenon serves as a continuous reminder of Finland's glaciated past.[2]

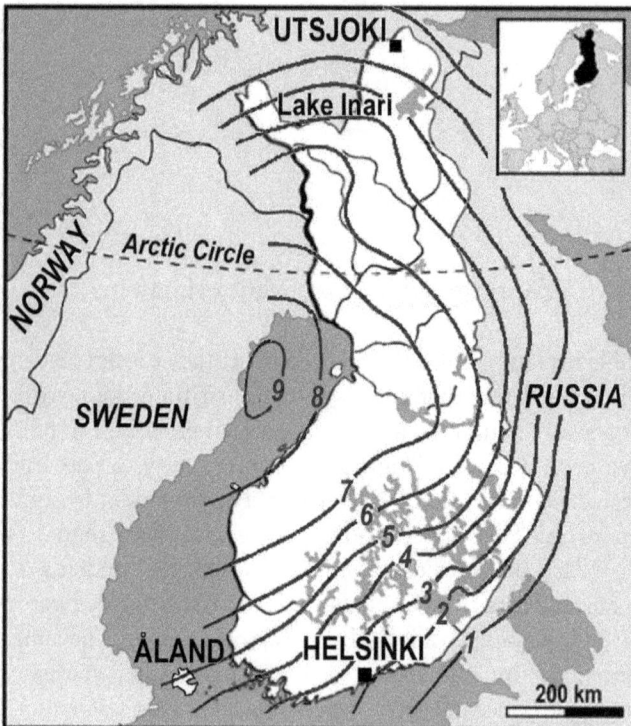

Figure 6.1. Geographical situation of Finland with places mentioned in the text and the isobases of isostatic uplift in mm/year or dm/century. J. Kakkuri, "Fennoskandian maakohoaminen," *Suomen kartasto*. Helsinki: Karttakeskus (1990).

Finland Today

Finland is a fairly large country situated between 60 and 70 degrees north. Being about 1160 kilometers long in a north-south direction, the country's temperatures, precipitation, and growing seasons vary accordingly.

The gradient in temperatures and growing season lengths is actually southwest to northeast, due to the favorable influence of the Gulf Stream, which literally drags Finland down into a much milder climatic zone than what one would expect from 60–70 degrees north latitude. For example, Finnish agriculture is possible at the 65th parallel and even beyond, whereas in Canada agriculture barely reaches the 55th parallel. Although seldom mentioned in connection to global warming, changes in the configuration of the Gulf Stream could have very negative consequences to Finland and Fennoscandia.

At about 11 million tons, Finland's per capita greenhouse gas (GHG) emissions are the highest of Fennoscandia and the 28 International Energy Agency countries.[3] This is generally blamed on the combination of cold climate, small and thinly spread population, and long distances between urban centers, as seen below. Most of Finland's GHG emissions indeed come from the energy used in electricity production, heating, and transportation.

Table 6.1. A few relevant facts about Finland

Population	5,426,674
Area	338,424 km^2
Population density	16 indiv./ km^2
Latitude	60–70°N
N-S length	c.1160 km
Mean annual temperature	5 to –4°C
Mean July temperature	17 to 12°C
Mean February temperature	–4 to –14°C
Mean annual precipitation	500–750 mm
Growing season	180–100 d
GHG emissions 2011	66.8 M tons

Climate Change Scenarios

A series of predictions and scenarios related to the effects of climate change in Finland have been advanced. In general, their local negative impacts are thought to be moderate and relatively easy to compensate through preventive and/or adaptive measures. Among the most important are the following:

- Higher temperatures and precipitation, mainly during the winter months;

- An increase in the frequency of extreme weather events;

- An increase of pests and diseases affecting crops, livestock, and humans; and,

- Baltic Sea conditions that might affect marine life and important fish stocks.

One major global consequence of climate change—sea level rise—is not thought to have the potential to greatly affect Finland (Figure 6.2). The isostatic uplift will supposedly compensate for that, as seen below. It is estimated that the Helsinki area would experience a water rise of only 30–40 centimeters by 2100, and it is calculated that coastal cities and areas where the uplift is more than 6.5 millimeters per year will not be affected by sea level rise.[4]

Indications of Ongoing Climate Change

On the whole, it can be said that earlier predictions seem to be holding, even if the observation period is rather short and the recorded trends are somewhat blurred by fluctuations and records of similar weather events in the past. For example, it is true that this century has seen some extreme events represented by mini-tornados and floods caused by strong winds in the coastal zone and by torrential rains inland. However, there are records of similar surges of destructive storms in the 1970s and 1980s[5] as well as earlier (though insurance companies have not reported them thoroughly enough for adequate comparison). Moreover, none of the twenty-first-century extreme weather events comes close to the legendary

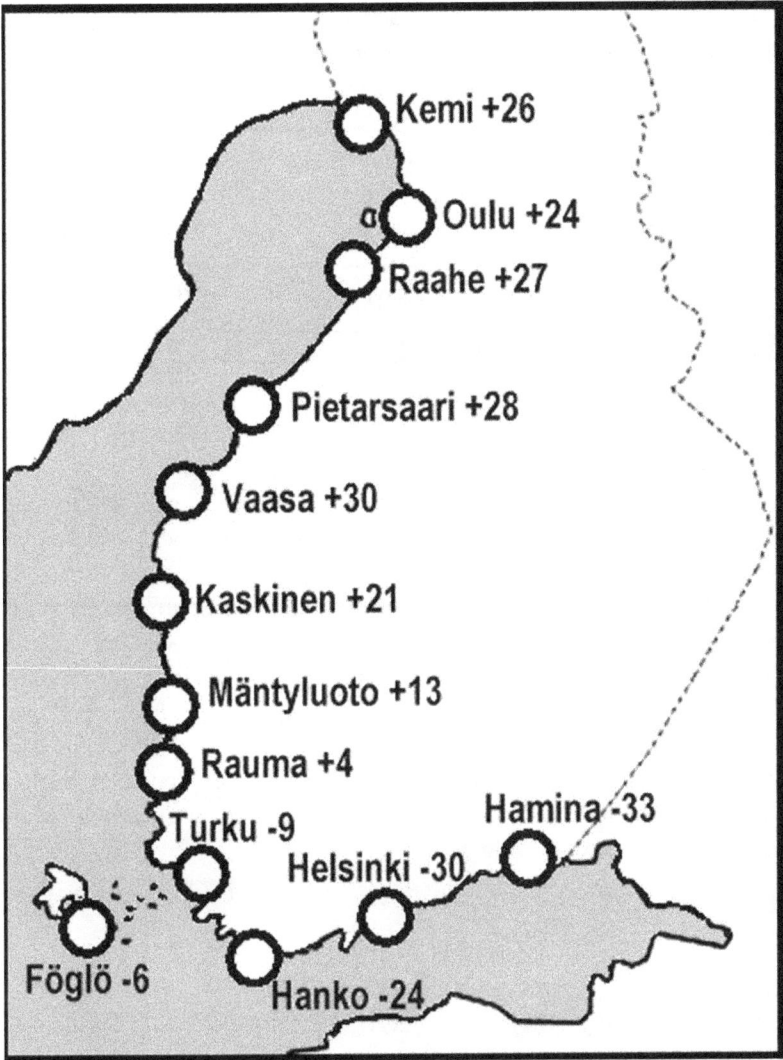

Figure 6.2. Sea level scenarios for 2100 in coastal cities/towns. The negative values (in cm) mark those towns where the rising sea level will overcome the local isostatic uplift by 2100. The positive values denote those towns where the uplift is expected to exceed the sea level rise. All values are weighted averages in centimeters. M. Johansson et al., "Global sea level rise scenarios adapted to the Finnish coast." *Journal of Marine Systems* 129 (Jan. 2014): 35–46; http://dx.doi. org/10.1016/j.jmarsys.2012.08.007. It is not clear whether this model takes into account the recently observed accelerated melting rate of polar ice.

storm of 1890, which supposedly reached winds of about 180 kilometers per hour.[6] Finally, the trend started by a series of mild winters at the beginning of this century was subsequently broken by cold snowy ones in the last three years.

Nevertheless, the Sámi reindeer herders have been facing problems due to increasingly later freezing and earlier thawing winters during the past two decades. This not only hampers their displacement during both fall and spring migrations, but also the melting and refreezing of the snow tends to create an icy crust layer that hinders the reindeer from feeding on lichens.[7]

But perhaps the most concrete indications of climate change can be seen in the northward spread of plant and animal species—local and foreign—during the past 15–20 years.[8] Migratory birds have been arriving increasingly earlier and leaving increasingly later. Some insect species have extended their range hundreds of kilometers north. Diversity is clearly on the rise, but at the same time, some of the local cold-adapted species might risk extinction.

An even more sinister development is the spread of new pests and diseases. Occurrences of new foreign crop pests have been increasingly reported lately. Disease-bearing ticks have spread their range from the southwest coast and archipelago to nearly half of the country (Figure 6.3). In view of all these developments, one wonders whether malaria will also return. The disease was fairly common in southern Finland until the onset of a cooler summer trend during the second half of the nineteenth century.[9]

What Is Being Done?

World Wide Fund for Nature (formerly the World Wildlife Fund) early warnings about the ongoing global warming combined with a series of hot summers and mild winters in the beginning of the twenty-first century[10] caused Finnish people to worry and made politicians react. Finland's national strategy for adapting to climate change was completed and published in 2005.[11] Regardless of whether this stemmed from a genuine desire to do something about the problem or from the government's wish to show it was doing the right thing, the creation of a national strategy was certainly an achievement. It was apparently the first of its kind in the European Union, soon followed by Spain in 2006 and by France[12] and Netherlands[13] in 2007.

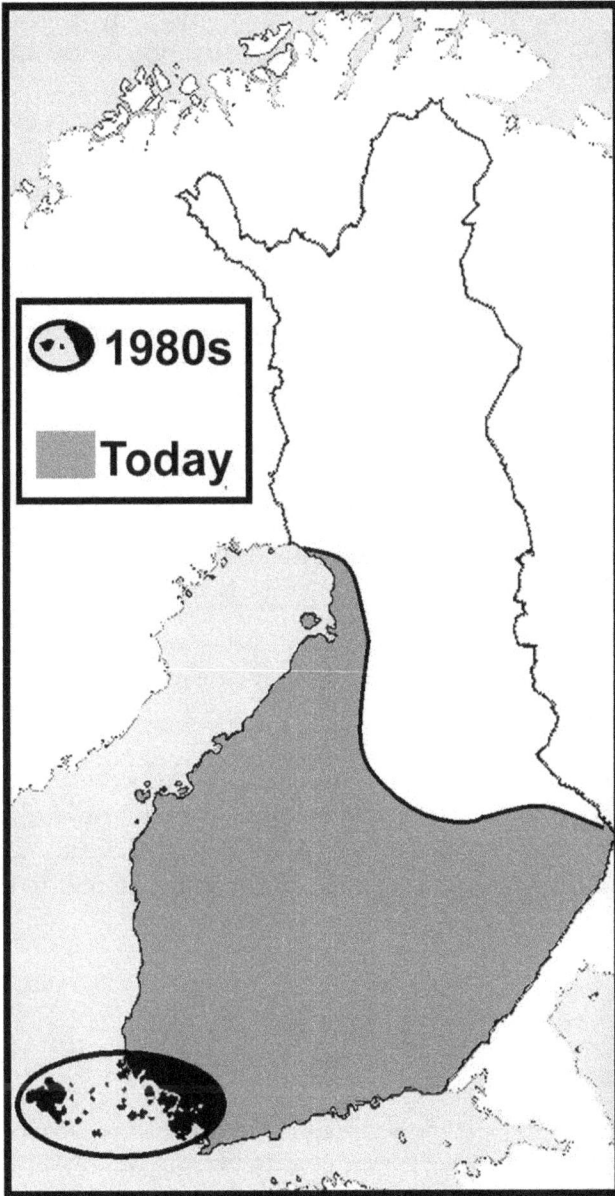

Figure 6.3. Distribution of Ixodes ricinus, the teak known to carry encephalitis (T.B.E.) and borreliosis, in the 1980s (black) and today (grey). T. Leino and O. Vapalahti, Puutiaisen levinneisyys sekä TBE-viruksen esiintyminen Suomessa, *Matkailijan terveysopas* (2012); http://www.terveyskirjasto.fi/terveyskirjasto/ktl. mat?p_artikkeli=mat00119.

Subsequently, Finland has published evaluations and updates at least in 2007, 2009, and as recently as March 2013.[14] These are publications with fine paper, lots of color pictures, and many graphs; all have also full English versions or summaries and popular outlines in booklets. Although Finland certainly deserves praise for the early reaction, one can also detect a certain air of propaganda and self-praise in some of these government publications, such as one proclaiming, "Finland is leading the way in adaptation policy."[15] Despite some achievement and the noise made about it, not all that could be done has been done.

The main goals described in the energy-climate update published by the Finnish Ministry of Employment and Economy in March 2013 can be summarized as follows:

1. By 2020, at least 38 percent of the energy used should come from renewable sources;

2. By 2020, energy consumption will be reduced to 310 TeraWatt hours through increased efficiency; and,

3. By 2050, GHG emissions will have been reduced by 80 percent through increased biofuel use and green commuting practices.

These commitments, if fulfilled, will be in accordance with the recommendations made by the European Union. Nevertheless, the strategy presented by the Finnish government at the end of 2012 has been criticized as insufficient by the Green Party, Finnish Greenpeace, and WWF.[16]

The Main Problem to Addressing Climate Change Is Politics

For the last 20 years, Finland's decision makers seem to have been dragging their feet with wind power. Despite big talk about support in the form of subsidies and tax cuts, bureaucracy has been a hindrance and the government's encouragement meager. All three major parties—Center, Conservatives, and Social Democrats—have traditionally been partial to nuclear power, which they see as the best way to curb GHG emissions regardless of possible radioactive-waste storage problems. A decision to build a new nuclear plant was made in 2002. It was supposed to be operational in 2012, but various technical problems have postponed it.[17] The construction of a sixth plant was approved in 2011, but the project has run into economic difficulties and, luckily, is still in limbo.[18]

This may be the reason for a recent more positive attitude toward wind power and other renewable energy sources. The government announced cutting the aid to renewable energy projects from €38 to €23 million in 2013, which was widely criticized both at home and abroad. In 2016, the Government of Finland "approved the investment aid scheme for renewable energy and new energy technologies as part of the country's ongoing efforts to achieve national and EU climate goals."[19]

The progress of wind power has been slow on the Finnish mainland, partly due to low support and partly to bureaucratic hurdles. On the other hand, the development of wind power has been more successful in the autonomous province of the Åland Islands, where it is responsible for generating about one-fourth of the local electricity. Nevertheless, in 2012 an application for financial aid from the state for the erection of a new wind power park that would raise local production to about 70 percent on Åland was denied based on the technicality that, according to the autonomy statutes, Åland is supposed to be responsible for its own energy. After the Parliament Constitutional Law Committee ruling that there were no legal impediments, it seemed that Åland would get its windcraft funding. Unfortunately, funds were nevertheless denied by Finland's central government.[20]

In contrast, there has been continuous support for peat power plants on the mainland. Peat power is a remnant of the 1970s energy crisis, and it is responsible for about 6 percent of Finland's energy production even today. Unfortunately, "peat is considered to be a slowly renewable biofuel" in Finland.[21] Despite its dubious renewable status, peat behaves much like fossil fuels, and peat power stands for about 12 percent of Finland's GHG emissions.[22] The industry employs more than 12,000 people, and it is the Center Party's protégé. During the last five years, peat energy production has been about 1,000 times greater than that of wind power.

What About Public Opinion?

Unfortunately, a continuous decline in the concern about climate change seems to have taken place during the past five years (Figure 6.4). A poll from 2008, shortly after the snowless winter of 2006–07, showed that more than 80 percent of Finns saw climate change as a threat. In 2012, only 23 percent did.[23] Why? There is more than one reason, including the following:

- Disappointment at the Copenhagen Summit failure;

- The current economic crisis and the fear of losing jobs;

- Disenchantment with government policies and its apathy on climate issues;

- Dissatisfaction with continuously hearing about climate change but little being done about it;

- Doubts raised about the reliability of the Intergovernmental Panel on Climate Change and local counterparts; and,

- A series of cold, snowy winters, causing many to question the claims of a warming trend.

All these issues have probably played a part, particularly as they apply to the economic crisis and the aftermath of climate change nego-

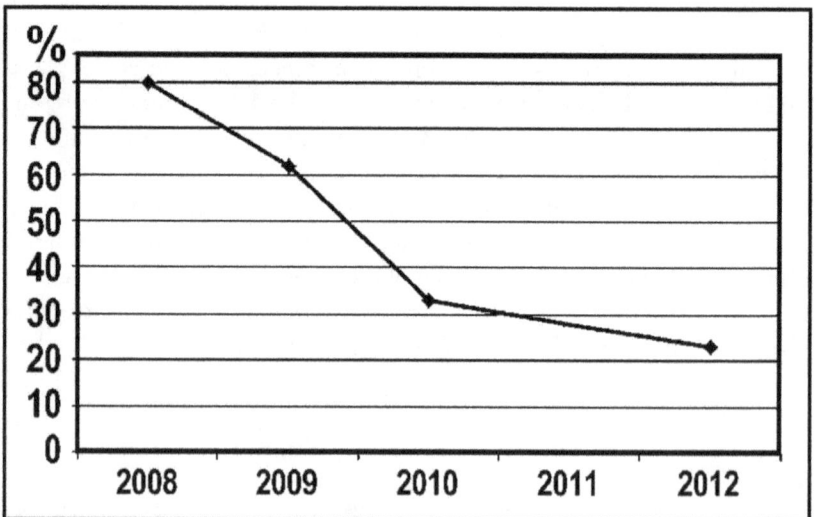

Figure 6.4. Results of 2008–2012 polls showing the proportion of Finns that regarded climate change as threat.

tiations in Copenhagen (sometimes referred to as the "Copenhagen fiasco").[24] There are the questions about the reliability of the Intergovernmental Panel on Climate Change.[25] For example, in Finland Prof. J. Kauppinen[26] has argued that carbon dioxide is only a minor agent and that the temperature rise observed in the last 100 years is the result of the combination of solar processes (0.47° Celsius), rainforest destruction (0.3° Celsius), GHG emissions (0.1° Celsius), and aerosols (0.06° Celsius). In any event, the recent series of cold winters has also influenced the public, who are already wary from overflowing climate change information. The feeling is best illustrated by an anonymous comment made in an internet discussion site in December 2012:

> A few years ago, all Helsinki was complaining and praying for snow. Now the last 3 winters have brought plenty of cold and snow to this city of climate freaks. It seems that the more that the climate supposedly gets warm, the more our summers and winters break cold records. There wasn't a single summer night last summer, and only on one day did the temperature reach 25°C. Have we been lied to about global warming? It's now being called climate change; terms are changed and lies get even bigger. Nature is the one that makes the climate to change and there is nothing we can do about it, even if the climate freaks would very much like to.[27]

Memory tends to be short-lived, and the series of alarming mild winters at the beginning of the century has been already forgotten. Moreover, those were not the first mild and snow-poor winters to be seen in Fennoscandia.[28] The main problem is that people generally tend to think in terms of specific weather manifestations, while climate researchers work with statistical trends of decades. At any rate, despite the confusing local weather fluctuations, the mentioned northward spread of plant and animal species in Finland during the past 20 years is a clear indication of a lengthier warming trend.

Final Remarks

I have tried to summarize various matters associated with climate change in Finland: its glaciated past, challenges due to geographical and demographic conditions, Finnish government policies concerning climate change, and the awareness and attitude of the public. As a whole, I must confess that it all seems rather complicated and messy.

Having said that, however, I must add that there is hint of light at the end of the tunnel. According to Prof. Raimo Lovio, Finland GHG emissions were clearly below the 1990 level in 2012.[29] This has happened before, but now there is one new, reassuring fact: for the first time, the production of carbon-neutral energy (nuclear and renewables) has been greater than that generated by fossil fuels and peat (Figure 6.5).

Also, after a rather cold winter when snow was still keeping southern Finland's farmers from their fields late in April 2013, there has been a record warm May. On May 31 and June 1 in 2013, the town of Utsjoki (70 degrees north) in northernmost Lapland was the warmest place in Europe with highs of 30.6° and 31.3° Celsius, respectively. Also, the water of Lake Inari, Lapland's largest lake, reached the all-time May record high of 16.6° Celsius, which is 10 degrees higher than the mean for this time of year. As a result of this wave of warm weather, Finns were still

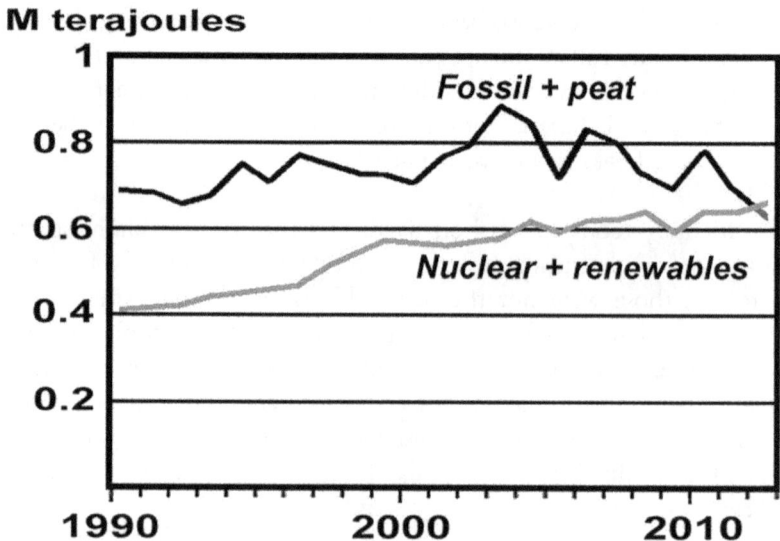

Figure 6.5. Comparison of the energy sources used in Finland 1990–2012. Observe that the use of nuclear and renewables (grey) have for the first time clearly surpassed fossil and peat (black) in 2012. H. Saavalainen, "Energiankulutuksen kasvu pysähtyi," *Helsingin Sanomat*, April 12, 2013; http://www.hs.fi/paivanlehti/kotimaa/Energiankulutuksen+kasvu+pys%C3%A4htyi/a1365653147084.

able to get their traditional "new potatoes" in time for Midsummer feast, and the strawberry harvest was at least one week earlier than normal. With more years like this, perhaps public opinion will swing once again.

Notes

1. E. Le Meur, "Isostatic Postglacial Rebound over Fennoscandia with a Self-Gravitating Spherical Visco-Elastic Earth Model," *Annals of Glaciology* 23 (1996): 318–27; J. Svendsen et al., "Late Quaternary Ice Sheet History of Northern Eurasia," *Quaternary Science Reviews* 23 (2004): 1229–71.

2. N. A. Mörner, "Glacial Isostasy and Long-term Crustal Movements in Fennoscandia With Respect to Lithospheric and Asthenospheric Processes and Processes and Properties," *Tectonophysics* 176 (1990): 13–24; M. Eronen, *Jääkausien jäljillä* (Helsinki: Ursan, 1991); M. Heikkilä and H. Seppä, "A 11,000 Year Palaeotemperature Reconstruction from the Southern Boreal Zone in Finland," *Quaternary Science Reviews* 22, no. 5 (2003): 541–54; H. Kallio, "The Evolution of the Baltic Sea—Changing Shorelines and Unique Coasts," *Geological Survey of Finland Special Paper* 41 (2006): 17–21.

3. J. Perttu, "IEA-järjestö listasi suomalaiset energia-ahmateiksi," *Helsingin Sanomat* (May 24, 2013); http://www.hs.fi/talous/IEAj%C3%A4rjest%C3%B6+listasi+suomalaiset+energia-ahmateiksi/a1369280756632?jako=2caa882f38988 4b6933c4d60506f334d.

4. M. Johansson et al., "Global Sea Level Rise Scenarios Adapted to the Finnish Coast," *Journal of Marine Systems* 129 (Jan. 2014): 35–46; http://dx.doi.org/10.1016/j.jmarsys.2012.08.007.

5. K. Pilli-Sihvola, H. Gregow, and P. Jokinen, "Impact of Climate-Change-Induced Storm Risk on the Optimal Rotation Period in Finnish Forests," Finish Meteorological Institute, n.d.; http://www.nordicadaptation2012.net/Doc/Poster_presentations/P38_Pilli-Sihvola.pdf.

6. H. Jokinen, "Major potentially climate induced changes in the coastal ecosystem of the western Gulf of Finland—a review," Tvärminne Zoological Station (2010).

7. J. Moen, "Climate Change: Effects on the Ecological Basis for Reindeer Husbandry in Sweden," *Ambio* 37 (2008): 304–11; http://dx.doi.org/10.1579/0044-7447(2008)37[304:CCEOTE]2.0.CO;2; M. Furberg, B. Evengård, and M. Nilsson, "Facing the Limit of Resilience: Perceptions of Climate Change among Reindeer Herding Sami in Sweden," *Global Health Action* 4 (2011).

8. P. Huuska, *Suomen lajisto muuttuvassa ilmastossa* (Helsinki: Suomen WWF, 2002); R. Heikkinen et al., "Ilmastonmuutos ja vieraslajien leviäminen Suomeen—Tutkimustiedon synteesi ja suurilmastollinen vertailu," *Suomen ympäristö* 7 (2012).

9. M. Núñez, X. Torres-Joerges, and M. Botella, "Evidencia de malaria endémica en Finlandia durante 1750–1850," in *Nuevas perspectivas del diagnóstico diferencial en Paleopatología*, ed. A. Cañellas Trobat (Mahón: AEP, 2005), 258–64.

10. See generally "WWF in the 60's"; http://wwf.panda.org/who_we_are/history/sixties/.

11. V. Marttila et al., eds., *Finland's National Strategy for Adaptation to Climate Change* (Helsinki: Ministry of Agriculture and Forestry, 2005); PNACC, *Plan Nacional de Adaptación al Cambio Climático* (Madrid: Ministerio de Medio Ambiente), http://www.magrama.gob.es/es/cambio-climatico/temas/impactos-vulnerabilidad-y-adaptacion/pna_v3_tcm7-12445_tcm7-197092.pdf.

12. ONERC, *Stratégie nationale d'adaptation au changement climatique* (Paris: ONERC); http://www.developpement-durable.gouv.fr/IMG/pdf/Strategie_Nationale_2-17_Mo-2-2.pdf.

13. VROM, *Maak ruimte voor klimaat!* (Amsterdam: Ministry of Housing, Spatial Planning, and Environment, 2007).

14. T. R. Carter, ed., *Suomen kyky sopeutua ilmastonmuutokseen*: FINADAPT (Helsinki: SYKE, 2007); Ministry of Agriculture and Forestry, *Adapting to Climate Change in Finland* (Helsinki: Ministry of Agriculture and Forestry, 2010); Ministry of Employment and Economy, *Kansallinen energia- ja ilmastostrategia* (Helsinki: Edita 2013).

15. Ministry of Agriculture and Forestry, *Adapting to climate change in Finland* (Helsinki: Ministry of Agriculture and Forestry, 2010), 3.

16. Greenpeace Finland, *Energia [vallan] kumous Suomen kestävän energian näkymät* (Helsinki: Greenpeace Finland & EREK, 2013); H-L. Kangas, *WWF: Suomi toivottaa ilmastonmuutoksen tervetulleeksi*; http://wwf.fi/jarjesto/viestinta/uutiset-ja-tiedotteet/WWF--Suomi-toivottaa-ilmastonmuutoksen-tervetulleeksi-1682.a; A. Koistinen, "Hallituksessa muhii kiista energiansäästöstä—Vapaavuori närkästyi vihreille," *Yle-uutiset* (January 22, 2013); http://yle.fi/uutiset/hallituksessa_muhii_kiista_energiansaastosta_-_vapaavuori_narkastyi_vihreille/6459308.

17. "Olkiluoto 3 delayed beyond 2014," World Nuclear News, July 17, 2012; http://www.world-nuclear-news.org/NN-Olkiluoto_3_delayed_beyond_2014-1707124.html.

18. www.worldnuclear.org, "Nuclear Power in Finland"; http://www.world-nuclear.org/information-library/country-profiles/countries-a-f/finland.aspx.

19. Tidal Energy Today, "Finland: €80 million for renewables and new energy technology," (2016); http://tidalenergytoday.com/2016/03/02/finland-e80-million-for-renewables-and-new-energy-technology/.

20. See generally Nordic Investment Bank, "Ensuring energy supply for the Åland Islands"; https://www.nib.int/news_publications/cases_and_feature_stories/1211/ensuring_energy_supply_for_the_aland_islands.

21. Ministry of Trade and Industry, *Outline of the Energy and Climate Policy for the Near Future—National Strategy to Implement the Kyoto Protocol*. Report to Parliament (Nov. 24, 2005); http://www.tem.fi/files/16129/jul27eos_2005_eng.pdf.

22. T. Lapveteläinen, K. Regina, and P. Perälä, "Peat-Based Emissions in Finland's Greenhouse Gas Inventory," *Boreal Environment Research* 12 (2007): 225–36.

23. H. Heikura, "Nelonen: Suomalaisten huoli ilmastonmuutoksesta vähentynyt," *Helsingin Sanomat* (April 22, 2012); http://www.hs.fi/kotimaa/ Nelonen+Suomalaisten+huoli+ilmastonmuutoksesta+v%C3%A4hentynyt+/a13 05560451278.

24. See, e.g., "Dismal outcome at Copenhagen fiasco," Financial Times opinion; https://www.ft.com/content/5b49f97a-ed96-11de-ba12-00144feab49a.

25. Q. Schiermeier, "Climate Body Slammed for Errors and Potential Conflicts of Interest," *Nature* 463 (2010): 596–97.

26. J. Kauppinen, J. Heinonen, and P. Malmi, "Major Portions in Climate Change: Physical Approach," *International Review of Physics* 5 (2011): 260–70.

27. Anonymous, "Missä ne leudot ja lumettomat talvet viipyvät? Agronet," (Comment on Dec. 2, 2012); http://keskustelukanava.agronet.fi/agronet/index. php?topic=41277.0.

28. C. Eriksson, *Characterizing and Reconstructing 500 Years of Climate in the Baltic Sea Basin* (Göteborg: Goteborgs Universitet, 2007); C. Eriksson et al., "Characterizing the European Sub-Arctic Winter Climate Since 1500 Using Ice, Temperature, and Atmospheric Circulation Time Series," *Journal of Climate* 20 (2009): 5316–34.

29. Academy of Finland, "A clear change taking place in the energy consumption of Finnish households"; http://www.aka.fi/en/about-us/media/ press-releases/2013/A-clear-change-taking-place-in-the-energy-consumption-of-Finnish-households/.

7

Teleconnecting the Great Thaw

Ezra B. W. Zubrow

Introduction

This paper is the result of a long-term interest in human adaptation to extreme environments by the author. It is partially based on the International Circumpolar Archaeological Project and its antecedents, Eurocores (Boreas Program) and Scenop, Social Change, and the Environment in Northern Prehistory. It also builds on and represents the work of a considerable team of scholars from McGill University, University of Oulu, University of Toronto, University of Cambridge, Lakehead University, Moscow University, and the Institute of Volcanology of Petropavlosk. Funding for the collaborative work has been provided by a series of grants from the National Science Foundation.

The International Circumpolar Archaeological Project has always been concerned with recognizing and confirming the similarities in human adaptations around the entire circumpolar area. Recently, its focus has expanded to considering the impact of the circumpolar area on more temperate areas. This recent focus recognizes several features of physical geography and climate change, including:

- The global atmosphere is a circulation system in which all parts of the atmosphere are connected;[1]

- The oceans are a global circulation system;[2]

- Changes in one location will create changes in another location, as the changes are disseminated through both of these circulation systems;

- Climate change in the Arctic is taking place approximately four times faster than in the temperate and tropical regions; and,

- Some changes in the temperate and tropical zones should be able to be traced to the previous changes in the Arctic through a process has generally been called teleconnection.[3]

History of Teleconnection

The study of teleconnection developed over time. This section discusses the history from the nineteenth century to modern times.

Nineteenth and Early Twentieth Century

In the late nineteenth and early twentieth century, many meteorologists unsuccessfully tried to predict monsoon weather. The first to succeed was a British mathematician turned meteorologist, Sir Gilbert Walker. As the third director of the Indian Meteorological Service and later as professor of mathematics at the Imperial College, London, he did time series correlations between atmospheric pressure, temperature, and rainfall. Examining time lags, Sir Gilbert was able to describe the oscillation in atmospheric pressure between the Pacific and Indian Oceans—the so-called Southern Oscillation. Later, he detected the Northern Atlantic Oscillation (NAO). Both impacted weather and rainfall patterns in many regions.[4]

Mid and Late Twentieth Century

Teleconnections in the mid- and late twentieth century were analyzed by idealized calculations of A. E. Gill and later through more complex models.[5] These complex models became known as the "proto-model," which assumed a barotropic, linearized model of atmospheric flow around a constant mean. In this model, the density depends only on pressure. Isobaric equals isopycnic equals isothermal, and the large geostrophic winds are independent of height. Resulting predictions offered by this model, however, were contradicted by subsequent observations because the teleconnection patterns did not change with the location of the forcing, as was expected.

Upon adoption of a more realistic background, the system became completely unstable.[6] The original false positives resulted from severely simplifying assumptions regarding barotropic systems.

Other work suggested that teleconnections at longer distances could be understood through wave theory. In particular, some analyses examined the dispersion of Rossby waves due to the spherical geometry of the Earth.[7] These planetary waves play an important role; atmospherically, they create vertical disturbances with highly variable air pressure, temperature, and winds, and they are responsible for the longitudinal variability. The waves can be stationary or travel for periods of one to a few weeks. They also define the marine response to atmospheric changes particularly at long time scales, such as the western boundary currents. Such early analyses are no longer used in most teleconnection climate change studies.

Present

Today, teleconnection is thought to be the result of the propagation of linear and planetary waves upon a three-dimensional seasonally varying base state. These patterns are persistent over time and "locked" to geographical features such as mountain ranges, meaning that these waves are stationary. Current analyses also find that teleconnection between tropical oceans and mid-latitude regions is symmetric along latitude circles (i.e., "zonal") and between hemispheres. There are transient eddies and mean atmospheric flow that are non-linearly mutually reinforcing.[8]

The Oscillations

Historically, scientists know that there have been climatic oscillations and that these oscillations have been documented. This section discusses the known configuration of these oscillations.

North Atlantic Oscillation

The first oscillation to consider is the NAO.[9] Studies have shown the teleconnection between the NAO for specific regional areas—Turkey,[10]

Azores,[11] Spain,[12] Norway,[13] Tibet,[14] Mediterranean,[15] and far-eastern Russia.[16] In addition, there are direct historical analyses of the NAO itself.[17] Furthermore, there are studies of NAO and particular economic and ecological impacts, for example insect damage,[18] ecological effects,[19] pollution,[20] and birds.[21]

The NAO has chronologically sequential positive and negative phases. The positive phase has above average temperatures in the eastern United States and across northern Europe. Simultaneously, it has below average temperatures in Greenland, southern Europe, and the Middle East. There is above average precipitation over northern Europe and Scandinavia in the winter, and below average precipitation over southern and central Europe.

The negative phase of the NAO is the reverse of the above for both temperature and precipitation. The oscillation is continuous. Most recently, the NAO was in a negative phase from 1955 to 1979, followed by a positive phase from 1980 to 1995.

Research Projects

My research group has been conducting teleconnection studies regarding the NAO for decades. We focus on using climatic data related to archaeological sites in order to show more directly how cultures have adapted to changing—and in particular—oscillating climatic conditions. This section of the chapter will explore three new studies: one based in the Yucatan, one based in Sri Lanka, and the third based in the circumpolar near Arctic.

The Yucatan Teleconnection

We have been working with the Foundation of Americas Research in the ancient Maya area around the site of Xcoch, near the famous site of Uxmal in the Yucatan Peninsula of Mexico. The Maya lived in what is called the Puuc area, which includes not only the Yucatan but Campache as well as parts of Belize and Guatemala. This area creates severe challenges because of seasonal aridity and the scarcity of surface water.[22]

We believe the problems the Maya faced were partially the result of the teleconnection from the NAO. The NAO's impact is reflected and correlates with the Atlantic Multidecadal Oscillation (AMO) index. The AMO's index shows the mode of variability occurring in the North Atlantic Ocean that has its principal expression in the sea surface tem-

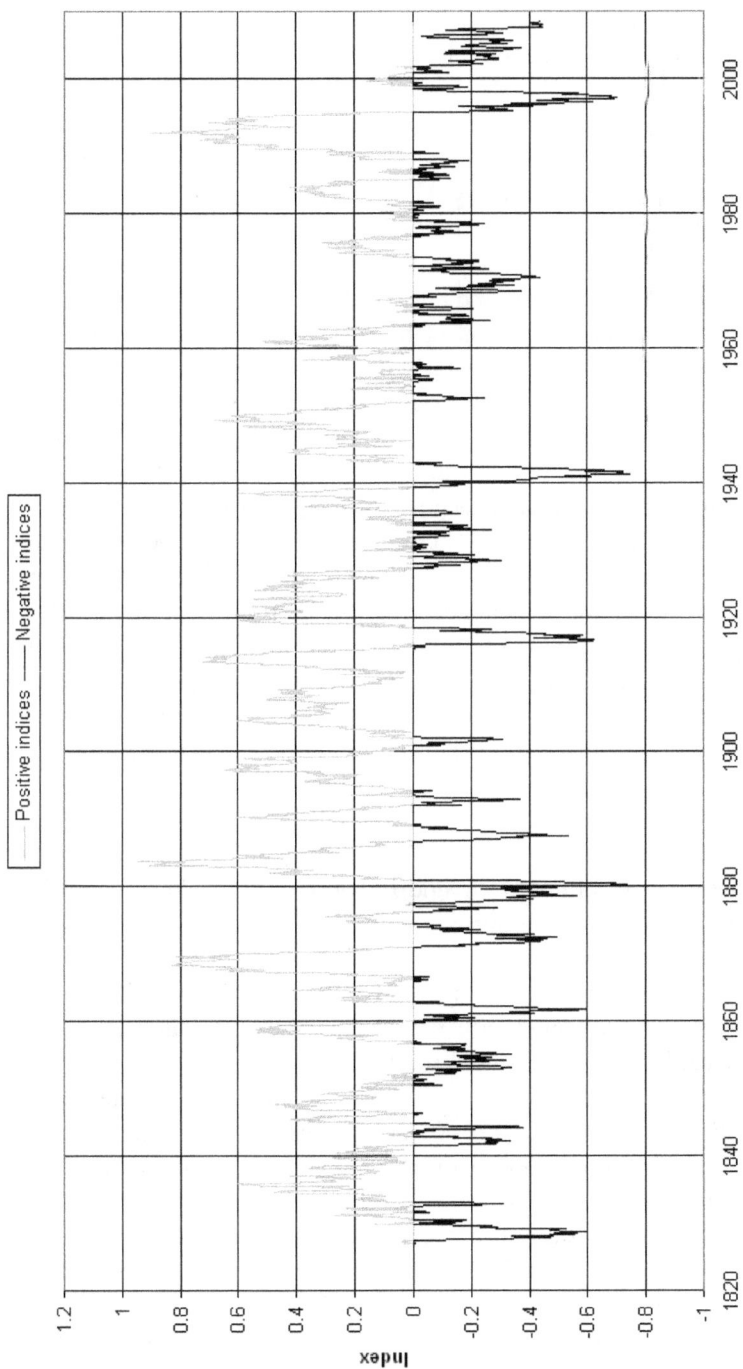

Figure 7.1. North Atlantic Oscillation based on calculations from the Climate Research Unit at the University of East Anglia using data from Iceland, Gibraltar, and Ponta Delgada

perature. The graph in Figure 7.2 shows the clear correlation between the AMO index and analogous changes in the NAO with the data from the Maya area from AD 1860 to AD 2000. It also shows the general direction of the temperature forcing.[23]

One series of drought cycles occurred near the end of the Preclassic period around the second century AD. A second period of droughts arose around the millennium during the Classic period.[24] Regional settlement history was conditioned by the distribution of natural water sources and the construction of reservoirs and cisterns. Dunning, Weaver, and Smythe suggest that the political control of these water sources appears to have limited the mobility of the regional population.[25] This author has previously argued the other side of the same coin. I assert that rather than restricting mobility, it increased mobility by making necessary the creation and use of more and more distant chultuns (underground water cisterns) and cenotes.

Noting that Xcoch has a deep-water cave, Smythe and Zubrow initiated a study designed to begin reconstructing climate change and human responses over the past 3,000 years. What is clear is that at Xcoch and in the surrounding Maya area, construction continued apace, regardless of whether there were droughts. Given the increased population pressure at Xcoch, massive efforts were made for rainwater capture in the form of hydraulic systems, such as aguadas (water ponds), massive catchment surfaces, drainage canals, water tanks and reservoirs, and chultuns.

Sri Lankan Teleconnection

Initial observations of an Arctic and Indian Ocean teleconnection that initiated human transitions during the middle-to-late Holocene in south Asia are currently being studied along the southeast coast of Sri Lanka. Priyantha Karunaratne, a postdoctoral fellow, and Hans Harmsen, a graduate student associated with this author's GIS[26] research group, are currently exploring how regional sea level change plays into the larger story of prehistoric peoples living along the coast approximately 7000 to 3000 BP. This work was part of Hans Harmsen's dissertation research and is his original contribution to Sri Lankan archaeology, climate history, and cultural heritage.

Initial evidence suggests a reasonable correlation among variations found between the Indian Ocean summer monsoon and the NAO. As Hong et al.[27] point out, each of the eight IRD events of the NAO over the last 12,000 years was followed by a significant decrease in Indian Ocean monsoon strength. This correlation may have had profound

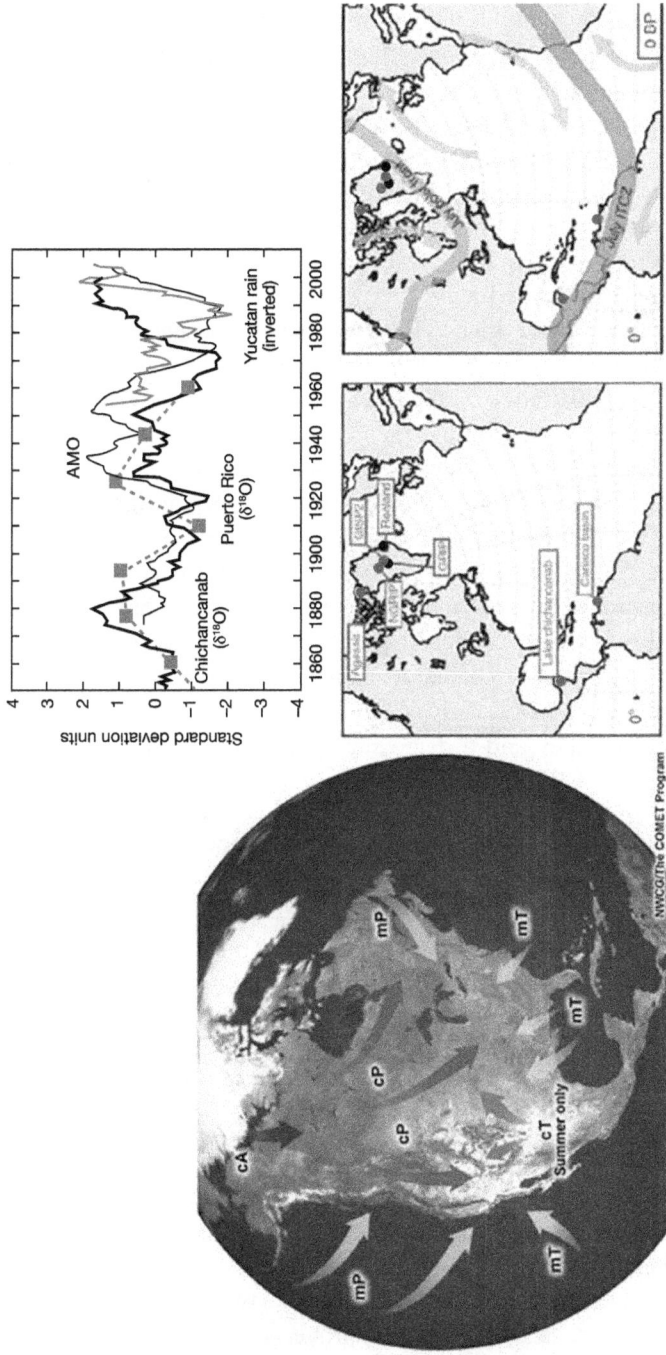

Figure 7.2. General North American Air Mass Patterns: The AMO index (thin black), precipitation record from the Yucatan Peninsula (gray), coral-based δ18O record from Puerto Rico14 (thick black), and the δ18O record from lake Chichancanab29 (dashed gray line) show the location of the climate proxy records (black and gray dots) and schematic major atmospheric systems. Note the close correlation and time lag between the general AMO index and the Mayan climate proxies.

implications for people living along the southeast coast of Sri Lanka during the middle-to-late Holocene. From about 8700–3600 BP, there was a progressive drying trend in Sri Lanka;[28] a trend that can be directly linked with decreasing Indian Ocean monsoon strength and supported by regional proxies' paleoclimate reconstructions for the whole of South Asia (for example, see Sukhija,[29] Sakar,[30] Chauhan,[31] and Thamban).[32]

Because monsoons are influenced by transequatorial pressure, Indian Ocean monsoonal changes are very useful in understanding long-term climatic changes related to Indian monsoon variation in South Asia.[33] For instance, based on the high resolution, oxygen isotope record from a Uranium-Thorium dated stalagmite from southern Oman, Fleitmann et al.[34] report a weakening of the Indian Ocean monsoon system by 8000 BP. This is supported by Thamban,[35] based on a high-resolution terrigenous multiproxy record from the Arabian Sea. Both studies suggest the weakening of monsoon strength occurring roughly during the fifth millennium BC (7000 BP) followed by a second weakening monsoon trend occurring between 6000–5500 BP. This is reinforced by Chauhan,[36] who offers that drought in southern India at 4800 BP may have reached its peak with the declining southwest monsoonal precipitation occurring at 3500 BP. Although still debated, a sudden environmental shift about 4200 BP appears to coincide with the decline of the Harappan civilization in the Indus Valley and a demographic shift of population to the Ganga Plains west of the Indus Valley.[37]

Based on geochemical climate proxies and landward cores derived from Panama, Kirinda, Okanda, and Vakarai along the southeast coast of Sri Lanka, Ranasinghage suggests a dry period between about 7000–3500 BP followed by an increase in rainfall until around 1000 BP.[38] Other proxy evidence from three sediment cores from different locations collected by Ranasinghage[39] indicate possible drought periods around 5500 BP, 4200 BP, 1500 BP, and 500 BP. He adds, however, that a more reliable age model is required for the Panama P13 core to confirm the dates of these events.

Along the southeast coast of Sri Lanka during the middle Holocene, from roughly 7000–4000 BP, a weaker monsoon regime and drying trend had important implications for prehistoric human communities in Sri Lanka as the landscape drastically underwent a dynamic transformation over a relatively short period of geologic time. Along the southeast coast, these trends are associated with sea level regression known to have formed dune systems, lagoons, and mangrove ecosystems. In addition, these drier periods were also indirectly responsible for the deposition of the now-submerged Holocene fluvomarine shell beds that are unique to the southeast coast of the island.[40]

Zubrow, Karunaratne, and Harmsen[41] have offered that changes in the North Atlantic teleconnection circa 5500 BP induced a decrease in the Indian Ocean monsoon strength, thereby increasing the archaeological visibility of four unique technocultural traits associated with coastal hunter-gatherer communities living along the southeast coast during the middle-to-late Holocene. These traits include the following:

- The appearance of new open-air settlements around shallow lagoons and on top of Holocene-deposited fluvomarine shell beds.

- The emergence of a transitional ceramic technology.

- New subsistence strategies that most likely included deep sea fishing.

- New mortuary practices, found in the form of flex burials.

Karunaratne and Harmsen have been recently gathering archaeological evidence along the southeast coast that has preliminary archaeological evidence regarding several hypotheses, discussed further in this section. The first, the shallow lagoon settlement hypothesis, offers initial evidence that suggests that "[p]rior to 3000 BP, prehistoric peoples along the southeast coast were aceramic and utilized a microlithic technology of quartz and chert. Some evidence of bone points and fishhooks exists as well. With the deposition of huge quantities of shell and coral were left on the beaches and bay lagoons as the sea level dropped, people quickly moved in and set up shop in these areas to take advantage of the high marine and terrestrial biomass."[42]

Caves and open-air encampments are the common denominator of the pre–Iron Age Mesolithic people of the island. Up to this point, there was no reason to refute that the current chronology of the Sri Lankan prehistoric and protohistoric periods. As Deraniyagala[43] has suggested, in approximately 3000 BP, iron-using farmers migrated from the north of India and settled the island. During this settlement, they appear to have pushed the native peoples farther and farther into the interior, thereby changing the settlement patterns from temporary encampments to more permanent settlements around coastal lagoons. Nevertheless, in addition to the north

Indian migrant populations, there were other iron-using peoples living in the Dry Zone lowland areas, reflecting cultural affinities to populations inhabited in the southern regions of the subcontinent on or before the north Indian migration. These populations too may have had contact with the late Holocene coastal groups, effecting major changes in the settlement patterns, subsistence technologies, and other cultural traditions.

Regarding the second Karunaratne and Harmsen hypothesis—the ceramic hypothesis—the only objects found prior to 3600 BP are clay balls that appear to have been fired at what are traditionally labeled aceramic sites. Although there is frequently surface ceramic scatter (i.e., black and red sherds) found in conjunction with microlithic flakes and cores that were once paleoshorelines, these are most likely disturbed areas and palimpsests of multiple occupations extending well into the Historic period. Currently, there is no concrete evidence to suggest that middle-to-late Holocene coastal hunter-gatherer populations engaged in ceramic production prior to the contact with early Iron Age populations. New observations in the interior of Sri Lanka, however, may shed additional light on the issue. Incipient agriculture and ceramic production may have been practiced by different communities at different times during the late Holocene. If these observations are correct, then ceramic production by coastal hunter-gatherer populations or exchange with interior agropastoral communities prior to the Early Iron Age contact period (c. 3000 BP) cannot be completely ruled out.

Regarding the third Karunaratne and Harmsen hypothesis—the subsistence change hypothesis—Harmsen has collected a number of soil samples that we hope will show evidence of the exploitation of deep sea fishing, such as skipjack and mackerel-tuna prior to 4500 BP. There is evidence of much later deep sea fishing at Pallemalala. Samples derived from the in situ layers of a shell mining pit at Kalamatiya may change the timeline for deep sea fishing in the region. Test samples at this site were collected at two meters below the surface. The shell layer itself is incredibly unusual in that it was found to be extremely deep and contained burnt bone, flakes, and charcoal. The implications of these tests are exciting and still currently under review.

Regarding the fourth Karunaratne and Harmsen hypothesis—the mortuary hypothesis—Karunaratne suggests the sites of Mini-athiliya and Pallemalala definitively demonstrate prehistoric people living on top of the shell mounds/beds and burying their dead in flex positions beneath the shell mounds, a practice not seen in later periods. The approximate radiocarbon date of 3600 BP (Kulatilake et al. 2014)[44] appears to be a little later than the preliminary estimates, which were thought to be somewhere between the third and fourth millennium BC. Harmsen has collected samples from two distinct cultural levels at two different locations approximately 50 meters away from the Mini-athiliya burial site, and he hopes to corroborate these earlier dates with the undisturbed shell layers that he found. In addition, he has samples taken from shell levels that he believes are coeval with Palemalala.

In short, the preliminary conclusion for this work regarding the larger global climatic process of an Arctic–Indian Ocean teleconnection is that linking the NAO to south Indian monsoon systems not only changed the weather patterns and displaced sea level, but that these phenomena were also heavily connected to the middle-to-late Holocene deposition and were instrumental in forming inland lagoon and barrier bay beaches from Tangalla to Kirinda. Moreover, these phenomena were critical in initiating changing subsistence, settlement, cultural, and technological patterns of the prehistoric people living along this coast three to five thousand years ago.

Arctic Teleconnection (Finland)

This author has had a long interest in the changing climatic and cultural adaptations in the Arctic, working in northern Norway, Finland, Russia, and Canada and running the International Circumpolar Archaeological Program.[45] In several of my works, I have tried to determine the regional patterns of climate change using direct variables as well as direct and indirect proxies and to compare the regional patterns across time. One set of studies made use of the European Pollen Database.

The most recent work has been with Michael Annese, another member of my research group. The graphs in the following section are his and represent continued research using the European Pollen Database. The fundamental question involved testing the relationship between the NAO and the climate as reflected in the pollen record at a variety of northern sites. The research focused on two species and genera of pollen: Pinus and Betula. Pinus is a relatively slow-growing and a long-term climax tree. Conifer trees are in the genus Pinus, in the family Pinaceae, and there are a large number of species. By contrast, Betula (Birch) is the opposite—a short-lived pioneer species common in the northern countries that flourishes in cold or boreal climates. A fast-growing secondary tree, it frequently enters "disturbed" areas, such as where there have been forest fires or tree harvesting.

We chose eight northern sites for the chronological depth and continuity of their deposits. Two were from Finland and one each from Sweden, Norway, Iceland, United Kingdom, Denmark, and Svalbard. They are briefly described by the following chart, which includes country, site, name, location by latitude and longitude, radiocarbon dating that partially underlies the chronological sequence, and a brief description.

For each site, we compared changes in both Pinus and Betula with the NAO. This chapter focuses on the two Finnish Sites, Masehjabri and Akuvaara.

Table 7.1. Descriptive attributes of eight northern archaeological sites

Country: Finland
Site Name: Masehjavri
Latitude: 69°3'0" N
Longitude: 20°59'0" E
Elevation: 685m

Brief Description:
Holocene pine and birch
limits near Kilpisjärvi,
western Finnish Lapland:
pollen stratigraphic
evidence

C14 Dates

Depth (cm)	Thickness (cm)	Datation Methode	Age (yearsBP)	Lab Number
5	10	C14	1680 ± 110	Hel-1037
25	14	C14	2620 ± 140	Hel-979
55	10	C14	3740 ± 130	Hel-978
85	10	C14	5770 ± 170	Hel-977
115	10	C14	8260 ± 170	Hel-976
143.5	7	C14	9690 ± 220	Hel-975

Country: Finland
Site Name: Akuvaara
Latitude: 69°7'30" N
Longitude: 27°41'0" E
Elevation: 170m

Brief Description:
Absolute and relative
pollen diagrams from
northernmost
Fennoscandia

C14 Dates

Depth (cm)	Thickness (cm)	Datation Methode	Age (yearsBP)	Lab Number
37.5	5	C14	2620 ± 170	Hel-525
67.5	5	C14	4180 ± 180	Hel-524
97.5	5	C14	6080 ± 170	Hel-523
125	5	C14	7770 ± 220	Hel-522
147.5	5	C14	8840 ± 170	Hel-521

Country: Sweden
Site Name: Fjällnas
Latitude: 62°33'0" N
Longitude: 12°10'0" E
Elevation: 780m

Brief Description:
The Fjällnäs project:
natural and cultural
components in landscape
formation. In: Königsson

C14 Dates

Depth (cm)	Thickness (cm)	Datation Methode	Age (yearsBP)	Lab Number
12	2	C14	50 ± 80	
14.5	1	C14	385 ± 60	
18.89	1	C14	590 ± 90	
20.5	1	C14	1145 ± 85	
27	1	C14	2370 ± 75	
29	1	C14	2230 ± 80	
39.5	1	C14	3230 ± 80	
42	2	C14	3225 ± 90	
51.5	1	C14	3480 ± 140	
54	2	C14	3460 ± 80	
56.5	1	C14	4025 ± 85	
58.5	1	C14	4255 ± 85	
63.5	1	C14	4725 ± 95	
65.5	1	C14	4725 ± 100	

Country: Norway
Site Name: Bruvatinet
Latitude: 70°11'0" N
Longitude: L28°25'0" E
Elevation: 119m

Brief Description:
Absolute and relative
pollen diagrams from
northernmost
Fennoscandia. Fennia

C14 Dates

Depth (cm)	Thickness (cm)	Datation Methode	Age (yearsBP)	Lab Number
58.75	7.5	C14	3890 ± 170	Hel-501
87.5	5	C14	4830 ± 190	Hel-500
117.5	5	C14	6970 ± 200	Hel-499
147.5	5	C14	8810 ± 190	Hel-498
177.5	5	C14	10280 ± 260	Hel-497
.5	5	C14	8810 ± 190	Hel-497

Country: Iceland
Site Name: Mosfjell
Latitude: 64°7'34" N
Longitude: 20°36'35" W
Elevation: 80m

C14 Dates

Depth (cm)	Thickness (cm)	Datation Methode	Age (yearsBP)	Lab Number
88.5	1	C14	1100 ± 45	Lu-1166
89.5	1	C14	1190 ± 50	Lu-1167
90.5	1	C14	1180 ± 50	Lu-1168
91.5	1	C14	1150 ± 50	Lu-1169
92.3	1	C14	1290 ± 50	Lu-1170

continued on next page

Table 7.1. Continued.

Country: United
Kingdom
Site Name: Abernethy
Forest
Latitude: 57°14'7" N
Longitude: 3°42'38" W
Elevation: 225

Brief Description:
Studies in the vegetation
history of Scotland Late
Devensian and early
Flandrian pollen and
macrofossil stratigraphy
at Abernethy forest,
Inverness-shire. New
Phytologist

C14 Dates

Depth (cm)	Thickness (cm)	Datation Methode	Age (yearsBP)	Lab Number
327.5	5	C14	6159 ± 100	Q-1272
355	5	C14	6803 ± 110	Q-1271
372.5	5	C14	7648 ± 120	Q-1270
430	5	C14	8670 ± 150	Q-1269
470	8	C14	9740 ± 170	Q-1268
510	8	C14	11115 ± 220	Q-1267
535	10	C14	11760 ± 250	Q-1266

Country: Denmark
Site Name: Lake Solso
Latitude: 56°8'0" N
Longitude: 8°38'0" E
Elevation: 41

C14 Dates

Depth (cm)	Thickness (cm)	Datation Methode	Age (yearsBP)	Lab Number
416	10	C14	3290 ± 80	K-5401
453	8	C14	3980 ± 80	K-5400
496	10	C14	4260 ± 85	K-5399
505	8	C14	4440 ± 85	K-5435
514	10	C14	5680 ± 70	K-5398
524	10	C14	6640 ± 105	K-5434
535	8	C14	7240 ± 110	K-5397

Country: Svalbard
Site Name: Semmel-
dalen
Latitude: 76°40'6" N
Longitude: 15°20'0" E
Elevation: 25

Brief Description:
Palynological investigation
of a Holocene peat
deposit from Spitsbergen.

C14 Dates

Depth (cm)	Thickness (cm)	Datation Methode	Age (yearsBP)	Lab Number
37.5	15	C14	1910 ± 110	GIN-413
111	18	C14	2500 ± 80	GIN-414
157.5	25	C14	2770 ± 110	GIN-415

First, systematic oscillation occurs in the NAO and in Pinus and Betula for each of the sites. The oscillations are clearly shown by the autocorrelations for each and demonstrate the amount of temporal lags (see Figure 7.3).

The autocorrelations are highest for the Masehjabi Pinus and for Akuvaara Pinus and Betula. The autocorrelation is lowest for the NAO. Furthermore, there is clearly at least one cycle in 10 lags. As expected, the autocorrelations show that the climate of one time period impacts

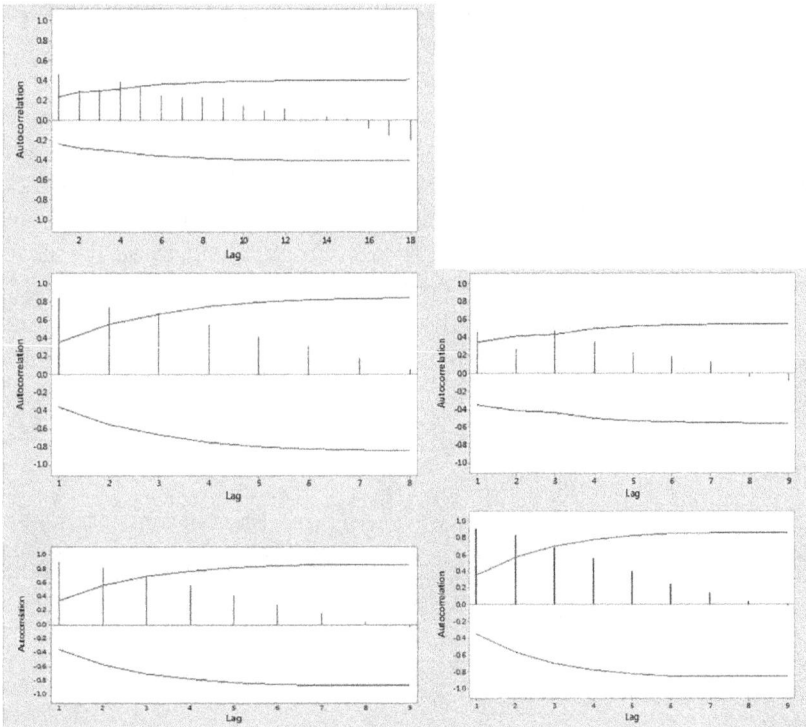

Figure 7.3. Autocorrelations of North American Oscillation, Pinus, and Betula from both Masehjarbi and Akuvaara. (1) Autocorrelation Function for NAO2 (with 5% significance limits for the autocorrelations) (2) Autocorrelation Function for MAS P COUNT (with 5% significance limits for the autocorrelations) (3) Autocorrelation Function for MAS B COUNT (with 5% significance limits for the autocorrelations) (4) Autocorrelation Function for AKU P COUNT (with 5% significance limits for the autocorrelations) (5) Autocorrelation Function for AKU B COUNT (with 5% significance limits for the autocorrelations)

the subsequent one. It is shown in all five autocorrelations. While not perfect, when it comes to climate, "like is near like."

Figure 7.4 shows the lagged cross-correlations. As one would expect, based on several structural reasons, the cross-correlations are not as high as the autocorrelations. First, the lag times between a change in NAO and its impact in Masehjabi and Akuvaara areas are not perfect nor necessarily standardized. These lags may be different in the same location chronologically and for the two locations spatially. In other words, a change in the NAO may not impact Masehjabi until 50 years later in one period and not until 150 years in another period. Given the difference in the spatial location, it also may make a difference for the teleconnection to impact at a greater distance.

Finally, there are at least three cycles in the climate record. Figure 7.5 demonstrates the clear correspondence between Pinus and Betula for both NAO sites. One should note that there is some standardization of the original values. There have been minimal transformations without changing the variables to make it possible to put the data on the same

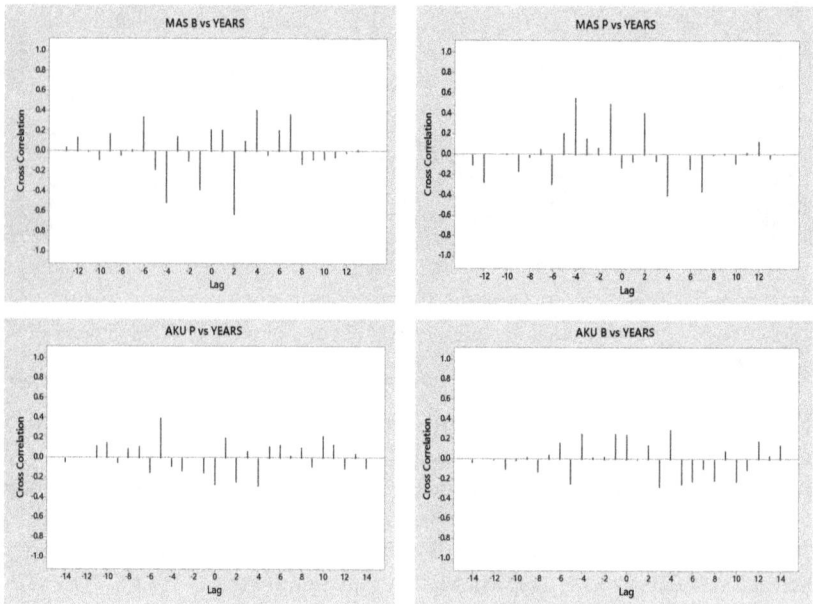

Figure 7.4. The lagged cross-correlations for Masehjabi Pinus and Betula and for Akuvaara Pinus and Betula with the North Atlantic Oscillation.

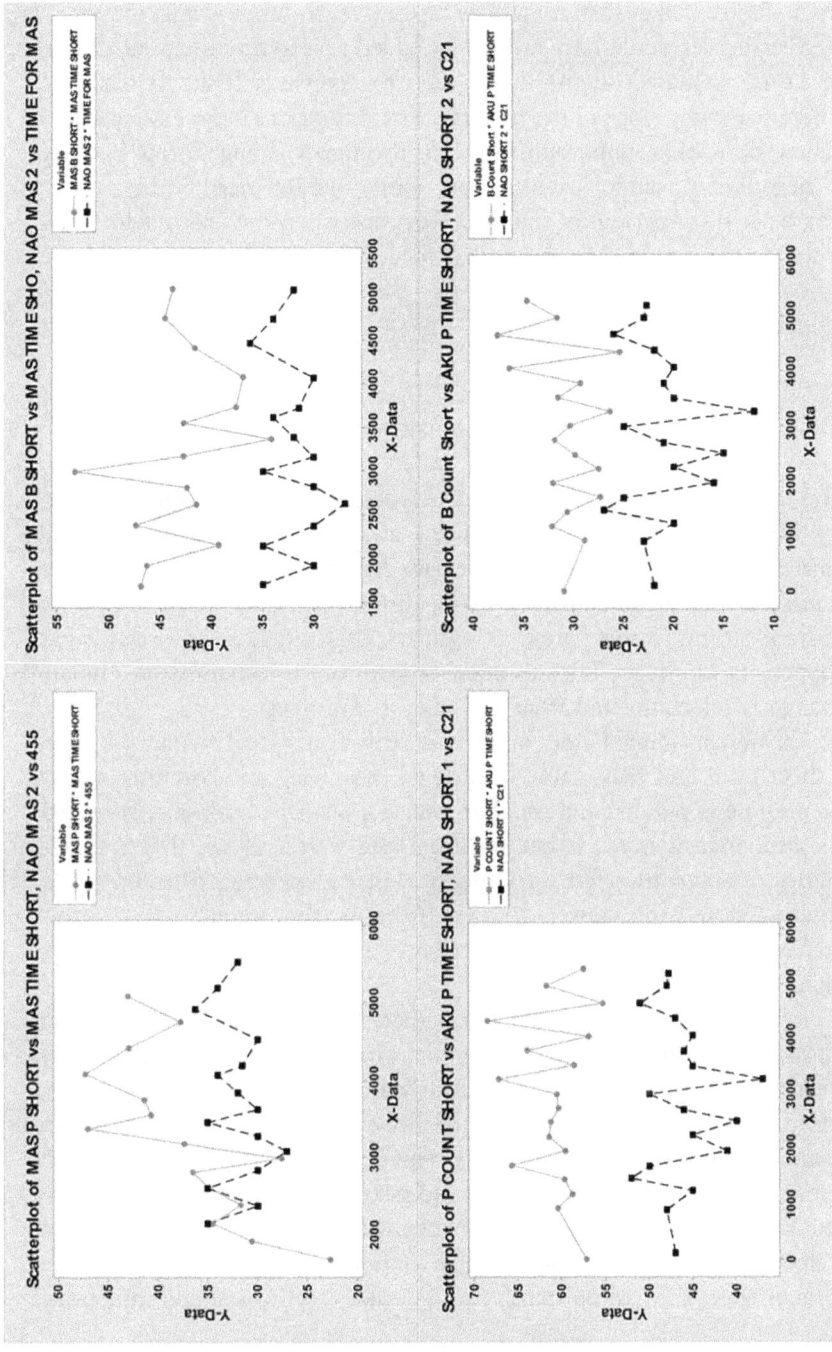

Figure 7.5. Scatter plots of Pinus and Betula versus the North Atlantic Oscillation. *Note*: There are somewhat different time scales shown in the upper versus the lower graphs.

graph and to make them roughly comparative. In other words, the entire NAO value set would have a constant added to it so that the results could be easily compared on the same graph to Akuvaara Pinus. It made no difference in the slope of the lines, nor the differences between sequential points, nor—most importantly—when the slopes changed from positive to negative. A careful examination points out the need to be careful. There are short periods of the time sequence when the changes in NAO postcede the changes in the pollen record, but for the vast majority, a change in the NAO will precede the changes in the climate record by a somewhat standardized amount.

Conclusions

The most important conclusions of this recent work are threefold. First, climate change has been taking place and creating significant cultural impacts for a long time. Second, the data demonstrate that climate change is not a local phenomenon. It is happening worldwide. Third (and what is the most innovative part of this paper), the evidence shows that what happens at one place impacts another location. In other words, climate change is teleconnected from one area to the next.

One can immediately understand this conceptual framework from a short-term and reasonably local level, watching and listening to the evening news pundits and weather forecasters since childhood. Forecasters announce a storm is coming from the west and say that the two inches of snow that fell on Chicago will be expected to move soon. Forecasters tell the viewers that in 10 hours, they should expect snow in Cleveland; in 18 hours in Pittsburgh; and in 24 hours expect six inches in Buffalo.

The same is true for more major aspects of climate change. Long-term (decades, centuries, and even millennia) changes covering relatively large areas will impact areas far away for relatively long periods. The atmosphere and the oceans are each a connected global system, and they are in turn connected into one grand global system. Like the snowstorm, change in one area may be teleconnected to the next area. However, when one is dealing with large-scale or long-term changes, one should not assume that a change in one location will swiftly cause a change at another. Rather, it takes time for it to be transferred—decades, centuries, and millennia.

Of more relevance to this book, the large-scale climate change that has been taking place in the Arctic has been taking place roughly four times more rapidly and four times more quantitatively than in the more temperate zones. It is thus not illogical to expect that one should see the same changes teleconnected—with a time lag—to the more temperate areas.

This paper began by outlining the history of the concept of teleconnection and providing a background to two major climate oscillations. The heart of the paper explored three recent case examples—one in the Yucatan, one in Sri Lanka, and one in Finland—presenting preliminary results for each. This author asserts that these studies demonstrate the importance of the teleconnection in understanding climate change developments in the Arctic and beyond.

Notes

1. Heat from the sun has an uneven distribution, with the equatorial areas receiving far more than the polar areas. Since the polar areas radiate more than they receive and the tropical areas receive more than radiate, the poles would get colder and colder and the equator hotter and hotter unless there was heat transfer. At both the north and south polar areas, cold air descends, building high pressure over both poles. Along the equator, hot air upsurges, creating contrasting low pressures. These hot and cold air bodies surge toward each other in an intricate but foreseeable pattern, depending on geographic features. The mid-latitudes have fronts, trade winds, and jet streams as a result of polar air meeting equatorial air. (Paraphrased from Espere Climate Encyclopedia; http://www.xplora.org/downloads/Knoppix/ESPERE/ESPEREdez05/ESPEREde/www.atmosphere.mpg.de/enid/0,55a304092d09/2__Circulation_Systems/-_Global_Circulation_18z.html).

2. The oceanic circulation system is a combination of the less important and more variable surface currents (wind and tidally driven), and the more important larger-scale density-driven currents caused by variations in the salinity and temperature. The density is not homogenous worldwide, and there are significant boundaries between water masses both spatially and stratigraphically.

3. M. Angulo-Martinez and S. Begueria, "Do Atmospheric Teleconnection Patterns Influence Rainfall Erosivity? A Study of NAO, MO, and WeMO in NE Spain, 1955–2006," *Journal of Hydrology* 450 (2012): 168–79; C. Raible, "Stability of Northern Hemisphere Teleconnection Patterns in Ensemble Simulations from 1000 to 2100," *Quaternary International* 279–280 (2012): 392; http://dx.doi.org/10.1016/j.quaint.2012.08.1228; N. Roberts et al., "Palaeolimnological

Evidence for an East-West Climate See-Saw in the Mediterranean Since AD 900," *Global and Planetary Change* 84–85 (2012): 23–34; C. Shen et al., "East Asian Monsoon Evolution and Reconciliation of Climate Records from Japan and Greenland during the Last Deglaciation," *Quaternary Science Reviews* 29, no. 23–24 (2010): 3327–35; http://dx.doi.org/10.1016/j.quascirev.2010.08.012; R. Izquierdo et al., "Effects of Teleconnection Patterns on the Atmospheric Routes, Precipitation and Deposition Amounts in the North-Eastern Iberian Peninsula," *Atmospheric Environment* 89 (2014): 482–90; http://dx.doi.org/10.1016/j.atmosenv.2014.02.057.

4. Warm water is less dense than cooler water, and less salty water is lighter than salty water. Since lighter water flows above denser water, there is "stable stratification." This major "conveyor belt" is caused by formation of deep water masses in the North Atlantic and by differences in temperature and salinity of the water in the southern Pacific. The cold water sinks in a relatively small polar area but the warm water rises in a much larger area. This conveyor belt is sometimes called the Thermohaline Circulation.

5. A. Gill, "Some Simple Solutions for Heat-induced Tropical Circulation," *Quarterly Journal of the Royal Meteorological Society* 106, no. 449 (1980): 447.

6. A. Simmons, J. Wallace, and G. Branstator, "Barotropic Wave-Propagation and Instability, and Atmospheric Teleconnection Patterns," *Journal of the Atmospheric Sciences* 40, no. 6 (1983): 1363–92,

7. T. Ambrizzi, B. Hoskins, and H. Hsu, "Rossby-Wave Propagation and Teleconnection Patterns in the Austral Winter," *Journal of the Atmospheric Sciences* 52, no. 21 (1995): 3661–72; P. Killworth, "Rossby Waves In S. A. T.," in *Encyclopedia of Ocean Sciences* ed. J. Steele and K. Turekian (New York: Academic Press, 2001): 2434–43.

8. P. Athanasiadis and M. Ambaum, "Do High-Frequency Eddies Contribute to Low-Frequency Teleconnection Tendencies?" *Journal of the Atmospheric Sciences* 67, no. 2 (2010): 419–33; D. Kim et al., "Effects of the North Atlantic Oscillation and Wind Waves on Salt Marsh Dynamics in the Danish Wadden Sea: A Quantitative Model as Proof of Concept," *Geo-Marine Letters* 33, no. 4 (2013): 253–61; M. Glantz, R. Katz, and N. Nicholls, *Teleconnections Linking Worldwide Climate Anomalies: Scientific Basis and Societal Impact* (Cambridge and New York: Cambridge University Press. 1991).

9. S. Baxter and S. Nigam, "A Subseasonal Teleconnection Analysis: PNA Development and Its Relationship to the NAO," *Journal of Climate* 26, no. 18 (2013): 6733–41; S. Blessing et al., "Daily North-Atlantic Oscillation (NAO) Index: Statistics and Its Stratospheric Polar Vortex Dependence," *Meteorologische Zeitschrift* 14, no. 6 (2005): 763–69; A. Dawson et al., "Complex North Atlantic Oscillation (NAO) Index Signal of Historic North Atlantic Storm-Track Changes," *Holocene* 12, no. 3 (2002): 363–69; S. Feldstein, "The Dynamics of NAO Teleconnection Pattern Growth and Decay," *Quarterly Journal of the Royal Meteorological Society* 129, no. 589 (2003): 901–24; N Jonsson and B. Jonsson,

"Size and Age of Maturity of Atlantic Salmon Correlate with the North Atlantic Oscillation Index (NAOI)," *Journal of Fish Biology* 64, no. 1 (2004): 241–47; K. Kodera, "Solar Cycle Modulation of the North Atlantic Oscillation: Implication in the Spatial Structure of the NAO," *Geophysical Research Letters* 29, no. 8 (2004); D. Luo and J. Cha, "The North Atlantic Oscillation and the North Atlantic Jet Variability: Precursors to NAO Regimes and Transitions," *Journal of the Atmospheric Sciences* 69, no. 12 (2004): 3763–87; M. Ogi, Y. Tachibana, and K. Yamazaki, "Impact of the Wintertime North Atlantic Oscillation (NAO) on the Summertime Atmospheric Circulation," *Geophysical Research Letters* 30, no. 13 (2003); M. Phillips, E. Rees, and T. Thomas, "Winds, Sea Levels, and North Atlantic Oscillation (NAO) Influences: An Evaluation," *Global and Planetary Change* 100 (2013): 145–52; T. Thomas et al., "Short-term Beach Rotation, Wave Climate and the North Atlantic Oscillation (NAO)," *Progress in Physical Geography* 35, no. 3 (2013): 333–52; N. Tisnerat-Laborde et al., "Variability of the Northeast Atlantic Sea Surface Delta C-14 and Marine Reservoir Age and the North Atlantic Oscillation (NAO)," *Quaternary Science Reviews* 29, no. 19–20 (2010): 2633–46; H. Zhao and G. Moore, "A Seasonally Lagged Signal of the North Atlantic Oscillation (NAO) in the North Pacific," *International Journal of Climatology* 26, no. 7 (2006): 957–70.

10. R. Acar and S. Senocak, "Annual Extreme Precipitation Trends for Western Turkey in Associated with North Atlantic Oscillation (NAO) Index," *Energy Education Science and Technology Part a—Energy Science and Research* 29, no. 1 (2012): 475–86.

11. C. Andrade et al., "Comparing Historic Records of Storm Frequency and the North Atlantic Oscillation (NAO) Chronology for the Azores Region," *Holocene* 18, no. 5 (2008): 745–54.

12. Angulo-Martinez and Begueria, 168–79.

13. A. Hindar et al., "The Significance of the North Atlantic Oscillation (NAO) for Sea-Salt Episodes and Acidification-related Effects in Norwegian Rivers," *Environmental Science & Technology* 38, no. 1 (2004): 26–33.

14. J. Li, R. Yu, and T. Zhou, "Teleconnection between NAO and Climate Downstream of the Tibetan Plateau," *Journal of Climate* 21, no. 18 (2008): 4680–90.

15. J. Lopez-Moreno et al., "Effects of the North Atlantic Oscillation (NAO) on Combined Temperature and Precipitation Winter Modes in the Mediterranean Mountains: Observed Relationships and Projections for the 21st Century," *Global and Planetary Change* 77, no. 1–2 (2011): 62–76; J. Lopez-Moreno, "Influence of Winter North Atlantic Oscillation Index (NAO) on Climate and Snow Accumulation in the Mediterranean Mountains," *Hydrological, Socioeconomic and Ecological Impacts of the North Atlantic Oscillation in the Mediterranean Region* 46 (2011): 73–89.

16. M. Ogi, Y. Tachibana, and K. Yamazaki, "The Connectivity of the Winter North Atlantic Oscillation (NAO) and the Summer Okhotsk High," *Journal of the Meteorological Society of Japan* 82, no. 3 (2004): 905–13.

132 / Ezra B. W. Zubrow

17. H. Linderholm and C. Folland, "An Annually Resolved Reconstruction of Summer North Atlantic Oscillation (SNAO) Variability for the Last 550 Years," *Geochimica Et Cosmochimica Acta* 72, no. 12 (2008): A553–A553; H. Linderholm, C. Folland, and A. Walther, "A Multicentury Perspective on the Summer North Atlantic Oscillation (SNAO) and Drought in the Eastern Atlantic Region," *Journal of Quaternary Science* 24, no. 5 (2009): 415–25.

18. V. Ducic et al., "North Atlantic Oscillation (Nao) and Insect Damage in Serbian Forests," *Archives of Biological Sciences* 64, no. 1 (2012): 215–19.

19. O. Gordo, C. Barriocanal, D. Robson, "Ecological Impacts of the North Atlantic Oscillation (NAO) in Mediterranean Ecosystems," *Hydrological, Socioeconomic and Ecological Impacts of the North Atlantic Oscillation in the Mediterranean Region* 46 (2011): 153–70.

20. M. Grundstrom et al., "Urban NO2 and NO Pollution in Relation to the North Atlantic Oscillation NAO," *Atmospheric Environment* 45, no. 4 (2011): 883–88 (2011).

21. A. Moller, "North Atlantic Oscillation (NAO) Effects of Climate on the Relative Importance of First and Second Clutches in a Migratory Passerine Bird," *Journal of Animal Ecology* 71, no. 2 (2002): 201–10.

22. M. Smythe et al., "Paleoclimatic Reconstruction and Archaeological Investigations at Xcoch and the Puuc Region of Yucatan, Mexico in 2009: Exploratory Research into Arctic Climate Change and Maya Culture Processes," *NSF Annual Reports* (2014); M. Smythe et al., "Paleoclimatic Reconstruction and Archaeological Investigations at Xcoch and the Puuc Region of Yucatan, Mexico in 2010: Exploratory Research into Arctic Climate Change and Maya Culture Processes," *NSF Annual Reports* (2010); M. Smythe et al., "Paleoclimatic Reconstruction and Archaeological Investigations at Xcoch and the Puuc Region of Yucatan, Mexico in 2011: Exploratory Research into Arctic Climate Change and Maya Culture Processes," *NSF Annual Reports* (2011).

23. D. Hodell et al., "Solar Forcing of Drought Frequency in the Maya Lowlands," *Science* 292 (2010): 1367–70.

24. H. Moyes et al.,"The Ancient Maya Drought Cult: Late Classic Cave use in Belize," *Latin American Antiquity* 20, no, 175–206 (2009).

25. E. Weaver, N. Dunning, and M. Smythe, "Preliminary Investigation of a Ritual Cave Site in the Puuc Region of Yucatán, Mexico: Actun Xcoch," *Society of American Archaeology* (2012).

26. K. M. S Allen and E. B. W. Zubrow, "Interpreting Space: GIS and Archaeology. Applications of Geographic Information Systems" (1990).

27. Ibid.

28. R. Premathilake and J. Risberg, "Late Quaternary History of the Horton Plains, Central Sri Lanka," *Quaternary Science Reviews* 22 (2003): 1525–41; P. Ranasinhage, "Holocene Coastal Development in South-Eastern Sri Lanka: Paleo-depositional Environments and Paleo-coastal Hazards." Unpublished PhD diss., Department of Geology, Kent State University, 2010.

29. B. Sukhija, D. Reddy, and P. Nagabhushanam, "Isotopic Fingerprints of Paleoclimates during Last 30 K Years in Deep Confined Groundwaters of Southern India, *Quaternary Research* 50 (1998): 252–60.

30. A. Sarkar et al., "High Resolution Holocene Monsoon Record from the Eastern Arabian Sea," *Earth and Planetary Science Letters* 177 (2000): 209–18.

31. O. Chaunan et al., "Late-Quaternary Variations in Clay Minerals along the SW Continental Margin of India: Evidence of Climatic Variations," *Geo-Marine Letters* 20 (2000): 118–22.

32. M. Thamban, H. Kawahata, and V. Rao, "Indian Summer Monsoon Variability during the Holocene as Recorded in Sediments of the Arabian Sea: Timing and Implications," *Journal of Oceanography* 63 (2007):1009–20.

33. D. Leuschner and F. Sirocko, "Orbital Insolation Forcing of the Indian Monsoon—A Motor for Global Climate Changes?" *Palaeogeography, Palaeoclimatology, Palaeoecology* 197, no. 1–2 (2003): 83–95.

34. D. Fleitmann et al., "Holocene Forcing of the Indian Monsoon Recorded in a Stalagmite from Southern Oman," *Science* 300 (1995): 1737–39.

35. Thamban, op. cit.

36. Chaunan, op. cit.

37. M. Staubwasser et al., "Climate Change at the 4.2 ka BP Termination of the Indus Valley Civilization and Holocene South Asian Monsoon Variability," *Geophysical Research Letters* 30, no. 8 (2003): 1425–29; M. Staubwasser and H. Weiss, "Holocene Climate and Cultural Evolution in Late Prehistoric–Early Historic West Asia," *Quaternary Research* 66 (2006): 327–87; A. Gupta et al., "Adaptation and Human Migration and Evidence of Agriculture Coincident with Change in the Indian Summer Monsoon during the Holocene," *Current Science* 90, no. 8 (2006): 1082–90; M. Madella and D. Fuller, "Palaeoecology and the Harappan Civilization of South Asia: A Reconsideration," *Quaternary Science Reviews* 25 (2006): 1283–1301.

38. Ranasinhage, op. cit.

39. Ibid., 203.

40. U. Weerakkody, "Mid-Holocene Sea Level Changes in Sri Lanka," *Journal of National Science Council of Sri Lanka* 16 (1988): 23–37; U. Weerakkody, "Geomorphological Evolution of the Southwest coast of Sri Lanka: Coastal Evolution since the Mid-Holocene Period and Historical Coastline Changes" (unpublished, 1990), Report submitted to Natural Resources, Energy and Science Authority of Sri Lanka, Colombo; U. Weerakkody, "The Holocene Coasts of Sri Lanka," *The Geographic Journal* 158, no. 3 (1992): 300–306; J. Katupotha, "Hiroshima University Radiocarbon Dates I: West and South-West Coasts of Sri Lanka," *Radiocarbon* 30, no. 1 (1988): 125–28; J. Katupotha, "Sea-level Variations: Evidence from Sri Lanka and South India," *Research in Geography—Disaster and Environment: Monitoring and Forecasting* 11 (1996): 143–53; J. Katupotha, "Evolution and Geological Significance of Holocene Emerged Shell Beds on the Southern Coastal Zone of Sri Lanka," *Journal of Coastal Research*

11, no. 4 (1995): 1042–61; R. Somadeva and S. Ranasinghe, "An Excavation of a Shell-midden at Pallemalla in Southern Littoral Area of Sri Lanka: Some Evidence of Prehistoric Chenier Occupation in c. 4th Millennium BC," *Ancient Asia* 1 (2006): 14–24.

41. E. Zubrow, P. Karunaratne, and H. Harmsen, "The North-Atlantic Teleconnection and Archaeological Visibility in Sri Lanka: Exploring the Effects of Climate Change on Coastal Mesolithic Communities circa 5500 BP," Friday 27 April 2012, The XII Nordic Theoretical Archaeology Group 25–28 April 2012. University of Oulu, Finland.

42. H. H. Harmsen, "Human Response to Environmental Change Along the Southeast Coast of Sri Lanka, ca. 7000–3000 cal yrs BP," State University of New York at Buffalo, *ProQuest Dissertations Publishing* (2017): 10255226.

43. S. Deraniyagala, "The Prehistory of Sri Lanka: An Ecological Perspective," 2nd ed., 2 vols. (Colombo, Sri Lanka: Dept. of Archaeological Survey, 1992).

44. S. Kulatilake et al., "The Discovery and Excavation of a Human Burial from the Mini-athiliya Shell Midden in Southern Sri Lanka," *Ancient Asia* 5, no. 3 (2014): 1–8.

45. E. Zubrow, "Social Change and Environment in the Nordic Prehistory: Evidence from Finland and Northern Canada (SCENOP)" (Funded $186,808) NSF; E. Zubrow, "International Collaborative Circumpolar Archaeological Project (ICCAP)": Joint Russian-American research in Kamchatka (Funded $845,769), Kamchatka, Siberia, Russia: NSF (2009); E. Zubrow, "International Collaborative Equatorial Climate Zone Archaeological Project (ICECZAP)": Joint Sri Lankan–American Research in the Southeastern Coastal Belt of Sri Lanka: NSF Polar Programs (2012); E. Zubrow et al., "Archaeological Survey of the Finnish-Russian Border and the Oulanka River Valley," *Oulanka Reports* 20 (1999): 5–60.

PART 2

8

One Law to Rule Them All

Arctic Climate Change Policy and Legal Realities

Kim Diana Connolly, Ezra B. W. Zubrow,
and Errol Meidinger

Law, at its core, often is designed primarily to provide structure and norms for human actions. Law and policy together are meant to create frameworks that can help us keep order, seek justice, and maintain peace. Law and policy are also used by leaders on many levels to balance benefits and burdens with varying approaches, ranging from efficiency to generational justice and many options in between. Climate change law is a new area. It is diffuse—those who are seeking to use the structure and norms to directly address, or indirectly control, the ramifications of climate change face conundrums that have been explored by many experts in recent decades. Most of that vital work, however, has not delved into Arctic-specific areas. Laws that actually govern human activity in the Arctic include international agreements, laws imposed on inhabitants by Arctic nations, local legislation, transactional agreements, and executive actions. There is no "one law" in the Arctic. Until recently, only a handful of scholars and specialists engaged in detailed assessment of sets of laws as they apply particularly to the Arctic.

As policymakers, scientists, and scholars have begun to explore climate change in the Arctic, we have learned an important truth.

Climate change, it turns out, isn't just transforming our Arctic ecosystems and cultures—it is simultaneously transforming the interpretation and application of existing and needed laws and policies that apply to the Arctic. This part of the book collects the work of authors who explore some of those legal and policy transformations.

This section opens with a chapter by climate change law expert Michael Gerrard. In his piece, Gerrard opens with a brief overview of some of the most recent climate science, contrasting the decline of Arctic sea ice with the role of solid fuel combustion in the increase of carbon dioxide, methane, and nitrous oxide concentrations. He goes on to explore the legal debates and conference structures that led to international agreements such as the Kyoto Protocol and the 1992 United Nations Framework Convention on Climate Change. He continues the chapter by evaluating the United States' domestic position by considering policies developed in all three branches of government, including the Federal Clean Air Act. He closes with a discussion of potential future strategies, from an affordable energy efficiency focus to pricier options, as well as the possibility that international competition can lead to collective gains.

Following that, Elizabeth Ann Kronk Warner writes of how the daily reality of climate change in the Arctic threatens the lifestyle, culture, and tradition of many indigenous groups. The chapter asserts that even if climate change mitigation efforts were undertaken with alacrity and commitment, threats to many Arctic indigenous ways of life remain. To that end, Kronk Warner explores adaptation strategies that may be helpful to indigenous communities in the Arctic, looking in particular at Alaska Native communities. Historic legal remedies and options are contrasted with climate adaptation strategies generally and as might be applied in the indigenous communities. The potential preference for mitigation efforts is discussed, but the chapter concludes that the harsh realities facing so many indigenous communities may mandate adaptation alternatives. In considering adaptation, Kronk Warner urges close attention to the sovereignty, human rights, and environmental justice of indigenous communities.

The next chapter, by Duncan Depledge, focuses on geopower. Depledge believes that the presence, absence, or melting of sea ice in the Arctic is not deterministic of economics, law, geopolitics, or society. Instead, he writes, like many human and nonhuman things, sea ice is constitutive of conditions of Arctic life. Building on the work of the feminist philosopher Elizabeth Grosz, Depledge applies a feminist geopolitical analytic to critical geopolitics with the aim of using the only ever partially realized materiality of the earth as a starting point for seeing the geopolitical differently. Ultimately, Depledge explores the notion of "Geopower" to call for a reexamination of the role sea ice is playing in constituting the Arctic as a geopolitical stage for the twenty-first century.

After that, a chapter by Kim Diana Connolly investigates the international governance of Arctic wetlands in an era of climate change. She notes that the quintessential Arctic tundra and permafrost are disappearing at an even more rapid pace than scientists predicted less than a decade ago. Exploring the Ramsar Convention, which is the international treaty dedicated to wetlands protection, Connolly concludes that as a treaty typical of its time (designed to encourage rather than mandate actions), this international agreement offers no meaningful enforcement or other mechanisms to direct or preclude actions to directly counteract the challenge of climate change. Connolly does acknowledge that the treaty and its governing secretariat should continue to draw up the convention's strong platform for education and messaging going forward, and leverage policy and norms (rather than enforceable law) to provide some helpful tools to preserve the thawing Arctic.

The final chapter in this part is by Cinnamon Carlarne. In assessing global climate change negotiations over the past several decades, she suggests that these negotiations have arrived at a crossroads. Carlarne urges policymakers not to focus on one single "right" pathway forward, but rather to aggressively pursue multiple pathways. She abjures a sharp focus only on an international, top-down system as it is no longer viable. Carlarne turns to adaptation and a more multifaceted system of climate governance as a matter of both efficacy and institutional integrity. She identifies as a key, practical challenge the tracking and coordination of any multilateral processes. Carlarne highlights in her chapter the benefits of a book bringing together lawyers, anthropologists, archaeologists, international relations theorists, filmmakers, and more to conceptualize and explore climate change in the Arctic as a unique opportunity to respond to the challenges that climate change poses in the region. Ultimately, however, Carlarne warns that unless the global community can collectively find ways (centralized or decentralized) to combat climate change, efforts to frame and respond to Arctic challenges will be futile.

The editors hope that the chapters in Part 2 will offer opportunities for readers to explore understandings of law and policy in several different venues and from varied viewpoints. Together, they touch on factors that will be important for collectively assessing how to use law to address climate change. Our existing laws were not designed for the crisis facing the Arctic caused by the changing climate. The authors present some ideas that can help us begin a necessary reconceptualization.

9

Regulating in the Face of a Changing World

Legal Regulation of Climate Change

MICHAEL B. GERRARD

An Overview of Recent
Climate Changes and their Causes

The Rising Sea Levels

Everyone knows that the temperatures have been going up. While temperatures bounce around from year to year, when looking at five-year averages, the trend is unmistakable.[1] A well-known adverse effect of these changes is that the Arctic is warming; the extent of Arctic sea ice declining had dipped to a record low in 2015.[2] A decreased level of sea ice has led to the rise of sea levels, which have increased at an accelerated pace.[3] There are a number of projections about what the future pace of sea level rise will be, but most scientists believe it most likely that the measured sea level near 2100 will be at least 1 or 2 meters higher than its current state.[4] Two meters is considerable, when taking into account the many flat areas of the world surrounded by the ocean. Historically, sea levels have risen about eight inches over the last century, already creating notable impacts.[5] These rising sea levels will have impacts that will require legal assessment and response.

The Greenhouse Gas Epidemic

Carbon dioxide levels have been measured continually from the top of a mountain in Hawaii since 1958; every year, these levels have increased.[6] In the summer, vegetation draws up a certain amount of carbon dioxide and, in the winter when the trees shed their leaves, this gas is released, leading to an annual fluctuation of carbon dioxide measurements. Overall, though, the increase monitored has been steadily growing every year.[7]

History has shown similar climate patterns, clearly apparent for three principal greenhouse gases: carbon dioxide, methane, and nitrous oxide.[8] Skeptics of climate change often reiterate that there are natural cycles of greenhouse gas progression and decline, which is true; for hundreds of thousands of years, there have been ups and downs. But, we are now at a level of carbon dioxide in the atmosphere that is higher than any time in more than 800,000 years, and the rise is exponentially greater than ever than has been experienced in geologic time.[9] This is different.

Causes of a Shifting Climate

Fossil Fuel Combustion

Dominated by carbon dioxide, the single leading cause of climate change is the increase in fossil fuel combustion, primarily coal, petroleum and natural gas. The greatest increase can most recently be traced to China. The emissions of carbon dioxide in the United States over the last three decades have held steady at a nearly flat rate, and in the last few years these emission levels have declined.[10] The trend in the European Union is similar, with focuses on a worldwide impact.[11] In comparison, China has experienced an enormous increase in carbon dioxide emissions.[12] Other large developing countries, such as India and Brazil, have experienced this to a lesser extent.[13] In 2006, China surpassed the United States as the world's largest emitter of greenhouse gases.[14] Other parts of the world are contributing very little to the greenhouse gas problem, with emissions from much of sub-Saharan African, other than South Africa, and from much of South America creating an inconsequential impact in comparison.[15] On the other hand, the booming Asian economies of Japan, South Korea, and Taiwan have large per capita emissions, although not at the output levels of China.[16]

Producers versus Consumers

A different perspective to be considered is not which countries are *producing* the most greenhouse gases, but which countries are *consuming* the byproducts of such gases. Emissions coming from major developed countries have held steady or gone down recently. But, the emissions that are attributable to major developed countries' consumption have skyrocketed. In contrast, for the developing world, the emissions that are attributable to those developing countries have been rapidly rising, yet only a portion of these emissions are attributable to the producing countries' consumption. Due to developed countries' propensity to export labor needs, a great deal of greenhouse gas generation that would have traditionally been attributable directly to our nations is now tied to places such as China and India, where the export of goods to the developed world has become commonplace. The per capita emissions in the United States have recently decreased, and although emissions from China are still lower than the United States, that is rapidly changing. India, in contrast, still only represents a small amount of per capita increases overall.[17]

International Cooperative Approaches to Climate Change

Overview

In 1992, the leaders of the world gathered in Rio de Janeiro and negotiated the United Nations Framework Convention on Climate Change.[18] It was first embraced by President George H. W. Bush, and then overwhelmingly ratified by the United States Senate. Despite its support, the Framework was not self-executing. The implementation details of the Framework were established in a number of conferences, most prominently in Kyoto in 1997, where the "Kyoto Protocol" was negotiated.[19]

The basic concept underlying the Kyoto Protocol was that the world would be divided between the rich and the poor. Rich countries would have to reduce their greenhouse gas emissions, but poor countries would not be obligated to reduce their emissions. Wealthy countries would assist in funding programs to the extent that the less-developed countries attempted to reduce their emissions. At the time, the list of poor countries included China and India. The objective of the Kyoto

Protocol was to begin the decline of emissions, and by the period 2008 to 2012 the levels would be several percentage points lower than the 1990 baseline.[20] The developed countries did not reach that goal by 2015, but were still moderately successful, with emissions leveling out slightly higher than the intended target goal.[21]

The rich countries, called the "Annex One" countries, might have nearly met their goal. The summation of all the countries in the world, however, is a much different story. The combined emissions of the developing countries excluded from the Kyoto Protocol, led by China, have increased, with their emissions, unconstrained by the agreement, more than offsetting the intended goals of the Kyoto Protocol.[22]

Failure to Implement and Attempts to Reconcile

The United States became the only major country in the world that never signed onto the Kyoto Protocol.[23] Although it was supported by President Clinton and Vice President Gore, the United States Senate by a vote of 95–0 refused to pass an agreement that did not impose significant emission reduction obligations on rapidly developing countries, and the Kyoto Protocol did not impose such restrictions.[24] Shortly after taking office in 2001, President George W. Bush explicitly repudiated the Protocol.[25]

Since the United States' failure to sign onto the agreement, there have been multiple attempts to discuss future agreements after Kyoto. At the annual United Nations Climate Conference in 2007, held in Bali, it was decided that a major new agreement would be achieved at the UN conference in Copenhagen in 2009, and the world would begin fulfilling it immediately.[26] However, no such agreement was established and implemented. Two years later at a 2011 conference in Durban, it was determined that the annual UN Climate Conference in 2015 would see to an agreement that would be employed by 2020.[27] The 2015 conference was held in Paris, and did result in a global agreement.[28]

That agreement, however, did not include any legally binding emission reduction commitments. Rather, almost every country submitted voluntary, nonbinding pledges called "intended nationally determined contributions." These pledges would theoretically lead to a world that is at least 2.7°C above preindustrial conditions—far above the international goals.[29] Even this might not be achieved, due to the nonbinding nature of the Paris Agreement, without any means to enforce the international policy or negative consequences for countries in violation of the agreement.

In the 2009 Copenhagen conference, it was agreed that the maximum tolerable increase in temperatures should be 2 degrees Centigrade (3.6 degrees Fahrenheit) above preindustrial levels.[30] If global average temperatures went above 2 degrees Centigrade, experts agreed that would be devastating to the world's climate. Small island nations argued heavily for a target goal to be no more than 1.5 degrees. These island nations believed such a limit imperative, because at 1.5 degrees, while these nations might still above water, at 2 degrees the islands would almost certainly be below water. In Paris, the international goals were set at a more ambitious level—well below two degrees, with an effort to keep to 1.5 degrees.[31] That, however, is merely aspirational; all combined national goals are nowhere near attaining an increase of less than 2 degrees. Instead, we seem to be on a path toward a rate of 3 or 4 degrees, drastic numbers with treacherous effects for more than small island nations.

Methods of Altering Our Destructive Course

International Energy Agency's Reduction Scenario

The most significant portion of greenhouse gases result from energy use. The International Energy Agency (IEA) has prepared a means of closing the gap between pledges and the temperature goals solely within the energy sector.[32] Of the needed emission reductions by 2050, a total of 19 percent would be achieved through carbon capture and sequestration—a means of capturing carbon dioxide before it is released from coal-fired power plants and other major sources. Although there have been various tests and experiments in smaller settings, on a commercial level there is only one example (in Canada) of technology that has been combined in such a way as to capture the carbon dioxide from a power plant and store it underground.

Carbon capture and sequestration, however, is only one essential element of the scenario prepared by the IEA. The second element focuses on renewable energy, accounting for 17 percent of needed emission reductions. This energy would be the result of wind, solar, hydroelectric, geothermal, and other types of naturally clean energy. The next focus category by the IEA is nuclear, a scenario that was prepared prior to the nuclear disaster in Fukushima, Japan. After that disaster, both Japan and Germany are slashing rather than increasing their use of nuclear energy. The next steps in the IEA scenario involve increasing power generation efficiency, and fuel switching (chiefly the conversion of power plants from coal to natural gas).

Easily the largest category considered in the International Energy Agency's scenario is energy efficiency. This category adds up to more than renewable energy and nuclear energy combined, even though it receives only a fraction of the consideration by the international community at large. In addition to having the largest potential to reduce greenhouse gas emissions and energy use, this category is also the most cost effective.

Examination of Alternative Energy Costs

The investment banking firm of Lazard has put together an analysis looking at the leveled costs of energy sources. In other words, Lazard examined the annual operating costs, such as buying fuel for fossil fuels, plus the capital costs amortized over the life of the particular type of facility to determine the overall cost of energy being produced. Lazard has shown a range in the dollar per gigawatt hour for each of the sources. This study examines the leveled costs of wind, biomass, natural gas, coal, nuclear, and solar photovoltaic energies. The type of energy Lazard determined costs the least? Not a type of energy at all. Instead, energy efficiency and conservation was shown to be much less expensive than any other method.[33]

A similar analysis was done by the McKinsey consulting firm, which examined numerous different options for reducing energy use and greenhouse gases, and arrayed them from those that saved the most money to those that cost the most money.[34] The items that save money are overwhelmingly energy efficient. For example: switching lighting from incandescent bulbs to LED bulbs, installing insulation in buildings, etc. These simple energy efficient actions would save a great deal of money. In determining the items that would cost the most, retrofitting plants for carbon capture and sequestration, although a powerful greenhouse gas reduction method, would prove inefficient in comparison with implementing energy efficiency.

The United States' Political Stance on Energy Efficiency

Legislative (In)Actions

The Clean Air Act of 1970 was passed essentially unanimously;[35] that Act's Amendments of 1977, which strengthened the statute, had tremendous bipartisan support.[36] The Clean Air Act Amendments of 1990 further strengthened the program by creating a cap and trade program for acid rain and many other actions, had overwhelming support by both the House and the Senate, and was signed by a Republican president, George H. W. Bush.[37] That was the last year that Congress enacted major new environmental laws: the Clean Air Act Amendments of 1990 and the Oil Pollution Act of 1990. When it came time to try to enact climate legislation, the bipartisan consensus of two decades had ended.

In 2009 the Waxman-Markey Bill, which would have created a comprehensive economy-wide cap and trade program,[38] barely passed in the House, by a vote of 219–212, and gained essentially no progress in the Senate.[39] The Congress that was elected in 2010, and those elected every two years since, have seen numerous bills passed in the House—and more recently in the Senate—going in the *opposite* direction. The EPA Regulatory Relief Act, better termed the "EPA Disempowerment Act," would take away considerable portions of the Environmental Protection Agency's power.[40] It passed the House overwhelmingly in October 2011, showcasing a complete shift in climate change perspective and bipartisan energy preservation cooperation.

As it currently stands, there are not enough votes in Congress to pass anything affirmative in regard to climate change. There also, however, are not enough votes to repeal any energy efficiency legislation previously enacted. As a result, the United States is faced with an old statutory structure based primarily on the Clean Air Act of 1970, a nearly half-century old statute enacted before the phrase "global climate change" or similar terms even existed.

Supreme Court Involvement

Despite the lack of action in Congress, the United States Supreme Court took action into its own hands. In 2007, the highest court declared that the Clean Air Act applies to carbon dioxide emissions and other greenhouse gas emissions.[41] Since then, the EPA has used the Supreme Court's decision as a stepping stone to authority, and during the Obama administration actively exercised such authority in the form of regulations. The most prominent effort established by the EPA since the Court's decision is the Clean Power Plan, which has been the subject of multiple lawsuits in the U.S. Court of Appeals for the District of Columbia Circuit. In 2016 the Supreme Court stayed the Clean Power Plan.

Presidential Environmental Action under the Obama Administration[42]

The largest greenhouse gas–producing source in the United States was for a long time coal-fired power plants. The second largest source of greenhouse gas was motor vehicles. (In the past year or two, the order has reversed, largely due to declining use of coal.) After that, carbon dioxide emissions from the burning of natural gas and oil are the culprits. The Obama administration has done a great deal to reduce motor vehicle emissions. Accordingly, the motor vehicle standards essentially became twice as efficient, assuming that plans continue through 2025, as had been anticipated. Due to the current cost of natural gas, launching new projects for the construction of coal power plants in the United States has essentially been halted. The goal of the EPA was to address the concern of existing coal-fired power plants emissions. In exercising its authority to address coal power plants, the EPA has encountered difficulty due to the fact that it must work through the individual states when imposing new standards.

[NOTE: This chapter is based on a talk given in April 2013 and has not been updated to reflect, among other developments, the election of Donald Trump as president in 2016; the subsequent reversal of many Obama administration climate initiatives; and new scientific studies that reflect an accelerating rate of climate change and its impacts.]

International and State Cap and Trade Action

Numerous greenhouse gas emissions-trading systems have emerged around the world, and more are emerging as time continues. The initial and most prevalent trading system started operation in Europe in 2005.[43] This was quickly followed by the Regional Greenhouse Gas Initiative, which was comprised of ten states in the mid-Atlantic and the northeast, until

New Jersey governor Christopher Christie decided to pull his state out of the Initiative.[44] The Regional Greenhouse Gas Initiative is a regional cap and trade program that regulates carbon dioxide emissions produced by power plants.

Similarly, New Zealand began its own platform, although without as much of a ripple effect as the United States regional state program or the European program, due to its limited greenhouse gas emissions.[45] The city of Tokyo also has a small initiative.[46]

In contrast, the California emissions project is exceptionally large. In 2006, Governor Arnold Schwarzenegger signed California's Assembly Bill 32 into law.[47] Its cap and trade program went into effect in January 2013, and the state has since linked with Quebec's cap and trade program, with plans to join Ontario's program as well. South Korea also has a trading system that is potentially very important, even though it hasn't received a great deal of international attention.[48] Australia instituted a "carbon tax," which was intended to be followed by a cap and trade program, although that program succumbed to political changes in the country.[49]

The most perilous energy problem is occurring in China. The growth of global greenhouse gas emissions has been dominated by China, yet there are a number of reasons that China would like to reduce its greenhouse gas emissions. The country's energy security relies on importing massive quantities of coal; levels of air pollution in cities throughout China have become stifling, with air quality in Beijing at some points reaching several times worse than the average air quality in an airport smoking lounge. Moreover, China has a massive coastline with hundreds of millions of people; when the sea levels rise, as anticipated over the next several decades, China will have the world's largest displacement problem. In seven cities and provinces, China has begun to create pilot programs on emissions trading.[50] The plan is to use the experiences in those seven programs and create a nationwide system that would become by far the world's largest carbon market. This carbon reduction or exchange program would considerably alter the emissions of greenhouse gases in China, thereby potentially altering the negative global impact of climate change. When China implements this nationwide program, the United States might someday follow with a similar program, thus changing the current global energy interface and altering the current climate change forecast.

Conclusion

A question still left unanswered by the overviews presented in this chapter is simple: How much higher will greenhouse gases increase in the coming decades and beyond? Never in known history, or in humankind's prehistory back to the emergence of our species, has there been a period when the increase in carbon dioxide levels has occurred at this pace. It is set for a destructive course, with a rate of increase faster than has ever been known to occur.

In answer to the climate change skeptic's counterclaim, yes, fluctuations of greenhouse gases are normal. It's the rate and magnitude of increase that are abnormal, and consequential proof of climate change. As presented, some changes in the legal system have been made, but not enough. In short, like other areas, the legal system must adapt.

Notes

1. "Global Land-Ocean Temperature Index," National Aeronautics and Space Administration, accessed June 4, 2016; http://data.giss.nasa.gov/gistemp/tabledata_v3/GLB.Ts+dSST.txt.

2. "Arctic Sea Ice Reaches Record Low after Record Hot January," The Weather Network, accessed June 4, 2016; https://www.theweathernetwork.com/news/articles/whats-up-in-climate-change-arctic-ice-cap-record-low-after-record-hot-january/63907.

3. "Global Mean Sea Level," Commonwealth Scientific and Industrial Research Organization, accessed June 4, 2016; http://www.cmar.csiro.au/sealevel/downloads/CSIRO_GMSL_1880_2015.pdf.

4. J. A. Church, P. U. Clark, A. Cazenave, J. M. Gregory, S. Jevrejeva, A. Levermann, M. A. Merrifield, G. A. Milne, R. S. Nerem, P. D. Nunn, A. J. Payne, W. T. Pfeffer, D. Stammer, and A. S. Unnikrishnan, "2013: Sea Level Change," in *Climate Change 2013: The Physical Science Basis. Contribution of Working Group I to the Fifth Assessment Report of the Intergovernmental Panel on Climate Change*, ed. T. F. Stocker, D. Qin, G.-K. Plattner, M. Tignor, S. K. Allen, J. Boschung, A. Nauels, Y. Xia, V. Bex, and P. M. Midgley (Cambridge and New York: Cambridge University Press, 2013), 1201.

5. "Global Average Absolute Sea Level Change, 1880–2014," United States Environmental Protection Agency, accessed June 4, 2016; https://www3.epa.gov/climatechange/science/indicators/oceans/sea-level.html.

6. "Full Mauna Loa CO2 Record," National Oceanic and Atmospheric Administration, accessed June 4, 2016; http://www.esrl.noaa.gov/gmd/ccgg/trends/full.html.

7. "Up-to-date Weekly Average CO2 at Mauna Loa: Last One Year," National Oceanic and Atmospheric Administration, accessed June 4, 2016; http://www.esrl.noaa.gov/gmd/ccgg/trends/weekly.html.

8. "Full Mauna Loa CO2 Record," National Oceanic and Atmospheric Administration, accessed June 4, 2016; http://www.esrl.noaa.gov/gmd/ccgg/trends/full.html.

9. J. A. Church et al., "2013: Sea Level Change," 1201.

10. "U.S. Energy-Related Carbon Dioxide Emissions, 2014," United States Energy Information Administration, accessed June 4, 2016; http://www.eia.gov/environment/emissions/carbon/.

11. "Greenhouse Gas Emission Statistics," Eurostat, accessed June 4, 2016; http://ec.europa.eu/eurostat/statistics-explained/index.php/Greenhouse_gas_emission_statistics.

12. Zhu Liu, "China's Carbon Emissions Report 2015," Report for Sustainability Science Program, Mossavar-Rahmani Center for Business and Government, Harvard Kennedy School, Energy Technology Innovation Policy research group, Belfer Center for Science and International Affairs, Harvard Kennedy School, Cambridge, MA, May 2015.

13. PBL Netherlands Environmental Assessment Agency, "Trends in Global CO_2 Emissions: 2015 Report," accessed June 4, 2016; http://edgar.jrc.ec.europa.eu/news_docs/jrc-2015-trends-in-global-co2-emissions-2015-report-98184.pdf.

14. "China Now No. 1 in CO2 Emissions; USA in Second Position," PBL Netherlands Environmental Assessment Agency, accessed June 4, 2016; http://www.pbl.nl/en/news/pressreleases/2007/20070619Chinanowno1inCO2emissionsUSAinsecondposition.

15. PBL Netherlands Environmental Assessment Agency, "Trends in Global CO_2 Emissions: 2015 Report," accessed June 4, 2016; http://edgar.jrc.ec.europa.eu/news_docs/jrc-2015-trends-in-global-co2-emissions-2015-report-98184.pdf.

16. Ibid.

17. Netherlands Environmental Assessment Agency, *Trends in Global CO_2 Emissions 2012*: Report, 28.

18. "First Steps to a Safer Future: Introducing The United Nations Framework Convention on Climate Change," United Nations Framework Convention on Climate Change, accessed June 4, 2016; http://unfccc.int/essential_background/convention/items/6036.php.

19. "Kyoto Protocol," United Nations Framework Convention on Climate Change, accessed June 4, 2016; http://unfccc.int/kyoto_protocol/items/2830.php.

20. Ibid.

21. Philippe Rekacewicz, "Global and Selected Annex 1 Countries Emissions of Greenhouse Gases (CO2, CH4, N20) in Projections," *COP 5 Emissions Graphics, UNEP/GRID-Ardenal*, 2006, accessed June 13, 2015; http://www.grida.no/graphicslib/detail/global-and-selected-annex-1-countries-emissions-of-greenhouse-gases-co2-ch4-n2o-in-projections_510c,

22. T.A. Boden, G. Maryland, and R.J. Andres, "Global, Regional, and National Fossil-Fuel CO2 Emissions," Carbon Dioxide Information Analysis Center, Oak Ridge National Laboratory, U.S. Department of Energy, 2015; doi:10.3334/CDIAC/0001_V2015.

23. Ibid.

24. Reginald Dale, "The Senate Hasn't Voted on the Kyoto Protocol," *The Washington Post*, November 14, 2009; http://www.washingtonpost.com/wp-dyn/content/article/2009/11/13/AR2009111303882.html.

25. Greg Kahn, "Fate of the Kyoto Protocol under the Bush Administration," *Berkeley Journal of International Law* 21, no. 548 (2003); http://scholarship.law.berkeley.edu/bjil/vol21/iss3/5.

26. Elizabeth Burleson, "The Bali Climate Change Conference," *ASIL Insights* 12, no. 4 (2008); https://www.asil.org/insights/volume/12/issue/4/bali-climate-change-conference#_edn1.

27. "Durban Climate Change Conference—November/December 2011," United Nations Framework Convention on Climate Change, accessed June 4, 2016; https://www.asil.org/insights/volume/12/issue/4/bali-climate-change-conference#_edn1.

28. "The Paris Agreement," United Nations Framework Convention on Climate Change, accessed June 4, 2016; http://unfccc.int/paris_agreement/items/9485.php.

29. "Paris Agreement: Stage Set to Ramp Up Climate Action," Climate Action Tracker, accessed June 4, 2016; http://climateactiontracker.org/news/257/Paris-Agreement-stage-set-to-ramp-up-climate-action.html.

30. "Copenhagen Climate Change Conference—December 2009," United Nations Framework Convention on Climate Change, accessed June 4, 2016; http://unfccc.int/meetings/copenhagen_dec_2009/meeting/6295.php.

31. "Summary of the Paris Agreement," United Nations Framework Convention on Climate Change, accessed June 4, 2016; http://bigpicture.unfccc.int/#content-the-paris-agreemen.

32. International Energy Agency, *World Energy Outlook Special Report* (Paris: International Energy Agency, 2015).

33. Lazard, "Lazard's Levilized Cost of Energy Analysis, Version 10.0," accessed June 4, 2016; https://www.lazard.com/media/438038/levelized-cost-of-energy-v100.pdf.

34. Tom Kiely ed., *Energy Efficiency: A Compelling Global Resource* (New York: McKinsey, 2010).

35. Heather Zichal, "Protecting Historic Progress on Clean Air," accessed June 4, 2016; https://www.whitehouse.gov/blog/2011/11/07/protecting-historic-progress-clean-air.

36. Jennifer Macedonia, "Supreme Court Validates EPA's Interpretation of Clean Air Act Authority," Bipartisan Policy Center, accessed June 4,

2016; http://bipartisanpolicy.org/blog/supreme-court-validates-epas-interpretation-clean-air-act-authority/.

37. "The Clean Air Act—Highlights of the 1990 Amendments," U.S. Environmental Protection Agency, accessed June 4, 2016; https://www.epa.gov/clean-air-act-overview/clean-air-act-highlights-1990-amendments.

38. Kevin Bogardus and Amanda Reilly, "7 Years Later, Failed Wax-man-Markey Bill Still Makes Waves," *E&E Daily*, June 27, 2016; http://www.eenews.net/stories/1060039422.

39. Ibid.

40. Michael McAuliff, "House Passes Incinerator Bill That the EPA Warns Will Kill Thousands," *The Huffington Post*, Dec. 13, 2011; http://www.huffingtonpost.com/2011/10/13/house-passes-incinerator-bill-epa_n_1010044.html.

41. Massachusetts v. Environmental Protection Agency, 549 U.S. 497 (2007).

42. This chapter was completed before President Trump took office, and was not updated.

43. "The EU Emissions Trading System," European Commission, accessed June 4, 2016; http://ec.europa.eu/clima/policies/ets/index_en.htm.

44. "Regional Greenhouse Gas Initiative," RGGI, Inc., accessed June 4, 2016; https://www.rggi.org.

45. "Reducing New Zealand's Greenhouse Gas Emissions," New Zealand Ministry for the Environment, accessed June 4, 2016; http://www.mfe.govt.nz/climate-change/reducing-greenhouse-gas-emissions.

46. "Tokyo's Cap and Trade Program," Siemens; http://www.siemens.com/press/pool/de/events/2014/infrastructure-cities/2014-06-CCLA/tokyo-climate-close-up.pdf.

47. "California's Global Warming Solutions Act," Center for Climate and Energy Solutions, accessed June 4, 2016; http://www.c2es.org/us-states-regions/action/california/ab32.

48. *Korea Emissions Trading Scheme* (International Carbon Action Part-nership, 2012).

49. Rob Taylor and Rhiannon Hoyle, "Australia Becomes First Developed Nation to Repeal Carbon Tax," *Wall Street Journal*, July 17, 2014.

50. Angeli Mehta, "China Launches Nationwide Emissions Trading Scheme," *Chemistry World*, October 6, 2015; http://www.rsc.org/chemistryworld/2015/10/us-china-emission-trading-scheme-climate-change.

10

Avoiding Genocide

Factors Applicable to Adaptation Planning for Arctic Indigenous Peoples

ELIZABETH ANN KRONK WARNER

Tribes in Alaska are facing nothing less than the loss of their entire culture.

—National Tribal Air Association, "Impacts of Climate Change on Tribes in the United States"

Introduction

More than 220 federally recognized indigenous groups reside in Alaska.[1] Given the sheer number and diversity of indigenous groups in Alaska, each group may be facing different impacts from climate change and may have different opinions about climate change.[2] Accordingly, this chapter generally discusses the impacts of climate change in Alaska and the Arctic and does not represent the opinions or circumstances of any one group.

Impacts of Climate Change in the Arctic

The impacts of climate change are being felt around the world. Indigenous peoples[3] in the Arctic are being particularly hard hit today by the impacts of climate change.[4] "The impact of climate change, while problematic for all peoples, falls disproportionately on Native peoples in regions such as the Arctic and Pacific, where the environment is closely tied to indigenous lifeways. Indigenous communities whose members predominantly practice traditional lifeways are particularly vulnerable to climate change."[5]

In the Arctic, climate change is causing indigenous peoples to lose land and natural resources that are crucial to their subsistence lifestyle. Increasing temperatures related to climate change have caused melting of sea ice and permafrost,[6] resulting in both global and local climate change impacts. Additionally, some of the changes being experienced by Alaskan indigenous groups include: (1) changing ocean pH levels that negatively impact species of fish and crustaceans that are relied upon by animals higher up the food chain (such as bowhead whales) that are in turn relied upon by subsistence communities; (2) thawing permafrost due to increased overall temperatures; (3) a reduction in sea ice that is relied upon by animals and communities for survival; (4) an increased abundance of water due to flooding that in turn causes erosion; (5) decreased water quality; and (6) changes in weather patterns.[7] Climate change has caused hunting, fishing, and travel in the Arctic to become more difficult, forcing some members to relocate after flooding.[8] Reindeer herders report declining populations because the animals find it increasingly difficult to access food and are more likely to fall through melting ice.[9] Some Arctic species such as caribou, upon which indigenous peoples rely heavily for their survival, have migrated away from their traditional habitats and ranges due to shifts in weather patterns. These impacts limit Arctic indigenous peoples' ability to rely upon these species because the indigenous peoples may be tied to specific areas for legal, cultural, and spiritual reasons, as described below.[10]

Because climate change is dramatically affecting the Arctic environment, the indigenous peoples who are reliant on subsistence foods are particularly hard hit.[11] Not only are the animals that subsistence hunters rely on more difficult to find because of climate changes,[12] but also subsistence hunting is much more dangerous, given the changing environment. For example, because of melting permafrost, it may be much more treacherous for hunters to travel previously relied-upon routes.[13] In Alaska, many indigenous communities rely on subsistence sources to some degree.[14] A reduction or even a perceived reduction in the availability of subsistence foods may also have a substantial impact on the mental health of reliant indigenous communities, given that subsistence foods play such an important role in the community.[15] Moreover, threats to traditional indigenous ways of life as a result of climate change may also endanger the indigenous knowledge of such communities, given that "[s]ubsistence activities require traditional knowledge based on the synthesis of observations and interpretations made over the past generations."[16] Because of these impacts, indigenous peoples in the Arctic, such as in Alaska, may be negatively impacted more than indigenous peoples elsewhere in the United States.[17]

Brief Introduction to the Law Applicable to Alaska Natives

Based on the foregoing, something must change if many Arctic indigenous peoples and their customs and traditions are to survive the onslaught of climate change. However, the legal scheme applicable in Alaska complicates the ability of Alaska Natives to adapt. Accordingly, this section provides a brief introduction into the law applicable to Alaska Natives in order to illustrate the legal constraints placed on these communities.[18]

Perhaps one of the most important laws impacting the legal rights of Alaska Natives is the Alaska Native Claims Settlement Act (ANSCA). On December 18, 1971, then-president Richard Nixon signed ANSCA into law.[19] ANSCA extinguished all aboriginal land title in Alaska[20] and established regional and village corporations, which are subject to Alaska state law, in which enrolled Alaskan Natives would receive corporate stock.[21] Village and regional corporations were able to select lands where they were already located as well as adjoining areas.[22] The Native corporations received title in fee to their lands.[23] Except for the Annette Islands Reservation, all reservations previously existing within Alaska were extinguished.[24] ANSCA does not provide special hunting rights for Alaska Natives.[25] Also, ANSCA created ambiguity as to whether the federal trust relationship applied to Alaska Natives.[26]

Whether land owned by Alaska Natives was "Indian country"[27] was an issue presented to the United States Supreme Court in *Alaska v.*

Native Village of Venetie Tribal Government.[28] Under ANSCA, fee title was conveyed from the United States to Native corporations, which in turn transferred title to the Native Village of Venetie tribal government. The issue of whether Indian country still existed in Alaska following passage of ANSCA arose when the Native Village of Venetie sought to tax private contractors building a public school in the area, and Alaska sued.

The Court evaluated whether the land owned in fee by the Village of Venetie was Indian country. The Court found that the land was not Indian country. First, ANCSA specifically revoked reservation and allotment land in Alaska. The Court therefore focused on whether the land in question was part of a dependent Indian community.[29] In deciding whether this was a dependent Indian community, the Court looked to whether the land was set aside by the federal government for the use of Indians and whether the land was under federal superintendence. The Court found that after passage of ANCSA, the lands were no longer set aside for Indian usage under the superintendence of the federal government, and, therefore, the Native Village of Venetie was not located within Indian country.[30]

As a result of the foregoing interpretation and subsequent developments, Alaska Natives are perhaps more constrained than other indigenous peoples living in the lower 48 states because of ANSCA and its legacy. Specifically, Alaska Natives do not have an aboriginal right to hunt or fish; Indian country (except as mentioned above) has been abolished, which in turn decreases Native jurisdictional authority in many instances; and ANSCA calls into question the application of the federal trust responsibility to Alaskan Natives. Accordingly, as discussed more fully below, the factors that should be considered when planning for climate change adaptation in Alaska may differ from factors applicable elsewhere.[31]

Previous Legal Efforts to Address the Impacts of Climate Change on Arctic Indigenous Peoples

Having evaluated the impacts of climate change of Arctic indigenous peoples and the law applicable to Alaska Natives specifically, it is now helpful to consider whether Arctic indigenous communities have previously used existing laws to attempt to combat the impacts of climate change.[32] Many Arctic indigenous communities have explored methods for dealing with the reality of climate change. For example, two of these communities, the Inuit Circumpolar Conference (now known as the Inuit Circumpolar Council [ICC]) and Native Village of Kivalina, explored legal avenues to hopefully address the impacts of climate change facing their respective communities. This section explores these legal claims and the results of such claims.

The ICC represents more than 150,000 Inuit residing in Canada, Greenland, Russia, and the United States.[33] As previously explained, the Inuit, along with other Arctic indigenous peoples, are experiencing profound changes in their environment. On December 7, 2005, the ICC filed a petition with the Inter-American Commission on Human Rights (IACHR), which is a commission of the Organization of American States.[34] The ICC brought its claim in the IACHR against the United States.[35] The ICC argued that as a significant contributor to climate change through its greenhouse gas emissions, the United States is a significant contributor to the negative environmental impacts affecting the Inuit in both Canada and the United States.[36] Because of the United States' significant contribution to climate change, the ICC asserted that Inuit rights under the American Declaration of the Organization of American States had been violated.[37]

The IACHR's response to the ICC's petition encompassed two paragraphs.[38] The IACHR determined that "the information provided [in the ICC's petition] does not enable us to determine whether the alleged facts would tend to characterize a violation of the rights protected by the American Declaration."[39] Ultimately, the IACHR found that "it will not be possible to process [the ICC's] petition at present because the information it contains does not satisfy the requirements set forth in those Rules and the other applicable instruments."[40] However, the IACHR did hold a hearing on the connection between climate change and human rights in March 2007 per the ICC's request.[41] Since the hearing in 2007, the IACHR has indicated that it remains interested in the rights of indigenous peoples within the Americas.[42]

The ICC is not the only Arctic indigenous community to seek legal redress for the impacts of climate change. Because the Native Village of Kivalina and City of Kivalina (Kivalina)[43] are also experiencing the profound impacts of climate change, as the sea ice protecting the community has melted leaving it vulnerable to severe erosion and storms,[44] the community brought a claim against various corporate defendants involved in the oil and gas business.[45] In light of the massive injuries Kivalina is suffering and the impending loss of the land upon which the community is located, Kivalina filed a complaint in the U.S. District Court for the Northern District of California (District Court) on February 26, 2008, against several private entities that allegedly contribute significantly to climate change through their emissions of greenhouse gases.[46] Kivalina included claims of federal public nuisance, state private and public nuisance, civil conspiracy, and concert of action. Kivalina requested monetary damages for current injuries sustained as well as a declaratory judgment "for such future monetary expenses and damages as may be incurred by Plaintiffs in connection with the nuisance of global warming."[47] On September 30, 2009, United States District Judge Saundra Brown Armstrong dismissed Kivalina's claim, finding that the complaint was precluded under the political question doctrine and that Kivalina lacked standing.[48] Furthermore, the district court determined that Kivalina did not meet the requirements of Article III standing.[49]

On March 10, 2010, Kivalina filed a brief in the U.S. Court of Appeals for the Ninth Circuit, appealing the district court's decision.[50] In a 3–0 decision, the United States Court of Appeals for the Ninth Circuit relied on federal displacement reasoning to affirm the district court's dismissal of the plaintiffs' claims.[51] Kivalina filed a petition for rehearing en banc with the Ninth Circuit. On November 22, 2012, the Ninth Circuit denied the petition.[52]

As can be seen from the foregoing discussion, to date, Arctic indigenous peoples have been unsuccessful in their efforts to compel action through the courts to address the impacts of climate change facing their communities. The results of the ICC petition and Kivalina's litigation may mean it is increasingly the case that Arctic indigenous communities will explore adaptation strategies to cope with climate change. Accordingly, the next section explores adaptation by first providing a brief introduction to adaptation generally and then considering the factors applicable to Arctic indigenous peoples considering adaptation strategies.

Arctic Indigenous Adaptation

To understand what adaptation is and the principles that generally guide adaptation development, this section begins with a brief introduction to climate change adaptation. With this framework in mind, the section then goes on to consider unique factors affecting Arctic indigenous peoples that should be included in any consideration of adaptive strategies for

Arctic indigenous peoples. Given that it is uncertain which governmental entity may be responsible for crafting adaptation strategies for Arctic indigenous peoples, the factors are crucial in the development of such strategies. This section concludes that, although adaptation and especially relocation may be less than ideal strategies to cope with climate change for indigenous peoples, by ensuring that certain factors are part of any discussion of climate change adaptation for Arctic indigenous peoples, hopefully the negative impact of such adaptation will be ameliorated.

Brief Introduction to Adaptation

As explained above, the impacts of climate change are dramatic and life altering for people around the world, but especially for Arctic indigenous peoples, who are already being hard hit by climate change. Today, strategies to cope with climate change can generally be categorized into one of two groups: adaptation[53] or mitigation.[54] Policymakers in the 1990s and early 2000s largely focused on mitigation policies.[55] For a wide variety of reasons, however, mitigation efforts proved largely unsuccessful in abating the impacts of climate change. As a result, "[a] comprehensive national strategy that successfully reduces greenhouse gas emissions to levels thought to be adequate to arrest climate change . . . quite clearly is not around the political corner."[56]

Given these truths, advocates, scientists, and politicians are increasingly considering adaptive strategies to cope with climate change.[57] Recognizing that the impacts of climate change are already occurring, adaptation is increasingly popular, given that it focuses on responses to climate change.[58] Adaptation efforts differ from mitigation efforts in several respects. For purposes of this paper, it is important to note that one of these differences is that "adaptation strategies are apt to be localized, and they may present opportunities for relatively quick action at the local level."[59] As Professor Robin Kundis Craig explains, "Climate change adaptation . . . requires continually evolving strategies to cope with continually changing locally and regionally specific socio-ecological conditions."[60] The localized nature of adaptive strategies is important when considering the role that indigenous governments play in developing such strategies, as discussed below.

Professor J. B. Ruhl, who has written widely on the subject of climate change adaptation, explains that the goals of adaptation planning are "[f]irst . . . to effectively and equitably manage the harms and benefits of climate change while mitigation does its work." He goes on to state that, second, adaptation planning must "supply interim strategies to put us in a position to resume long-term planning for sustainable development when climate change is 'over.'"[61] Professor Ruhl also notes that the international law community has identified climate change adaptation as a human rights issue.[62] This is consistent with the use of international human rights norms as a factor in any adaptive planning and the ICC's petition to the IACHR, as discussed above.[63]

Ultimately, however, adaptation should not be the sole focus of any community. This is the case in part because some communities are more vulnerable to climate change and less able to adapt. For example, scholars caution against policies focusing only on adaptation. Caution may be warranted because such policies have a tendency to hit the poor the hardest, because the poor generally have the most difficulty adapting due to lack of resources.[64] Successful adaptation is a product of socioeconomic factors as well as physical, environmental factors.[65] Ultimately, because "[i]n the United States, poor and marginalized communities without sufficient financial and social resources will face significant adaptation challenges,"[66] Professor Alice Kaswan concludes that "equity considerations should play a vital role in emerging U.S. adaptation initiatives."[67]

In order to ensure that indigenous communities engage in successful adaptation, it is helpful to use an integrated method of adaptation that takes into consideration ecological, social, and economic factors.[68] Yet, communities cannot be treated the same by adaptation planners: not only will such actions will result in inequity;[69] also, as explained above, there is wide diversity among the Arctic indigenous communities. Furthermore, in the case of indigenous communities, it is also crucial that indigenous sovereignty—the right to self-determination, human rights, environmental justice, and the unique connection to land and the environment possessed by many indigenous communities—be taken into consideration.

There are two types of response orientation to adapting to climate change: either be proactive[70] or reactive.[71] Because of the intensity of the impacts of climate change already affecting Alaskan indigenous peoples, the majority of Alaskan Natives may use reactive adaptive strategies. For example, several indigenous villages in Alaska are already experiencing flooding and erosion, including Kivalina, Koyukuk, Newtok, and Shishmaref, and as a result, these communities are actively considering relocation, and in the case of Newtok, have already begun relocation efforts.[72] In this regard, use of adaptive strategies in Alaska may differ from the lower 48, where the impacts are not yet so dramatic. There may be more opportunity for proactive development of adaptation strategies in the lower 48 states not available to Alaska Natives and others living in the area.

Finally, it is important to note that adaptation strategies include the possibility of relocation. When indigenous communities face relocation, such as Newtok and Kivalina currently face, additional legal challenges arise unique to their status as indigenous communities.

Even community relocation is no panacea, as Professor Kaswan explains. Relocation requires substantial resources, an appropriate relocation site, and, such as in the case of many indigenous communities whose cultural identities are tied to a geographical place, the risk of cultural disruption. Professor Kaswan posits that a political decision over whether to protect or retreat has significant social justice implications, and that differences in political power are likely to determine who receives protection and who must leave.[73]

Moreover, relocation is very expensive. For example, the cost to relocate the Native Village of Kivalina is estimated to cost between $95 and $400 million.[74] Given the foregoing, it may be that indigenous communities try to avoid relocation whenever possible. The complexities articulated above are only intensified by the fact that many indigenous peoples have unique connections to their land and environment, as discussed below.

At the end of the day, "[c]limate change will require people to develop new strategies for avoiding and recovering from its harms and capturing and harnessing its benefits."[75] Adaptation inevitably results in winners and losers as resources are reallocated in the face of climate change.[76] Accordingly, to help ensure that Arctic indigenous peoples are not climate change losers, this next subsection discusses factors that should be included in a discussion of adaptive strategies for Arctic indigenous peoples.

Indigenous Adaptation

With a background in climate change adaptation now in hand, this portion of the chapter considers what a domestic climate justice policy, as it applies to indigenous peoples, might consider. As explained above, communities, including Arctic indigenous communities, are increasingly looking to adaptive strategies.[77] As indigenous communities consider and implement adaptive strategies, a question arises as to who will be responsible for crafting such adaptive strategies.[78] For example, in the case of Alaska Natives, should it be the federal, state, or Native government that makes decisions regarding the appropriate adaptation strategy? Ideally, as explained below, it should be the Alaska Native governments that make these decisions. However, given the uncertainty of the ultimate decision maker, this section develops factors that should be taken into consideration by any decision maker acting within Alaska Native communities. Specifically, the factors that should be taken into consideration include international human rights norms, environmental justice, tribal sovereignty, and the unique connection that many Arctic indigenous communities possess with their land and environment.

One factor that Arctic indigenous communities should take into consideration when planning their adaptive strategies is the application of the international human rights framework. Given the human rights dimensions of climate change—as noted above in the discussion of the ICC's petition to the IACHR—numerous scholars have called on governments to assist indigenous peoples with adaptation.[79] Furthermore, as Professor Rebecca Tsosie concluded, an international human rights approach is appropriate to address the impacts of climate change on indigenous peoples, given that domestic solutions will not adequately address such impacts.[80]

Notably, adopting human rights approaches to issues affecting indigenous communities as a result of climate change may require varying approaches, as some indigenous communities may consider such rights, for example those related to subsistence, to be communal rights.[81] In considering the application of human rights norms to indigenous adaptation, it is important to distinguish sovereignty from self-determination, as indigenous communities may have rights based in both. "[S]overeignty is a substantive legal status while self-determination is a political right that stems from an underlying moral claim."[82]

In considering what law applies to their adaptive efforts and specifically thinking about international human rights, Arctic indigenous communities may want to consider the United Nations Declaration on the Rights of Indigenous Peoples (UNDRIP).[83] UNDRIP addresses international expectations of the basic rights enjoyed by indigenous peoples. Although not a binding legal document, the UNDRIP is helpful in providing a baseline as to what the United Nations and its member states believe are the rights (or should be the rights) of indigenous peoples. Of particular importance in assessing rights are the UNDRIP's statements with regard to indigenous self-determination, property, and redress. UNDRIP Article 3 states, "Indigenous peoples have the right to self-determination."[84] UNDRIP Article 10 states, "Indigenous peoples shall not be forcibly removed from their lands or territories. No relocation shall take place without the free, prior and informed consent of the indigenous peoples concerned and after agreement on just and fair compensation and, where possible, the option to return."[85] UNDRIP Article 26 states, "Indigenous peoples have the right to the lands, territories and resources which they have traditionally owned, occupied or otherwise used or acquired. . . . States shall give legal recognition and protection to these lands, territories and resources."[86] And, finally, UNDRIP Article 28 states that

> [i]ndigenous peoples have the right to redress, by means that can include restitution or, when this is not possible, just, fair and equitable compensation, for the lands, territories and resources which they have traditionally owned or otherwise occupied or used, and which have been confiscated, taken, occupied, used or damaged without their free, prior and informed consent.[87]

Furthermore, given the human rights perspective that must be incorporated into any discussion of indigenous adaptation, indigenous communities must be given an opportunity to actively participate in the dialogue on adaption. This is consistent with the general guideline that communication regarding adaptation is essential for any community, indigenous and nonindigenous, to adapt.[88] The right to participate is also consistent with UNDRIP and the general international human rights framework.

Indigenous adaptation to climate change should also consider the application of environmental justice. Native communities can be environmental justice communities.[89] "Even before climate change came into the picture, an environmental justice theme emerged around the inequitable burdens the poor and people of color have sustained in terms of disproportionate exposure to pollutants, proximity to industrial sites and contaminated lands, and limited access to environmental amenities."[90] "[T]he term 'environmental justice' has been used to highlight the distributional impacts of the dominant society's environmental decision-making process on disadvantaged communities, including poor and racial minorities."[91] In this regard, environmental justice is certainly applicable to Arctic indigenous peoples, who have contributed little if anything to the problem of climate change but are disproportionately bearing its negative impacts.

Climate change and its impacts on indigenous peoples are environmental justice issues, because "[t]he disproportion between tribal contributions to global warming and the negative impacts on tribes qualifies this as an environmental justice issue."[92] Although the law applicable in Alaska differs from the law applicable to the lower 48 states, the existing law applicable in Alaska may still be used to further any environmental justice claim or perhaps more specifically, climate justice claims of Alaska Natives.[93] Ultimately, assuming that the factors discussed are taken into consideration when examining adaptation measures for indigenous communities, it may be possible that "[a]daptation law can play a significant role in furthering climate justice."[94]

Another factor to be considered when choosing adaptive strategies for Arctic indigenous communities, especially those is Alaska, is indigenous sovereignty. Notably, "[t]ribal self-determination mandates that adaptation strategies in Indian country be decided by the governing tribes."[95] As noted above, the vast majority of Indian country in Alaska was eradicated as a result of ANSCA. Yet, tribal self-determination and sovereignty demand that indigenous communities be the decision makers in adaptation planning, as explained above under international human rights law. Moreover, adaptive measures, more so than mitigation measures, can be developed on a local level, which calls for increased participation for local governments—here, indigenous governments.

Native nations differ from other communities that may be impacted by climate change because of their status as sovereigns. Tribes' legal rights flow as an initial matter from their sovereignty and their related historical management of the land and resources. Native nations exist as entities separate from state and federal governments. Myriad historical legal developments led to this separateness.[96] Although the nature of tribal sovereignty has changed over the ensuing decades since the founding of the United States, tribal sovereignty remains in place today.[97]

Accordingly, claims raised by Native nations "must be consistent with the promotion of tribal self-governance."[98] An injustice occurs if courts or policymakers fail to consider the sovereignty of Native nations, because Native nations cannot meaningfully participate in the legal process if courts fail to consider something so essential to Native nations as their sovereignty.[99] Consistent with the necessity to recognize indigenous sovereignty to prevent injustice as well as international human rights norms, any adaptation policy applicable to indigenous peoples must provide for broad participation by the indigenous community. Generally, scholars have noted that community participation is necessary for successful climate change adaptation.[100] Such participation from indigenous communities is particularly important for the reasons already discussed. Also, consistent with the variety in indigenous governments and cultures, climate change impacts are variable,[101] and therefore any adaptation plans should address the individual needs of the indigenous community being impacted. Allowing for indigenous participation also helps ensure that these crucial differences are taken into consideration during adaptation planning. Notably, however, consideration of tribal sovereignty alone cannot ensure justice for Arctic indigenous communities considering climate change adaptation. Professor Tsosie explains that "the problem of climate change cannot be resolved through recognition of Native sovereignty, because the environmental harms are largely occurring beyond the boundaries of their lands."[102] Accordingly, all factors discussed here should play a role in adaptation planning.

Finally, adaptation planning for Arctic indigenous communities should also take into consideration the unique cultural and spiritual connection that many indigenous communities have with their land and environment. Professor Tsosie explains that the importance of land is particularly vital to most indigenous communities.

> There is no other place that indigenous people can go and still continue to practice their unique lifeways and cultural practices. Geographical location is essential to indigenous identity. History has demonstrated time and again that the forcible removal of indigenous communities from their traditional lands, resources, and lifeways results in immeasurable harm.[103]

Beyond legal considerations discussed above, many indigenous peoples also have a strong spiritual and cultural connection to the land upon which they reside or to their traditional homelands. For many indigenous peoples, their spirituality is intimately connected to the Earth and their environment.[104] As a result, as the effects of climate change ravage their environment, indigenous peoples may experience both a physical and a spiritual loss connected with the negative impact on the environment. Similarly, because of the close spiritual connection that many indigenous peoples have with the environment, their culture and traditions are also intimately connected to the larger environment.[105] It is commonplace in many indigenous communities for annual traditions and customs to be tied to certain environmental occurrences. As climate change threatens to dramatically change the environment, culture and tradition may also therefore be threatened.

In part because of this strong connection to place, Professor Tsosie concludes that "[t]he international dialogue on climate change is currently focused on a strategy of adaptation to climate change that includes the projected removal of entire communities, if necessary. Such a strategy will prove genocidal for many groups of indigenous peoples."[106] Because of the strong connection many indigenous communities have with a particular space, Professor Sarah Krakoff explains that "[t]he option of relocating is certainly as available to tribal communities as to others, but relocation has a different meaning if the cultural definition of a people is bound to a location and its unique ecological offerings."[107] Given the harsh realities of climate change, especially those faced by Arctic indigenous communities, as discussed above many Alaskan Native communities (such as the Native Villages of Kivalina and Newtok), are actively considering relocation. Hopefully, if the factors discussed above are included in any discussion of adaptive strategies that include relocation, such relocation will not prove "genocidal." For example, when considering relocation, it may be possible to keep indigenous communities within their traditional homelands.[108]

Conclusion

Climate change is drastically affecting the Arctic environment. Because of these drastic changes, Arctic indigenous peoples' lifestyles are being dramatically altered, and as a result, Arctic indigenous cultures and traditions are threatened as well. Given that it is unlikely that mitigation efforts will be able to redress the situation currently facing these communities and that previous legal claims—such as the ICC petition and Kivalina complaint—have proven largely unsuccessful, many Arctic indigenous communities may increasingly consider adaptive strategies.

Although such strategies certainly have the potential to be very helpful to indigenous communities trying to survive climate change, adaptation is not without its risks for indigenous peoples, as highlighted by Professor Tsosie. Accordingly, adaptive planners working with Arctic indigenous communities are encouraged to incorporate a number of factors into any adaptation planning. Adaptation planning for these communities should include considerations of international human rights law, environmental justice, tribal sovereignty, and the unique connection that many indigenous communities have with their homeland and environment. Hopefully, by incorporating these factors into adaptation planning, climate change adaptation will not prove "genocidal" for Arctic indigenous peoples.

Notes

1. Indian Entities Recognized and Eligible to Receive Services from the Bureau of Indian Affairs, 77 Fed. Reg. 47, 868 (2012). In addition to the number of federally recognized Alaska Native tribes, "[t]here are eleven distinct groups of Alaska Natives who are divided into five groups based on geographic proximity or cultural affinity: (1) the Athabascan in the east and interior; (2) the Yup'ik and Cup'ik in the west; (3) the Inupiaq and St. Lawrence Island Yupik of the north and northwest; (4) the Aleut and Alutiiq of south central Alaska and the Aleutian islands; (5) the Eyal, Tlingit, Haida and Tsimshian of the southeastern archipelago." Sarah Krakoff, "American Indians, Climate Change, and Ethics for a Warming World," *Denver University Law Review* 85 (Sept. 9, 2008): 879.

2. Elizabeth B. Ristroph, "Alaska Tribes' Melting Subsistence Rights," *Arizona Journal of Environmental Law and Policy* 1 (Sept. 18, 2010): 49. Moreover, it is not the intent of this author to "invoke the mythic, romantic Indian, perpetually at one with nature and free of taint and pollution." Krakoff, "American Indians," 868. Rather, while noting that differences exist and trying to avoid the perpetuation of stereotypes regarding indigenous peoples and their connection to the environment, this chapter seeks to find some commonality of experience and apply legal principles to these instances of commonality. In order to account for the differences between communities, climate change adaptation strategies should be developed for the specific indigenous community being impacted.

3. The term *indigenous peoples* refers to a broad group of people. Professor S. James Anaya explains that "[t]he rubric of indigenous peoples includes the diverse Indian and aboriginal societies of the Western Hemisphere, the Inuit and Aleut of the Arctic, the aboriginal peoples of Australia, the Maori of Aotearoa (New Zealand), Native Hawaiians and other Pacific Islanders, the Sami of the European far North, and at least many of the tribal or culturally distinctive

non-dominant people of Asia and Africa. They are *indigenous* because their ancestral roots are embedded in the lands on which they live, or would like to live, much more deeply than the roots of more powerful sectors of society living on the same lands or in close proximity. And they are *peoples* in that they comprise distinct communities with a continuity of existence and identity that links them to the communities, tribes, or nations of their ancestral past." S. James Anaya, *International Human Rights and Indigenous Peoples* (New York: Aspen Publishers, 2009), 1.

4. Markedly, however, some scholars have noted that what is currently occurring in the Arctic merely foreshadows what may happen to indigenous peoples of the lower 48 states. Rebecca Tsosie, "Indigenous People and Environmental Justice: The Impact of Climate Change," *University of Colorado Law Review* 78 (2007): 1646.

5. Ibid., 1628.

6. "Alaska may be experiencing the impacts of global warming more than any other place on Earth, and Alaska Native tribes are among the first American populations to feel the effects of global climate change. Erosion and flooding affect 86 percent of Alaska Native villages to some extent, with the greatest effects felt along the coast." Daniel Cordalis and Dean B. Suagee, "The Effects of Climate Change on American Indian and Alaska Native Tribes," *Natural Resources and Environment* 22 (2008): 47; Anu Mittal and Jeffery D. Malcolm, *Alaska Villages: Most Are Affected by Flooding and Erosion, but Few Qualify for Federal Assistance* (GAO-04-142) (Washington, DC: U.S. General Accounting Office, 2003); http://www.gao.gov/assets/250/240810.pdf.

7. Ristroph, "Alaska Tribes,'" 51–58.

8. Ibid.; Azadeh Ansari, "'Climate Change' Forces Eskimos to Abandon Village," *CNN.com/technology*, April 28, 2009; http://www.cnn.com/2009/TECH/science/04/24/climate.change.eskimos/.

9. International Arctic Science Committee, "Case Study: Kola: The Saami Community of Lovozero Climate Change Case Study," *Encyclopedia of Earth*, February 8, 2010; http://www.eoearth.org/view/article/154043/.

10. Alaska Native Claims Settlement Act of 1971, 43 U.S.C. § 1603 (1971); Cordalis, "Effects of Climate Change," 47; General Accounting Office, *Alaska Villages*.

11. "Climate change impacts the availability and safety of subsistence foods, the costs and risks of subsistence activities, and the very knowledge on which subsistence depends." Ristroph, "Alaska Tribes,'" 47–48. "Subsistence uses" have been defined as "the noncommercial, customary and traditional uses of wild, renewable resources by a resident domiciled in a rural area of the state for direct personal or family consumption as food, shelter, fuel, clothing, tools, or transportation, for the making and selling of handicraft articles out of non-edible by-products of fish and wildlife resources taken for personal or family

consumption, and for the customary trade, barter, or sharing for personal or family consumption." Alaska Stat. § 16.05.940 (2009).

12. "During the winter, Alaska's caribou herds must dig through snow to find lichens to eat. When there is rain instead of snow, it can freeze into a nearly-impenetrable sheet of ice, and caribou may starve. Arctic marine mammals adapted to spending most of their lives on sea ice may not be able to adapt to the rapid changes taking place to the sea ice." Ristroph, "Alaska Tribes,'" 59.

13. "North Slope whalers have reported that they must now travel farther out to hunt. Increased travel time and distances add to fuel and maintenance costs and increase the risk of an accident occurring far from home. Changes in snow cover can make snow-machine travel difficult. . . . Less sea ice cover and more broken ice have made spring whaling more difficult for North Slope residents, as the water is rougher and more perilous to navigate. . . . More rapid ice recession and thinner ice conditions have also affected walrus hunting, such that hunters are more often butchering walruses in the water." Ibid., 60–61.

14. Ibid., 50–51.

15. Ibid., 64. In general, vulnerable income groups and minorities may suffer greater psychological impacts when disasters, such as those related to climate change in the Arctic, occur. "While disaster is not easy for anyone, there is evidence that lower income groups and minorities suffer disproportionately greater psychological impacts, likely associated with serious disasters. Lower income groups are also less likely to have access to mental health resources." Alice Kaswan, "Domestic Climate Change Adaptation and Equity," *Environmental Law Reporter News and Analysis* 42 (2012): 11133.

16. Ristroph, "Alaska Tribes,'" 64.

17. Ibid.

18. A full discussion of the law applicable to Alaska Natives is beyond the scope of this chapter. For a more complete discussion, see David S. Case and David S. Voluk, *Alaska Natives and American Laws* (Fairbanks: University of Alaska Press, 2002).

19. Alaska Native Claims Settlement Act of 1971, 43 U.S.C. § 1601–28 (1971).

20. Ibid., § 1603.

21. Ibid., § 1606.

22. Ibid., § 1611.

23. Ibid.

24. Ibid., § 1618.

25. "All aboriginal titles, if any, and claims of aboriginal title in Alaska based on use and occupancy, including submerged land underneath all water areas, both inland and offshore, and including any aboriginal hunting or fishing rights that may exist, are hereby extinguished." Ibid., § 1603(b).

26. Ibid., § 1601(b). As explained by Ray Halbritter, Nation Representative of the Oneida Indian Nation of New York: "[T]he trust obligation of the Federal government to Native people is fundamentally different from any other relationship the United States has with any other distinct group of people and carries elevated obligations. . . . The purpose behind the trust is and always has been to ensure the survival and welfare of Indian tribes and people. This includes an obligation to provide those services required to protect and enhance Indian lands, resources, and self-government, and also includes those economic and social programs that are necessary to raise the standard of living and social well-being of the Indian people to a level comparable to the non-Indian society." *Fulfilling the Federal Trust Responsibility: The Foundation of the Government-to-Government Relationship, Hearing Before the Committee on Indian Affairs,* 112th Cong. (2012) (statement of Ray Halbritter, Oneida Indian Nation Representative). A complete discussion of the federal trust relationship is beyond the scope of this chapter. For a more complete discussion of the federal trust relationship, see Elizabeth Ann Kronk, "Indian Claims and the Court of Federal Claims: A Legal Overview, Historical Accounting and Examination of the Court of Federal Claims' and Federal Circuit's Impact on Federal Indian Law," *Journal of the Federal Circuit Historical Society* 6 (2012): 59.

27. Indian Crimes Act of 1976, 18 U.S.C. § 1151 (1976). Section 1151 provides that Indian country includes: (1) all land within a reservation, notwithstanding issuance of a patent and including rights of way; (2) dependent Indian communities; and (3) all allotments.

28. Alaska v. Native Village of Venetie Tribal Gov't, 522 U.S. 520 (1998).

29. Indian Crimes Act, § 1151. "Indian country" includes dependent Indian communities.

30. Ristroph, "Alaska Tribes,'" 75–76.

31. For example, it may be that the federal trust relationship would not play a significant role in the development of adaptation strategies in Alaska.

32. Limited portions of this chapter have been taken from Elizabeth Ann Kronk, "Application of Environmental Justice to Climate Change–Related Claims Brought by Native Nations," in Tribes, Land and the Environment, ed. Sarah A. Krakoff and Ezra Rosser (Burlington: Ashgate, 2012), 75; and an article coauthored with Randall S. Abate, pending at the time of writing with the University of Ottawa Law Journal.

33. "Eleventh Conference of the Parties to the UN Framework Convention on Climate Change Montreal," Sheila Watt-Cloutier, Inuit Circumpolar Conference, accessed Oct. 17, 2012; http://www.inuitcircumpolar.com.

34. Although the ICC represents Inuit living in Greenland and Russia as well as in Canada and United States, the ICC's 2005 petition was limited to those Inuit living in Canada and the United States, as the IACHR's jurisdiction is limited to nation-states within the Americas. Sheila Watt-Cloutier, "Petition

to the Inter American Commission on Human Rights Violations Resulting From Global Warming Caused by the United States" petition, Dec. 7, 2005; http:// earthjustice.org/sites/default/files/library/legal_docs/petition-to-the-inter-american-commission-on-human-rights-on-behalf-of-the-inuit-circumpolar-conference.pdf. The Organization of American States is composed of all of the nations of North and South America. Organization of American States, accessed Dec. 5, 2012; http://www.oas.org/. The IACHR is headquartered in Washington, D.C. Ibid.

35. Watt-Cloutier, "Petition to the Inter American Commission," 132. The ICC petition focused on the United States in part because of the American withdrawal from Kyoto, "a decision which the petition argues forms a key part of the US failure to control its greenhouse gas emissions adequately." Hari M. Osofsky, "Complexities of Addressing the Impacts of Climate Change on Indigenous Peoples Through International Law Petitions," in *Climate Change and Indigenous Peoples: The Search for Legal Remedies*, ed. Randall S. Abate and Elizabeth Ann Kronk (Northampton: Edward Elgar, 2013), 313. The United States remains outside of the Kyoto Protocol as of this writing; Ibid., 505. Overall, some commentators have concluded that the United States has been the slowest nation to respond to the global problem of climate change. Sarah Nuffer, "Human Rights Violations and Climate Change: The Last Days of the Inuit People?" *Rutgers Law Record* 37 (2010): 184.

36. Watt-Cloutier, "Petition to the Inter American Commission," 132.

37. "[T]he petition relied upon rights contained in the regionally-based American Declaration of the Rights and Duties of Man because the United States is not party to the American Convention on Human Rights." Osofsky, "Complexities," 514–15.

38. Organization of American States, Letter to Sheila Watt-Cloutier et al., November 16, 2006; http://graphics8.nytimes.com/packages/pdf/science/16commissionletter.pdf.

39. Ibid.

40. Ibid.

41. Ibid., 498–99.

42. Osofsky, "Complexities," 499.

43. The Native Village and City of Kivalina "are the governing bodies of an Inupiat village of approximately 400 people . . . located on the tip of a six-mile barrier reef located . . . some seventy miles north of the Arctic Circle." Native Village v. ExxonMobil, No. 4:08-cv-01138-SBA, 2008 U.S. Dist. Ct. Pleadings LEXIS 16355 (N.D. Cal. Feb. 26, 2008).

44. Ibid., 1. "Houses and buildings are in imminent danger of falling into the sea. . . . Critical infrastructure is imminently threatened with permanent destruction." Ibid.

45. Kivalina filed its complaint against numerous private corporations who contributed substantial quantities of greenhouse gases to the environment,

including: ExxonMobil Corporation, BP PLC, BP America, Inc., BP Products North America, Chevron Corp., Chevron U.S.A., Inc., ConocoPhillips Comp., Royal Dutch Shell PLC, Shell Oil Comp., Peabody Energy Corp., AES Corp., American Electric Power Comp., Inc., American Power Services Corp., DTE Energy Comp., Duke Energy Corp., Dynegy Holdings, Inc., Edison International, MidAmerican Energy Holdings Company, Mirant Corp., NRG Energy, Pinnacle West Capital Corp., Reliant Energy, Inc., The Southern Comp., and XCEL Energy, Inc. Ibid.

46. Kivalina's complaint asserts that "[d]efendants in this action include many of the largest emitters of greenhouse gases in the United States." Ibid. The complaint then goes on to detail the actual greenhouse gas emissions for each defendant during certain years. Ibid., 6–30, 39–44. For example, in 2006, BP emitted "65 million tons of carbon dioxide equivalent greenhouse gases," Chevron "emitted 68 million tons of carbon dioxide equivalent," and Conoco Phillips emitted "62.3 million tons." Ibid., 6–8.

47. Ibid., 67.

48. Order Granting Defendants' Motions to Dismiss for Lack of Subject Matter Jurisdiction, Native Village of Kivalina v. ExxonMobil Corp., 663 F. Supp.2d 863 (2008), http://www.shopfloor.org/wp-content/uploads/kivalina-order-granting-motions-to-dismiss.pdf.

49. Ibid., 15–22.

50. Appellant's Opening Brief, No. 09-17490, Native Village v. ExxonMobil Corp., 663 F. Supp.2d 863 (2008); http://www.law.uh.edu/faculty/thester/courses/Climate-Change-2012/Kivalina%20Appellants'%20Brief.pdf.

51. Ibid.

52. "The panel has voted to deny the petition for rehearing en banc. The full court has been advised of the petition for rehearing en banc, and no judge of the court has requested a vote on the petition for rehearing en banc." Order on Petition for Rehearing, Village of Kivalina v. Exxon Mobil Corp., No. 4:08-cv-01138-SBA, Nov. 27, 2012; http://www.climatelawyers.com/file.axd?file =2012%2f12%2f20121127+Order+(denying+rehearing+en+banc)%2c+Kivalin a+v.+ExxonMobil.pdf.

53. The World Health Organization defines adaptation as: "Adjustment in natural or human systems to a new or changing environment. Adaptation to climate change refers to adjustment in response to actual or expected climatic stimuli or their effects, which moderates harm or exploits beneficial opportunities. Various types of adaptation can be distinguished, including anticipatory and reactive adaptation, public and private adaptation, and autonomous and planned adaptation." "Climate Change and Human Health," *World Health Organization*, accessed May 30, 2013; http://www.who.int/globalchange/publications/cchhsummary/en/. The Intergovernmental Panel on Climate Change defines adaptive practices as "actual adjustments, or changes in decision environments,

which might ultimately enhance resilience or reduce vulnerability to observed or expected changes in climate." W. Neil Adger et al., "Assessment of Adaptation Practices, Options, Constraints and Capacity," in *Climate Change 2007: Impacts, Adaptation and Vulnerability*, ed. M. L. Perry et al. (New York: Cambridge University Press, 2008), 720; http://www.ipcc.ch/pdf/assessment-report/ar4/wg2/ar4-wg2-chapter17.pdf.

54. Mitigation has been defined as "options for limiting climate change by, for example, reducing heat-trapping emissions such as carbon dioxide, methane, nitrous oxide, and halocarbons, or removing some of the heat-trapping gases from the atmosphere." Thomas R. Karl et al., eds., *Global Climate Change Impacts in the United States* (New York: Cambridge University Press, 2009), 10–11; http://downloads.globalchange.gov/usimpacts/pdfs/climate-impacts-report.pdf.

55. J. B. Ruhl, "Climate Change Adaptation and the Structural Transformation of Environmental Law," *Environmental Law* 40 (2010): 368.

56. Ibid.

57. "[T]he cold war between mitigation and adaptation is finally thawing. Climate change is already happening, and more is yet to come no matter what, thus a consensus is building that mitigation needs adaptation, and vice versa, even if they fundamentally are different and sometimes competing policy thrusts." Ibid.

58. Judith V. Royster, "Climate Change and Tribal Water Rights: Removing Barriers to Adaptation Strategies," *Tulane Environmental Law Journal* 26 (April 20, 2012): 199. Ultimately, although increased attention is being paid to adaptation strategies, "[m]itigation and adaptation are both essential parts of a comprehensive climate change response strategy." Karl et al., *Global Climate*, 11. This is because "[n]either approach is effective alone. Mitigation alone only stabilizes or reduces the impacts of climate change, but adaptation by itself accepts the inevitability of climate change's adverse effects." Royster, "Climate Change," 199.

59. Shelley Ross Saxer and Carol M. Rose, "A Prospective Look at Property Rights," *George Mason Law Review* 20 (May 1, 2013): 724.

60. Robin K. Craig, "The Social and Cultural Aspects of Climate Change Winners," *Minnesota Law Review* 97 (July 16, 2013): 1419.

61. Ruhl, "Climate Change," 375.

62. Ibid., 403.

63. "[T]he petition relied upon rights contained in the regionally-based American Declaration of the Rights and Duties of Man because the United States is not party to the American Convention on Human Rights." Osofsky, "Complexities," 514–15.

64. Tsosie, "Indigenous People," 1660. "[W]hether burdens have a greater effect on minority groups or those living in poverty, the costs are most often endured by the poorest members (socially, economically, politically) of our society."

"Environmental Justice: Factors and Influences," *Virginia Natural Resources Leadership Institution*, Aug. 2010, 1. Ultimately, "[c]atastrophe is bad for everyone. But it is especially bad for the weak and disenfranchised." Robert R. M. Verchick, *Facing Catastrophe: Environmental Acton for a Post-Katrina World* (Cambridge: Harvard University Press, 2010), 106.

65. "Although the relevant factors vary by the type of climate change impact at issue, sensitivity is determined by such features as elevation, the quality of the housing stock, underlying health conditions, and proximity to other hazards. The capacity to cope is a function of such factors as a community's financial and social resources, access to health care, and geographic mobility. In other words, the extent of adverse consequences is not only a function of geographic location and physical attributes, but of socioeconomic conditions." Kaswan, "Domestic Climate Change," 11126.

66. Ibid., 11125.

67. Ibid., 11126.

68. Ibid., 11138. "An integrated ecological, social and economic approach to adaptation planning, like that suggested by Rob Verchick and by Manuel Pastor and his co-authors in the disaster planning context, is essential to equitable adaptation efforts." Manuel Pastor et al., *In the Wake of the Storm: Environment, Disaster, and Race After Katrina* (New York: Russell Sage, 2006), 30–31; Verchick, *Facing Catastrophe*, 165.

69. "Adaptation policies that attempt to treat everyone the same, regardless of underlying demographic characteristics, will result in substantial inequality given underlying differences." Kaswan, "Domestic Climate Change," 1139.

70. "Proactive strategies anticipate climate change impacts to design measures that will reduce harm or harness benefits in the future, such as crop and livelihood diversification, seasonal climate forecasting, community-based disaster risk reduction, famine early warning systems, insurance, water storage, supplementary irrigation, and so on." Ruhl, "Climate Change," 382.

71. "[R]eactive strategies design responses based on observed climate change impacts as they occur through measures such as emergency response, disaster recovery, and migration." Ibid.

72. General Accounting Office, *Alaska Villages*, 3.

73. Kaswan, "Domestic Climate Change," 11134.

74. Ibid., 11138; Randall S. Abate, "Public Nuisance Suits for the Climate Justice Movement: The Right Thing and the Right Time," *Washington Law Review* 85 (May 17, 2010): 207.

75. Ruhl, "Climate Change," 380.

76. Ibid., 366.

77. Notably, this chapter does not argue that indigenous communities should focus all of their attention on adaptation policies. Rather, this chapter

advances factors that should be incorporated into discussions focused on indigenous adaptation.

78. "Given that adaptation strategies are a necessary part of the response
to climate change, an issue arises as to whether strategies within Indian country
will be developed and chosen by the federal government on a national scare
of developed and chosen by each tribe to meet the particular needs of each
reservation." Royster, "Climate Change," 199–200.

79. Ruhl, "Climate Change," 407; Randall S. Abate, "Climate Change, the
United States, and the Impacts of Arctic Melting: A Case Study in the Need for
Enforceable International Environmental Human Rights," *Stanford Environmental
Law Journal* 26A (2007): 71–72; James D. Ford, "Supporting Adaptation: A
Priority for Action on Climate Change for Canadian Inuit," *Sustainable Develop-
ment Law and Policy* 8 (Spring 2008): 25; Donald M. Goldberg and Tracy Badua,
"Do People Have Standing? Indigenous Peoples, Global Warming, and Human
Rights," *Barry Law Review* 11 (Fall 2008): 61; Jesse Hohmann, "Igloo as Icon: A
Human Rights Approach to Climate Change for the Inuit?," *Transnational Law
and Contemporary Problems* 18 (April 23, 2009): 295; Margueritte E. Middaugh,
"Linking Global Warming to Inuit Human Rights," *San Diego International Law
Journal* 8 (Fall 2006): 207; E. Rania Rampersad, "Indigenous Adaptation to
Climate Change: Preserving Sustainable Relationships Through an Environ-
mental Stewardship Claim & Trust Fund Remedy," *Georgetown International
Environmental Law Review* 21 (2009): 613; Tsosie, "Indigenous People," 1676;
Erika Zimmerman, "Valuing Traditional Ecological Knowledge: Incorporating the
Experiences of Indigenous People into Global Climate Change Policies," *New
York University Environmental Law Journal* 13 (2005): 846.

80. "Thus, if there is to be any greater understanding of the need to
protect indigenous cultures, it must come from some authority outside domestic
law. This is the prospective role of international human rights." Tsosie, "Indigenous People," 1651.

81. Ristroph, "Alaska Tribes,'" 49–50.

82. Tsosie, "Indigenous People," 1663.

83. United Nations General Assembly, Resolution 61/295 and Annex,
"Declaration on the Rights of Indigenous Peoples," Sept. 13, 2007; http://www.
un.org/esa/socdev/unpfii/documents/DRIPS_en.pdf.

84. Ibid., Art. 3.

85. Ibid., Art. 10.

86. Ibid., Art. 26.

87. Ibid., Art. 28.

88. "Communication is key to effective adaptation and, given the diversity of population, community and demographic-specific strategies are necessary. . . . In addition to identifying language needs, adaptation planners need to

identify culturally appropriate modes of communication considering newspapers, radio, television, e-mail, social media, or door-to-door outreach. . . . Given the importance of community-specific information to designing appropriate substantive adaptation measures and communication strategies, adaptation planning processes require bottom-up participatory mechanisms." Kaswan, "Domestic Climate Change," 11141.

89. "First, virtually all Indian tribes clearly fit into Getches and Pellow's definition of groups who come to the table with 'palpable and endemic disadvantage,' stemming from a long history of discrimination, exclusion, and deliberate attempts to destroy their cultural and political communities. Second, the obvious disproportionate environmental harms borne by Native peoples have meant that they are *already* a part of the discussion—to let them continue to be so without a conscious articulation of the role of tribal sovereignty would be counterproductive to determining appropriate remedial strategies." Ibid., 162. Therefore, for Native nations, meaningful participation includes an acknowledgment of their sovereignty. Therefore, courts considering claims brought by Native nations, like the one brought by Kivalina, must consider tribal sovereignty in order to effectively view the matter from an environmental justice lens. In *Village of Kivalina v. Exxon Mobil Corp.*, the district court, as previously discussed, failed to consider the Nation's sovereignty, especially in its discussion of the Nation's standing in the matter. And, as a result, Kivalina was deprived of an environmentally just outcome.

90. Ruhl, "Climate Change," 405.

91. Tsosie, "Indigenous People," 1627.

92. Sarah Krakoff, "American Indians, Climate Change, and Ethics for a Warming World," *Denver University Law Review* 85 (2008): 865.

93. "Several other federal statutes reinforce Alaska Native subsistence rights by preempting state regulation of certain activities such as game hunting, reindeer herding, and whaling. While these rights arguably have less bite than treaty rights, they nonetheless contribute to the justice claims that Alaska Natives may assert in response to climate change, and at a minimum should put lawmakers on notice that serious legal issues will be on the horizon even if we act swiftly to mitigate global warming." Ibid., 882.

94. Kaswan, "Domestic Climate Change," 11127. Environmental justice and climate justice are related concepts, but slightly different. As Professor Judith Royster explains, "[j]ust as the environmental justice movement focused attention on the disproportionate environmental harms visited on minority and low-income communities in the United States, the related concept of climate justice focuses on the inequitable effects of climate change worldwide. While environmental justice is concerned with environmental quality, climate justice is concerned with the 'equitable distribution of the benefits of climate change

adaptation.'" Royster, "Climate Change," 198. In this regard, climate justice is linked to climate change adaptation.

95. Royster, "Climate Change," 200.

96. American Indian tribes are extraconstitutional, meaning that tribes exist apart from the American Constitution. Ann Tweedy, "Connecting the Dots Between the Constitution, The Marshall Trilogy, and the *United States v. Lara*: Notes Toward a Blueprint for the Next Legislative Restoration of Tribal Sovereignty," *University of Michigan Journal of Law Reform* 42 (Spring 2009): 656; Gloria Valencia-Weber, "The Supreme Court's Indian Law Decisions: Deviations from Constitutional Principles and the Crafting of Judicial Smallpox Blankets," *University of Pennsylvania Journal of Constitutional Law* 5 (2003): 417. In the early nineteenth century, the U.S. Supreme Court affirmed the separateness of Native nations. In *Cherokee Nation v. Georgia*, the U.S. Supreme Court held that American Indian tribes were "domestic dependent nations," highlighting their separateness from both state and federal governments. 30 U.S. 1 (1831). In *Worcester v. Georgia*, the U.S. Supreme Court further clarified the separateness of American Indian tribes, finding that the laws of the states shall have "no force or effect" within the exterior boundaries of American Indian tribal territory. 31 U.S. 515 (1832). Although the breadth of tribal sovereignty has certainly changed in the intervening decades, today, the majority of matters handled by tribal courts include issues of property and family law. Nell Jessup Newton, "Tribal Court Praxis: One Year in the Life of Twenty Indian Tribal Courts," *American Indian Law Review* 22 (1998): 308. This is consistent with the general policy of the American federal government to leave issues related to American Indian tribal members solely within the inherent tribal sovereignty of tribal governments. Worcester v. Georgia, 31 U.S. 515 (1932); Santa Clara Pueblo v. Martinez, 436 U.S. 49 (1978). Moreover, Congress has indicated its recognition of tribal sovereignty through passage of the Indian Self-Determination and Educational Assistance Act and by subsequently amending various federal statutes to allow for increased tribal governance. 25 U.S.C. § 450 (2006).

97. Santa Clara Pueblo v. Martinez, 436 U.S. 49 (1978).

98. Ibid.

99. "Such a notion of justice must incorporate an indigenous right to environmental self-determination that allows indigenous peoples to protect their traditional, land-based cultural practices regardless of whether they also possess the sovereign right to govern those lands or, in the case of climate change, prevent the practices that are jeopardizing those environments." Tsosie, "Indigenous People," 1652.

100. Ruhl, "Climate Change," 406.

101. Ibid., 415; Karl et al., *Global Climate Change*, 154.

102. Tsosie, "Indigenous People," 1644.

103. Ibid., 1645. Professor Tsosie goes on to explain that "Indigenous peoples and the lands that sustain them are closely linked through ancient epistemologies that organize the universe quite differently than Western epistemology does." Ibid.

104. Not every indigenous person has a close connection with his or her environment.

105. "[M]any sources of international law concerning indigenous human rights recognize that the cultural survival of indigenous peoples is centrally linked to the integrity of their land base." Armstrong Wiggins, "Indian Rights and the Environment," *Yale Journal of International Law* 18 (1993): 347–48.

106. Tsosie, "Indigenous People," 1675.

107. Krakoff, "American Indians," 872.

108. "[J]ustice can only be achieved by an affirmative commitment to protect indigenous peoples within their traditional lands." Tsosie, "Indigenous People," 1676.

11

Geopower and Sea Ice

Encounters with the Geopolitical Stage

Duncan Depledge

Introduction

When practitioners and experts of foreign policy speak of "geopoliti-cal change," it is typically in reference to certain geographical features gaining or losing influence over the course of international relations and global politics. Such thinking is part of a tradition of classical geopolitical thought (hereafter Geopolitics) dating back to the late nineteenth and early twentieth centuries.[1] From this perspective, the dominant feature of Geopolitics in the Arctic being sea ice (indeed the very idea of the Arctic as a fixed and knowable quantity) was for a long time taken for granted. Before and during much of the Cold War, sea ice was widely regarded as a barrier to the interests and activities that nation-states might seek to pursue in the region, whether searching for resources, trade routes, or encounters with the sublime. As a geopolitical stage, the Arctic was thus largely separated (in geopolitical terms) from the rest of the world, despite increasing scientific, military, and economic activity during the twentieth century. Eventually, this was viewed as an opportunity: A speech by Mikhail Gorbachev in 1987 marked the Arctic as a different kind of geopolitical stage, one where nation-state activity was defined more in terms of international cooperation and institution building instead of conflict. However, in the early twenty-first century, with Arctic sea ice thinning more and more each summer, a number of commentators expect the behavior of nation-states to "revert to form."[2] They argue that the essential features of the international system are extending into the Arctic; what was once regarded as a different kind of geopolitical stage, due to the presence of sea ice, is being brought back into line with the "natural laws" of the international system.

"Critical" Geopolitics has, since the 1980s, sought to challenge Geopolitics by reconceptualizing it as a "discursive practice by which intellectuals of statecraft 'spacialize' international politics and represent it as a 'world' characterised by particular types of places, peoples and dramas."[3] Geopolitics is treated as a "problematic set of discourses, representations, and practices" in order to expose the ways geographical knowledge is used to justify relations of power between "selves" and "others"—relations that are subsequently reinforced and legitimated through a range of texts, images, performances, and practices.[4] The perceived openness of the Arctic and indeterminacy of geographical space in general is thus read by Critical Geopolitics as suggestive of a *vulnerability* to enrollment not just in various state-building projects (most prominently in Canada, Russia, Norway, Denmark/Greenland, and the United States), but also in schematics for how international relations should be orchestrated (in the Arctic, this is centered largely on the privileges of a combination of the five Arctic Ocean littoral states, the eight Arctic states, indigenous peoples groups, and the Arctic Council). The term *vulnerability* is important here, as it implies that the Arctic (and geographical space more broadly) is powerless to resist the ways in which it is put to use as a stage for geopolitical machinations.

Thus, in both "Classical" and "Critical" formulations of geopolitics, geography essentially provides the stage on which various political dramas can unfold. In the former, the stage is relatively stable, resting on claims about enduring and objectively knowable geographies, which naturally direct the course of international relations and global affairs. In the latter, the stage is still relatively stable, but direction comes from how *vulnerable* geographies are invested with meaning and used to justify certain power relations by human actors occupying the stage. This has led a number of geographers to ask, "What does the 'geo' in 'geo-politics' actually do?"—the point being to consider whether there is more that the "geo" does than simply constitute the stage for human "politics," and more specifically in the case of this chapter, what this "geo-power" would mean for how we approach the geopolitics of the Arctic in the early twenty-first century.[5]

The purpose of this chapter is to elaborate on the concept of geopower rooted in the work of the feminist philosopher Elizabeth Grosz.[6] Moreover, the chapter takes a cue from feminist geographers who have sought to bring a feminist geopolitical analytic to Critical Geopolitics with the aim of "adding a potentially reconstructive political dimension to the crucial but at times unsatisfactory deconstructionist impulses."[7] However, rather than use the materiality of the human body, "not fully produced by or absorbed into discourse, to forge a space for a feminist, non-essentialist notion of 'political,'" my concern here is to consider the potential of using the only ever partially realized materiality of the earth as a starting point for seeing the geopolitical differently. The point is that Hyndman's call for feminist geopolitics (and Critical Geopolitics more broadly) to displace and resituate geopolitical scripts "in order to foreground the security of people on the ground" can be assisted by attending to how the ground itself is encountered as a never fully realized stage.[8]

Geopower

Elizabeth Grosz, renowned feminist, and Gearóid Ó Tuathail, a formative figure in Critical Geopolitics, both use the term *geopower* in a way that belies a shared concern for "geo-politics." For Ó Tuathail (drawing on Foucault), geopower concerns the way in which human actors use the relationship between power and geographical knowledge to produce and manage physical space (for example, through institutionalized or taken-for-granted ways of seeing, displaying, and marking the earth). Ó Tuathail argues that with the emergence of a world of "closed space" at the end of the nineteenth century, when there was virtually nothing left of value to discover or occupy, geopower became Geopolitics: "governmentalized forms of geographical knowledge" expressed in universal terms.[9] As such, Geopolitics must be regarded as an overdetermined form of "geo-politics," in which the unnamed practices that make Geopolitics possible are hidden from view.[10]

Grosz's use of geopower is markedly different. While in Ó Tuathail's account geopower marks a human force over the earth, for Grosz geopower refers to earthly forces that are entangled and interfere (precede, enable, provoke, and restrict) with life in all its forms, whether human or nonhuman. For Grosz, life both emerges from and capitalizes upon these forces, transforming "the world into *its world*."[11] Our understanding of the world around us thus rests on both an encounter with the world and a capitalization of that encounter, which attempts to reconfigure the world on our own terms. However, in the process of attempting to reconfigure the world, new conditions emerge for how the world is encountered, producing new combinations and new modes of organization and understanding that ultimately transform life itself. Thus, as life and earth continue to mingle, new forces are unleashed that provoke and incite new forms of life by "generating problems, questions and events that must be addressed and negotiated, symbolised or left unrepresented."[12] For Grosz, geopower is therefore always provoking life to overcome itself, to vary itself and to change across space and time: "The natural is *not* the inert, passive, unchanging element against which culture elaborates itself but the matter of the cultural, that which enables and actively facilitates cultural variation and change, indeed that which ensures that the cultural, including its subject-agents, are never self-identical, that they differ from themselves and necessarily change over time."[13]

The perpetual push of Grosz's geopower works against the *negentropy* of geopolitical practices that attempt to fix geographical fixtures in space and time, either to determine their influence over international relations and global affairs or to invest them with meaning. Negentropy describes emergent levels of organization where each level builds upon the achieved orderings of the preceding level and provides the ground for the next level to emerge. Successive orders are thus reliant on what has gone before and put to use in what comes after.[14] To illustrate this crudely, we might consider how the contemporary international system is not an enduring ordering of international relations but an emerging order that has evolved from the Cold War, which itself evolved out of World War II, and so on. Although these historical divisions are somewhat arbitrary, the point is to emphasize that *wherever* the dividing lines are drawn, certain elements (such as geopolitical tropes about the ongoing civilizational conflict between the "West" and the "Axis of Evil") may become so pervasive that they influence the shape of what follows. In building on past relations among various elements, the negentropy of geopolitical practices is working constantly to close down the possibility of alternative orderings and constrains political debate. Geopower opens up such alternatives.

Grosz's work draws heavily on the writings of Charles Darwin (as opposed to Social Darwinism) as well as Michel Foucault, who has also been influential in Critical Geopolitics. As Grosz notes, both retained "[a] fundamental commitment to the intangibility of the hold of domination and its ongoing and transforming susceptibility to resistance and realignment by virtue of the very forms of distribution or patterning that power itself takes . . . domination remains precariously dependent on what occurs not only 'above' but also 'below.' "[15]

The implication for Geopolitics, we might infer, is that the seemingly enduring features of the geopolitical stage are always dependent on the ongoing subordination of earthly forces "below": forces that constantly recombine with life in ways that threaten to reconstitute the geopolitical itself. As in Ó Tuathail's account, Geopolitics may be posited as an overdetermined form of geopolitics. The difference between Grosz and Ó Tuathail is that in Grosz's case, the hidden practices that make Geopolitics possible are found in a common realm where life (human and nonhuman) and earth are intermingled, rather than in an exclusively human social realm. Geopolitics might therefore usefully be (re)conceptualized as an attempt to arrest geopower (earthly forces) and subordinate it to the power of people (for example, foreign policy practitioners) or things (for example, enduring geographical features). Such a (re)conceptualization would also draw attention to the capacity of the "geo" to subvert or resist dominant forms of power, forcing us to reconsider whether the material world is as vulnerable to geopolitical machinations as Critical Geopolitics suggests, with the implication that earthly forces are taken more seriously as constituents in the production of the geopolitical, without returning to the geographical determinism associated with Geopolitics, classically formulated.

Arctic Geopolitics

In the early-twenty-first-century Arctic, Geopolitics remains highly prevalent in the texts, practices, and performances of foreign policy elites, political commentators, and the mainstream media, whether in North America, Europe, Russia, or Asia. In particular, the thinning of Arctic summer sea ice (the ten lowest minimum Arctic sea ice extents since the satellite record started in 1979 have all occurred since 2007) has one way or another been described as an opening up of the Arctic.

Geographical features (sea ice, water columns, continental shelves, and sea beds), which were once literally frozen or partly frozen, are being held responsible for determining the course of international relations in the region. According to the worst-case scenario, the decline of sea ice threatens to engulf the Arctic in resource scrambles and armed conflict unless law and order are imposed, either by Arctic nation-states or, more broadly, the international community. Such accounts are girded by an "uneasy synthesis between liberalism and neo-realism," where the existence of the Arctic as an objectively knowable space—its essential features and exceptionalisms—and the practices and interests of nation-states and other actors are largely taken for granted.[16] However, in presupposing the existence of the Arctic as a stage for these machinations, both the labor and the provocations posed by the humans and nonhumans involved in assembling the Arctic-as-stage are hidden from view, constraining the possibility of providing alternative geopolitical accounts of change and the possibilities of life in the Arctic more broadly.

Assembling the Arctic Stage

"Stage making" has long been at the heart of classical geopolitical thought. As Ó Tuathail noted, the West continues to retain a will to survey the world in order to sight (recognize and render space visible), site (delimit global political space), and cite (judge and textualize place) the realities of global political space.[17] Foreign policy experts and practitioners attempt to simplify and stabilize the global stage in such a way that the actions of nation-states may appear rational. However, stage making is an ongoing process, one that continually provokes and incites further kinds of encounters between earth and life while at the same time trying to contain potential outcomes: "to slow them, to put them in service of life's [in this case the nation-state's] provisional interests."[18]

Contrary to the expectations of Geopolitics, the Arctic-as-stage is therefore far from a permanent reality waiting to be discovered or, in the case of Critical Geopolitics, invested with meaning. The Arctic-as-stage is a specific ordering of life and earth, and as such is constituted from a common realm of both human and nonhuman elements including, but not limited to, sea ice, sea beds, water columns, continental shelves, mineral resources, and myriad different plants and animals as well as people and their various technologies, institutions, interests, and fantasies.

As such, the Arctic-as-stage might more usefully be conceptualized as an "assemblage" of life and earth.

The term *assemblage* is ill-defined in the social sciences, owing to the diversity with which it has been deployed by various scholars. However, within geography, the term has generally been used to encourage us to be "deliberately open as to the form of unity, its durability, the types of relations and the human and non-human elements involved."[19] More specifically, as geographers Ben Anderson and Colin McFarlane argue, the term seeks to account for four relational processes: the coming together, realigning, and/or dispersal of various elements at specific junctures in space and time; the distribution of agency across multiple elements within a collective; the ongoing emergence rather than resultant formation of assemblages; and the provisionality with which elements gather and disperse.[20]

Significantly, assemblages direct attention toward processes of territorialization and deterritorialization, or what I here refer to as stage (un) making. Assemblages always attempt to "claim" territory from combinations of earth and life as parts are gathered, marked, and held together. However, this territory can also collapse as the same parts recombine or disperse, ultimately leading, in this case, to the reterritorialization of the stage in novel ways. Stage making in Geopolitics is simultaneously an attempt to capitalize upon and bracket out this process of assembly.

To describe the assembly of an Arctic "stage" is thus to describe the coming together of heterogeneous forms of earth and life into a provisional order. This assemblage, or stage-assemblage, is then used by experts and practitioners of Geopolitics to constrain the conditions under which further encounters occur as well as how they come to be known. The relative success of gGeopolitics is thus found in the way seemingly essential features of the international system (nation-states, anarchy) have remained central to assemblages of Arctic geopolitics, while novel interactions involving indigenous peoples, transnational oil companies, and environmental NGOs—as well as ecosystems, ice, and the global climate—have been suppressed, despite their importance to how change in the Arctic is encountered, managed, and understood by practitioners and experts of foreign policy.[21] Crucially, this staging of Arctic geopolitics—that is, the conditions provided by the stage—has been used to justify the privileges of Arctic states to dictate the terms of Arctic governance according to a specific understanding of the international system that excludes other actors (indigenous people, non-Arctic states), the most recent being the Ilulissat Declaration signed by the five Arctic coastal states (Canada, Russia, Norway, Denmark, and the United States) in 2008. At the same time, such accounts reinforce the negentropy of geopolitical practice and close down the possibility of alternative orderings of Arctic geopolitics.

The Demands of Geopower in the Arctic

The negentropy in Geopolitics is part of the hidden, unnamed workings of geopolitics—what Ó Tuathail calls a convenient fiction—that suppresses accounts of novel encounters between life and earth driven by geopower (earthly forces) in order that they might be displaced by more conventional understandings of the essential features of international relations and global politics.[22] However, what Elizabeth Grosz argues is that there are some forces of geopower that Geopolitics must always respond to: the forward drift of time, the force of variation and proliferation of natural differences, and relations between the self and others.[23] These forces provoke and incite responses from geopolitics by "generating problems, questions, events that must be addressed and negotiated, symbolized or left unrepresented."[24] They create moments where gGeopolitics is exceeded by a geo-politics that has been brought into the open, however temporarily. It is in these moments that the geopolitical stage is subject to change.

The Forward Drift of Time

The Arctic is far from an unchanging, enduring stage where Geopolitics plays out. This may sound surprising, since for more than 2,500 years the Arctic has appeared relatively stable from a Western (nonindigenous) perspective. However, there are at least four factors that have helped produce and maintain this assumption about the relative stability of the Arctic stage in Western history.

The first factor is that over the period that explorers from Pytheas (320 BC) to Peary (1909) "discovered" the Arctic, from a geological perspective the Arctic has changed very little.[25] According to data taken from ocean cores in the Arctic, the last major warm period (when the extent of summertime ice was likely less than it is today) in the region was 5,000–8,000 years ago. This is significant since it meant that despite warming events around AD 500 and 1500, the major period of European and North American exploration from the seventeenth to the nineteenth centuries coincided with the Little Ice Age (circa 1600–1850), when ice conditions, particularly in the high Arctic, remained especially prohibitive to the navigational technologies of the period.[26] Although there would have been variation over this period, overall, the Arctic that European (and later North American) explorers would have encountered (at least in terms of its most dominant geopolitical feature, sea ice) would have appeared relatively stable. Accounts producing the Arctic stage-assemblage as a barrier to (nonindigenous) human activity in the North were therefore largely uncontroversial throughout this period of discovery.

The second factor was that the earth adjacent to the Arctic was also remarkably stable over this period. The earth that physically constitutes the Arctic is incredibly sensitive to changes in the earth that surrounds it (note that earth as it is used here includes the atmosphere and oceans). For much of the past two millennia, and again overlapping with the major period of European and North American exploration, there was relatively little variation in the earth surrounding the Arctic. The overall stability of the global climate, levels of pollution, and oceanic temperatures thus contributed to maintaining the stability of Arctic earth in geopolitical terms, since there was relatively little in the way of detectable shifts in the stage-assemblage (despite incidents such as the collapse of the seal population in the Bering Strait area in the 1890s).

The third factor was that for much of the 2,500-year period in question, the Arctic was encountered with only limited human technology, the effects of which were so localized that the overall stability of the earth constituting the Arctic was not significantly disrupted. Sea ice alone presented a formidable barrier to the wooden vessels that attempted to navigate passages around and through the Arctic Ocean, while the region itself was too distant to be significantly impacted by pollution from the preindustrial centers of Europe. Despite the presence of highly mobile indigenous communities capable of traversing the ice, in the Western geopolitical imagination, the Arctic stage-assemblage was still regarded as an obstacle to (or, in the case of the English at least, an affront to—see below) human activities.

Lastly (although there are likely other factors as well), there were limits to Western interest in the Arctic—limits to the imagination about what kind of place the Arctic could be. In the sixteenth century, sea routes from Europe to Asia were sought in the Arctic by the English and

the Dutch in order to overcome Spanish and Portuguese naval dominance in the Atlantic Ocean. However, as noted above, they lacked the
technology to overcome the Arctic they encountered in any significant
way, and aspirations to turn the Arctic into a "polar Mediterranean"
dissipated.[27] By the nineteenth century, the Arctic was more a space of
Western masculinist fantasy, in part linked to economic activities involving hunting for furs, whale oil, and baleen. Overcoming the Arctic for
the most part meant surviving limited and highly localized encounters
with what was increasingly regarded as a hostile space. For the English
at least, the Arctic came to be seen as a sublime and monstrous space
that threatened humanity to its core.[28] Rumors of cannibalism among
John Franklin and his crew fed fears of humans being consumed by
nature in their encounters with the Arctic.[29] However, while the Arctic
stage-assemblage was invested with fantasy and fear, these ideas were not
enough to physically transform the Arctic—if anything, they reinforced
the stability of the Arctic-stage by discouraging further encounters.

And yet, despite the relative stability of the Arctic stage-assemblage during this period, time continued to press on. By the end of the
nineteenth century, encounters with the Arctic stage-assemblage were
accelerating and intensifying in a variety of ways.[30] Rapid industrialization in the nineteenth century was accompanied by the development
of new technologies and renewed fantasies, such as those of Vilhjalmur
Stefansson about the Arctic as a potential polar Mediterranean and the
northward course of empire, which to a lesser or greater extent have
been sustained through the twentieth and early twenty-first centuries.
As the global atmosphere has warmed, the earth around the Arctic has
also changed, affecting atmospheric, oceanic, and cryospheric systems on
a global scale. The diffusion of pollution from industrial development
continues to alter the chemical composition of the earth that physically
constitutes the Arctic. Sea ice, the dominant geopolitical feature of the
Arctic stage-assemblage, is disappearing at an unprecedented rate as
the ocean and atmosphere warm. All of these factors are implicated in
further encounters between earth and life in the Arctic, a process that
is also transforming life and earth beyond the Arctic.

The Arctic, or more specifically, the earth constituting it (land,
sea, ice, tundra, permafrost), is always physically changing over time,
whether we consider it in terms of temperature, chemical composition,
or state of matter (for example, gas, solid or liquid). This means that
the stage, as an assemblage, is inherently unstable, shifting with changes

in the physical condition of the earth. Time therefore provides an irre-sistible push to the future, forcing the stage-assemblage to constantly overcome itself as elements combine, shift, and recombine. However, as the above account has shown, although many of these changes may seem inconsequential to human affairs, over time they may drastically alter our perception of the kind of stage the Arctic represents. We see this today in claims that the Arctic Ocean is undergoing a fundamental state (stage) change from being permanently ice covered to seasonally ice free with tremendous implications for the kinds of lives (human and nonhuman) that can be lived there.[31]

Over time, the effectivity of individual elements within a stage-assemblage may also be overcome. For example, over time, the physical effects of the Little Ice Age during the Middle Ages on the extent of sea ice in the Arctic will become minimal as other elements in the stage-assemblage come to exert a greater influence. The loss of human effectivity is overcome through the creation of collective forms of organization that allow action and meaning to be sustained over time in the same way that a ball is passed in rugby in order to keep it moving (to use one of Bruno Latour's metaphors).[32] One way classical theories of geopolitics have been sustained over generations is through the teaching and dissemination of texts and practices among students. However, time poses a constant provocation to these geopolitical texts and practices because over time, the further intermingling of earth and life invariably exceeds the boundaries established by taken-for-granted geopolitical tropes. This excess is found in encounters with the stage-assemblage that undermine what has previously been taken for granted: encounters brought about by new technologies, new ideas, as well as changes in the environment both in and beyond the Arctic. This excess, brought about by change over time, is thus a resource that creates the space to rethink the stage-assemblage so that the Arctic is no longer regarded as an obstacle or a monstrous place but a knowable quantity where, for foreign policy practitioners and experts, the interests of nation-states (largely associated with nation building and economic activity) can be more easily pursued and justified, albeit in novel ways.

The Force of Variation

Life, both human and nonhuman, does not emerge from or encounter the earth that constitutes the Arctic in any prescribable fashion. Natural differences among various forms of life therefore pose a further provoca-tion to geopolitics and the Arctic stage-assemblage. Variation propels life toward a variety of encounters with the stage-assemblage, producing novel interactions that, like time, may exceed geopolitical discourses. For example, the relative success indigenous communities have had living in the Arctic over thousands of years contradicts long-standing Western assumptions about the inhospitability, if not hostility, of Arctic space, a situation that is now being reversed as novel forms of Western life (facilitated by new technology and new ideas combining to create an "urban Arctic") and changes in the environment encounter the region and cause the stage-assemblage to shift, at times endangering indigenous lives in the process.

The relative stability of the Arctic stage-assemblage (from a Western perspective) over the past 2,500 years owes much to the limited presence of nonindigenous peoples in the region that lasted into the twentieth century.[33] It was not until the sixteenth century that the exploration of the Arctic even became an imperative for some emerging nation-states and their empires.[34] However, when it did become an imperative, it did so for a variety of reasons. Encounters with the Arctic produced markedly different reactions among Westerners alone. Imperial navies and explor-ers were interested in the possibility of discovering and utilizing passages to Asia through the sea ice.[35] Whale hunters from Europe and America followed after the discovery of huge whale populations in and around the Arctic seas. Resource exploitation also became a theme on land as the fur trade expanded northward in Russia and North America, often following land-based explorations tied to nation-building projects. Exploitation, trade, settlement, and exploration were all examples of the various forms of life that emerged from Western encounters with the Arctic.

For the nation-state, containing this variation in ways that suited national interests was relatively straightforward as exploitation, trade, settlement, and exploration facilitated and benefited one another as well as the state. Increased human presence in the North facilitated deeper explorations, which in turn had the potential to uncover new routes and resources that could be exploited for trade and provide the foundations for new settlements. Despite the different objectives, actors, and sites involved in these cross-territorial activities, the central role of the nation-state in both facilitating and benefiting from such encounters allowed for this variation to be viewed by foreign policy practitioners and experts collectively in terms of the national interest.

However, while Geopolitics may attempt to contain or manage variation, it cannot prevent it. The unstoppable proliferation of variation that inevitably occurs over time ensures that life and the earth that constitutes the Arctic are constantly encountering each other in novel ways, threatening the stability of the Arctic stage-assemblage. Since the beginning of the twentieth century, the proliferation of variation has increased rapidly. This proliferation is associated with the acceleration and intensification described earlier of activities that have brought the Arctic stage-assemblage into more frequent encounters with both humans and nonhumans. Over the past century, as more interest has developed in the Arctic, the environment has changed and new technologies and ideas have been deployed. The region has been physically transformed, through encounters with different actors, into a variety of cross-cutting stages for resource exploitation—shipping; tourism; indigenous life; monitoring climate change; environmental stewardship; and military-strategic operations, tests, and exercises. Pollution, development, and changes in the atmosphere and oceans both in and beyond the Arctic have further contributed to the physical transformation of the Arctic stage-assemblage. This in turn has facilitated novel encounters with forms of life keen to explore, exploit, manage, preserve, and ultimately capitalize on the changing qualities of the stage-assemblage to support various interests. Geopolitics has therefore also been precariously balanced on an ability to manage excesses of variation (as well as time) in ways that allow the overall stability of the Arctic stage-assemblage to be sustained in spite of constant encounters with difference, for example, by continuing to emphasize the central role of national territory and sovereignty and the essential laws of the international system while at the same time suppressing, ignoring, and forgetting the variation that exists among different interest groups.

Relations between Self and Other

The variation described in the previous section propels Arctic earth into a multitude of different encounters with life. In attempting to account for these differences, distinctions between "self" and "other" or "us" and "them" begin to emerge. The elaboration of these differences poses a number of challenges to Geopolitics: Specifically, how do self and other interact and how should this relationship be managed? While the Arctic stage-assemblage does not determine the formation of self and others—or relations between them (and thus my argument should not be confused with geographical determinism)—it does condition the kinds of encounters that can occur. For example, the disappearance of summertime sea ice in the Arctic affects how both humans and animals encounter the Arctic and other kinds of life in the region. This is the Arctic at its most stage-like. With Geopolitics, foreign policy practitioners and experts attempt to structure relations between the self and other by claiming knowledge of the essential nature of these relations, often in ways "which privilege the bodies and activities of some at the expense of others."[36] Through discourse, practice, and performance, these practitioners and experts attempt to fix in place and manage relations between the elements that constitute not just the stage-assemblage, but also life on that stage. However, as with the forces of time and variation, uncontrolled relations among different elements always threaten to go beyond established geopolitical tropes centered on interstate relations and the rules that govern them.

In the Arctic, relations between the West and the Arctic have changed considerably over the centuries since European explorers first sought to navigate passageways through the sea ice. The Arctic is implicated in these changes to the extent that it has been enrolled in different ways to provide the stage on which encounters between self and other have been elaborated. By way of example, three prominent (if oversimplified) accounts of the Arctic stage-assemblage have been particularly important to how relations between the West and the Arctic are constructed and managed in the early twenty-first century. The first has cast the Arctic as a resource base, primarily in terms of its potential offshore hydrocarbon deposits, which are only just starting to be tapped.[37] As a resource base, the Arctic has been used by some commentators as a stage for competition among nation-states. Encounters among nation-states have subsequently been elaborated in terms of a zero-sum free-for-all competition over access to resources. In the second, the Arctic provides the stage for international scientific cooperation. This has facilitated a very different kind of encounter between nation-states based on collaboration and seemingly universal common interest where self and other are engaged in positive-sum cooperation. The third account of the Arctic stems from the Cold War. The Arctic is presented as the stage for interstate conflict, a military-strategic theater where the qualities of the Arctic stage-assemblage are felt in terms of their implications for military installations, operations, and exercises. Encounters between nation-states on opposing sides tend to be characterized by displays of power and acts of secrecy by the self, while the other is treated with suspicion and fear.

These various accounts of the Arctic as a stage for encounters between self and other illustrate how, as in the case of Heidegger's Greek Temple, the Arctic has in different ways been presented as a familiar, if not taken-for-granted structure that foreign policy practitioners and experts confidently know their way around. The various elements and relations that comprise the stage-assemblage disappear from view, and what remains becomes the paradigm through which to understand Arctic affairs, rendering visible some actors, voices, relations, and features while suppressing others. However, by drawing attention to the excesses produced by geopower (time, variation, relations), it is possible to foreground the elements and relations that comprise the stage-assemblage. In doing so, we find that although these elements and relations have been used in specific ways to create the stage for the elaboration of a geopolitical discourse, they have not been used up; they are only partially realized.[38] The stage-assemblage therefore cannot be taken for granted, since it is constantly being undermined by geopower. The constant provocation posed by geopower creates a space and an opportunity for elaborating the stage-assemblage (and relations on it) in different terms. And since the physical material that comprises this stage is only ever partially realized, it matters to the possibilities of assembling a stage (and the possibilities of life on it) whether this material, or earth, is in the case of the Greek Temple, marble or plastic, or in the case of the Arctic, whether there is sea ice, open water, tundra, or permafrost.

Containing Geopower

Containing the excesses of geopower (time, variation, relations) has always been at the core of writing a geopolitics that reifies enduring features of the geographical landscape as the basis for the geopolitical stage. Geopolitics has helped produce a stable picture of Arctic history in the West that is regularly used by foreign policy practitioners and experts to reinforce ideas of change in present while suppressing the considerable amount of variation that has gone on over time, including, for example, in the extent and thickness of sea ice; in the ecosystem (for example, species collapse and migration); in indigenous habitation and use of the Arctic;

and in motivations for different kinds of nation-state activity. However, since encounters between earth and life cannot be repeated, the only way that the stage-assemblage can be stabilized is by sustaining the outcomes of specific encounters (reduced to their lowest common denominator such as the national interest) through some form of collective or institutional structure or legal regime (the nation-state, international law, academic institutions, the media), which is then used to discipline further encounters between earth and life so that they appear to produce the same outcome each time. In trying to fix the Arctic as a specific kind of geopolitical stage (through discourse, practice, and performance), Geopolitics thus works to suppress the provocations of geopower described above.

Consequently, there is a politics to how the Arctic is encountered, organized, mapped, and used to facilitate certain kinds of life at the expense of others that have been used, for example, by nation-states to forcibly relocate indigenous peoples, or, in the case of the European Union, to impose restrictions on certain economic activities linked to sealing. To presuppose a natural order to these encounters is to hide the technical labor as well as the provocations that this labor has had to overcome, involved in establishing the Arctic as a specific kind of stage for specific kinds of life. Alternative possibilities for life are closed down in the process. However, it is more than likely that over the coming years, there will be yet more novel encounters between earth and life as new elements emerge and arrive in the Arctic and old ones dissipate.

This, Grosz argues, is the challenge that all cultures (geopolitical or otherwise) are presented with in the face of geopower.[39] Grosz has developed Darwin's work on the struggle for existence in nature to show that all culture is engaged in a similar struggle. When the boundaries of a culture, in this case Geopolitics, are exceeded, the only way to survive is through self-transformation: the adoption of "ever more viable and successful strategies" for containing geopower, which over time may leave a geopolitical culture completely unrecognizable from itself.[40] The success of Geopolitics is therefore only ever provisional, dependent on an ability to cohere in spite of internal tensions brought about by the suppression of geopower.[41] It is this ability to still cohere that allows Geopolitics to arrest geopower and stabilize the geopolitical stage over the *longue durée*—by accommodating variation and change without exposing it. However, when the tension becomes too great, the only way Geopolitics can survive is through a self-transformation capable of providing new solutions to the problem of geopower.

Conclusion

If we take geopower seriously, it should become evident that as life and earth in the Arctic continue to encounter one another in novel ways, our experiences of geopower—of time, variation, and relations between selves and others—in the Arctic should be provoking us to consider the possibility of alternative solutions to how the Arctic is set up as a stage and how encounters between different forms of life on that stage are elaborated. This chapter has sought to reconceptualize geopolitics as an attempt to arrest geopower and subordinate it to the power of people or seemingly enduring geographical features to determine the course of human affairs. An alternative "geo-politics" has been proposed to place encounters with geopower to the fore of geopolitical analysis. Three forms of geopower have been considered (time, variation, and relations), and each has been shown to be provocative to the extent that they provide a constant pressure to the kinds of stage-assemblages established through geopolitical discourses, practices, and performances. "Geo-politics" should be understood as an attempt to manage and contain this pressure: a provisional solution that allows for a geopolitical discourse to be asserted in spite of the fact that earth and life are constantly encountering one another in novel ways.

To this end, geopolitics/geo-politics might fruitfully be conceived as what Grosz calls a "style of living" that prompts "innovation and ingenuity" in response to the "endless generation of problems" geopower creates in order that a stage-assemblage (and relations on it) can be constructed, constrained, and capitalized upon.[42] Geopolitics therefore leads to the suppression of the ways in which the Arctic has varied over time (for example, in terms of the extent to which sea ice has been a persistent feature) and across space (for example, that sea ice is thicker in some parts of the Arctic, making those parts less accessible than others), as well as suppressing and constraining the variety of ways in which the Arctic has been encountered and experienced, usually to the detriment of indigenous cultures and local knowledge. What is left is a simplistic constitution of the Arctic as an imagined stage, dominated by the presence and interests of states, relations between which tend toward conflict or cooperation depending on the volume of sea ice present (as measured by satellite) or the strength of international institutions or legal regimes.

To the extent that our understanding of geopolitics as a style of living means foreign policy choices and limits are rooted in knowledge of earth and life, the means we use to acquire this knowledge matters whether it occurs through direct encounters with the Arctic or forms of what the political geographer Anssi Paasi has called "geopolitical remote sensing" from afar.[43] Earth and life constitute fields of technical uncertainty that must be brought under control if they are to be made useful. Geopolitics therefore emerges as a technical solution to the problem of containing geopower and building negentropic structures that are then used to inform and legitimate foreign policy. Competing assemblages of the Arctic emerge because every encounter between life and the Arctic is a historically and geographically localizable response to uncertainty, the elaboration of which relies on what is encountered, modes of technological development, and the human imagination. Throughout history, indigenous cultures, nation-states, international institutions, and nonstate actors have all produced very different accounts of their encounters with the Arctic.

At the same time, by conceiving of geopolitics as a style of living, we might recognize the imperative for Critical Geopolitics to not only deconstruct Geopolitics, but also to chart alternatives for different ways of seeing the world. There is obviously a need to generate knowledge from past encounters and experiences in order to help us understand the present and guide policy decisions about the future. However, it is important that we do not fall into the trap of forgetting that other possibilities, including ones that may not have been encountered before, could exist. It is in these alternatives, in novel encounters with the only-ever-partially realized materiality of the earth, that we might find a valuable political resource for interrogating other ways of imagining the Arctic, facilitate the elaboration of alternative accounts and experiences, and seriously begin to question what kind of taken-for-granted stage is being constituted in the Arctic (including the various roles and relations of those who occupy it). Foregrounding the stage in this way might just provide a new basis for displacing dominant geopolitical scripts and start a more dynamic and, ultimately, more positive set of discussions about the future of political, economic, legal, social, and cultural activities in the Arctic.

Notes

1. G. Ó Tuathail, S. Dalby, and P. Routledge, eds., *The Geopolitical Reader* (London: Routledge, 2006).

2. S. Borgerson, "Arctic Meltdown: The Economic and Security Implications of Global Warming," *Foreign Affairs* 87, no. 2 (2008): 63–77; R. Howard, "Russia's New Front Line," *Survival* 52, no. 2 (2010): 141–56.

3. G. Ó Tuathail and J. Agnew, "Geopolitics and Discourse: Practical Geopolitical Reasoning in American Foreign Policy," *Political Geography* 11, no. 2 (1992): 192.

4. M. Power and D. Campbell, "The State of Critical Geopolitics," *Political Geography* 29, no. 5 (2010): 243.

5. UCL Department of Geography and ESRC, "Terra Infirma: Experimenting with Geo-Political Practices" (workshop, The Arts Catalyst, London, UK, Jan. 27, 2012).

6. E. Grosz, *Time Travels: Feminism, Nature, Power* (London: Duke University Press, 2005); E. Grosz, *Chaos, Territory, Art: Deleuze and the Framing of the Earth* (New York: Columbia University Press, 2008).

7. J. Hyndman, "Mind the Gap: Bridging Feminist and Political Geography Through Geopolitics," *Political Geography* 23, no. 3 (2004): 309.

8. Ibid., 311.

9. G. Ó Tuathail. *Critical Geopolitics* (Minneapolis: University of Minnesota Press, 1996): 15.

10. Ibid.

11. E. Grosz, "Geopower," *Environment and Planning: Society and Space* 30 (2012): 974.

12. Grosz, *Time Travels*, 51.

13. Ibid., 47.

14. N. Clark, *Inhuman Nature: Sociable Life on a Dynamic Planet* (London: Sage, 2011): 45.

15. Grosz, *Time Travels*, 29.

16. J. Dittmer et al., "Have you Heard the One About the Disappearing Ice? Recasting Arctic Geopolitics," *Political Geography* 30, no. 4 (2011): 203.

17. G. Ó Tuathail, "Problematizing Geopolitics: Survey, Statesmanship, and Strategy," *Transactions of the Institute of British Geographers* 19, no. 3 (1994): 259–72.

18. Grosz, *Time Travels*, 42.

19. B. Anderson and C. McFarlane, "Assemblage and Geography," *AREA* 43, no. 2 (2011): 124.

20. Ibid.

21. See, e.g., Heather Nicol, "Reframing Sovereignty: Indigenous Peoples and Arctic States," *Political Geography* 29, no. 2 (2010): 78–80.

22. Ó Tuathail, *Critical Geopolitics*.

23. Grosz, *Time Travels*.

24. Ibid., 51.

25. D. S. Kaufman et al., "Recent Warming Reverses Long-Term Arctic Cooling," *Science* 325 (2009): 1236–39.

26. L. Polyak et al., "Quaternary History of Sea Ice in the Western Arctic Ocean Based on Foraminifera," *Quaternary Science Reviews* 79 (2013): 145–46.

27. A. Craciun, "The Scramble for the Arctic," *Interventions: International Journal of Postcolonial Studies* 11, no. 1 (2009): 103–14.

28. A. Craciun, "The Frozen Ocean," *PMLA* 125, no. 3 (2010): 693–702.

29. F. Spufford, *I May Be Some Time: Ice and the English Imagination* (London: Faber and Faber, 1996).

30. K. Dodds, "From Frozen Desert to Maritime Domain: New Security Challenges in an Ice-Free Arctic," *Swords and Ploughshares* 17 (2010): 11–14.

31. P. Berkman and O. Young. "Governance and Environmental Change in the Arctic Ocean," *Science* 324 (2009): 339–40.

32. B. Latour, *Science in Action: How to Follow Scientists and Engineers Through Society* (Cambridge: Harvard University Press, 1987).

33. T. Koivurova, H. Tervo, and A. Stepien, "Indigenous Peoples in the Arctic," *Arctic Transform* (Sept. 4, 2008); http://Arctic-transform.org/download/IndigPeoBP.pdf.

34. D. Avango, L. Hacquebord, and U. Wrakberg, "Industrial Extraction of Arctic Natural Resources since the Sixteenth Century: Technoscience and Geo-Economics in the History of Northern Whaling and Mining," *Journal of Historical Geography* 44 (2014): 15–30.

35. Ibid.

36. Grosz, *Time Travels*, 28.

37. F. Beauregard-Tellier, "The Arctic: Hydrocarbon Resources," Parliament of Canada Info Series, Oct. 24, 2008.

38. M. Inwood, *Heidegger: A Very Short Introduction* (Oxford: Oxford University Press, 1997).

39. Grosz, *Time Travels*, 28.

40. Ibid.

41. J. Allen, "Powerful Assemblages?" *AREA* 43, no. 2 (2011): 154–57.

42. Ibid., 25.

43. Power and Campbell, "The State of Critical Geopolitics," 244.

12

Arctic Wetlands and Limited International Protections

Can the Ramsar Convention Help Meaningfully Address Climate Change?

Kim Diana Connolly

Climate Change and Arctic Wetlands

Climate change is transforming the planet,[1] and the Arctic is on the front lines.[2] Those seeking tools to slow or alter this transformation are searching everywhere.[3] Some are looking to international treaties as potential tools.[4] In keeping with the theme of the Big Thaw Conference, this chapter explores the current and potential role of the Ramsar Convention (formally known as the Convention on Wetlands of International Importance especially as Waterfowl Habitat)[5] in this effort, particularly for Arctic wetlands.

The only international environmental treaty to focus on a specific ecosystem, the Ramsar Convention defines wetlands very broadly, to include "areas of marsh, fen, peatland or water, whether natural or artificial, permanent or temporary, with water that is static or flowing, fresh, brackish or salt, including areas of marine water the depth of which at low tide does not exceed six metres."[6]

The Arctic, by its nature, contains a very high percentage of wetlands: its land mass is well over one-half wetlands.[7] These wetlands are of different types, from tidal systems at sea level to moist tundra in high alpine zones. Many Arctic wetlands are underlain and maintained by permafrost (perennially frozen ground), though others are supported by rainfall, snow melt, springs, and tidal waters.[8] National leaders have identified wetlands of the Arctic as vital, such as when U.S. Secretary of State John Kerry told reporters on a summer 2016 trip to Alaska that Arctic wetlands are "the center of change within the center of change."[9]

Arctic wetlands may be particularly susceptible to climate change, because science shows the Arctic is likely to experience more climate change impacts than the other areas on the planet.[10] Rising temperatures threaten ecosystems such as Arctic peatlands.[11] Consequently, many animal species—including waterfowl, a central concern of the Ramsar Convention—are expected to struggle in seeking to adapt to changing habitats and food sources.[12] The issue of Arctic wetland conservation extends beyond the region, however, as a change to Arctic wetlands—and in particular peatlands—may accelerate the rate of climate change the world over.[13]

The Ramsar Convention and its Mandates

There are 169 contracting parties to the convention, including the United States, which joined in 1987. Presently, there are almost 2,300 Ramsar Sites worldwide, covering more than 216,000,000 hectares. Ramsar encourages nations to protect wetland resources; the convention provides "the Contracting Parties shall formulate and implement their planning so as to promote the conservation of the wetlands included in the [Ramsar Site] List, and as far as possible the wise use of wetlands in their territory." All Arctic nations (Canada, Denmark, Finland, Iceland, Norway, Russia, Sweden, and the United States) are members of the convention.

The Ramsar Convention works with various stakeholders, such as the Arctic Council, to address the threat of climate change to Arctic Wetlands. Formed in 1996 as a high-level intergovernmental forum comprised of Arctic states,[14] the Arctic Council provides a direct and focused means of cooperating to further Arctic issues.[15] Member states have granted full consultation rights to "organizations of indigenous peoples with majority Arctic indigenous constituency,"[16] which they call

"Permanent Participants." An organization seeking Permanent Participant status must represent either a single indigenous population living in more than one of the Arctic states, or more than one indigenous people in a single Arctic state.[17] Of principal concern to both the member states and the Permanent Participants are sustainable development and protection of the Arctic environment. Indeed, in 2018 the Ramsar Conference of the Parties issued a resolution that noted, "Arctic and sub-Arctic wetlands are of global significance not only for their biodiversity and their ecosystem services, especially for indigenous peoples and local communities, but also for other services, such as their roles as sinks or stores of carbon."[18]

The Arctic Council has six working groups tasked with following specific mandates to achieve the goals of the council.[19] One of these groups, Conservation of Arctic Flora and Fauna (CAFF),[20] focuses on Arctic biodiversity and seeks to increase member states' ability to protect native plant and animal species.[21] To meet this mandate, CAFF gathers data and provides that data (along with accompanying reports) to member states, allowing those governments to take actions to preserve the Arctic environment.[22] Further, CAFF provides Arctic states an avenue for cooperative management and decision making.[23]

Given that 60 percent of the Arctic is made up of various kinds of wetlands, it is not surprising that the Ramsar Convention and the Arctic Council have increasingly engaged in team efforts to protect Arctic ecosystems.[24] On July 12, 2012, during the 11th Conference of the Parties in Bucharest, Romania, the Ramsar Secretariat and the CAFF National Representative for Greenland signed a Resolution of Cooperation "to raise awareness and promote the importance of Arctic wetlands."[25] In reaching this agreement, Ramsar and CAFF acknowledged their cooperation had the potential to contribute to the conservation of Arctic wetlands by sharing knowledge and broadening the base of decision makers to whom this information is available and understandable.[26] Benefits of this relationship are already evident, and include the availability of CAFF's "Arctic Biodiversity Assessment" report[27] to the Ramsar Contracting Parties.[28] The convention had also approved 68 Ramsar Sites featuring Arctic ecosystems.[29]

The Ramsar Convention itself emerged in 1971 after more than eight years of work by concerned nations and nongovernmental organizations.[30] First signed by representatives of 18 countries in Ramsar, Iran,[31] in February 1971,[32] it entered into force in 1975.[33] The convention represented a dramatic shift from historic perspectives on wetlands as "disastrous realms, sources of disease, [and] obstacles to any form of positive development."[34] The convention[35] has been amended twice,[36] and signatories regularly come together in conferences of the parties to negotiate and agree to other important guidance documents.[37]

The Ramsar Convention has five goals: "(1) To work towards achieving the wise use of all wetlands . . . ; (2) To develop and maintain an international network of wetlands that are important for the conservation of global biological diversity . . . ; (3) To enhance the conservation and wise use of wetlands using effective international cooperation . . . ; (4) To progress towards fulfillment of the Convention's mission by ensuring that it has the required mechanisms, resources, and capacity to do so. . . . and, (5) To progress towards universal membership of the Convention."[38] Unaffiliated with the United Nations system of Multilateral Environmental Agreements,[39] the Convention Secretariat is headquartered in Switzerland,[40] and receives intercessional guidance from a standing committee.[41] The secretariat and signatories also receive expert scientific and policy guidance from its Scientific and Technical Review Panel (STRP).[42] Member countries are encouraged to create National Ramsar Committees,[43] which tend to vary from country to country in terms of composition and role in meeting the convention's obligations.[44] Arctic wetlands of international importance receive some level of support through these Ramsar goals and structures, though as is true of wetlands worldwide, the wetlands of the Arctic receive only indirect protections.

There are few direct requirements under the Ramsar Convention. One absolute obligation is that each party designate at least one site of international importance. Designation requires meeting official criteria, and completing a Ramsar Information Sheet (RIS) with data on and support for the proposed site.[45] Once approved, sites join the List of Wetlands of International Importance.[46] After listing, a party is obliged "to promote the conservation of the site."[47] However, the convention provides that listing a site "does not prejudice [a party's] exclusive sovereign rights."[48] This lack of external control on designated wetlands under Ramsar is in keeping with many of the agreements and cross-nation work that touches Arctic ecosystems.[49]

The convention also puts forth a requirement that each party apply "wise use" to all wetlands in a party's territory.[50] As explained by the Ramsar Secretariat, "[t]he Convention defines wise use of wetlands as 'the maintenance of their ecological character, achieved through the implementation of ecosystem approaches, within the context of sustainable development.' Wise use can thus be seen as the conservation and sustainable use of wetlands and all the services they provide, for the benefit of people and nature."[51] Yet one internationally known expert in the field identified this directive as presenting somewhat of a paradox, stating that "[t]hrough the resources of the Ramsar Convention we have seen 267 decisions that, in one way or other, have extolled Governments and others to conserve and make wise use of all wetlands, and yet, in many instances, we still witness ongoing wetland loss and/or degradation."[52]

Likewise, international cooperation is identified as a Ramsar Convention cornerstone, and has led to various relationships with related instruments and organizations with similar goals.[53] Yet some analyses question the ability to assess effectiveness of the cooperative work, such as a comment that noted "[w]ork relating outcomes to Convention implementation is expected to show that a constant or worsening rate of biodiversity decline is occurring even in some cases where diligent implementation on agreed actions is being undertaken by relevant governments."[54]

Of relevance to this chapter, some international cooperative efforts fostered by Ramsar have directly involved the Arctic. Pursuant to the July 2012 Resolution of Cooperation between the Ramsar Convention and CAFF, the Nordic-Baltic Wetlands Initiative (NorBalWet) invited CAFF to "share its circumpolar knowledge and experience" and "explore possibilities for professional collaboration" at a NorBalWet conference in September 2013 in Ilulissat, Greenland.[55] NorBalWet is an initiative that acts as "an operational mean" in the Nordic-Baltic region "to provide effective support for improved implementation of the objectives of the Ramsar Convention."[56] There is considerable—but not total—overlap among NorBalWet member countries and members of the Arctic Council.[57] At the September 2013 conference, topics of discussion included "relevant Ramsar resolutions regarding wetlands, climate change, and Ramsar sites," as well as "recommendations for improving collaboration and information exchange" in the region.[58]

CAFF also initiated an Arctic Migratory Birds Initiative (AMBI), a project designed "to address urgent conservation needs of declining migratory bird populations in the Arctic."[59] AMBI focuses on "birds that depend on the Arctic tundra to breed, but spend the rest of the year on migration across the globe," aiming to conserve "important refueling sites" for "Arctic migrating shorebirds," some of whom are members of an endangered species.[60] CAFF looks to "provide an international forum to convince the countries at lower latitudes to find sustainable solutions" to the problems such birds face, enlisting "the help of the Arctic Council's diplomacy."[61] These CAFF efforts support the wise use model underlying the Ramsar approach.

As mentioned above, each member nation must designate at least one Wetland of International Importance, or Ramsar Site. Designated sites must meet at least one of nine official criteria: (1) contain representative, rare, or unique wetland types; (2) support vulnerable, endangered, or critically endangered species; (3) support plant or animal populations important for regional biodiversity; (4) support plant or animal species at a critical stage in the life cycle; (5) regularly support 20,000 or more waterbirds; (6) regularly support 1 percent of the population of a waterbird species or subspecies; (7) support a significant proportion of indigenous fish species that are representative of wetland benefits and values; (8) be an important source of food for fish, spawning ground, nursery, and/or migration path; and (9) regularly support 1 percent of the population of a species or subspecies of wetland-dependent, non-avian animal species.

Although there is no onerous enforcement that results if a party allows someone to impact designated wetlands of international importance, there is a public information component. When a proposed project might impact listed wetlands of international importance, the convention has a process whereby third parties[62] can bring this potential impact to the attention of the Ramsar Secretariat.[63] Article 3.2 of the convention provides that "each Contracting Party shall arrange to be informed at the earliest possible time if the ecological character of any wetland in its territory and included in the List has changed, is changing or is likely to change as the result of technological developments, pollution or other human interference. Information on such changes shall be passed without delay to the [Ramsar Secretariat]."[64] Pursuant to a subsequent resolution,[65] "[e]cological character is the combination of the ecosystem components, processes and benefits/services that characterise the wetland at a given point in time" and that "[f]or the purposes of implementation of Article 3.2, change in ecological character is the human-induced adverse alteration of any ecosystem component, process, and/or ecosystem benefit/service."[66] Accordingly, based on "informed, authoritative or expert judgement,"[67] human-induced[68] changes (on-site or off-site)[69] can be brought to the attention to both the Ramsar Secretariat and the national authority responsible to the secretariat.[70] Upon receipt of the Article 3.2 report, the secretariat may then inquire as to the status and request an update from the party,[71] and report back to the all parties at the next Conference of the Parties.[72] Whether climate change could be considered such an alteration has not been fully tested.

Wise use is a concept interpreted as applying to all wetlands and water resources in a contracting party's territory, not only to those sites designated as Wetlands of International Importance. The third Conference of the Parties, held in Regina, Canada, in 1987, provided a revised definition through Resolution IX.1 Annex A (2005): "Wise use of wetlands is the maintenance of their ecological character, achieved through the implementation of ecosystem approaches, within the context of sustainable development."

Viewed as predecessor of what we now term "sustainability" concepts,[73] the wise use of wetlands is one of the Ramsar Convention's so-called three pillars.[74] "Wise use" requires contracting parties to develop plans to protect all wetlands in their territories, when possible.[75] "Wise use" includes maintaining the ecological character of the wetlands "within the context of sustainable development,"[76] which may be similar to the public interest review concept.[77] Always fundamental to the convention, its importance was recently highlighted by listing it as the top goal in the convention's recent strategic plan.[78]

Ramsar focuses modern concepts of wise use on the promotion of ecosystem services,[79] generally viewed as the benefits of healthy and intact wetlands that flow to people and nearby ecosystems.[80] The convention also calls for increased participation in the restoration and protection of wetlands at the local level.[81] This objective can be achieved by focusing on the economic and health benefits functioning wetlands provide for local populations.[82] The strategic plan lays out 11 strategies for furthering the wise use of wetlands, primarily involving information gathering and development of protective national policies.[83] This is a potential avenue for exploration in the realm of Arctic wetlands, though policies would need to proceed through the various Arctic nations individually. Yet even if adopted as Arctic policy, this new commitment may not overcome lingering concerns about the wise use concept in practice being insufficient to provide meaningful protection in some settings. As one set of scholars noted, "Regulatory systems which do not constrain the discretion of decision-makers drawn from the current generation seem unlikely to serve the interests of future generations very effectively."[84]

Even if the wise use obligation does not yield protections, of potential benefit to Arctic wetlands is an absolute mandate that convention members catalogue and assess their wetlands,[85] and thereafter share that data (including via the secretariat's website).[86] Knowledge sharing is viewed by the convention as key to involving organizations and government entities not traditionally involved wetland protection.[87] This mandate could perhaps be better coordinated to further complement other data assessment regarding climate change that proceeds through bodies such as the Intergovernmental Panel on Climate Change (IPCC).[88]

The secretariat encourages use of compiled information to develop appropriate policies designed to satisfy wise use and other obligations.[89] All policies must take advantage of "best available scientific knowledge,"[90] and should support approaches that acknowledge wetlands ecosystem services, such as the relationship of wetlands to a nation's water resources available for human use.[91] Parties are also obligated to assess the impact of individual projects that might compromise the character of wetlands.[92] To provide contracting parties guidance on how to implement the wise use concept for all 11 strategies, the secretariat of the convention has produced a series of handbooks, which can be found on the convention's website and are intended to be used as a "toolkit" to promote wise use.[93] A firm dedication to implementing wise use of Arctic wetlands by all Ramsar contracting parties thus could, theoretically, provide some hope for climate change mitigation.

The Potential Role of the Ramsar Convention in Protecting Arctic Wetlands

As the previous sections demonstrate, the Arctic contains many wetlands, and the Ramsar Convention has a role in protecting wetlands including those in the Arctic. Unfortunately, however, while the convention relies on a lot of process involved in designation and hosts regular international gatherings, the convention was drafted and is implemented in such a way as to preclude formal protection for any wetlands through Ramsar itself. In fact, the United States highlights this limitation in its public statements, noting that "Ramsar does not impose restrictions on nations and landowners. Ramsar is not a regulating entity, nor is it a United Nations Convention."[94]

Ramsar is, instead, a treaty typical of its time, designed to encourage rather than mandate actions. As a tool, it is therefore limited to a supporting role in the climate change challenge. But though lamented as insufficient in and of itself by some,[95] perhaps its very limitations can be viewed as a potential strength.

As one scholar wrote in 2012, "[t]he Convention has garnered a degree of trust through its 40 year history. In 1971 the world could not have imagined the nature of today's environmental problems, especially through the lens of climate change. The Convention persists and has evolved with the times. Its key strength is the ecosystem-based approach to conservation and the capacity to address trans-national issues, enabling it to help solve the linked environmental problems between development and security. The Convention has all the tools needed for an increased role in water diplomacy. Nevertheless, the question that exists is whether the infrastructure of the Convention is adaptable enough to meet coming environmental challenges. Whether the treaty can adequately address future pressures on transboundary wetland resources, given the increased rate of change from climate change impacts, compounded by conflict that is exacerbated by such change, is the challenge for the treaty."[96] Building on this assessment by the secretariat, it is possible that the Arctic can still fashion a way to further benefit from Ramsar in the context of climate change.

The Ramsar Convention has a long-standing program entitled CEPA, which stands for communication, capacity building, education, participation and awareness. Updated through a resolution adopted in 2015, Resolution XII.9 at COP12,[97] CEPA relies on local implementation based on a planned systematic approach, which reflects the interests of stakeholders and beneficiaries but is specifically tailored to local context, culture, and traditions.[98] Nations of the Arctic employ CEPA, but might consider further leveraging designations (and statements regarding mandatory wise use) into motivations for climate-protective treatment of Ramsar and nearby wetlands.

Ramsar's CEPA approach and links to other work internationally have some potential for cross-nation work that might benefit Arctic wetlands. For example, the Habitat Contact Forum (HCF) held its seventh meeting in Bodo, Norway, in June 2013.[99] HCF is part of the Nature Protection Subgroup of the Barents Euro-Arctic Council's Working Group on Environment.[100] The Ramsar Secretariat sent a representative to the meeting, because several topics of discussion were "closely related to the work of the Ramsar Convention."[101] In particular, HCF is "focused on the establishment of new protected areas, management of existing protected areas, and other measures that will contribute to the conservation of biological diversity" in the region.[102] The assistant advisor for Europe at the Ramsar Secretariat stressed the importance of designating new Ramsar sites, developing policies for wise use of wetlands, partnering with "other sectors of government, focal points of other MEAs, NGOs and civil society in order to ensure that the role and importance of wetlands is fully recognized," and "using the tools provided by the Ramsar Convention" to communicate effectively "in order to achieve a good understanding in all sectors of our societies of the value of wetlands" and "recognize the important role of wetlands in climate change mitigation and adaptation."[103]

Likewise, the attention on a subset of wetlands, peatlands, may increase attention to the possibilities for connecting with Ramsar when it comes to Arctic wetlands in the years ahead. In November 2016, at the Marrakech United Nations Climate Change Conference (COP 22), the Global Peatlands Initiative was launched.[104] Peatlands "contain almost 100 times more carbon than tropical forests," and the Initiative "seeks to mobilize governments, international organizations and academia" to protect the vital peatlands.[105] Global warming leads to thawing of permafrost, causing Arctic peatlands to change "from carbon sinks to sources."[106] Head of UN Environment Erik Solheim supported the Global Peatlands Initiative, warning that we must avoid reaching "the tipping point that will see peatlands stop sinking carbon and start spewing it into the atmosphere, destroying any hope we have of controlling climate change."[107] In May 2017, scientists reported that the Arctic frozen tundra is "warming so rapidly that it now is emitting more carbon than it captures."[108]

As the secretary general of Ramsar remarked in November 2016 in Marrakech, "It is now time for action and wetlands can play a key role in this regard, as nature-based solutions for adaptation and mitigation. Adaptation cannot happen without water. Wetlands are the primary source of water for human consumption, energy and agriculture. Billions of people depend also on wetlands for their livelihoods. Wetlands make communities more resilient to the impacts of climate change. They provide buffers against sea level rise and storm surges, and reduce the impacts of floods, droughts and cyclones. Wetlands also play a major role in mitigation as they are the planet's most effective carbon sinks. . . . Yet, despite all the critical services that wetlands provide, 64% of the world's wetlands have been lost in the last century. We continue to lose wetlands at the rate of 1% per year—which is faster than the current rate of deforestation. Today we have the knowledge, and we have the tools, to reverse this process. Wetlands need to be factored into the Nationally Determined Contributions and in the implementation of the Sustainable Development Goals."[109] Parties to the Ramsar Convention should take these exhortations to heart in the months and years to come, particularly parties who are Arctic nations.

There is no doubt that the Arctic is in a time of deep trouble. In May 2017, the Arctic Council held its 10th Ministerial Meeting in Fairbanks, Alaska.[110] There, ministers from member nations signed the council's third binding agreement, the "Agreement on Enhancing International Arctic Scientific Cooperation," as well as the Fairbanks Declaration.[111] During this meeting, council leadership transferred from the United States of America to Finland.[112] Finland will lead the Arctic Council until 2019.[113] The Fairbanks Declaration reviews the council's work during the past two years of the United States' leadership, and "provides guidance" for the next two years of Finland's leadership.[114] That declaration cited "activities taking place outside the Arctic region" as "the main contributors to climate change effects and pollution in the Arctic,"[115] but noted that Arctic temperatures are increasing at more than double the rate of Earth's average rate of warming.[116] The "Big Thaw" is real, and leaders know it.

While Ramsar as a treaty offers no definitive tools to help affirmatively protect Arctic wetlands directly, it nevertheless provides opportunities through both its educational programs and public relations opportunities to vigorously encourage protections. As the center of change, the Arctic deserves all the vigorous encouragement it can get. Accordingly, the Ramsar Secretariat and parties to the convention should continue to draw up the convention's strong platform for education and messaging going forward, and maximize its potential for making meaningful impact for our thawing Arctic.

Notes

1. See generally the Intergovernmental Panel on Climate Change (IPCC)'s website, https://www.ipcc.ch/; National Aeronautics and Space Administration (NASA), "The consequences of climate change," https://climate.nasa.gov/effects/ (Global climate change has already had observable effects on the environment.

Glaciers have shrunk, ice on rivers and lakes is breaking up earlier, plant and animal ranges have shifted and trees are flowering sooner.).

2. See World Wildlife Federation, "Arctic Climate Change," http://wwf.panda.org/what_we_do/where_we_work/arctic/what_we_do/climate, "Arctic Climate Research at the University of Illinois"; http://arctic.atmos.uiuc.edu.

3. See, e.g., Ross Koningstein and Davide Fork, "What It Would Really Take to Reverse Climate Change: Today's renewable energy technologies won't save us. So what will?" IEEE Spectrum, Nov. 18, 2014; http://spectrum.ieee.org/energy/renewables/what-it-would-really-take-to-reverse-climate-change; David Biello, "7 Solutions to Climate Change Happening Now," *Scientific American,* Nov. 17, 2014; https://www.scientificamerican.com/article/7-solutions-to-climate-change-happening-now/; Simon Worrall, "100 Practical Ways to Reverse Climate Change," *National Geographic,* May 28, 2017; https://news.nationalgeographic.com/2017/05/climate-change-global-warming-drawdown-hawken/.

4. For an overview of environmental governance in the Arctic, see Joseph F. DiMento, "Environmental Governance of the Arctic: Law, Effect, Now Implementation," *UC Irvine Law Review* 2016; https://papers.ssrn.com/sol3/papers.cfm?abstract_id=2853673.

5. Convention on Wetlands of International Importance especially as Waterfowl Habitat (Feb. 2, 1971), T.I.A.S. No. 1084, 996 U.N.T.S. 245 (amended 1982 & 1987) [hereinafter Ramsar Convention]. A current copy of the Ramsar Convention text can be found at http://www.ramsar.org/cda/en/ramsar-documents-texts/main/ramsar/1-31-38_4000_0__.

6. Ramsar Convention, Article 1. This is much broader than the definitions of wetlands used under United States regulations and guidance. See generally U.S. Environmental Protection Agency; http://water.epa.gov/lawsregs/guidance/wetlands/definitions.cfm.

7. U.S. Fish and Wildlife Service, "2013 NWI Alaska Mapping Status Alaska Region," *Alaska National Wetlands Inventory*; https://www.fws.gov/alaska/fisheries/nwi/pdf/2013_status_update.pdf.

8. Jonathan V. Hall, W. E. Frayer, and Bill O. Wilen, "Status of Alaska Wetlands," U.S. Fish and Wildlife Service, 1994; https://www.fws.gov/wetlands/Documents/Status-of-Alaska-Wetlands.pdf.

9. Matthew Lee, "Kerry tours Arctic Circle to see climate change impact," *PBS News Hour*, June 16, 2016; http://www.pbs.org/newshour/rundown/kerry-tours-arctic-circle-to-see-climate-change-impact/.

10. See, e.g., Megan Scudellari, An Unrecognizable Arctic, NASA (July 25, 2013); http://climate.nasa.gov/news/958.

11. *See,* CONTRIBUTION OF WORKING GROUP II TO THE FOURTH ASSESSMENT REPORT OF THE INTERGOVERNMENTAL PANEL ON CLIMATE CHANGE 553, ed. M. L. Parry et al., 2007 (hereinafter WORKING GROUP II); http://www.ipcc.

ch/publications_and_data/ar4/wg2/en/ch12s12-4-5.html (noting that although some Arctic wetlands may realize increased productivity, some peatlands will suffer a loss of permafrost and become drained, which may even cause the former wetlands to catch fire during dry years). The relationship between increasing temperatures and Arctic wetlands is complex. Generally, as permafrost melts, wetlands form, only to be drained later as the thawing and drying cycle progresses. Thus, although at times it may appear climate change is a boon to Arctic wetlands, in the end Arctic wetlands are likely to suffer from unprecedented drainage. However, it is difficult to predict exactly the outcome of these, and other, competing forces. See, e.g., U.S. CLIMATE CHANGE SCIENCE PROGRAM, ABRUPT CLIMATE CHANGE, 196 (John P. McGeehin et al., eds., 2008); http://www.climatescience.gov/Library/sap/sap3-4/final-report/#finalreport.

12. See e.g., Arctic Change—Land: Waterfowl, NOAA, http://www.arctic.noaa.gov/detect/land-duck.shtml (last visited Sept. 8, 2013).

13. See, e.g., WORKING GROUP II, supra note 11 hypothesizing warmer temperatures will increase the rate of peat decomposition, releasing additional carbon emissions into the atmosphere).

14. The Arctic Council is composed of Canada, Denmark, Finland, Iceland, Norway, Russian Federation, Sweden, and the United States. About the Arctic Council, ARCTIC COUNCIL (April 7, 2011); http://www.arctic-council.org/index.php/en/about-us/arctic-council/about-arctic-council.

15. Ibid.

16. The Permanent Participants Are Arctic Athabaskan Council, Aleut International Association, Gwich'in Council International, Inuit Circumpolar Council, Russian Association of Indigenous Peoples of the North, and Saami Council. Permanent Participants, ARCTIC COUNCIL (April 27, 2011); http://www.arctic-council.org/index.php/en/about-us/permanent-participants.

17. Ibid.

18. 13th Meeting of the Conference of the Contracting Parties to the Ramsar Convention on Wetlands, Resolution XIII.23: Wetlands in the Arctic and sub-Arctic, Oct. 29, 2018; https://www.ramsar.org/sites/default/files/documents/library/xiii.23_arctic_subarctic_wetlands_e.pdf.

19. Working groups consist of representatives from sectoral ministries, government agencies, and researchers. Working Groups, ARCTIC COUNCIL (April 15, 2011); http://www.arctic-council.org/index.php/en/about-us/working-groups.

20. See CONSERVATION OF ARCTIC FLORA AND FAUNA, CAFF; http://www.caff.is/.

21. CAFF—Conservation of Arctic Flora and Fauna, ARCTIC COUNCIL (April 15, 2011); http://www.arctic-council.org/index.php/en/about-us/working-groups/conservation-of-arctic-flora-and-fauna-caff.

22. Ibid.

23. Ibid.

24. *Resolution on Cooperation (RoC) between the Ramsar Convention and the Conservation of Arctic Flora and Fauna (CAFF) Working Group*, RAMSAR (July 18, 2013); http://www.ramsar.org/cda/en/ramsar-news-archives-2012-caaf-cop11/main/ramsar/1-26-45-520%5E26110_4000_0__.

25. Press Release, Conservation of Arctic Flora and Fauna, CAFF Signs Resolution of Cooperation with Ramsar and AEWA (July 16, 2012); http://www.arctic-council.org/index.php/en/resources/news-and-press/news-archive/142-wg-news/572-caff-signs-resolution-of-cooperation-with-ramsar.

26. Ibid.

27. See Press Release, Ramsar Convention, The Arctic Biodiversity Assessment (May 21, 2013); http://www.ramsar.org/cda/en/ramsar-news-arctic-biodiversity-assessment/main/ramsar/1-26%5E26187_4000_0__. The report can be downloaded without charge. ARCTIC BIODIVERSITY ASSESSMENT; http://www.arcticbiodiversity.is/ (last visited Sep. 8, 2013).

28. Contracting Parties, or Member States, of the Ramsar Convention; http://archive.ramsar.org/cda/en/ramsar-about-parties/main/ramsar/1-36-123_4000_0__.

29. Press Release, supra note 24.

30. G. V. T. Matthews, *The Ramsar Convention on Wetlands: Its History and Development* (1993) (recounting that "[i]t took just over eight years of conferences, technical meetings and behind the scenes discussions to develop a convention text"); http://www.ramsar.org/cda/en/ramsar-pubs-books-ramsar-convention-on-21313/main/ramsar/1-30-101%5E21313_4000_0__.

31. The convention's short form is not an acronym, but rather signifies name of the town (Ramsar, Iran) where it was originally signed.

32. The original 1971 version of the Convention can be found at http://www.ramsar.org/cda/en/ramsar-documents-cops-1971-final-act-of-the/main/ramsar/1-31-58-136%5E20803_4000_0__.

33. By its terms, the Ramsar Convention was to enter into force four months after seven parties had ratified it. Ramsar Convention, supra note 2, at art. 10. For a current introduction to the history of the Convention, see A *Brief History of the Ramsar Convention*; http://www.ramsar.org/cda/en/ramsar-about-history/main/ramsar/1-36-62_4000_0__. The United States became a party in 1987 during the Reagan administration. See Contracting Parties in Order of their Accession; http://www.ramsar.org/cda/en/ramsar-about-parties-parties-in-order/main/ramsar/1-36-123%5E20715_4000_0__.

34. G. V. T. Matthews, supra note 3.

35. For a superb overview of the convention, including its history and modern implementation, see the 2006 edition of *The Ramsar Convention Manual—A Guide to the Convention on Wetlands* (Ramsar, Iran, 1971) (6th ed. 2013); http://www.ramsar.org/pdf/lib/manual6-2013-e.pdf.

36. The actual language of the incorporated amendments can be found at the official documents site: http://www.ramsar.org/cda/en/ramsar-documents-texts/main/ramsar/1-31-38_4000_0__.

37. "The Guidelines adopted by the Conference of the Contracting Parties to the Ramsar Convention on Wetlands"; http://www.ramsar.org/key_guidelines_index.htm. Another website from the Ramsar Secretariat e provides links to operational information including various guidance documents officially adopted during meetings of the Conference of the Contracting Parties, available at http://www.ramsar.org/about/the-conference-of-the-contracting-parties.

38. The Ramsar Strategic Plan 2009–2015 as adopted by Resolution X.1 (2008) and adjusted for the 2013–2015 triennium by Resolution XI.3 (2012); http://www.ramsar.org/pdf/strat-plan-2009-e-adj.pdf.

39. See generally Basic Information on Secretariats of Multilateral Environmental Agreements, Mission, Structure, Financing and Governance; http://www.un.org/ga/president/60/summitfollowup/060612d.pdf.

40. See Ramsar, The Ramsar Secretariat; http://www.ramsar.org/cda/en/ramsar-about-bodies-secr/main/ramsar/1-36-71-77_4000_0__.

41. See Ramsar, The Standing Committee; http://www.ramsar.org/cda/en/ramsar-about-bodies-standing/main/ramsar/1-36-71-73_4000_0__.

42. See Ramsar, The Scientific and Technical Review Panel (STRP), Ramsar's scientific subsidiary body; http://www.ramsar.org/cda/en/ramsar-about-bodies-strp/main/ramsar/1-36-71-74_4000_0__.

43. See Ramsar, Resolution 5.6: The wise use of wetlands, Annex A, http://www.ramsar.org/cda/en/ramsar-documents-resol-resolution-ix-1-annex-a/main/ramsar/1-31-107%5E23536_4000_0__ suggesting that establishment of national wetland committees can assist with meeting "wise use" obligations). See also United States National Ramsar Committee; http://www.ramsarcommittee.us/.

44. See Ramsar, National Ramsar Committees; http://www.ramsar.org/cda/en/ramsar-activities-nationalramsarcommittees/main/ramsar/1-63-516_4000_0__.

45. See Ramsar, Information Sheet on Ramsar Wetlands (RIS); http://www.ramsar.org/cda/en/ramsar-documents-info-information-sheet-on/main/ramsar/1-31-59%5E21253_4000_0__. A new process for completing and updating future RIS's was approved in 2012. Resolution XI.8, Streamlining procedures for describing Ramsar Sites at the time of designation and subsequent updates; http://www.ramsar.org/pdf/cop11/res/cop11-res08-e.pdf.

46. The current list of sites is maintained by the nongovernmental partner Wetlands International; http://ramsar.wetlands.org/.

47. Ramsar Convention, supra note 2, at art. 3.1.

48. Ibid. at art. 2.3.

49. Timo Koivurova Erik J. Molenaar, "International Governance and Regulation of the Marine Arctic: I. Overview and Gap Analysis" WWF Inter-

national Arctic Programme (2010); file:///Users/kimconno/Downloads/3in1_final.pdf.

50. See Ramsar Manual, supra note 11 at 47.

51. Ibid.; see generally Ramsar, "The Wise Use of wetlands"; http://www.ramsar.org/about/the-wise-use-of-wetlands.

52. C. Max Finlayson, Editorial, "Forty years of wetland conservation and wise use" Aquatic Conserv: Mar. Freshw. Ecosyst. 22: 139–143 (2012); www.wileyonlinelibrary.com.

53. Related instruments and organizations include: The United Nations Environment Programme (UNEP), The Convention on Biological Diversity (CBD), The Convention on Conservation of Migratory Species of Wild Animals (CMS), The UNESCO World Heritage Convention, the United Nations Convention to Combat Desertification (UNCCD), the United Nations Framework Convention on Climate Change (UNFCCC), UNEP's Convention for the Protection and Development of the Marine Environment of the Wider Caribbean Region and other regional conventions, UNESCO Man and the Biosphere Programme, Global Terrestrial Observing System (GTOS), and others. See Ramsar, Memoranda of understanding and cooperation with other conventions and international organizations; http://www.ramsar.org/cda/en/ramsar-documents-mous/main/ramsar/1-31-115_4000_0__.

54. "The Ramsar Convention on Wetlands and its indicators of effectiveness" presented at the International Expert Workshop on the 2010 Biodiversity Indicators and Post-2010 Indicator Development, a workshop convened by the UNEP World Conservation Monitoring Centre (UNEP-WCMC) in cooperation with the Convention on Biological Diversity (CBD), hosted by the UK Department for Environment, Food and Rural Affairs (Defra), with funding provided by the European Commission (EC), the UK Joint Nature Conservation Committee (JNCC), and the United Nations Environment Programme (UNEP) (2009); https://www.cbd.int/doc/meetings/ind/emind-02/official/emind-02-08d-en.pdf.

55. Arctic Council. "Arctic Wetlands in a Time of Change," last modified November 4, 2016; http://www.arctic-council.org/index.php/en/our-work2/8-news-and-events/175-arctic-wetlands-in-a-time-of-change.

56. NorBalWet. "Welcome to NorBalWet," accessed June 6, 2017; http://www.norbalwet.org.

57. See ibid.; Arctic Council. "The Arctic Council: A backgrounder," last modified May 26, 2017; www.arctic-council.org/index/php.en/about-us.

58. Arctic Council, "Arctic Wetlands in a Time of Change," (updated 2016); https://www.arctic-council.org/index.php/en/our-work2/8-news-and-events/175-arctic-wetlands-in-a-time-of-change.

59. Ibid.

60. Ibid.

61. Ibid.

62. Ramsar Handbook 19 notes, however, that "[i]n practice . . . this very seldom occurs, and most Article 3.2 reports received by the Ramsar Secretariat come from third parties."

63. Resolution VIII.8 urged Parties to "to put in place mechanisms in order to be informed at the earliest possible time, including through reports by national authorities and local and indigenous communities and NGOs, if the ecological character of any wetland in its territory included in the Ramsar List has changed, is changing or is likely to change, and to report any such change without delay to the Ramsar Bureau so as to implement fully Article 3.2 of the Convention."

64. Ibid.

65. Resolution IX.1 Annex A (2005).

66. Ibid.

67. COP10 Document 27 (2008), an information paper on "Background and rationale to the Framework for processes of detecting, reporting and responding to change in wetland ecological character," observes that "[n]o guidance has been given on what degree of 'likelihood' or confidence is sufficient to require the triggering of the Article 3.2 process. Clearly it would defeat the aim of this provision if strict standards of evidence and substantiation were imposed. On the other hand, the system might be open to abuse (or at least ineffectiveness) if the merest suggestion or anxiety on the part of one person were enough to create the legal reporting obligation. The appropriate approach will lie somewhere in a middle ground of informed, authoritative or expert judgement." Ibid.

68. To trigger the Article 3.2 process, the change in ecological character must be human-induced and not the result of natural evolutionary change occurring in wetlands. See COP10 Document 27 which advises, "There is, however, no guidance provided to Parties on how to distinguish human-caused changes from naturally-occurring changes. In practice this can be difficult, since, for example, an apparently natural change to a site may in practice be the consequence of a human-caused ex situ change, such as changes in the water management elsewhere in a river basin." Ibid.

69. Resolution XI.9 (2012) recognized "that changes in the ecological character of wetlands may be due to in situ or ex situ activities."

70. Ibid.

71. Once the secretariat receives an Article 3.2 report from an NGO, the secretariat will pass it along to the party's Administrative Authority (AA), assuming that it comes from a reputable group and contains credible information. The AA is asked whether the party is aware of the matter and requests the party to advise the secretariat on the status of the situation.

72. See Resolution XI.4 (2012) for an example of such a report.

73. Ibid.; see generally Ramsar, "What is the 'wise use' of wetlands?"; http://www.ramsar.org/cda/en/ramsar-about-faqs-what-is-wise-use/main/ramsar/1-36-37%5E7724_4000_0__.

74. Royal C. Gardner and Kim Diana Connolly, "The Ramsar Convention on Wetlands: Assessment of International Designations Within the United States," 37 Envtl. Law Reporter 10089 (Feb. 2007).

75. Convention on Wetlands of International Importance especially as Waterfowl Habitat, Feb. 2, 1971, T.I.A.S No. 11084, 996 U.N.T.S. 245; http://www.ramsar.org/cda/en/ramsar-documents-texts-convention-on/main/ramsar/1-31-38%5E20671_4000_0__.

76. *Ramsar Handbooks for the Wise Use of Wetlands*, 4th Edition, 2010, Book 1, RAMSAR CONVENTION; http://www.ramsar.org/pdf/lib/hbk4-01.pdf.

77. 33 C.F.R. § 320.4. See ch. 4.

78. Ramsar Resolution X.1, The Strategic Plan 2009–2015; http://www.ramsar.org/pdf/strat-plan-2009-e-adj.pdf. The most recent strategic plan was adopted in 2008 and amended in 2012.

79. *Ramsar Handbooks for the Wise Use of Wetlands*, 4th Edition, 2010, Book 1, supra note 76.

80. Ibid. For links to helpful resources about Ramsar's conception of ecosystem services provided by wetlands, see http://www.ramsar.org/cda/en/ramsar-pubs-info-ecosystem-services/main/ramsar/1-30-103%5E24258_4000_0__.

81. Ramsar Resolution X.1, The Strategic Plan 2009–2015, supra note 78.

82. Ibid.

83. *Ramsar Handbooks for the Wise Use of Wetlands*, 4th Edition, 2010, Book 1, supra).

84. D Farrier, L Tucker, "Wise use of wetlands under the Ramsar Convention: a challenge for meaningful implementation of international law," *Journal of Environmental Law* (2000); https://academic.oup.com/jel/article/12/1/21/438292.

85. Ramsar Resolution X.1, The Strategic Plan 2009–2015, *supra* note 78.

86. Ibid.

87. Ibid.

88. International Panel on Climate Change; http://www.ipcc.ch/index.htm.

89. Ramsar Resolution X.1, The Strategic Plan 2009–2015, *supra* note 78.

90. Ibid.

91. Ibid.

92. Ibid.

93. *Ramsar Handbooks for the Wise Use of Wetlands*, 4th Edition, 2010, Ramsar Convention; http://www.ramsar.org/cda/en/ramsar-pubs-handbooks/main/ramsar/1-30-33_4000_0__.

94. U.S. Fish and Wildlife Service International Office, "Ramsar Convention"; https://www.fws.gov/international/pdf/factsheet-ramsar.pdf.

95. Aziza Saud Al Adhoobi, "Influences on the Successful Implementation of the Convention on Wetlands of International Importance (Ramsar) among Member Countries," Louisiana State University Digital Commons (2016) ("Several prior studies and national reports to the Convention by Member Countries highlighted some of these influences factors associated with governance issues inside each individual country, funding issues, information limitation and dissemination issues, lack of experts and resources, socioeconomic stresses and environmental pressures that contribute to more degraded wetlands within Ramsar designated sites." Ibid. at 50 (citing multiple other sources).

96. Pamela Griffin, "The Ramsar Convention: A new window for environmental diplomacy?," Institute for Environmental Diplomacy and Security, University of Vermont (2012); http://www.uvm.edu/ieds/sites/default/files/Ramsar_IEDSResearchSeries.pdf.

97. "The Ramsar Convention's Programme on communication, capacity building, education, participation and awareness (CEPA) 2016–2024"; http://www.ramsar.org/sites/default/files/documents/library/cop12_res09_cepa_e_0.pdf.

98. "The Ramsar CEPA Programme"; http://www.ramsar.org/activity/the-ramsar-cepa-programme.

99. Ramsar Convention Secretariat. "Strengthening wetland conservation in the Barents Euro-Arctic Region," accessed June 6, 2017; http://www.ramsar.org/news/strengthening-wetland-conservation-in-the-barents-euro-arctic-region.

100. Ibid.

101. Ibid.

102. Ibid.

103. Ibid.

104. United Nations. "New UN initiative aims to save lives and cut climate change by protecting peatlands," accessed June 6, 2017; http://www.un.org/apps/news/story.asp?NewsID=55585#.WS7zjmNjGFI.

105. Ibid.

106. Ibid.

107. Ibid.

108. William Yardley, "Tillerson, at Arctic meeting, signs document affirming need for action on climate change," Los Angeles Times, May 11, 2017, accessed June 6, 2017; http://www.latimes.com/nation/la-na-arctic-council-20170511-story.html.

109. Ramsar, "IGO Statement to UNFCCC COP22 on behalf of the Ramsar Convention on Wetlands Secretary General Martha Rojas-Urrego," November 17, 2016; http://www.ramsar.org/news/wetlands-crucial-in-addressing-climate-change.

110. Arctic Council. "Arctic Council Ministers meet, sign binding agreement on science cooperation, pass Chairmanship from U.S. to Finland,"

last modified May 13, 2017; http://www.arctic-council.org/index.php/en/
our-work2/8-news-and-events/451-fairbanks-04.

    111. Ibid.

    112. Ibid.

    113. Ibid.

    114. Ibid.

    115. Yardley, "Tillerson, at Arctic meeting, signs document affirming need for action on climate change," supra note 108.

    116. Mike Blanchfield, "Freeland praises Tillerson's work on Arctic Council climate change statement," CBC News, May 12, 2017; http://www.cbc.ca/news/politics/freeland-tillerson-arctic-council-1.4111883.

13

Climate Governance and Arctic Governance

You Can't Have One Without the Other? Or, What Dual Governance Failures Look Like

CINNAMON CARLARNE

In the absence of urgent action on climate change, there may be a number of tipping points in climate-driven systems in the Arctic, which threaten to rapidly escalate the danger for the whole planet. A collapse of summer sea-ice, increased methane emissions from thawing permafrost, runaway melting of the Greenland ice-sheet, and a collapse of the thermos-haline circulation, may all be approaching in the Arctic and will have disastrous consequences for global climate and sea levels. These together comprise a wake-up call to reinvigorate efforts to tackle climate change. A lack of consensus on precisely how fast any tipping points are approaching in the Arctic should not be used as an argument for inaction.

—Environmental Audit Committee, *Protecting the Arctic*, Report, 2012–13, H.C. 171-I, at 21 (U.K.)

I. Introduction

The theme of this book is *The Big Thaw*, referring, of course, to the rapid and impactful thawing of the Arctic region as a result of anthropogenic climate change. With climate change proceeding at an estimated twice the pace in the Arctic as compared to the rest of the planet, and with the ice loss of recent years putting Arctic melt decades ahead of model predictions, the Arctic has become the bellwether for the rest of the planet for climate change.[1] The global community, thus, looks to the Arctic as a symbol of what is to come. For this reason, not only is the Arctic a research hub for climate scientists and anthropologists, but it is also the subject of great debate concerning the adequacy of existing governance structures. Yet, the global dimensions are just one piece of the Arctic climate picture, with the other pieces being the direct impacts of the thaw on the human and nonhuman systems that make up the Arctic landscape. These impacts, many of which we have already started to witness, may have devastating effects on human communities,[2] flora, and fauna.[3]

In light of all this, perhaps rather tritely, one could say that we stand at the precipice of change, "change" meaning many things: a changing climate; a changing Arctic environment; changing social, cultural, economic, and political realities—all of this and more. Perhaps, even more tritely, one could say that in the face of all of this change—some of which is rapid and some of which is slow or, at least, imperceptible—our governance responses at every level have failed to keep pace with either the rapid or the slow changes. We could say that after 20-plus years of efforts to develop a traditional treaty-based framework to address climate change, we have largely failed and that the early costs of this ongoing failure are being borne in significant part by the human and nonhuman inhabitants of the Polar North where, in turn, efforts to structure local and regional governance responses have also largely come to naught. Yes, perhaps it is trite to say this. Maybe we know this all too well, so one should refrain from flogging the proverbial horse. Yet, with atmospheric greenhouse gas emissions exceeding 400 ppm in May 2013 and with Inuit communities watching their landmass erode and disappear before their eyes and with the now infamous but none-the-better-for-it polar bears clinging to the edges of the disappearing ice, perhaps it is not trite but rather urgent that we say that we stand at the precipice of change and that, before the ice melts from beneath our feet, we need to examine what role law and larger governance systems can play at every level in addressing this challenge. In the particular context of *The Big Thaw*, this means examining both the larger system of global climate change governance and the regional system of Arctic governance to explore how the failings of one—the global climate change regime—necessitate the rapid evolution of the other: the Arctic governance regime.

This chapter offers an overview of the dual governance challenges that frame the more discreet problems that will be examined in the chapters that follow. In examining the juxtaposition of the climate change and Arctic governance challenges, this chapter suggests that in both contexts, adaptation and multilevel governance approaches must be prioritized alongside ongoing more traditional mitigation and management efforts. Part II begins by offering a brief chronicle of the history of the global climate change regime to reveal how negotiations have evolved while greenhouse gas emissions have continued to rise. This part suggests that the global climate change regime has arrived at a critical juncture and that future negotiations must facilitate polycentric approaches in both the mitigation and adaptation contexts, but with an increasing focus on adaptation. Part III examines climate-related challenges to Arctic governance systems, revealing how climate change is exacerbating existing social, cultural, and environmental stresses in the Arctic and highlighting long-standing political tensions over Arctic management strategies. Finally, Part IV concludes by emphasizing how the essential linkages between global efforts to address climate change and regional efforts to govern the Arctic reveal larger challenges to structure governance systems that enable shared global goals to be translated into meaningful actions at multiple levels of governance.

II. Climate Governance

The United Nations Framework Convention on Climate Change (UNFCCC)[4] forms the core of the global climate change regime and establishes the underlying objective of stabilizing "greenhouse gas concentrations in the atmosphere at a level that would prevent dangerous anthropogenic interference with the climate system."[5] Following the entry into force of the UNFCCC in 1994, global negotiators began the process of agreeing upon the terms of a protocol to the treaty that would delineate state roles and responsibilities with regard to combatting climate change, with particular focus on delineating a regime for ensuring global reductions in the emissions of greenhouse gases. Ultimately, these negotiations culminated in 1997 with the adoption of the Kyoto Protocol.[6] The Kyoto Protocol, drawing upon the earlier successes of the 1987 Montreal Protocol on Substances that Deplete the Ozone Layer,[7] adopted a targets-and-timetables approach to reducing global greenhouse gas emissions by at least 5 percent below 1990 levels in the first commitment period, 2008–2012.[8] With regard to commitments during this period—again taking a cue from the Montreal Protocol—the UNFCCC and, in turn, the Kyoto Protocol differentiated roles and responsibilities according to the economic status of the state parties, thus creating a system of emissions reductions obligations founded on the notion of common but differentiated responsibilities.[9]

Together, the UNFCCC and the Kyoto Protocol established the overarching obligations and framework for the global climate change regime. However, even before negotiations for the Kyoto Protocol were complete, divisions between key state players prefigured the conflict, chaos, and frustration that would plague the next 15 years of efforts: first, to bring the protocol into force and second, to achieve measurable progress in mitigating climate change. One of the first signs of serious trouble came when the United States quickly signaled that it would not be ratifying the protocol in the near term based, at least in part, on a Senate Resolution stating that the United States should not be a signatory to *any* protocol that exempted developing countries from legally binding obligations.[10] The United States' decision not to support the protocol revealed not only widespread resistance to aggressive efforts to address climate change, but also the way in which tensions between emissions reductions and economic development would come to shape and, more often than not, inhibit progress in halting climate change.

Yet, despite early signs that the United States would refrain from supporting the protocol, the global community existed in a state of limbo for many years following its adoption. Questions remained as to whether the United States would eventually ratify the agreement, thus creating the much-needed momentum that would incentivize concerted global action on what was now understood to be one of the most critical collective action problems of our time. Eventually, despite continued U.S. entrenchment, first Japan and later Russia ratified the Kyoto Protocol as a result of European Union–led efforts. Consequently, the agreement entered into force in 2005.[11] Despite this hard-fought legal success, during this critical period, 1997–2005, global greenhouse gas emissions continued to rise and, in part, the greenhouse gas footprint of the rapidly developing economies grew exponentially.[12]

Just two years later, in 2007—15 years after the adoption of the UNFCCC and 10 years after the adoption of the Kyoto Protocol—not only had the major developed nations done little to address climate change, but the role of the rapidly developing economies, particularly China, had also become one of utmost importance. In 2007, China surpassed the United States as the largest net emitter of greenhouse gas emissions,[13] and the U.S. Energy Information Administration (EIA) projected that "by 2030, carbon dioxide emissions from China and India combined are projected to account for thirty-one percent of total world emissions, with China alone responsible for twenty-six percent of the world total."[14] The EIA report further noted that China was experiencing the largest annual global growth in energy-related carbon dioxide emissions and that China and India together accounted for 72 percent of the projected global growth in coal-related carbon dioxide emissions.[15] In the wake of unprecedented rates of emissions growth in the developing economies, the global community had to adjust to a new reality—achieving meaningful emissions reductions could not be accomplished without full engagement on the part of the rapidly developing economies. And, yet, at this point—more than a decade and a half into global efforts to address climate change—the largest developed country emitter remained outside the fold of the climate change agreement, while even those developed countries within the fold could point to little measurable success[16] in reducing greenhouse emissions or otherwise structuring effective climate change mitigation or, even, adaptation strategies.

The seeming futility of the first decade of the protocol sparked frustration during the 13th annual meeting of the Conference of the Parties (COP) to the UNFCCC and the third annual Meeting of the Parties (MOP) to the Kyoto Protocol in Bali, Indonesia, in 2007. The objective of the Bali Conference was to create a roadmap for negotiating a new post-2012 climate treaty, even as the parties tried to invigorate the only recently enacted yet already seemingly obsolete Kyoto Protocol. Between December 3 and 15, 2007, more than 10,000 participants representing 180 countries as well as numerous nonstate actors came together in Bali to debate the future of the global climate change regime—or, really, to try to give a future to the global climate change regime.[17] At the culmination of the Bali Conference, the participants ultimately succeeded in negotiating a roadmap and an action plan for long-term cooperative action under the UNFCCC with the ultimate goal being to negotiate a post-Kyoto agreement by 2009.[18]

While the year 2009 did not hold any magical significance, it did represent a good place to draw the line, being one year into the first Kyoto Protocol compliance period—not too early to consider bringing to life a new framework, but early enough to go back to the drawing board should the first round of negotiations fail. And by now, the latter scenario seemed increasingly likely.

Between 2007 and 2009, global climate negotiations continued and progress was made in developing negotiating texts for the much-anticipated 2009 meeting of the UNFCCC COP and the Kyoto Protocol MOP in Copenhagen. Following multiple years of stalled negotiations, 2009 brought a semblance of hope. With a new Democratic president in the White House in the United States,[19] and with the new administration instigating small but meaningful steps to jump start U.S. climate change law and policy,[20] waves began to appear in the previously still and stagnant waters of global climate negotiations. Sparked in part by change in the United States and in part by increasing urgency surrounding climate change, the United States, China, India, and Brazil—all of whom were now considered key emitters but none of whom were subject to any meaningful international or national emissions reductions obligations—offered evidence that they were willing to actively engage in the climate negotiations as the 2009 meeting neared.[21]

The ensuing Copenhagen Climate Change Conference (COP-15/ MOP-5) represented at once the nadir and at the same time a critical turning point for global climate change negotiations. The 2009 Conference represented the first time since the meeting in Kyoto that all major emitters expressed the intent to attend, to actively engage in the negotiations, and to send a head of state. Yet, by 2009, the pool of major emitters had grown to include a number of developing countries, including China, India, Brazil, and South Korea. So, while the United States—at least at the executive level—showed a long-awaited willingness to re-engage with global negotiations, this was far from enough to guarantee a successful outcome at the conference. And, as quickly became clear during the tumultuous meeting, there was no longer a single hegemony or even a pact of powerful players that could effectively direct the negotiations or lead the way in efforts to negotiate a collective response to climate change.[22] Rather, what emerged during the Copenhagen meeting were the new contours of global climate politics. The re-engagement of the United States was met with the emergence of China and, to a lesser degree, India as dominant players in establishing the parameters of climate governance.[23] The Copenhagen Conference demonstrated that a new political paradigm had emerged and that it, in key part, represented a shift away from developed country–led negotiations,[24] away from developed country–focused emissions reductions, and away from top-heavy, monolithic solutions to a problem defined by complexity.[25]

Thus, when the U.S. climate negotiator characterized the Copenhagen Conference as a "snarling, aggravated, chaotic event,"[26] he was really describing the larger field of global climate negotiations both past and present. Yet, just as the negotiations crashed among discord, they also released a spark of hope. The hope came in an unexpected and, at least initially, unwanted form—the Copenhagen Accord.[27] The Copenhagen Accord did not originate from the Conference of the Parties plenary sessions nor did it reflect the multilateral nature of UNFCCC negotiations or anything close to global consensus. Rather, the Copenhagen Accord was drafted by the heads of state of the United States, China, India, Brazil, and South Africa during the course of a private (read: exclusive) meeting.[28]

The Copenhagen Accord, extending a mere three pages in length, committed parties to continuing efforts to facilitate long-term cooperative action to combat climate change and provide "[s]caled up, new and additional, predictable and adequate funding"[29] while also calling for the establishment of a new "Green Climate Fund."[30] The accord, on its own, had no official status. Further revealing the divides separating parties to the convention, the COP could not garner the consensus vote needed to approve the accord as an official UNFCCC decision.[31] In the end, the COP voted to "take note" of the accord, making it a part of an official UNFCCC COP-15 decision.

This final product neither brought to life the vision articulated by the Bali Roadmap nor provided anything approximating a guide for short-term efforts to mitigate or adapt to climate change. What it did provide, however, was a tool for reframing global climate change negotiations in light of changing notions—or realities, really—of what a global agreement on climate change could and should be doing. In other words, it provided a starting point for an ongoing process of institutional revaluation. This re-evaluation characterizes current negotiations, focusing on the question of: When confronted by a massive[32] problem such as global climate change that involves heterogeneous needs, capacities, and responsibilities and that implicates short- and long-term economic, political, and social stability as well as fundamental questions of equity and basic human rights, what *should* and, equally importantly, what *can* an international agreement do to facilitate effective efforts to address the problem at every level of governance?

While the Copenhagen Accord did not make much headway in answering this question, it did start to push back on traditional notions of success and failure in the institutional context. In addition, the accord gave the COP several important tools to use in future negotiations. First, the Copenhagen Accord called for deep cuts in emissions premised on the need to "[h]old the increase in global temperature below two degrees Celsius."[33] This notion has since been embedded as an underlying goal in climate negotiations. Second, the accord emphasized the need for "enhanced action and international cooperation on adaptation,"[34] revealing an ongoing trend to push institutional efforts beyond mitigation. Third, as previously mentioned, the accord called for the creation of a "Green Climate Fund" as the operating entity of the financial mechanism for the convention. Finally, the accord called for the creation of a new mechanism for enhancing technology development and transfer while also establishing a framework for developed and developing countries to voluntarily take measures to reduce greenhouse gas emissions in the interim period, during which negotiations for a new agreement proceeded. Although the accord did little to flesh them out in its three pages, each one of these initiatives has since become a key part of ongoing institutional efforts.

Copenhagen marked a turning point. In the years since, we have seen the initiation of a new phase in global climate change negotiations. Beginning in Cancún[35] in 2010 and continuing in Durban[36] (2011) and Doha (2012), the parties to the UNFCCC and the Kyoto Protocol have begun the process of re-envisioning the role of the global climate change regime in every aspect of climate policy, from mitigation to adaptation to technology transfer.

In key part, the Cancún Agreements and the Durban Platform for Enhanced Action reaffirmed, as originally advanced in the Copenhagen Accord, the need to achieve cuts in greenhouse gas emissions "deep enough to hold the increase in global average temperature below 2°C above preindustrial levels."[37] They also developed the contours of the new Green Climate Fund,[38] created a new technology mechanism to facilitate enhanced technology development and transfer,[39] and established a new framework to facilitate action on adaption, including the creation of a new Adaptation Committee. In addition, in Durban, the parties created the Ad Hoc Working Group on the Durban Platform for Enhanced Action, which was charged with the task of "develop[ing] a protocol, another legal instrument or a legal outcome under the Convention applicable to all Parties"[40] no later than 2015 in order for that agreement to come into effect and begin to be implemented in 2020.[41]

As the post-Copenhagen negotiations have continued, the emphasis has been on enhancing funding for mitigation and adaptation through the Green Climate Fund;[42] improving mechanisms for technology transfer and for measuring, reporting, and verifying countries' greenhouse gas emissions and the actions that they take to reduce them;[43] developing a more comprehensive system for facilitating adaptation efforts;[44] and considering options for creating a new international mitigation strategy.

All in all, the steps taken since Copenhagen have created political breathing room for negotiations on a new international legal instrument that focuses on mitigation obligations while simultaneously reframing institutional efforts around an agenda based on facilitating a more diverse set of actions the majority of which envision the UNFCCC as an enabler for interinstitutional, multilevel, and multiscale governance efforts. That is, the post-Copenhagen process has "underscored the continuing importance of and potential of multilateral engagement"[45] while revealing the extent to which multilateral negotiations have broadened the focus beyond finding a centralized solution[46] to include more concerted efforts to facilitate the creation of a set of support systems for mitigation and adaptation efforts at multiple levels and on multiple scales. This is an important shift, but one that is still being realized. At the time of this writing, the global community continues to wrangle over fundamental questions of rights and responsibilities and procedural questions of whether and how to frame future legal emissions-reductions obligations. Yet, among all of this wrangling, through a series of post-Copenhagen decisions, global climate negotiators have begun to re-envision the role that the UNFCCC will play in facilitating what is increasingly becoming a much more polycentric[47] set of climate governance systems, particularly with regard to adaptation.

The emerging contours of the system are unrefined and untested, but they offer opportunities for enabling mitigation and adaptation actions to be taken at an optimal level of governance with optimal levels of external support.[48]

Facing a failing global governance framework, we are beginning to witness the creation of a more pluralistic regime. Yet, even as this regime evolves and takes shape, we are confronted with the reality that very little has been done to curb global reliance on fossil fuels and that, at least for the foreseeable future, global greenhouse gas emissions are anticipated to continue rising. Thus, 20-plus years into the fight against global climate change, we now realize that we are committed to at least some degree of warming. As a result, we must confront the wicked nature[49] of climate change in both its most direct and immediate form and in terms of the spin-off governance challenges[50] to which it gives rise. The spin-off challenges arise in a variety of contexts, raising questions as varied as how to treat climate-displaced people (i.e., environmental refugees),[51] to how to respond to the legal gaps and overlaps between climate change and the numerous fields of law with which it interacts, to how to improve governance regimes in areas where climate change is exposing fundamental gaps and flaws. Within the latter category, we are confronted with vast new and intensified challenges, particularly in the context of structuring climate change adaptation strategies at every level of governance, but also in relation to more discreet challenges, such as whether and how to govern evolving techniques and technologies of geoengineering[52] and how to craft governance regimes for the sovereign and contested areas of the Arctic, where geophysical and geopolitical[53] characteristics are changing rapidly as a result of climate change.

III. Arctic Governance

With the global community slowly fumbling forward with efforts to address climate change, the Arctic community is left with the difficult task of deciding how it will handle the regional implications of climate change.

As previously discussed, the Arctic is our planetary tell-tale for climate change.[54] And, as will be discussed in great detail in subsequent chapters of this book, the effects of climate change are being felt in many and varied ways in the Arctic region, creating challenges that range from understanding how climate change will affect the health and availability of fish and marine mammals upon which indigenous and local peoples rely, to the ability of nomadic communities to keep Caribou meat frozen, to who is responsible for aiding or otherwise compensating climate-displaced peoples, to more macro-level controversies about who has a right to access waterways and mineral resources, to global-level debates about whether climate change demands a rethinking of the entire Arctic governance strategy.

It is beyond the remit of this chapter to chronicle in detail these challenges and how they give rise to governance challenges from the local to the global level.[55] Instead, the section that follows very briefly highlights several of these challenges to reveal how the Arctic is a microcosm for the climate-related governance challenges that the rest of the planet will face as global warming continues and suggests that, in common with global climate change governance writ large, in thinking through Arctic governance responses, the focus should be on creating governance structures that enable polycentric responses to emerging challenges, with an emphasis on adaptation.

Arctic Governance: A Brief Background

As background, in contrast to the youthful, hard-working, and centralized global climate governance regime, the Arctic governance regime is older,[56] slower moving, and piecemeal.[57] Thus, unlike the climate change regime, which revolves around the UNFCCC, the Kyoto Protocol, and related COP/MOP decisions, the governance framework for the Arctic[58] involves a dizzying patchwork of bilateral, regional, and international agreements that rely primarily on "soft"[59] law but also encompass key "hard" law components.[60] Components of this extensive framework address issues ranging from natural resource management[61] to research cooperation,[62] territorial sovereignty,[63] maritime access and control,[64] and regulation of the deep seabed.[65] And, of course, the array of global, regional, and bilateral agreements exists alongside the applicable sovereign legal regimes of the Arctic states.[66]

The development of the Arctic governance regime, including its component parts, largely predates the emergence of climate change as a global problem with significant regional implications. With global efforts to address climate change over the last 20 years largely coming to naught in terms of either slowing or reversing the pace of climate change, however, this regime, which already struggles to address conventional problems,[67] is now being called upon to address the earliest effects of climate change in the Arctic, including ongoing ecosystem changes[69] and the rapid loss of sea ice.[69] As a result of this convergence, the Arctic has become a global "governance barometer in the sense that it is an area generating early indications of the growing need for innovation in governance systems worldwide."[70]

232 / Cinnamon Carlarne

Arctic Governance Challenges

As the global governance barometer, the Arctic reveals the importance of triage and embracing polycentricity. In other words, because state and regional efforts cannot cure the cause of the problem (global emissions of greenhouse gases), these efforts must focus on addressing discrete and region-specific challenges and, in doing so, must embrace the reality and possibilities of legal pluralism. At the highest level, these include addressing long-standing tensions over multiple claims to the outer continental shelf that converges in the middle of the Arctic Ocean—claims that are not yet settled nor capable of being fully settled under existing international agreements[71] in their current form—and managing Arctic waters beyond the jurisdiction of existing institutions.[72] Similarly, as discussed in Mark Roberts's chapter,[73] another macro-level challenge involves addressing the effects of short-lived climate pollutants,[74] such as black carbon soot, on the Arctic environment.[75] At this level, the governance challenges involve analyzing the utility of existing international agreements—such as the United Nations Convention on the Law of the Sea and the Montreal Protocol on Substances that Deplete the Ozone Layer[76]—in their current form or as modified to address an emerging problem versus the ability to use regional agreements to address a problem of global origin. In this context, we are asked to consider not only the utility of our international instruments in relation to regional responses, but also to inquire whether problems such as governance of the disputed areas of the Arctic Ocean are more appropriately dealt with by the nation-states claiming sovereignty over the region or, given the importance of this ecosystem to the larger global community, whether it is desirable and possible to reconceptualize the area as part of the global commons.[77] That is, do we need to ask the larger question of whether Arctic governance should continue to revolve around—and be decided by—the interests of the Arctic states, or should Arctic governance be reconfigured around the notion that this area is the "common heritage of mankind" as applied to the high seas and the moon, or the "common concern" of humankind as applied to climate change and conservation of biological diversity? Yet, in asking this question, it must be juxtaposed against the stark failure of the global community to address climate change and the reality that this global failure is what is driving efforts to craft regional responses to climate-induced threats.

Moving down a step, more distinctly regional challenges include improving and modifying governance structures for fisheries,[78] ecosystem and biodiversity management,[79] and oil spill preparedness[80] as climate change multiplies threats in each of these contexts. Here, the origins of the threats to environmental resources are both regional (e.g., overfishing and state-based natural resource management policies) and global (e.g., climate change alters and exacerbates threats to existing ecosystems and results in the opening of new ocean areas to natural resource exploitation). The intersection of global and regional pressures creates a complex environment in which to develop governance and management systems. This complexity and fundamental inability to conceptualize the nature of the threats to the underlying natural systems forces decision makers to operate in a context of even greater uncertainty than what has traditionally characterized environmental decision making.[81]

Finally, at the state and local levels, the acute nature of climate-induced threats to human health and well-being becomes even more visible as Arctic communities and, in particular, indigenous populations[82] struggle to survive in a world characterized by rapid change. As the Arctic ecosystem evolves, local communities confront food shortages, new health-related threats,[83] and, more dramatically, permanent displacement.[84] At this level, local challenges can be dealt with through subnational, national, or regional responses. But even here, with respect to threats to local well-being, there is an acute awareness that the threats derive from both the individual and collective behavior of the global communities and, accordingly, there are increasing efforts to use international legal tools to hold states responsible for their part in contributing to these local harms.[85] Further, in this context, the challenge is often framed less as what types of governance efforts are needed to prevent the harm and more in terms of what types of governance efforts are necessary to facilitate adaptation and, in some circumstances, compensation for the inevitable harms that will accompany the regional effects of global climate change.

The above description offers a very brief sketch of some—but far from all—of the governance challenges that climate change is either creating or exacerbating in the Arctic region. In light of this dizzying array of challenges, saying that we stand at the precipice of change sounds much more like an understatement than mere melodramatics. Instead, perhaps we should say that we are sliding down the precipice and desperately trying to grasp onto the soft ice with our axes and crampons while we still have a chance. In the governance context, this grasping must take place at multiple levels and in multiple contexts (i.e., within the larger climate change context and within the more specific Arctic context), and the efforts that ensue must prioritize adaptation efforts at every level of governance based on the reality that we have "entered the era of climate change adaptation, which is most fundamentally about coping with continual, and often unpredictable, change."[86]

IV. Governance in a Thawing World

As this chapter has sought to demonstrate, the challenges that the Arctic communities face must be contextualized within the larger efforts and, for the most part, failures of the global community to address climate change. With international efforts to develop a consensus-based approach to climate change struggling to make even a dent in net global emissions of greenhouse gases and with international negotiations caught up in a crisis of confidence over the ability to define the ethical and procedural parameters for moving forward with efforts to use international law as a central tool in addressing climate change, the governance challenges associated directly and indirectly with climate change are multiplying exponentially. As such, we have "passed, definitively, the point of avoiding climate change impacts,"[87] and we are now confronted with a thawing world. Within this world, the original governance challenge remains: find ways to mitigate and adapt to anthropogenic climate change.

With this task in mind, it is worth returning to the specific mandate of the 1990 UN General Assembly resolution that initiated global efforts to address climate change.[88] There, the General Assembly tasked the global community with developing "a framework convention on climate change, and other related instruments, containing appropriate commitments for action to combat climate change and its adverse effects."[89] We have the framework convention. We have other related instruments, principally the Kyoto Protocol. Yet, we neither have appropriate commitments for combatting climate change, nor do we have appropriate commitments for combatting the adverse effects of climate change. Putting aside commitments for a moment, we do not even have appropriate actions or frameworks or strategies—legally binding or not—for combatting climate change and its adverse effects.

With the mandate of the General Assembly in mind and, more importantly, with human and ecosystem health and well-being in mind, the discussion in Section II suggested that we need to continue to push back against the notion that combatting climate change and its adverse effects can or should be done based on the centralized, consensus-based set of rules that we originally envisioned as providing a consolidated and comprehensive framework for responding to global climate change. As we grasp the complexity of the causes and consequence of climate change as well as the complexity of the global world in which we operate, the need for novel governance approaches based on an appreciation for legal pluralism and the potential power—and, often, necessity—of polycentric responses[90] is gradually influencing the tone and shape of climate negotiations in nearly every context.

Yet, even as the nature of global climate negotiations evolve, we are left not only with the original governance challenge as described by the UN General Assembly, but also with the secondary governance challenges to which climate change gives rise. Lest the term *secondary* be misunderstood, these challenges implicate basic human rights and the continued existence of countless species of plants and animals. And, in the context of the Arctic, the gravity of these challenges emerges from questions of delineating sovereign rights; to finding solutions to regional warming; to preventing and responding to regional marine and terrestrial management; to responding to immediate threats to indigenous health, well-being, and basic survival. The Arctic governance challenges are *Arctic* only in the sense that they are issues that pose immediate challenges to peoples of the Polar North. In terms of cause and consequence, however, many of these challenges are attributable to, and consequential for, the larger community. As such, the governance systems that emerge—or that fail to emerge—from the macro to the micro level in the Arctic are of practical and symbolic importance well beyond the region.

Returning to where we began, the ongoing failings and evolution of the global climate change regime both necessitate and inform the evolution of the Arctic governance regime. In both contexts, little progress has been made and the core challenges remain; in both contexts, the problems become more acute with time and inaction; in both contexts, the failure of the one heightens the urgency of the other; in both contexts, there is a need to triage government responses and, in so doing, to focus on adaptation and enabling multilevel and multiscale responses that enable discreet if insufficient actions while awaiting macro-level changes.

In bringing together lawyers, anthropologists, archaeologists, international relations theorists, filmmakers, and more to explore how climate change has, is, and will impact the Arctic region, this text makes a significant contribution toward efforts to conceptualize and, thus, better respond to the challenges that climate change poses in the Arctic region. Ultimately, however, unless the global community can collectively find ways—whether centralized or, as is more likely, decentralized—to combat climate change, efforts to frame and respond to Arctic challenges will be futile. Equally, however, the heightened nature of the threats to the Arctic offers unique opportunities to mobilize regional and even global action around issues (e.g., black carbon) that could have lasting effects for the larger global community. This book highlights the range of threats and opportunities that exist; let us hope that it can serve as one of many tools that we use to make progress in addressing climate change in all of its varied forms.

[Please note: This chapter is current as of April 2016.]

Notes

1. See, Thomas Homer-Dixon, "Nonlinearity, Uncertainty, and Time Lags: Why We Must Start Planning Now to Geoengineer Earth Soon," paper prepared for delivery at the annual meeting of the American Political Science Association, Toronto, Ontario, Sept. 3–6, 2009).

2. See, e.g., Robin Bronen, "Climate-Induced Community Relocations: Creating an Adaptive Governance Framework Based in Human Rights Doctrine," *New York University Review of Law & Social Change* 35 (2011); Robin Bronen, "Forced Migration of Alaskan Indigenous Communities Due to Climate Change," in *Force Migration and Social Vulnerability*, ed. Tamer Afifi and Jill Jäger (Heidelberg: Springer, 2010).

3. See, e.g., Sam Welch, "The Scared Bear: Imminence, Climate Change, and the Endangered Species Act," *Ecology Law Quarterly* 39, no. 2 (2012); Christine Hunter et al., "Climate Change Threatens Polar Bear Populations: A Stochastic Demographic Analysis," *Ecology* 91, no. 10 (2010).

4. United Nations Framework Convention on Climate Change, opened for signature May 9, 1992, 1771 U.N.T.S. 107 (entered into force March 21, 1994) [hereinafter UNFCCC].

5. Ibid., art. 2.

6. Kyoto Protocol to the United Nations Framework Convention on Climate Change, opened for signature March 16, 1998, 37 I.L.M. 22 (entered into force Feb. 16, 2005).

7. Montreal Protocol on Substances that Deplete the Ozone Layer, opened for signature Sept. 16, 1987, 1522 U.N.T.S. 3 (entered into force January 1, 1989).

8. Supra note 7.

9. See, e.g., UNFCCC art. 4(2) (dividing developed and developing nations into separate categories, Annex I and Annex II, respectively based on the notion of differentiated responsibilities); Kyoto Protocol art. 3(1) (establishing binding emissions reductions obligations for Annex I countries). See also, United Nations Conference on Environment and Development, Principle 7, Rio de Janeiro, Braz., June 3–14, 1992, *Rio Declaration on Environment and Development*, A/CONF.151/26 (Vol. 1), Annex I (Aug. 12, 1992) (for the most frequently cited definition of CBDR); Christopher D. Stone, "Common but Differentiated Responsibilities in International Law," *American Journal of International Law* 98, no. 2 (2004).

10. Byrd-Hagel Resolution, S. Res. 98, 105th Cong. (as passed by Senate, July 25, 1997) (enacted). The U.S. Senate passed the Byrd-Hagel Resolution by a margin of 95–0. Its passage virtually precluded the possibility that the United States subsequently would ratify the drafted Kyoto Protocol.

11. Supra note 7.

12. See, e.g., U.S. Department of Energy, Energy Information Administration, *International Energy Outlook 2008*, DOE/EIA-0484(2008); http://www.tulane.edu/~bfleury/envirobio/readings/International%20Energy%20Outlook%2008.pdf; U.S. Department of Energy, Energy Information Administration, *International Energy Outlook 2007*, DOE/EIA-0484(2007): 74–80; http://www.env-edu.gr/Documents/International%20Energy%20Outlook%202007.pdf; U.S. Department of Energy, Energy Information Administration, *World Carbon Dioxide Emissions from the Consumption and Flaring of Fossil Fuels (Million Metric Tons of Carbon Dioxide)* 1980–2006; http://www.eia.gov/cfapps/ipdbproject/iedindex3.cfm?tid=90&pid=3&aid=8&cid=regions&syid=1980&eyid=2006&unit=MMTCD. See also, Cinnamon Carlarne, "The Glue that Binds or the Straw that Broke the Camel's Back?: Exploring the Implications of U.S. Reengagement in Global Efforts to Address Climate Change," *Tulane Journal of International & Comparative Law* 19 (2010): 123–24 (describing the rapid growth in China's greenhouse gas emissions over the past decade).

13. See, e.g., John Vidal and David Adam, "China Overtakes US as World's Biggest CO2 Emitter," *The Guardian*, June 19, 2007, accessed July 2, 2016; "Gas Exchange: CO2 Emissions 1990–2006," *Nature* 447, no. 7148 (2007).

14. DOE/EIA-0484(2007): 74.

15. Ibid., 76.

16. There are exceptions to the overarching failure, of course, including progress in the European Union to develop a comprehensive climate change regime. See, e.g., Cinnamon Carlarne, "Law and Policy in the European Union," ch. 5 in *Climate Change Law and Policy: EU and US Approaches* (Oxford: Oxford

University Press, 2010); see also, Cinnamon Carlarne, "Member State Laws and Policies," chap. 6 in *Climate Change Law and Policy: EU and US Approaches* (Oxford: Oxford University Press, 2010).

17. Lin Feng and Jason Buhi, "The Copenhagen Accord and the Silent Incorporation of the Polluter Pays Principle in International Climate Law: An Analysis of Sino-American Diplomacy at Copenhagen and Beyond," *Buffalo Environmental Law Journal* 18, no. 1 (2010–11): 18–20.

18. See generally, United Nations Framework Convention on Climate Change Conference of the Parties, *Report of the Conference of the Parties on its thirteenth Session, held in Bali, from 3 to 15 December 2007*, Addendum, Part II: Action taken by the Conference of the Parties at its thirteenth session, 3–7, FCCC/CP/2007/6/Add. 1 (March 14, 2008) [hereinafter Bali Action Plan]; http://unfccc.int/resource/docs/2007/cop13/eng/06a01.pdf. The creation in Bali of the new Ad-Hoc Working Group on Long-Term Cooperative Action under the Convention complimented the work of the preexisting Ad Hoc Working Group on Further Commitments under the Kyoto Protocol.

19. "Barack Obama and Joe Biden: New Energy for America," (2008); http://www.barackobama.com/pdf/factsheet_energy_speech_080308.pdf.

20. See, e.g., Macon Philips, "From Peril to Progress (Update 1: Full Remarks)," *The Whitehouse Blog*, Jan. 26, 2009.

21. See Carlarne, "The Glue that Binds," 135–36 (discussing the announcements that the United States, China, India, Brazil, and the European Union made about their negotiating positions leading up to the Copenhagen meeting).

22. Ibid., 139.

23. For helpful overviews of the Copenhagen Conference, see Daniel Bodansky, "The Copenhagen Climate Change Conference—A Post-Mortem," *American Journal of International Law* 104 (2010); Radoslav S. Dimitrov, "Inside Copenhagen: The State of Climate Governance," *Global Environmental Politics* 10, no. 2 (2010); Meinhard Doelle, "The Legacy of the Climate Talks in Copenhagen: Hopenhagen or Brokenhagen?" *Carbon & Climate Law Review* 4 (2010).

24. See, e.g., Robin Lustig, "Copenhagen: The Dawn of a New Political Reality," *BBC Radio Blog*, Dec. 21, 2009.

25. See generally, Cinnamon Carlarne, "The Future of the UNFCCC: Adaptation and Institutional Rebirth for the International Climate Convention" (working paper no. 172, Ohio State Public Law, 2012).

26. Neil MacFarquhar and John M. Broder, "U.N. Climate Chief Resigns," *New York Times*, Feb. 18, 2010; http://www.nytimes.com/2010/02/19/science/earth/19climate.html (quoting U.S. negotiator Todd Stern).

27. United Nations Framework Convention on Climate Change Conference of the Parties, *Report of the Conference of the Parties on its fifteenth session, held in Copenhagen from 7 to 19 December 2009*, Addendum, Part II: Action taken by

the Conference of the Parties at its fifteenth session, FCCC/CP/2009/11/Add.1 (March 30, 2010); http://unfccc.int/resource/docs/2009/cop15/eng/11a01.pdf.

28. See, e.g., Philip Sherwell, "Barack Obama Denies Accusations that He 'Crashed' Secret Chinese Climate Change Talks," *The Telegraph* (London), Dec. 19, 2010. But see Lindsey Ellerson, "High Drama in Copenhagen (per Administration Officials)," *ABC News Blogs: Politics*, Dec. 18, 2009 (offering a different account of the incident).

29. FCCC/CP/2009/11/Add.1, page 6.

30. Rob Fowler, "Analysis of the Copenhagen Accord: An Initial Assessment of the Copenhagen Outcomes," *Teaching Climate/Energy Law & Policy* (blog), Dec. 20, 2009.

31. See, FCCC/CP/2009/11/Add.1, 4. It was critical to recognize the accord in some official manner in order to take any further efforts to operationalize its financial provisions.

32. See, Richard J. Lazarus, "Super Wicked Problems and Climate Change: Restraining the Present to Liberate the Future," *Cornell Law Review* 94, no. 5 (2009): 1159.

33. See, FCCC/CP/2009/11/Add1, 5.

34. Ibid., 6.

35. United Nations Framework Convention on Climate Change Conference of the Parties, *Report of the Conference of the Parties on its sixteenth session, held in Cancún from 29 November to 10 December 2010*, Addendum, Part II: Action Taken by the Conference of the Parties at its sixteenth session, Decision 1/CP.16, 2–25, FCCC/CP/2010/7/Add.1 (March 15, 2011); http://unfccc.int/ resource/docs/2010/cop16/eng/07a01.pdf; United Nations Framework Convention on Climate Change Conference of the Parties serving as the Meeting of the Parties to the Kyoto Protocol, *Report of the Conference of the Parties Serving as the Meeting of the Parties to the Kyoto Protocol on its sixth session, held in Cancún from 29 November to 10 December 2010*, Addendum, Part II: Action Taken by the Conference of the Parties Serving as the Meeting of the Parties to the Kyoto Protocol at its sixth session, Decision 1/CMP.6, 3–4, FCCC/KP/CMP/2010/12/ Add.1 (Mar. 15, 2011); http://unfccc.int/resource/docs/2010/cmp6/eng/12a01.pdf.

36. See generally, United Nations Framework Convention on Climate Change Conference of the Parties, *Establishment of an Ad Hoc Working Group on the Durban Platform for Enhanced Action*, Proposal by the President, Draft decision -/CP.17, FCCC/CP/2011/L.10 (Dec. 10, 2011); http://unfccc.int/resource/ docs/2011/cop17/eng/l10.pdf.

37. Ibid.

38. FCCC/CP/2010/7/Add.1, 17.

39. See ibid., 19.

40. FCCC/CP/2011/L.10, ¶ 2–3.

41. Ibid. ¶ 4.

42. United Nations Framework Convention on Climate Change Conference of the Parties, *Green Climate Fund—Report of the Transitional Committee,* Proposal by the President, Draft decision -/CP.17, FCCC/CP/2011/L.9 (Dec. 10, 2011); http://unfccc.int/resource/docs/2011/cop17/eng/l09.pdf. The Green Climate Fund was created to "meet the financing needs and options for the mobilization of resources to address the needs of developing country Parties with regard to climate change adaptation and mitigation" (ibid., ¶101).

43. United Nations Framework Convention on Climate Change, *Revision of the UNFCCC reporting guidelines on annual inventories for Parties included in Annex I to the Convention,* Draft decision -/CP.17 (2011); http://unfccc.int/files/meetings/durban_nov_2011/decisions/application/pdf/cop17_annual_inventories.pdf.

44. Based on the proposition set forth at COP-16 in Cancún that "[a]daptation must be addressed with the same priority as mitigation and requires appropriate institutional arrangements to enhance adaptation action and support." FCCC/CP/2010/7/Add.1, 3. See also, United Nations Framework Convention on Climate Change, *Outcome of the Work of the Ad Hoc Working Group on Long-term Cooperative Action under the Convention,* Draft decision -/CP.17, 17–20; http://unfccc.int/files/meetings/durban_nov_2011/decisions/application/pdf/cop17_lcaoutcome.pdf#page=17l; see generally, United Nations Framework Convention on Climate Change, *National adaptation plans,* Proposal by the President, Addendum, Draft decision -/CP.17, FCCC/CP/2011/L.8/Add.1 (Dec. 10, 2011), http://unfccc.int/resource/docs/2011/cop17/eng/l08a01.pdf.

45. Scott Shackelford, "Governing the Final Frontier: A Polycentric Approach to Managing Space Weaponization and Orbital Debris," *American Business Law Journal* 51, no. 2 (2014): 471.

46. See, e.g., William Hare et al., "The Architecture of the Global Climate Regime: A Top-Down Perspective," *Climate Policy (Special Issue),* no. 6 (2010). doi: 10.3763/cpol.2010.0161 (suggesting that a centralized approach is preferable).

47. See Carlarne, "The Future of the UNFCCC."

48. Here, the suggestion is not that there is always one, clear optimal level at which a particular action takes place and that a blanket decision to decentralize decision making to the regional, national, or local level will resolve governance issues. Rather, the suggestion is that centralized decision making generally is not viable and that decisions about the optimal level for various adaptation actions should be made based on the best available information. For a discussion of the dangers of suggesting that there is one panacea—or "blueprint for a single type of governance"—within the context of a complex problem such as climate change, see Elinor Ostrom, Marco A. Janssen, and John M. Anderies, "Going Beyond Panaceas," *Proceedings of the National Academy of Sciences* 104, no. 39 (2007): 15176, doi: 10.1073/pnas.0701886104. See also, William A. Brock and Stephen R. Carpenter, "Panaceas and Diversification of Environmental Policy,"

Proceedings of the National Academy of Sciences 104, no. 39 (2007), doi: 10.1073/pnas.0702096104; Elinor Ostrom, "A Diagnostic Approach for Going Beyond Panaceas," *Proceedings of the National Academy of Sciences* 104, no. 39 (2007), doi: 10.1073/pnas.0702288104.

49. See generally, Horst W. J. Rittel and Marvin M. Webber, "Dilemmas in a General Theory of Planning," *Policy Sciences* 4 (1973); Richard James Lazarus, "Super Wicked Problems and Climate Change: Restraining the Present to Liberate the Future," *Cornell Law Review* 94, no. 5 (2009).

50. See generally, Cinnamon Carlarne, "Arctic Dreams and Geoengineering Wishes: The Collateral Damage of Climate Change," *Columbia Journal of Transnational Law* 49, no. 602 (2011).

51. See generally, Oliver Bakewell, "Research Beyond the Categories: The Importance of Policy Irrelevant Research into Forced Migration," *Journal of Refugee Studies* 21, no. 4 (2008), doi: 10.1093/jrs/fen042; Norman Myers, "Environmental Refugees: An Emergent Security Issue," Doc No EF.NGO/4/05 (paper presented at the 13th Meeting of the Organization for Security and Co-operation in Europe Economic Forum, Prague, Czech Republic, May 22, 2005); Stephen Castles, "The International Politics of Forced Migration," *Palgrave Macmillan Journals: Development* 46, no. 3 (2003), doi:10.1057/palgrave.development.1110462; Richard Black, "Environmental Refugees: Myth or Reality" (working paper no. 34, New Issues in Refugee Research, United Nations High Commissioner for Refugees, 2001).

52. See, e.g., Frank Gervais, Ulf Riebesell, and Maxim Y. Gorbunov, "Changes in Primary Productivity and Chlorophyll a in Response to Iron Fertilization in the Southern Polar Frontal Zone," *Limnology and Oceanography* 47, no. 5 (2002), doi: 10.4319/lo.2002.47.5.1324 (discussing several iron enrichment experiments in the Southern Ocean). See also Quirin Schiermeier, "Ocean Fertilization Experiment Draws Fire: Indo-German Research Cruise Sets Sail Despite Criticism," *Nature*, Jan. 9, 2009, doi:10.1038/news.2009.13 (discussing a controversial ocean iron fertilization experiment sponsored by the German science ministry).

53. Duncan Depledge, "Geo-power and Sea Ice: Encounters with the Geopolitical Stage," in *Big Thaw* (2016).

54. See Homer-Dixon, "Nonlinearity, Uncertainty, and Time Lags."

55. The challenges relate to questions of human rights, environmental management, and maritime rights and responsibilities. See, e.g., "Inuit File Petition with Inter-American Commission on Human Rights, Claiming Global Warming Caused by United States Is Destroying Their Culture and Livelihoods," *Center for International Environmental Law*, Dec. 7, 2005; Hari Osofsky, "Inuit Petition as a Bridge? Beyond Dialectics of Climate Change and Indigenous Peoples' Rights," *American Indian Law Review* 31 (2007) (exploring the challenges posed to the Inuit by rapid climate change and the legal implications of

the Inuit Petition to the Inter-American Human Rights Commission alleging that acts and omissions on the part of the United States violated Inuit human rights); "Nobel Prize Nominee Testifies About Global Warming: Inuit leader Sheila Watt-Cloutier's Testimony Before the Inter-American Commission on Human Rights Put Spotlight on Climate Change and Indigenous Peoples," *Center for International Environmental Law*, March 1, 2007; E. J. Molenaar, "Arctic Marine Shipping: Overview of the International Legal Framework, Gaps and Options," *Florida State University Journal of Transnational Law & Policy* 18, no. 2 (2009); McKenzie Funk, "Healy Mapping Mission: Arctic Landgrab," *National Geographic*, May 2009.

56. The extensive range of governance agreements applicable to the Arctic reflects the range of issues that have challenged domestic and international affairs in the area since the end of World War II.

57. Numerous complementary institutions offer overarching but soft governance institutions for the region, such as the 1991 Arctic Environmental Protection Strategy (AEPS) and the Arctic Council. The AEPS, for example, establishes action plans and working groups on particular issues but was never intended to create a legally binding framework. Similarly, the Arctic Council was created to facilitate monitoring and implementation of AEPS but has had limited functionality.

58. For a brief overview of formal and informal governance efforts in the Arctic, see "Arctic Governance in an Era of Transformative Change: Critical Questions, Governance Principles, Ways Forward, Report of the Arctic Governance Project," *The Arctic Governance Project* (2010): 3, 4–5; http://img9.custompublish.com/getfile.php/1219555.1529.wyaufxvxuc/AGP+Report+April+14+2010[1].pdf?return=Arcticgovernance.custompublish.com. See also, U.S. Department of Energy, Energy Information Administration, *Arctic Oil and Natural Gas Potential* (2009); http://www.eia.doe.gov/oiaf/analysispaper/Arctic/index.html (providing a factual overview of the area and discussing the fact that "[j]urisdictionally, the Arctic contains portions of eight countries—Canada, Denmark (Greenland), Finland, Iceland, Norway, Russia, Sweden, and the United States. Finland and Sweden do not border the Arctic Ocean and are the only Arctic countries without jurisdictional claims in the Arctic Ocean and adjacent seas").

59. See, e.g., U.S. Department of State, "Agreement between the Government of the United States of America and the Government of the Russian Federation on the conservation and management of the Alaska-Chukotka polar bear population," Oct. 16, 2000, http://pbsg.npolar.no/en/agreements/US-Russia.html/ [hereinafter Polar Bear Population Agreement]; "About the Arctic Council," The Arctic Council, accessed July 2, 2016; http://www.Arctic-council.org/index.php/en/about-us/Arctic-council/about-Arctic-council (established by the Ottawa Declaration of 1996 "as a high level intergovernmental forum to provide a means for promoting cooperation, coordination and interaction among

the Arctic States, with the involvement of the Arctic Indigenous communities and other Arctic inhabitants on common Arctic issues, in particular issues of sustainable development and environmental protection in the Arctic"); Barents Euro-Arctic Council, *Cooperation in the Barents EuroArctic Region, Conference of Foreign Ministers in Kirkenes*, Declaration, Jan. 11, 1993; http://www.barentsinfo.fi/beac/docs/459_doc_KirkenesDeclaration.pdf (established in 1993 to "provide impetus to existing cooperation and consider new initiatives and proposals" in the Barents Region of the Arctic. *Id.* at 2); "About CAFF," Conservation of Arctic Flora and Fauna Program, accessed July 2, 2016, 2014; http://www.caff.is/about-caff (noting generally that the goals of CAFF include monitoring Arctic biodiversity, conserving Arctic species and their habitats, considering the establishment of protected areas, conserving nature outside of protected areas, and integrating conservation objectives and measures for economic sectors of the society); "Circumpolar Areas Protected Network (CPAN) Home," Conservation of Arctic Flora and Fauna Program, accessed July 2, 2016; http://www.caff.is/protected-areas-cpan (stating CPAN was "was operational from 1996–2010 and was designed to oversee and advance the CPAN program and to provide the CAFF Board with advice on needed actions. It aimed to ensure sufficient protection of all habitat types in the Arctic"). The five Arctic nations have also entered into various natural resources management regimes for reindeer, fisheries, and polar bear.

60. See, e.g., "Treaty concerning the Archipelago of Spitsbergen and Protocol," Feb. 9, 1920; http://www.aeco.no/wp-content/uploads/2013/06/TheSvalbardTreaty.pdf (the parties to the treaty agreed to recognize Norway's sovereignty over the Archipelago of Spitsbergen in return for a commitment from Norway to demilitarize the area and allow all parties equal access to the area's natural resources, encourage scientific research, and establish an equitable administrative system) [hereinafter Treaty of Spitsbergen]; United Nations Convention on the Law of the Sea, Dec. 10, 1982, 1833 U.N.T.S. 397; Convention on the International Maritime Organization, March 6, 1948, 9 U.S.T. 621, 289 U.N.T.S. 48, at art. 52.

61. See, e.g., Polar Bear Population Agreement.

62. See, e.g., Canada and United States of America, "Agreement on Arctic Cooperation," Jan. 11, 1988, TIAS no. 31529, United States Treaties and Other International Agreements; https://treaties.un.org/doc/publication/unts/volume%201852/volume-1852-i-31529-english.pdf; Canada and the United States, "Agreement Between the Government of Canada and the Government of the United States of America on the Conservation of the Porcupine Caribou Herd," July 17, 1987, TIAS no. 11, 259; http://www.treaty-accord.gc.ca/text-texte.aspx?id=100687. This agreement gave rise to the Plan for the International Conservation of the Porcupine Caribou Herd; http://www.wmacns.ca/pdfs/13_PCH%20International%20Conservation%20Plan.pdf.

63. See, e.g., Treaty of Spitsbergen.
64. See, e.g., UNCLOS.
65. See ibid. Part XI. See also, James Harrison, "The International Seabed Authority and the Development of the Legal Regime for Deep Seabed Mining" (working paper no. 2010/17, University of Edinburgh School of Law, 2010); http://ssrn.com/abstract=1609687 (providing an excellent overview of the issues surrounding future governance decisions of the deep seabed).
66. Components of these sovereign legal regimes will be discussed in subsequent chapters of this book.
67. For a more thorough discussion of the Arctic legal regime, see Donald Rothwell, *The Polar Regions and the Development of International Law* (Chicago: University of Chicago Press, 1996). See also, Linda Nolan, "Arctic Legal Regime for Environmental Protection," (paper no. 44, at 5, IUCN Environmental Policy and Law, 2001); http://weavingaweb.org/pdfdocuments/EPLP44EN.pdf (describing gaps in the existing Arctic governance regime).
68. See, e.g., Oran Young, "Arctic Stewardship: Maintaining Regional Resilience in an Era of Global Change," *Ethics & International Affairs*, no. 26.4 (Jan. 7, 2013) (suggesting that prominent among expected effects in the Arctic "are rising surface temperatures, a deepening of the active layer of the permafrost, the collapse of sea ice, increases in the intensity of coastal storm surges made possible by the retreat of the sea ice, accelerated melting of the Greenland ice sheet, and the acidification of marine systems").
69. See, e.g., John Walsh et al., "Ongoing Climate Change in the Arctic," *Ambio* 40 (2011), doi: 10.1007/s13280-011-0211-z; Funk, "Arctic Landgrab." As the sea ice melts and/or thins, vast new tracts of water emerge. As a result, the global community anticipates obtaining access to deep sea resources and new shipping routes, creating a series of new governance challenges related to maritime access, ecosystem management, the well-being of indigenous peoples and safety and environmental issues surrounding the growth of the Arctic tourism industry. See also, The Ilulissat Declaration (in which the Arctic Coastal States declare that "[t]he Arctic Ocean stands at the threshold of significant changes. Climate change and the melting of ice have a potential impact on vulnerable ecosystems, the livelihoods of local inhabitants and indigenous communities, and the potential exploitation of natural resources").
70. *The Arctic Governance Project*, "Arctic Governance in an Era of Transformative Change."
71. The United Nations Convention on the Law of the Sea is the most relevant international agreement in this regard, but it does not regulate areas beyond national jurisdiction, for example, the high seas. This means—absent the settlement of continental shelf claims—much of the high seas of the Arctic are "open," or beyond national control or international regulation. There are

no well-defined, widely agreed upon guidelines for managing these areas or for protecting them from present or future misuse. See UNCLOS.

72. Recognizing potential limitations of the existing governance system, in May 2008—following Russia's decision to plant a flag in disputed Arctic territory—the five Arctic coastal states (Canada, Russia, Denmark, Norway, and the United States) with potential jurisdictional claims over the contested area of the Arctic Ocean negotiated the Ilulissat Declaration. Noting the changing conditions in the Arctic and the possibility of overlapping jurisdictional claims raising legal disputes in the future, the parties declared that "an extensive international legal framework applies to the Arctic Ocean" and that "[b]y virtue of their sovereignty, sovereign rights and jurisdiction in large areas of the Arctic Ocean the five coastal states are in a unique position to address these possibilities and challenges" within the legal framework that exists. By endorsing the continuing validity of existing legal instruments as the basis for settling existing and future disputes, the five nations sought to ensure that they would maintain primary—but not exclusive—responsibility for managing activities in the region, including questions of development and environmental protection. In this way, the declaration not only establishes a diplomatic framework for future peaceful negotiations, but also constitutes an effort, albeit discreet and indirect, to deter the negotiation of an alternative governance regime for the Arctic Ocean that might open governance of contested areas in the Arctic Ocean to a larger group of actors. See the Ilulissat Declaration, 1–2.

73. Mark Roberts, "Will Action on Short-Lived Climate Forcers Give the Arctic Time to Adapt?" in *Big Thaw* (2016).

74. See generally, Laura Boone, "Reducing Air Pollution from Marine Vessels to Mitigate Arctic Warming: Is It Time to Target Black Carbon?" *Carbon & Climate Law Review* 6, no. 1 (2012) (discussing the nature of the threat that black carbon poses to the Arctic and examining potential governance responses).

75. For an overview of the effects of short-lived pollutants, see "Integrated Assessment of Black Carbon and Tropospheric Ozone, UNEP/WMO Report," *United Nations Environment Program/World Meteorological Organization* (2011); http://www.unep.org/dewa/Portals/67/pdf/BlackCarbon_report.pdf.

76. See, Anjali D. Nanda, "India's Environmental Trump Card: How Reducing Black Carbon Through Common but Differentiated Responsibilities Can Curb Climate Change," *Denver Journal of International Law & Policy* 39, no. 3 (2011): 533–34 (explaining that while no international agreement currently addresses black carbon there are calls to address it through existing international agreements).

77. That is, would it be possible to reconceptualize Arctic governance more in line with AntArctic governance? See generally, The AntArctic Treaty, Dec. 1, 1959, 402 U.N.T.S. 71; http://www.ats.aq/documents/ats/treaty_original.

pdf. See also, Scott J. Shackelford, "The Tragedy of the Common Heritage of Mankind," *Stanford Environmental Law Journal* 27 (May 19, 2009): 123; http://ssrn.com/abstract=1407332.

78. See, e.g., Jennifer Jeffers, "Climate Change and the Arctic: Adapting to Changes in Fisheries Stocks and Governance Regimes," *Ecology Law Quarterly* 37, no. 1–2 (2010), doi: 10.1080/1088937X.2011.591919.

79. E.g., "Arctic Biodiversity Assessment: Report for Policy Makers," *Conservation of Arctic Flora and Fauna* (2013); http://www.Arcticbiodiversity.is/the-report/report-for-policy-makers.

80. "Agreement on Cooperation on Marine Oil Pollution Preparedness and Response in the Arctic," *The Arctic Council* (2013); http://www.Arctic-council.org/eppr/agreement-on-cooperation-on-marine-oil-pollution-preparedness-and-response-in-the-Arctic/.

81. See, e.g., Robin Kundis Craig, "Becoming Landsick: Rethinking Sustainability in an Age of Continuous, Visible, and Irreversible Change," in *Rethinking Sustainable Development to Meet the Climate Change Challenge*, ed. Jessica Owley and Keith Hirokawa (Environmental Law Institute, 2014 forthcoming); http://papers.ssrn.com/sol3/papers.cfm?abstract_id=2270076 (discussing how the "reality of constant change and threatened disruption" necessitates changes in how we think about environmental decision making).

82. See generally, Randall S. Abate and Elizabeth Ann Kronk, "Commonality Among Unique Indigenous Communities: An Introduction to Climate Change and its Impact on Indigenous Peoples," *Tulane Environmental Law Journal* 26 (Feb. 7, 2013); http://ssrn.com/abstract=2213506.

83. See, e.g., Mark Nuttall et al., "Hunting, Herding, Fishing, and Gathering: Indigenous Peoples and Renewable Resource Use in the Arctic," in *Arctic Climate Impact Assessment Scientific Report* (Cambridge: Cambridge University Press, 2005): 649–90.

84. See, e.g., *Native Village of Kivalina v. ExxonMobil Corp.*, 663 F. Supp.2d 863 (N.D. Cal. 2009) (wherein the native Village of Kivalina—the governing body for an Inupiat Eskimo village—"alleges that as a result of global warming, the Arctic sea ice that protects the Kivalina coast from winter storms has diminished, and that the resulting erosion and destruction will require the relocation of Kivalina's residents."); Ibid., 868.

85. Petition to the Inter American Commission on Human Rights Seeking Relief From Violations Resulting from Global Warming Caused by Acts and Omissions of the United States, *The Inuit Circumpolar Conference*, Dec. 7, 2005; http://earthjustice.org/sites/default/files/library/legal_docs/petition-to-the-inter-american-commission-on-human-rights-on-behalf-of-the-inuit-circumpolar-conference.pdf.

86. Kundis Craig, "Becoming Landsick," 79.

87. Ibid.

88. United Nations General Assembly, *Protection of Global Climate for Present and Future Generations of Mankind*, A/RES/45/212 (Dec. 21, 1990); http://www.un.org/documents/ga/res/45/a45r212.htm.

89. Ibid., preamble.

90. See generally, Carlarne, "The Future of the UNFCCC."

PART 3

14

Polar Communities and Cultures in Addressing Climate Change

Errol Meidinger, Ezra B. W. Zubrow,
and Kim Diana Connolly

How we humans respond to climate change varies greatly among different cultural groups and communities. Our responses reflect differing experiences, traditions, and approaches to problem solving, particularly with respect to nature.

Although they face many similar problems, local cultures in the polar regions vary widely. That variability is likely to be both a challenge and a strength in addressing climate change. It will be a challenge to achieving shared understandings and coordination among the diverse cultures. But that diversity may also be a strength because of the range of experiences and understandings that polar communities can bring to the effort. The rich variability of polar cultural traditions also adds an essential layer to the operation of the governance institutions and challenges presented in Part 2. Cultural orientations will be decisive in the project of achieving effective polar governance to address climate change.

The chapters in this Part explore community understandings of nature in several different places and times. They are intended suggest the kinds of factors that will be important in harnessing community capacity to address climate change. We are now in a time where many more such studies will be essential to effectively addressing climate change in the Arctic.

We begin with three historical studies. In the first, T. L. Thurston provides an analysis of societal adaptation in "Livelihood and Resilience in a Marginal Northern Environment: 1,000 Years on the Småland Plateau." After making a strong plea for better incorporation of social science findings into climate change adaptation studies prepared by physical scientists, Thurston presents a rich synthesis of research on climate adaptation in an agriculturally marginal region subjected to sharp ecological swings. The Småland Plateau cooled markedly and became relatively depopulated between 400 to 800 CE; subsequently, the region experienced sustained warming (although it is still relatively "cool" for a temperate region). Throughout the period, it built a resilient culture of solidarity, entrepreneurship, and independence, maintaining a degree of autonomy from the state and expanding citizen participation and activism in the face of the industrial revolution. Thurston ventures the hope that, on the cusp of another, and probably greater set of climate change challenges, Småland society will be able to achieve the increased collaboration and partnerships necessary to sustain itself in a new normal.

In "The Holocene Catastrophe," André Costopoulos contrasts the Holocene, the relatively long and stable period we appear to be transitioning out of, with the period 18,000 to 10,000 years ago, when sea levels rose 125 meters and human populations necessarily relocated and reorganized, and did so quickly. They were able to adapt in part because they were hunter-gatherers intent on solving their immediate problems—finding food and shelter—and did not tie themselves or their self-understandings to fixed locations. In contrast, during the relatively stable Holocene, societies have tied themselves to territories through elaborate property, governmental, and cultural structures, and have made major investments in the places they inhabit. They identify places by who lives there and who "owns" them rather than how they can best be lived in. Costopoulos argues that, as presently constituted, our understandings of place are likely to severely hobble our adaptation to climate change, and that much adaptation is likely to be highly conflictual as refugees from climate change are rejected and possibly subjected to violence by other settled societies. Costopoulos hopes that we might learn from the pre-Holocene period to "value problem solving algorithms rather than the specific solutions" they generated.

In "Effects of Natural and Social Stressors on Human Biology: Northern Sweden in the Little Ice Age," Theodore Steegmann presents early results from a study using historic data to examine climate change in northern Sweden, its impact on humans, and how they responded between the fourteenth and nineteenth centuries. The chapter catalogues the multiple additional stressors affecting the medieval Norse population of the region, including epidemics, poor land, misguided governance institutions, and war. It then argues that by learning how they managed to navigate those challenges the research can contribute valuable findings on how to foster resilience in the face of the current era of rapid climate change. Like Thurston, Steegmann argues that the "collapse" scenario popularly associated with the work of Jared Diamond does not take adequate account of the record of human resilience and resourcefulness in northern societies.

The struggle for resilience in today's polar world was vividly illustrated at the conference in "Surviving Climate Change," a film produced by Sarah Elder in collaboration with members of the Yup'ik Eskimo community of Emmonak, Alaska. Elder's paper in this volume draws upon film footage to document Yup'ik people's perceptions and responses to climate change in this remote sub-Arctic village, which is only two meters above sea level in the huge Yukon River Delta. Arctic life has always been a delicate balance between great food abundance one moment and the threat of nonsurvival the next. Yup'ik culture encompasses this tension with alert appreciation. While the sense of threat is rising, it is not totally new. Residents talk about how they plan to stay and adapt, basing their hopes for successful adaptation on long experience while acknowledging that the threats are new and unsettling.

In "Resilience, Reindeer, Oil, and Climate Change: Challenges Facing the Nenets Indigenous People in the Russian Arctic," Maria S. Tysiachniouk, Laura Henry, and Svetlana A. Tulaeva present their research on another northern indigenous group, reindeer herders in Arctic Russia. Representing four different communities and organized in forms ranging from private brigades to collective farms, the herders face common challenges arising from rapidly changing economic and political conditions, as well as significant oil and gas development on their territory. They are only beginning to recognize the dangers posed by climate change. In seeking to assess the degree and nature of the herders' resilience to these challenges the authors find that the herders' effectiveness in seeking compensation for the effects of oil and gas development and in managing their relations to the local and regional authorities depends on their ability to document damage to the tundra and their familiarity with their rights under different models of corporate social responsibility and Russian law. However, even the most capable communities are at risk of hobbling dependency on financial support from the oil and gas sector and have little control over how the resources transferred to them are used in practice.

Extending the examination of modern culture to an urban context, Enrique del Acebo Ibañez explores how young urban dwellers can become more attentive to climate change. The chapter focuses particularly on the requirements and effects of human rootedness, which involves linking social imaginaries (shared cultural visions of life) with everyday living patterns. Findings from a survey of young inhabitants of Buenos Aires highlight the primary role of mass media in individual perceptions of environmental issues. The research also indicates that individuals feel more responsible for environmental problems when they are rooted in the community where such issues take place. Many survey participants did not feel there was a link between environmental problems in their home country and similar issues in other countries. Acebo Ibañez ultimately highlights the problem of cultural disconnect, which may impede meaningful transboundary discourse on climate change in the Arctic, an issue that inherently requires both local and global cooperation.

Finally, in "Future?" Torill Christine Lindstrøm shifts our attention to modern Norwegian society and the question of how to motivate behavior more attentive and adaptive to climate change among people living developed lifestyles. Arguing that sanctions and threats are ineffective, Lindstrøm advocates the importance of human contact with nature in motivating desirable behavioral changes such as reduced consumption, collective commuting, recycling, reduced population, and increased energy prices. Lindstrøm draws on her experience in Friends of the Earth-Norway to illustrate the centrality of nature in Norwegian culture. She argues that particular types of increased contact with nature, such as child care and nature schooling, will result in changed environmental and political positions, as well as new adaptive behaviors for Arctic societies. To facilitate this process, Lindstrøm calls for new legislation allowing everyone to be free in nature and mandating outdoor activities tied to nature.

In closing, as editors we note that the chapters in this Part suggest only a few of the potential lessons that can be drawn from local polar cultures in addressing climate change. We hope they will help provoke a much more extensive, highly imaginative inquiry into our cultural algorithms of adaptation, survival, and care.

15

Livelihood and Resilience in a Marginal Northern Environment

1,000 Years on the Småland Plateau

T. L. Thurston

Introduction

This long-term analysis of human, climate, and environmental interactions in a marginal northern environment—the Småland Plateau in central Sweden (Figure 15.1)—is presented with the hope of demonstrating how deeply one must dig into the past to understand the present. This involves examination of current and historic documents, the exegesis of ancient texts, the record of climate and ecological data, and archaeological evidence. Beginning in the present and moving back through multiple examples of what others have deemed "starting points" for understanding current issues reveals flaws inherent in some approaches.

While there are a number of highly technical accounts of socio-ecological sequences in the distant past—written by archaeologists for other archaeologists—most material presented for public consumption has been produced by nonarchaeologists, typically written to sell books, and are consequently shallow and full of errors or omissions.

Critique of such publications has been substantial and long standing,[1] yet has had little impact on the public's thirst for good stories. Rather

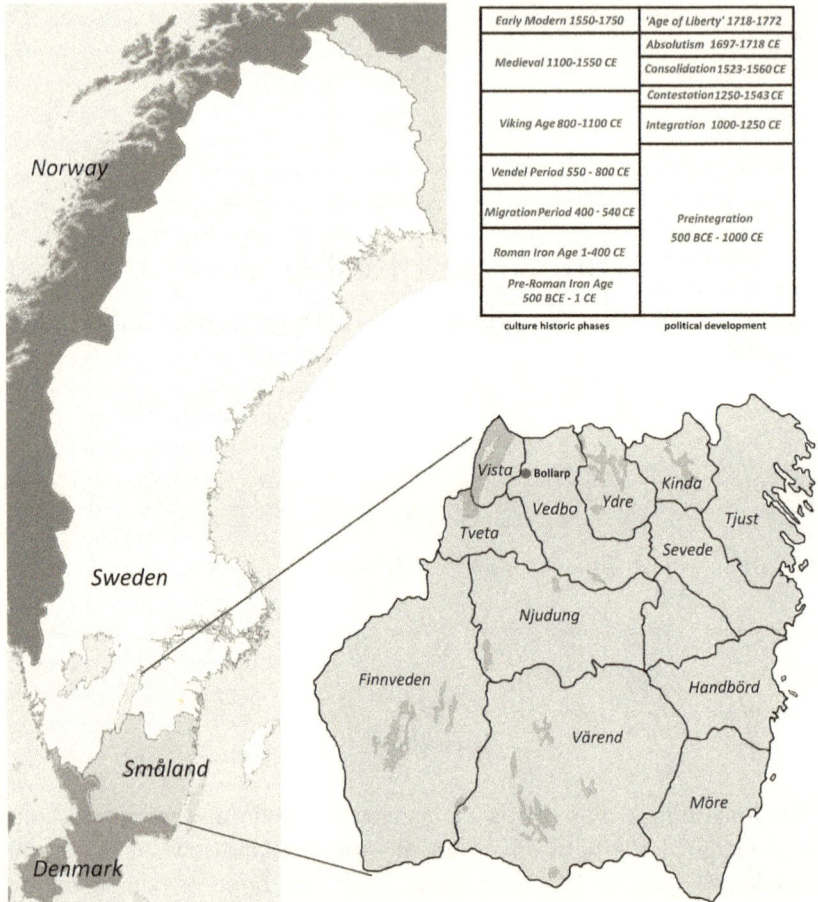

culture historic phases	political development
Early Modern 1550-1750	'Age of Liberty' 1718-1772
	Absolutism 1697-1718 CE
Medieval 1100-1550 CE	Consolidation 1523-1560 CE
	Contestation 1250-1543 CE
Viking Age 800-1100 CE	Integration 1000-1250 CE
Vendel Period 550 - 800 CE	
Migration Period 400 - 540 CE	Preintegration 500 BCE - 1000 CE
Roman Iron Age 1-400 CE	
Pre-Roman Iron Age 500 BCE - 1 CE	

Figure 15.1. Sweden and Småland in geographic and chronological context.

than adding to the critique, I present a new case study from a context less familiar, avoiding any doomsday or utopian scenarios.

An Urgent Expedition into the Past, Unfortunately without a Time Machine

Just as debates over climate change started to feel "tired" to much of the public, the observable and sometimes painful impacts of increased and intensified storminess, drought, flooding, and unusual heat or cold have created a new urgency surrounding the historical context of human-environment interactions. This has led the natural sciences community on a renewed quest for better historical understanding of climate change, with the expectation that it will produce tools for prediction of future impacts on human life.

It is therefore somewhat disappointing that when climate and other geophysical scientists consider human action and reaction to shifting conditions, their projections frequently lack expertise on actual human behavior. While a small number seek social science data to flesh out their theoretical models, the majority are uninterested. A number of organizations have attempted to bridge this gap.

The issues? A 2004 workshop at Australia's Queensland University, focused on uniting the social and natural sciences, produced the following:

ANTHROPOLOGIST: "So, how are you integrating the social sciences into your research programme?"

REGIONAL CATCHMENT GROUP MANAGER: "Well . . . er . . . we are talking to a lot of people, so we figure we have got that covered."[2]

Despite the group manager's amusing cluelessness about what social scientists do or what importance it might have, it is actually a rather positive response: that of a self-selected workshop attendee. We are just as likely to hear, "Why would anyone want to do that?" or "I'm very busy and don't have time for this."

Understandably, this has much to do with the heavy expectations for publishing and research within the narrow bounds of each discipline, especially when university and government research funding is rarely classified or offered in trans/inter/cross-disciplinary formats, terms that in themselves have been poorly defined, although there have been attempts.[3] Most urgent calls for saving the planet through such collaborations come from the social sciences.[4] Fischer et al. (2011) reviewed and analyzed 81 papers with similar themes and found that outside of more and more "reviews" of the issues and problems, there was almost no actual collaborative work. The authors point out the danger of the mounting number of review articles—they give the impression that more is happening when it is not. Others have called for training in interdisciplinary competency, but studies reveal that social science components in natural science coursework largely consist of "an add-on in the final session of a natural science based component of the programme or module. Niesenbaum and Lewis (2003)[5] concluded that 'interdisciplinary' aspects tended to be marginalized rather than integrated throughout, leading them to state that interdisciplinarity is being 'ghettoized.' "[6]

This is also strikingly apparent when moving from theoretical to specific cases. A lack of reasonable perspective about the difference between the time scale of the human lifespan and the geological process is often lacking. For example, on the scale of a human lifetime, deglaciation after the last Ice Age occurred in a highly varied manner—one valley before another nearby, one coastline earlier than one only 50 miles away—creating unique human patterns directly related to local iterations of planetary climate processes. Hence, for example, as part of a specific discussion of *human action* in a landscape, some humor greets the geophysicist's pronouncement that an archaeological interpretation is clearly "wrong" because deglaciation impacted an entire latitude "at the same time." Yes, "at the same time" when the increment of time is 1,000 years, but no, when archaeological data show the successive occupation of newly de-iced territory with every 20- or 30-year generation, revealing the ways in which people pioneer and inhabit newly available land. Would this not be relevant to understanding what is likely to happen in our lifetimes as the Arctic ice melts and people begin to establish along newly open polar shipping lanes?

It is inherent in most social sciences to consciously consider how multiple temporal and spatial scales operate simultaneously. We are taught this as graduate students and take it to heart. It is not the fault of the natural scientists that they are not taught this and rarely consider it. The unfortunate outcome, which eventually disseminates to the public, is research about hypothetical actors that lacks data on real people, yet makes many implicit and explicit assumptions about what humans "have done" and "will do."

The social sciences can be similarly myopic. In many instances, researchers look at the recent past to understand the consequences of climate and environmental changes, such as desertification, habitat destruction, shifting food supply, and water access on the human population, using short-term (decadal) indicators of change. Their themes are steeped in detailed knowledge about human motives and intentions but tend to cast problems as quite "suddenly" occurring. The longer-term perspective of many geological, biological, *and* human social processes is missing. Among historians, the boundary between the historic periods and their preceding prehistoric or protohistoric antecedents sometimes forms an intellectual barrier to studying the long record of continuity or change; a curtain comes down between processes occurring in historic and prehistoric times, as if there were no connections between them simply because people did not write things down.

Despite the inertia of individual disciplines, the last two decades have seen the appearance of a small but vocal advocacy for unified research and a number of funding sources that promote it, such as the National Science Foundation's programs in Arctic Social Sciences; Dynamics of Coupled Natural and Human Systems; Science, Engineering, and Education for Sustainability; and Infrastructure Management and Extreme Events.

It is the nature of anthropological archaeology to more intentionally and substantively unite the social and natural and the long and short term, especially for those specializing in environmental or landscape archaeology. A large, specifically archaeological literature addressing socionatural processes can be attributed to environmental archaeologists. Some of these have garnered extradisciplinary attention by publishing in *Nature, Science,* and *Proceedings of the National Academy of Sciences.*[7]

In addition, many archaeologists have collaborated in syntheses with other scientists around issues of climate, weather, and environmental change.[8] As an analogue, several organizations have appeared to unite the disciplines more effectively: the Association for Environmental Studies and Sciences, The Integrated History and Future of People on Earth, The Resilience Alliance, The North Atlantic Biocultural Organization, The International Network of Research on Coupled Human and Natural Systems, and the National Science Foundation's Arctic Social Science–sponsored Global Human Ecodynamics Alliance initiative.

In Europe, there has been success with connecting research with policy. Archaeologist Sander van der Leeuw directed a multimillion-euro project for the European Union from 1992–1999 seeking the origins of poverty and land degradation in southern Europe. The project coordinated 65 natural and social sciences researchers from 11 institutions and traced the ecological and social roots of the issues as far back as the Neolithic period 6,000 years ago. This work included a subproject on the problems that scientists encounter in communicating important findings and guidance to politicians. After chairing numerous scientific councils in Europe, van der Leeuw is now based in the United States, but it is doubtful whether he or others will be tapped for reinventing future policy in North America. Despite this, as public anxiety about climate change increases, we find it more and more common to field questions from the general public.

Resilience, Panarchy, Adaptation, and Remembering

The analysis of socionatural problems rarely concerns *only* the climate, or culture, or history. Human/nature interactions are among the most complex relationships one can hope to untangle. The following case study illustrates the particular ways in which archaeologists focus on the theorization and reconstruction of human behavior in the past, behavior vis-à-vis not only other humans, but also the natural world. This means nature not only as a source of resources, food, and shelter, but also as an experienced sensory world, a nature commoditized, politicized, sacralized, gendered, and otherwise manipulated: physically constructed through labor and ideationally constructed through beliefs, rituals, rules, and concepts and other often-intangible influences.

In this context, climate change is about much more than phenomena such as rising sea levels, drought, or the immediate impacts of unanticipated environmental realities on human communities. One of the most successful unifying conceptual constructs is Resilience Theory, which stems from the notion that nature, once characterized by eighteenth- and nineteenth-century European scientists as hierarchic, is now understood to be far from it—in fact, it is heterarchic, with many separate miniature hierarchies, all working at the same time, interdependent yet independent of each other's internal workings.

Gunderson and Hollings (2002)[9] use the example of sea ice changes, fisheries failures, desertification, and agricultural failures, which appear to be related to independent local conditions but are in reality all connected through underlying causes. In order to unify understanding of social and natural causes and outcomes, they recast the old term *panarchy* as a way of understanding interrelatedness on many temporal and spatial scales and among many types of dynamic process.

The world is a type of laboratory of human behaviors and responses, a culmination of all the trial and error in particular sets of circumstances. People connect their understanding of their current conditions with their remembrance of past events to help them make decisions that keep society stable and uninterrupted. We must imagine that there are two scales of human action, a cycle of quick responses and experiments dealing rapidly with events as they occur, and a longer cycle of stability in human organization, based on remembering and applying accumulated experience, even as experimentation continues.

At a point where change is occurring, two concepts are important: *remember* and *revolt*.[10] *Remember* is long-term accumulation of knowledge and slow processes of stability. *Revolt* occurs when the fast actions, decisions, and experiments overwhelm the slow, stabilizing cycles. An immediate response is needed to a quick-moving problem, and stabilization and continuity are temporarily discarded.

Yet these quick decision-making cycles often result in adjustments to the long stabilizing cycles through adaptation to new conditions or change in the relationships among people, other people, and nature. When we are lucky, our way of life is altered but not beyond recognition. We eventually will run out of fossil fuels, for example, but the relatively quick phase of experimentation and development of alternative energy may allow us to survive it relatively unscathed, even though life will be somewhat different than it is right now. Then, we will enter a new stability phase in our use of energy until some future time when revolt must again occur.

There are some processes and events, however, that are so destabilizing that there is no renewal after revolt but instead a "release"—the system and everything about it collapses and must be entirely reorganized.[11] Sometimes the human desire for short-term social and economic expedience leads to longer-term collapse and release, since the source of the expedient solution is "brittle" or "fragile"—reliance on a scarce or dwindling resource or an unsustainable way of life. The best-case scenario is to avoid this by making the right decisions during revolt phases, leading to renewal rather than release. Within the framework of Resilience Theory, the ability to do this is described as resilience.

When we examine any long-term sequence of human/nature interaction, we have to make sure we are not looking only at a single "revolt" cycle—a short-term flurry of activity—but also understand what came before and what happened after. Otherwise, it is impossible to determine the connection between long-term interrelationships and *why things happen*. We can keep this in mind as we examine the long-term processes and the events that impacted the people of the Småland Plateau over a period of 1,000 years and more.

Time Depth and Recursive Processes

Archaeologists, even those studying the more recent past, look at much longer time frames than other social scientists, especially in terms of identifying the origins and trajectories of socionatural processes. We try to think not only in terms of environmental impacts on humans, but also human impacts on the environment.[12] This includes human ingenuity in creating practices that can mitigate or overcome environmental and climate challenges as well as human failures and, much more often, the tenuous maintenance of an imperfect status quo.

To an agricultural economist, contemporary African migrations due to desertification might seem to be a problem that begins when regional desiccation and deforestation affects the soils, moisture regime, and the cereal farming livelihood of large groups of people, and they are uprooted. To a cultural anthropologist or rural sociologist, the process might begin in nineteenth-century colonial times as a result of European intervention. Varied agricultural economies were reduced to monocropping for export production, with introduced species and methods unsuitable to the local habitat. This in turn disrupted cultural traditions and food production methods, leading to hunger and overexploitation of land.

To an archaeologist, in addition to these essential observations, the climate record, the paleoecological record, and the archaeological record must be studied in terms of centuries or millennia—as far back in time as possible—to understand the way of life in a particular land-scape through time. We might first ask, does today's population have deep ancestral roots in the region? If not, when did they first arrive and who was there a thousand years before? What where the environmental conditions a millennia or two or five millennia ago, when they first took up residence in the area? We might ask what livelihoods were apparent in the region through time—foraging, herding, farming? Have there been other periods of migration? What were the causes? Have people responded to prehistoric episodes of desertification in the same way, or were there other solutions, such as landscape manipulation or changes in livelihood? Were the alternatives open to local people narrowed by processes related to Modernity, and thus no longer available as possible recourse to cope with environmental challenges? It might have been much easier to change a way of life or use a new technology three thousand years ago than within today's sharply bordered nation-states.

The study of the current and the recent past are both important, but they do not answer all our questions or provide a context from which long-term extrapolations can be made. Archaeology adds depth through the integration of different types of data and allows us to move much farther back, ask bigger questions, and create a broader and more meaningful picture than studies of the decades immediately surrounding some episode of change or even a few preceding centuries. Livelihood failure is never attributable solely to external factors such as climate change and should always be viewed in the context of social processes. It is also rare for such processes to consist only of reaction or response to such change—there is always proaction, even if it is counterproductive.

Modern sustainable entrepreneurship is a concern of science, government, and business leaders. To succeed in the present, we need to understand long-term cycles of socionatural resilience in the past. It takes centuries of trial and error to create flexible, adaptable strategies and avoid a way of life that is " 'overconnected' or 'brittle,' allowing small-scale transformations to 'revolt' and explode into larger-scale crises."[13] The livelihood systems in much of the developed and developing world are overly brittle, and we do not have centuries to alter our way of life. We can, however, learn from the study of other people's failures and successes over long sequences of time.

Livelihood and Resilience in a Marginal Northern Environment

The Småland Plateau in south-central Sweden has a long history of marginality: a high latitude; extremely rocky, boulder-strewn upland with low temperatures; a brief growing season; and thin moraine soils beneath ubiquitous swamps and heavy forests (Figure 15. 1). Since the beginning of farming here five thousand years ago, and in all the subsequent eras, every slight or major climate downturn has seen widespread abandonment,[14] and toward the end of the Little Ice Age in the nineteenth century, the vast majority of Swedish emigration originated here, making Småland the ancestral home for most Swedish American communities in North America. It remains a hard place to be a farmer. Yet at some point, the population developed a livelihood that allowed a viable persistence for those who remained, and as textual evidence accumulated through the centuries, it becomes clear that they remained on the Småland Plateau not only out of necessity but because they were very much attached to it.

Despite the difficulty of life in such rugged terrain and unfavorable climate, contemporary Småland is also known today as a region of high tech companies, advanced research and development, and a "knowledge economy" that spawns successful entrepreneurs at an unusual rate. According to the European Union, Småland ranks high among "the top twenty 'knowledge economies' in Europe [that] are accounted for by Sweden (7 locales), the UK (6 locales), Germany (2 locales), Belgium (2 locales), France and Italy (1 each)."[15]

The growth of such an economy in this particular region of Sweden has taken researchers by surprise, as it has occurred mainly during a period when Swedish industrial manufacturing has declined. Upon closer examination, the modern focus on high tech, information technology, business to business, and supply line industries is only the latest in a series of transformative reinventions of livelihood in the region, precipitated by climate change, difficult environmental conditions, and in response to governmental demands for taxes and labor, no matter how poor the taxpayer.

The most well-known recent example of a Småland success might be the career of Ingvar Kamprad,[16] who as a boy in the 1930s sold matches, fish, Christmas tree decorations, seeds, pencils, and chairs from his bicycle in order to fund his entrepreneurial ideas and eventually the IKEA concept. Due to the heavily forested landscape, many other large furniture concerns originated here as well.

Småland's Kosta Boda glass company was founded in 1742 and its rival Orrefors in 1898, pyrotechnic industries enabled by the wall-to-wall carpet of forest covering the region. The Paris Exhibition of the 1920s made Småland's glass industry world famous, and the brands continue to succeed today, their cachet connected to perception of superior Swedish design.[17] Within Sweden, 15 glass manufacturers were born and remain in Småland.

Still earlier, the large-scale mechanized manufacture and distribution of safety matches was developed in mid—nineteenth-century Jönköping, Småland's largest urban center. Using the plentiful wood supply and hydropower from the many steep waterfalls cascading off the plateau, the Lundström brothers exported the product globally beginning in 1855. This made Jönköping the "match capital" of the world at a time when this was a leading-edge technology.[18] Eventually, matchstick conglomerates were formed under industrialist Ivar Kreuger, with more than 170 factories in production. In each of these cases, someone's good idea was copied by others, competing against each other, yet all succeeding.

Even farther back in time, abundant hydropower, iron ore, and charcoal production made Småland a hub for iron production and manufacturing. Industrial-scale iron production was established in the Viking Age, becoming a state interest when warfare with neighboring Denmark became a concern for the Swedish state between 1448 and 1790. What is today called Scania, the southernmost part of Sweden, belonged to Denmark until 1658.

This made Småland the border between two warring nations for centuries, making life miserable for those in the path of constant burning and pillaging. Yet it also made Småland the most convenient place to produce both iron and weapons in the region, rather than from similar resources in the far north of Sweden. Beginning in 1620, the Swedish crown established the Jönköping Rifle Factory, expanding it in 1689 to the city of Husqvarna, the near neighbor of Jönköping, which became home to the Husqvarna Company. As a private enterprise from 1757 onward, it grew to be the "factory to the world"[19] in the nineteenth and twentieth centuries, expanding from weaponry to cook stoves, sewing machines, bicycles, and today's chainsaws, snow blowers, lawnmowers, and motorcycles.

It can therefore be argued that the region has a long history of what were, each in its own time, major innovations and technological advances based on local industries developed originally as small-scale enterprises. Each enterprise then spawned friendly competitors. The industrial history of this unlikely marginal area—and its impacts at home and abroad throughout time—have been the subject of scores of theses and dissertations from academics in business, accounting, and related areas of study. The reality of the success is especially reflected in the recent European Union studies that place Småland so high in the rankings of knowledge economies, vital not just to Sweden but also to European information technology industries.[20]

Economic Development in the "Kingdom of Stones"

Yet at the same time, Småland was and continues to be a symbol of harsh living conditions for the majority of its inhabitants—small farmers seen as hardy and resourceful. Vilhelm Moberg, Sweden's best-known twentieth-century novelist, wrote about the hardships of life in his native province and labeled it *Stenriket*, or "the kingdom of stones," where people of the *stengardar* or "stone farms" scratched out a living (Moberg 1949).[21] More frequently, it is called *morka Småland*, or dark Småland, due to the forest that covers 90 percent of the modern and ancient region.

This characterization, like the region's industrial history, also goes far back in time. In 1890, the Swedish encyclopedia *Nordisk Familjebok*, a Victorian household staple,[22] noted that "The Smålandian is by nature alert and clever, diligent and hard-working, yet compliant, cunning and crafty, which gives him the advantage of being able to move through life with little means."[23]

In fact, economic success and tenacity are often linked to this history of a difficult livelihood in a harsh environment that left a mark on local character: free enterprise, hardiness, thrift, inventiveness, and the ability to make something out of nothing. In Ceccato and Persson's (2002, 2003)[24] work on economics in peripheral regions, a number of interviews reflect this notion, such as this respondent identified as a "local entrepreneur":

> I have felt this, as an inhabitant of Småland province. The Smålanders have never got anything for free. We have always been prepared to drudge and toil for our way of living, and being able to live where we want. We want to maintain what we have. That is why I have the position I do today and try to forge together various authorities and pull them in the same direction.[25]

Likewise, this "representative of a local organization": "Put a Smålander on a boulder in the sea and he will manage. Another sign of a Smålander is that he only opens his wallet to put money into it."[26]

Ceccato and Persson[27] (2003, 14–15) also note that "compared to other 'deprived regions' in Sweden, [Småland] is known as 'an independent region'—always receiving very little help from the central government and laterally from the EU (especially compared to the northernmost regions)" with very similar conditions and economy. Many authors, and most Smålanders, have noted this contrast—that the region has been, and still is, considered to be "deprived" yet always overcomes its own drawbacks.

A once widely held paradigm attributed current Swedish attitudes to the post–World War II "welfare state," yet current research on the socioeconomic legacy of early Sweden does not support this. Today, most historians, economists, and sociologists examining the relationship among industrialists, the government, and the working class point to cultural traditions stretching far back in time: a political system where the ability to stay in power has long been reliant on the good will of the laboring and farming sectors.[28]

More recently, business researcher Nuur (2005) has added to the contemporary theory[29] that this is generally a manifestation of local culture: Life as a farmer in tight-knit communities combined with the harsh living conditions of the sixteenth and seventeenth centuries fostered mental hardiness and community ties that were conducive to productive entrepreneurship. "In Sweden, the Gnosjö region located in the province of Småland in southeast Sweden showed the pattern . . . of generating small enterprises . . . shown to combine competition and collaboration. The presence of socio-economic networks that created a breeding ground for entrepreneurship was observed."[30]

> The ability of the region [is] to foster entrepreneurial activi-
> ties and nurture a climate of trust between the economic
> actors *through embedded relations that span through the commu-*
> *nity*. . . . According to Gummesson (1997), the foundations
> of this spirit started in the sixteenth century when a weapon
> factory was established in the scarcely populated, small-farming
> area.[31] (my italics)

This climate of trust between economic actors with commu-
nity-embedded relations is referred to as "the Gnosjö Spirit," which according to Gummesson (1997) started in the sixteenth century as the iron industry and weapons trade began to rise and foreign gunsmiths were brought into the region and taught new methods to locals. After the death of the warmongering Swedish king Charles XII and Sweden's defeat in the Great Northern War, Gummesson (1997) argues that the now self-employed local blacksmiths, experiencing a steep drop off in demand for weaponry, were motivated to band together to expand their

craft into a number of other manufacturing areas. This, it is argued, explains the region's unique entrepreneurial history.

Yet the belief that "the Gnosjö Spirit" originates in the Early Modern era is a shallow perspective. Important threads of Småland's history are found in the centuries when the Husqvarna company was established, a good example of a relationship among marginalized farmers, shrewd craft specialists, government, and "big business," but to claim that this is the root of the relationship is myopic—unmindful of any processes or events before the sixteenth and seventeenth centuries—and a familiar issue for scholars who study long-term cycles.

The Ever-Present Past

If we return to the notion that the social and natural environments of Småland have a relationship to its people's many unexpected successes and somewhat unusual livelihoods, we can deconstruct the nineteenth and twentieth centuries' popular description of the Smålander cited above. *Thriftiness* describes the seeking of income and advantage in any way possible. *Alert and clever, diligent and hardworking*, often coupled with the idea of free enterprise, were commentary on the popular perception that the region suffered extreme poverty. *Compliant, cunning, and crafty* are euphemisms for stubborn resistance to unwanted restrictions while giving the impression of submission, a typical strategy employed by oppressed people and often found among the "weapons of the weak."[32]

Nevertheless, there are many parts of Sweden—and the world— where industries take advantage of resources, but do not create entrepreneurs out of their most deprived populations. Farming aside, the nature of Småland's environment—and its mineral, biological, and hydrological wealth—has been exploited since the earliest occupation of the uplands. These conditions are necessary but not sufficient to explain the strategies and nature of the Småland people.

I would argue that there is another important ingredient in the region's development in addition to the natural environment and the industries well suited to that environment's resources. This important ingredient is *conflict*: a long history of antagonism toward the state, over integration itself, and then unwanted surveillance, laws, taxes, trade regulation, even religion, leading to successful attempts to conceal, evade, deny, and take up arms, individually and collectively. Many of the region's notable social strategies are as old as the Swedish state, when the Smålanders first learned to thrive despite the imposition of laws and taxes imposed from above. This tradition continues today. Many natives of the Småland upland continue to deprive authority by any means possible as well as challenge administrative structures that intrude, unwanted, on their way of life.

Småland before Modernity

Much of Sweden's history in which Småland's is enfolded is a struggle between royal authority and ordinary people. There are, however, differences between Småland and other provinces that proved significant. First we must examine the important governing role of the ordinary people, or *folk*, that extends far back in time. To begin, we can look to the establishment of the first *Riksdag*, or parliament, in Sweden, which occurred in 1435. Its first iteration was an invention of the nobility as resistance to royal excesses, and under government authority in 1527, it was explicitly directed to represent four groups: aristocrats, clergy, merchants, and farmers.

Yet, this was preceded by the so-called Swedish Magna Carta—the 1319 Charter of Liberties—between the king and the nobles, who claimed to protect the peasantry. In 1330, this document was amended to include a written and spoken oath, taken upon election—yes, kings were popularly elected—that the king would obey the law, especially in regard to taxation.[33] This oath was incorporated into national law in 1350.

One might point out that Magna Carta–like documents were presented to rulers all over Europe in the thirteenth through the sixteenth centuries and that many regions had local assemblies. While these formats were found in many parts of Europe, Scandinavia—including Sweden—differed substantively because there was a traditionally "electoral monarchy, the lack of true feudalism and serfdom, and the strong position of a landowning yeoman-type of peasantry . . . [and] lay dominance in the judiciary [that] came to be one of the cornerstones of Swedish legal cultural identity."[34]

Yet, the idea of lay commoners as participants in their own government was itself not at all novel; it was rooted in a far older system, that of the Nordic/Germanic "public territorial assemblies (e.g., *moots* or *things*) [which] formed the main venues for administration or legal affairs, resolving individual disputes as well as making more general rules. Such traditions of "participatory justice" continued at the local level until the High Middle Ages."[35] Kings—and before them, chieftains—were called upon to stand before the assembly and justify actions affecting the community, such as warfare or changes in the law. If the vote of the *thing* went against them, the ruler was expected to stand down and abandon his plans.

Småland before History

The *thing/ting/moot* assembly was active in the medieval era and later, but is far older, stretching back into prehistoric times. It was emphasized and further encoded in the fourteenth and fifteenth centuries because of royal attempts to erode these rights as kingship in the region developed and changed. The reason the format is indeed seen across Europe is that it was not especially endemic to the North, or to Nordic or Germanic people, but rather to the Iron Age, as previously discussed.[36]

Because of the Roman conquest of much of Europe, the tradition of political assembly was abrogated, surviving only in its very local forms. In Scandinavia and northern Germany—which never were conquered by the Romans—and in England—which was de-Romanized by "Anglo-Saxon" immigration from Scandinavia, Germany, and the Netherlands—the notion of the nested assembly continued. Local, regional, and national king-electing assemblies all operated simultaneously, at different locales and frequencies, addressing different levels of jurisprudence and decision making. Similar forms survived in both Scotland and Ireland, among Celtic-speaking rather than Germanic-speaking peoples, also lying outside former Roman imperial borders.

Let us then discover the true origin of the distributed system of governing power, which in turn created an independent and resistant Småland. "Sweden" developed from an earlier polity known as the Svear state or kingdom, which formed in the later part of the Iron Age (500 BCE–800 CE). In the earlier period, the Bronze Age (1700–500 BCE), society in northern Europe (and beyond) exhibited clear distinctions between elite and common in both wealth and symbolic status. A small minority displayed large houses, enormous cattle sheds indicating owner-ship of massive herds, monumental grave mounds, distinctive exotic and local wealth items, and restricted access to metals and weapons.

Across much of Europe, the Bronze Age ended in upheaval, with signs of conflict and violence against the upper classes, from which many prehistoric archaeologists conclude that the era's rulers were not only socially distant from the rest of the population, but that they also must have wielded a generally unwanted form of authority. Across much of the continent, including Scandinavia, the period closed at around 500 BCE with a collapse of visible elite culture, often interpreted as an outright rejection of the system.[37]

The earliest Iron Age is, conversely, characterized archaeologically by an era of social and political flattening, with figures of authority almost invisible, materially speaking. The Early Iron Age, from 500 BCE to around 1 CE is marked by the disappearance of obvious status markers, large dwellings, and monumental tombs with wealthy goods, which were everywhere apparent in the Late Bronze Age.[38] No burial elaboration, luxurious living conditions, or overt signs of wealth are seen for many generations.

As the Iron Age progressed and contact was established between southern Europe and western/northern European peoples, literate Mediterraneans with firsthand knowledge—such as Julius Caesar, Cassius Dio, Diodorus Siculus, Pliny, Strabo, Tacitus, and others—described "primitive democracies" in the Celtic- and Germanic-speaking spheres of the late centuries BCE through the early centuries CE. Many archaeologists, however, feel that this "democratic" format was established much earlier, during the Bronze Age/Iron Age transition with its remarkable changes in the material expression of internal social differentiation.[39]

Tacitus, especially—in some of the most critically examined passages of Roman writing—around 98 CE described Germanic society, including what he depicted as the far northern great islands and peninsulas of Scandinavia, where three separate internal structures co-governed society: military professionals, sacred specialists, and an assembly of the people who met at predetermined times and places to prosecute the law and discuss community or regional concerns. Based largely only on the text of Tacitus, this idea was supported by many archaeological theses in the past, now considered overly simplistic.[40]

More recently, Tacitus has been critically revisited by historians, philologists, and archaeologists, and while the notions of ethnicity and migration as described by the Romans are still much debated (e.g., Bowlus 2002[41] versus Steuer 2006),[42] this form of sociopolitical organization has been largely affirmed.[43]

What Tacitus described was a more collective form of leadership in which leaders required support from the assembly for initiating military or other civic actions; if there was disapproval from the assembly, presided over by the religious specialists, his plans were scuttled. Furthermore, these leaders and soldier followers had reciprocal obligations in which a warlord supported his fighters, but they were able to legally abandon his service if they perceived arrogance, avarice, or ineptitude. On the broader level, allied groups might elect a paramount to lead collectively against outside threats, but refusal to relinquish power led to fully sanctioned overthrow or assassination of such high-level elites (a good current exposition of Tacitus and other evidence is offered by Wells 1999).

Such a sociopolitical organization with three "stand-alone" power structures—legislative, warrior, and religious—is termed a *heterarchy* by Crumley (1995, 2003, 2005) and defined as consisting of separate institutions, unranked against each other (no one more "important" or primate than another), yet each one internally ranked and each having checks and balances on the others.[44]

This is not particularly unusual; there are many contemporary examples of such organization, for example, any current nation-state with mutually regulating legislative, judicial, and executive branches. It is an inherently more flexible and resilient system of government, a "complex adaptive system" to which the successes of "barbarian" groups in defeating the highly skilled, organized, and rigidly structured Roman armies and military machinery is often attributed.[45]

Despite the low visibility of elites in the earlier Iron Age, it is probable that there were leadership figures at this time, but their strategy was to suppress any flaunting of such a status. According to one notion (Blanton et al. 1996),[46] there is a contrast between styles of leadership. One is an "elite network" with large displays of wealth and power, bought into and mutually legitimated by a network of upper classes across a broad area: the Bronze Age. The Iron Age, in contrast, was marked by "corporate" leadership—meaning more self-rule by ordinary people—and leaders who purposely maintained a lower, less visible profile, in keeping with the overarching political philosophy of the era, probably to keep their heads on their shoulders, if nothing else more ideological. This generally agrees with archaeological evidence for a more collective system seen in a more egalitarian material culture, reduced stratification in sociopolitical and settlement indicators, more egalitarian burial rites,[47] and the appearance of assembly-places seen through textual records, place names, and archaeological evidence.[48]

By the time Tacitus was writing in the first century, more than five centuries had passed, and warlords were reasserting themselves slowly over the course of the first few centuries. Despite this slow reemergence of stratification, the assembly remained powerful, if not in preventing the development of an elite, then in protecting everyone else against their potential excesses.

Development of Regional and National Laws

Some social codes and behaviors observed by the Romans continued, albeit in shifting form, in the intervening centuries when there are no textual records, only to emerge again in the documentary sources when literacy broadened from rune stones to texts around 1000–1100 CE. The assembly occurred at marked and repeatedly used outdoor areas such as a hill with a standing stone, or sometimes a built structure, which served as a place to meet and discuss community concerns as well as a legal forum (specific to the region discussed here: Iversen 2013;[49] Oosthuizen 2013;[50] Riisøy 2013; Smith 2013).[51]

By this time, the tradition of assembly at a *thing*-place was less about entering into war and more coincident with legal proceedings: presence of a formal law speaker who committed the law code to memory to prevent covert changes or amendments. There were different tiers of assemblies: local places and district places were trumped by "national" thing-places, where kings were elected by popular vote.

Some kings ran unopposed, but there are notable cases where two candidates debated before a huge crowd as the kingship was contested and won.[52] Should there be any doubt of the continuity of this tradition, a mid—fourteenth-century law code in Sweden recommended that the king be elected from among the king's sons, but if there were none, any man born in Sweden could be elected.[53] Common people and nobility relied on protection through this system, where kings were bound to obey the will of the public, and the laws against excessive taxation, conscription, and other abuses allowed for the removal—or even mur-der—of abusive rulers.

Yet at the same time, there were forces at work that would remove the consent and participation of the less wealthy and the farmer class in the construction and maintenance of legal protections. In 1296, for example, a request came to the Swedish king from one of the prov-inces asking for his authority to amend and update a particular regional

Swedish law code. The king assigned a lawman to oversee this, who in turn selected a panel of 12 men who had knowledge of the law and comprised nobility, clergy, wealthy non-nobles, and peasants.[54] When the reform was complete, the 12-man panel accepted and approved it.

However, in 1327, after a period of royal infighting, a similar request to amend a different regional law code was submitted with an almost identical letter of request, but in this case the lawman selected only secular aristocracy, with no members who were real experts in the law. Non-nobles, peasants, and those intimately familiar with old laws were now excluded. Furthermore, while in 1296 the panel of 12, including peasants, approved the final revision, in 1327 it was simply read and proclaimed at many local assemblies, so "while the drafting of the law of Södermanland may have been more firmly in the hands of the elite as representatives of the people, the confirmation emphasized more, or at least paid lip service to, the joyful acceptance of the law by the people of Södermanland at multiple assemblies."[55]

What this reveals is an Iron Age society with invisible and highly limited leadership, developing slowly into one dominated by a political-military elite, but with strong and sophisticated leveling mechanisms: "checks and balances" from across society. The persistence of such sociopolitical traditions is discernable in the archaeological record throughout the course of the Iron Age, most strongly in the early Iron Age but continuing into the later Iron Age and Viking Age, despite the redevelopment of more visible and more powerful rulers. In the thirteenth century, controls on the king and in the formulation of new laws *and* the preservation of old laws were still partly in the hands of the farmer class. In an attempt to discourage kings from reckless behavior, stronger controls in the fourteenth century, such as the Charter of Liberties, were enacted. However, at the most basic level, the fourteenth century brought challenges to farmers' ability to participate in the ancient tradition of shared governance and shared legal jurisprudence.

Småland and the Swedes:
Forest Farmers in the Distant Past

If instead of looking backward from our own time we begin in the past and work forward, we find that in the late prehistoric era, alluded to in early historic traditions, the Småland Plateau consisted of 12 self-governing small polities (Swedish *lands*). These can be seen both historically, in the sixth-century writings of Jordanes,[56] and through archaeological evidence, such as bounded and regionalized mortuary customs,[57] as cohesive and identifiable between 500 and 1000 CE. In fact, the name *Småland* derives directly from this tradition: It means "the small kingdoms."

The Swedish, or *Svear* kingdom expanded from the area around Stockholm. In the ninth and tenth centuries, this brought the kingdom into conflict with the *Götar* kingdom to the south. Farther south still were the 12 small realms of Småland. The Svear and Götar eventually merged around 1000 CE, agreeing to draw kings alternately from each region. This protohistoric era produced few documents, but from rune stones, inscribed coinage, and heroic sagas, we can gather that while Småland was not a part of Götaland, the two realms may have been allies. After the merger created the proto-Swedish state, it simply claimed Småland as a part of its political body.

The archaeological research program funded by the National Science Foundation, titled *Forest Farmers of the Small Lands*, has studied the livelihood of ordinary people on Småland's upland Plateau as the state attempted to incorporate their region. On the broader level, it investigates the problem of resistance to state authority through the lens of Collective Action Theory and the notion that political formations that provide "voice" in the management of public goods, supported by fair and foreseeable taxation, are the most successful in harnessing the resources, labor, and revenue of their populations, while those that do not provide "voice" predictably foment resistance, recalcitrance, and sometimes violent rebellion.[58]

In most parts of Sweden, as it slowly unified, the assembly system was in full force, although it was modified through time. If the public took issue with taxes and/or had legal disputes, the matter was taken to the local or regional assembly, depending on its import, and was petitioned before the king if it was of broad consequence. There are many examples of both farmers and nobles bringing issues before the assembly and the lawmen for resolution.

While claims of unification with Småland began around 1000 CE, the state had no physical presence in the region. The Smålanders did not accept the claims and kept to themselves, carrying on as in the past. They preferred to take their issues to local courts rather than to the Swedish king.[59] More than in other parts of Sweden, "in Småland in particular, local and regional unwritten customs were important means of regulating land rents, forest rights, tenurial relations, dues and fees, etc., all matters which were either not regulated by written laws, or for which such laws as existed had never been applied."[60] Thus, in a way they excluded themselves from the ability to meet the Swedish king face to face and negotiate what taxes and laws were acceptable to them, which other regions took full advantage of.

When the Svear began to assert authority in Småland, especially in the area of tax collection, the inhabitants had no systematized channel to the royal court and did everything they could to evade the eventual ramifications of this relationship. The collection of taxes was among the primary objectives of the state. With no physical presence in Småland— and given the rough terrain and heavy forestation—the state authorized tax farmers, who were tasked to extract some sum above and beyond what was owed to the state and keep the difference as their pay. This system, while cheap for the state, has a global history of fostering not only corruption, but also unlawful, often violent means to collect. It was no different in early Sweden. The tax farmers attempted to collect as much as they could with impunity, frequently demanding double the already high tax burden and imposing brutal retaliatory punishments among those who would not pay. Among the forest farmers of the Plateau, surplus was not only hard won from the difficult environment, but also closely held among tightly knit kinfolk living in the high, heavily forested valleys of the Plateau.

Climate and Environment in a Marginal Upland

The environment of the Plateau must be examined in order to understand the cooperative and collective nature of the uplanders. The Småland Plateau is formally classified as a marginal upland lying at 300 to 400 meters ASL, at the 57th to 58th parallels. While only moderate in elevation, the environment is rendered much harsher than lowlands only 100 km due east because of the combined elevation and latitude. July temperature only reaches around 14 °C, comparable with regions above the Arctic Circle (SMHI 2009).[61] The soil in the small valleys where most settlements were and continue to be located is often less than 5 centimeters (2 inches) deep, and between the areas where farms are found, most of the land is characterized by dense forest amid huge up-thrusting boulders and bedrock, swamp, and thousands of large and small lakes.

The uplands have always been subject to stark swings in ecological conditions, responding more drastically than surrounding lowlands to climate change. Pollen profiles from lake cores, showing conditions over thousands of years, reveal shifts in vegetation associated with land use, for example, succession from "slash and burn" clearance, to fallow, and eventual reuse. First inhabited in the Neolithic (4000–1700 BCE) by the Late Bronze Age to Early Iron Age transition around 500 BCE, there was a humanly managed forest and a moving system of settlements, pasture, and horticultural or garden-style fields in artificial openings.[62] During climate optimums, such as the so-called Roman Warm Period from about 150–400 CE, many settlements were in evidence that practiced a largely pastoral economy supplemented with forestry.

The region saw a severe lowering of temperature and rise in moisture between 400 and 800 CE, and by around 500 CE, much of the Plateau had been almost totally abandoned, coinciding with the dramatic climate downturn across Europe known as the Post-Roman Climate Minimum. This was probably accompanied by plague; while Sweden was preliterate, nearby regions recorded astounding levels of mortality from the epidemic disease, which followed the widespread sociopolitical and economic upheavals in Europe after the Roman collapse. Reforestation of the upland then occurred where people had once lived.[63]

Archaeological and paleoecological data show that between 600–1000 CE, there was an agrarian expansion in nearby lowlands with nucleation of small settlements into larger villages. In contrast, on the Plateau, 400–800 CE saw minimal occupation and sporadic forest grazing. It is tempting to imagine that people from the now-uninhabitable uplands flooded into the closely neighboring lowlands, swelling the population and precipitating settlement changes seen through archaeological studies.[64]

During the Viking Age, beginning around 800 CE, a newly warming climate led to recolonization, and between 800 and 1000 many new settlements appeared. By proxy, populations began to increase in the uplands[65] around the time that the Swedish state began to encroach and incorporate the region.

From 1200 to 1500, colonization in the higher elevations continued to expand, even in the face of the Little Ice Age between 1350–1850 CE, although the climate impacts were drastic.[66] In the mid-fourteenth century, the Black Death killed one-third of Sweden's population. Some villages were abandoned, but thereafter and through the 1600s, waves of settlement foundations occurred in the uplands, not only within the larger lower valleys, but also in increasingly higher terrain.

Economic Strategies on the Småland Plateau: Cooperative Labor and Occupational Pluralism

Cooperative labor and occupational pluralism are the two clear liveli-hood strategies associated with the high latitude, high elevation, and forested upland. These can be viewed both as responses to climate and environmental conditions and also to social conditions as the Swedish state penetrated and consolidated power in the region.

Occupational pluralism[67] refers to the constant combining and shifting of resources, processing technologies, and land/labor rights and strategies.[68] McCann (1999) notes that "occupational pluralism represents a strategy for family survival in a marginal world of work. It is a response to those situations in which no single activity provides an adequate income to meet family needs. To this end, contributors to the family's economic welfare might follow a number of seasonal activities—some subsistence, some that earn cash—as they try to gain a modicum of well-being." Occupational pluralism, relying on food and nonfood forest products, is seen with clarity in the archaeological record.

To farm in the forest, clearings needed to be created. In early historic times, the practice called *svedjebruk,* or slash and burn, was undertaken by formal cooperatives of many farms and villages in which all ages and sexes worked together. The *svedjebruk* system was made of obligations and tightly knit relationships—formal agreements on cutting and burning trees and then beating the fires to stop them spreading too far, clearing stones and boulders, and meticulously dividing the products according to effort, sometimes years after the cycle had begun.

Analogous to this practice and around the territories of archaeo-logical settlements, thousands of stone heaps called clearance cairns are found. These were formed during the creation of pasture, when as in historic times, trees were felled and burned in place and stones were collected and piled up. The charcoal from burning was swept up into the stone heaps, which facilitates their dating by ^{14}C.[69] The ability to radiocarbon date the cairns shows that the practice goes back into Iron

Age times. The scale of clearance in the Iron Age and Viking Age was as great or greater than in the later historic period, and by inference, the labor cooperation to accomplish this was similar. There are also groups of cairns that originate in the waves of settlement in the thirteenth to sixteenth centuries.

Farmers from the earliest occupation and onward relied on stock-breeding multiple species in the tiny, rocky valleys. Animal bones in archaeological sites attest to this activity throughout the Iron Age and medieval periods. The pastoral round, with the maintenance of many breed-specific schedules, was already very complex and interdependent. Each type of animal had its own need for tending, feeding, and scheduling of labor.

Arboriculture for animal leaf fodder is evident,[70] which by the eighteenth century was recorded as reaching thousands of tons, as are pollarding and coppicing[71]—the practice of pruning and trimming trees in order to create thin, uniform branches used for basketry, furniture, and other crafts. This can be seen by studying macrobotanical remains, that is, the charred preserved remains of twigs, stems, and withies, which show distinctive shapes and forms associated only with human propagation to furnish specifically sized and shaped material. There is also evidence of other arboriculture for animal fodder as well as tree-based human food.[72] Acorn, beechnut, and hazelnut propagation, both to feed large herds of pigs and for human consumption,[73] is indicated—a practice that continued into the Middle Ages, Early Modern, and Modern eras.

The tools found at archaeological farm sites, combined with the evidence for forestry and the manipulation of wood, aligns with various early historic records of woodworking, furniture making, and other industrialized crafts utilizing forest products. Another important market craft was leather working. Additionally, Smålanders were known to produce a market surplus of eggs, honey, and preparations such as fruit preserves from early times.

The huge number of small and large lakes and bogs on the plateau provided millions of tons of bog iron ore, which precipitates within water as minerals filter down to lower levels and consolidate. This can be collected in chunks and smelted, producing iron of quality comparable to mined ore. A lake or bog can be emptied of ore and reharvested a couple of centuries later. Geological ore that is unearthed from subterranean mines is also ubiquitous in the region, the main source for the later Husqvarna Company's production activities. But long before this, in the twelfth century, iron industries were run as peasant cooperatives[74] of up to eight households, each headed by a man with knowledge of smithcraft.[75] Some of the legal regulations relating to the details of owning and running such cooperatives still survive in the Swedish archives.

In order to smelt iron ore into iron and steel, farmers established and carried out an enormous charcoal industry. Like stone clearance cairns, pits where charcoal was produced can also be dated, as they are made from the most typically archaeologically dated material, the charcoal itself.[76] As with clearance features, they fall into eras from the early Iron Age and onward, beginning with smaller features and developing into what archaeologists have called industrial production levels from the late Viking Age forward. Similarly, as the state's naval and shipbuilding activities increased, tar was produced in much the same manner.[77]

Many practices had impacts on labor, seasonality, and organization. Archaeologists are able to understand the time depth of productive processes and the levels of change and continuity in the past by studying many settlements in the uplands, revealing people's livelihood practices, and dating the lifespan of the settlements. The productive activities were performed by farm families, interspersed with their herding and forestry tasks. Much more was produced than was necessary for subsistence; the surplus was sold in lowland market towns in order to supplement the household with things that could not be produced on the farm: silver, glass, beads, and mass-produced ceramics.

Coordination between place name types, which went in and out of fashion through time, and radiocarbon dating enables our picture of expansion and pioneering. The village structure between the fourteenth and sixteenth centuries, known from tax rolls and later cadastral maps, reflects the low carrying capacity of this marginal land. As opposed to fertile lowland areas where villages held 15–20 or more farms, upland villages usually consisted of between two and six farms very loosely combined into an agglomerated community.[78]

In parts of southern Scandinavia, including lowland Småland, small plowed and manured "infields" were created around villages between 1100 and 1300. In the study region, this did not happen, and slash and burn remained the primary farming method until after 1550, mostly for creating pasture.[79] Planting around the upland farms was mostly of a horticultural nature before this time. Only after 1550 were upland "infields" more frequently planted with cereals.[80]

A Razor's Edge on the Interface of Climate, Economy, and State

The inhabitants of the chilly kingdom of stones were thus resourceful and entrepreneurial even in the earliest times. Yet the history of their relationship with the state shows a legacy of resistance, protest, and violence. Around 1000 CE, the Svear kings first claimed to rule the region. There was no actual Svear state presence in Småland until 1134 and it remained self-governing, but the ramifications were instantaneous: Småland became the border between Sweden and Denmark and thus embroiled in many issues surrounding centuries of warfare between them. Impacts included conscription of local men and invasion by troops who raped local women and fired the landscape, laying waste to the region at the borderland. As pressure rose on the aristocracy to fight or else supply armed warriors to take their place, the local nobility pressed the farming population for more funds to pay for this expense. The state also increased demands for higher war-related taxes from the villagers, thus squeezing them from both sides.

The fifteenth and sixteenth centuries saw many conflicts over tax evasion by the peasantry. Tax farming collectors grew more aggressive, reportedly leading to local atrocities, and in turn, many taxmen were murdered in the forest. Because the dispersed population occupied small clearings in dense dark forest among almost impassible rocky and con-voluted terrain, they could effectively hide people and their assets from prying eyes. The extraction of goods or coins from the forest population required territorial control and the close surveillance of trade, which the state did not have.

Over the next centuries, the crown took steps to remedy this. Around 1140, a royal castle was constructed in the heart of the region that became the permanent year-round residence of the King of Sweden for almost 200 years. In 1284, the state appropriated the local Iron Age–Viking Age marketplace and chartered it as a royal market town on a crossroads between East and West Götaland, calling it Jönköping, which became a levy place and garrison for armies involved in warfare against Denmark. This activity also created vulnerability, making it a target for Danish attacks. During fourteenth-to-sixteenth-century warfare, suffering in the town and surrounding countryside was great enough to be mentioned in the scanty texts, and the city was fortified in the sixteenth century.

In the same period, Swedish ruler Gustav Vasa enacted a series of directives that unequivocally and negatively impacted the forest farmers' way of life. First, he outlawed trade between Denmark and Sweden, and commercial activity across the border—a millennia-old tradition—was rendered illegal, leading to the Smålanders' refusal to recognize the Swedish-Danish border at Småland's southern edge.[81] This was partly aimed at disrupting any economic benefit the trade brought to the Danes but also because trade through the cover of the forest landscape was largely untaxed.

The ties between Småland's forester-pastoralists and their Danish counterparts on the other side of the border were much stronger than allegiance to their respective kings or acknowledgment of an arbitrary border. During the Danish-Swedish wars, "farmers' peace treaties" or *bondefred* were drawn up, which were formal written agreements to continue trade and provide mutual warning against incursions from their own homelands. Actual collusions are documented for both sides.[82] This treasonous activity resulted in furious retribution from the Swedish king.

In addition to the trade ban, the king also banished Catholicism, had priests humiliated and imprisoned, and ordered the pious Smålanders to adopt Lutheranism.[83] The upland forest population had been living for centuries in hidden forest strongholds and in close cooperation, with mechanisms for communicating and collaborating despite the barriers of physical geography. The cumulative effect of these perceived oppressions was rebellion.

In 1542, Niels Dacke, an impoverished local farmer magnate who had already paid blood money for killing a sheriff over tax collection, appears in historic texts as a general in command of a farmer army. Dacke's rebellion (*Dackefejden*) spread through Småland and along the border, and Vasa's army of foreign mercenaries was massacred by crossbow-armed farmers in steep rocky forests.

Vasa, who was himself put in power by an *earlier* farmer army, signed a peace treaty with Dacke, who raised the ban on trade, lowered taxes, and restored the Catholic Church according to local desires. When Vasa broke the treaty and Dacke's forces were decimated, Dacke was wounded, outlawed, and died on the border of Småland and Denmark in 1543; his family was executed shortly thereafter.

Despite Dacke's demise, the representative, decentralized, Iron Age–rooted mode of governance survived. Rather than more strongly suppress the Smålanders, the ruler brought them further into the system

of decentralized governance, where there were conduits for the negotiation of taxation and other obligations as well as recourses for resolving
disputes with the state. To ensure the security of the throne, he and
his descendants continued to participate in this more collective form of
government where farmers, despite the increased power of the crown,
could resume the tradition of bringing issues of concern directly before
the crown.[84]

Can We Expect Resilient Recycling or Release in Marginal Northern Europe?

The link between entrepreneurship and the marginal upland of the
Småland Plateau, the collective nature of farming the forest, and the
need for occupational pluralism is clear. Economists and business scholars
have correctly identified some of these factors, although perhaps not in
exactly the right sequence.[85] The linkages between these factors and
the willingness of the uplanders to subvert government authority and
then take up arms against the state is also predictable in light of a vast
literature on pastoralists, peasants, and the state in the social sciences.

The error creeps in when the seventeenth century is identified
by historians, economists, and industrialists as the era of "creation" for
the Smålander's solidarity, entrepreneurship, and independence. It was,
rather, the moment in which they *reclaimed* their rights and autonomy,
hoping to return to the system of government that was rooted in Iron
Age traditions. This was a reaction against a central government that
was attempting to mimic the Early Modern continental imperial rulers
of France, Russia, and Britain, who were then exercising absolute and
sometimes dissolute power over their people. Their political tradition
had been established in the Iron Age and been slowly eroded through
the medieval period, until the environmental, social, political, and
economic conditions of the Plateau's inhabitants fomented opposition,
resistance, and rebellion as a rational response according to Collective
Action Theory.[86]

Because of their defense of a cherished political form established and
developed between 500 BCE and the ninth-to-eleventh-century Viking
Age, ordinary farming people found the ability to resist exploitation in
the sixteenth century. Following from this, the abuses of the Industrial
Revolution, as we traditionally characterize them, began very late in the

nineteenth century, and their negative effects were less severe than in many world regions. Overly asymmetrical conditions were again challenged and a more egalitarian system restored in the twentieth century. Because of citizen activism, instead of a steady worsening of conditions, Sweden saw a rise in the standard of living after 1840, when mortality was dramatically lowered and birth rates rose. This was accompanied by a 30 percent increase in agricultural production between 1830 and 1860,[87] in tandem with rising iron and textile production—increased economic indicators combined with increased public well-being rather than at its expense. Unlike emigration from other parts of Europe, the late—nineteenth-century Swedish emigration to the United States and Canada is attributed to the lure of cheap farmland, higher wages, and the low cost of transatlantic passage rather than to extreme hardship or suffering in the homeland (Gjerde 1995; Norman and Runblom 1987; Runblom and Norman 1976).[88] Voluntary migration (as opposed to one forced by starvation or persecution) led to the almost idealized immigrant story of Swedish Americans. Those who remained at home in Småland persisted in their concealed and insular way of life, predicated upon the strategies of occupational pluralism and cooperative labor. This way of life endures in current times; the Smålanders do not want to leave their challenging terrain.

The era that Nuur and other analysts refer to as the origin of the "Gnosjö Spirit" and the "beginning" of Smålanders' ability to become cohesive, to compete while also working together, and to learn from each other, is in fact only a single point of "renewal" on a much longer resilient trajectory. Because of a lack of expertise (or interest) in the earlier chain of events, many scholars miss the real root causes. By the time of the sixteenth- and seventeenth-century conflicts, the Smålanders had already dealt with several acute climate shifts, epidemic diseases, economic challenges, political oppression, and religious persecution: sequences of *remember, revolt,* and *reorganize*—without ever having a true *release.* This represents resilience in terms of the theoretical approach in long-term human ecodynamics that posits a cycle of change in which socionatural relationships build, sustain, adjust or fail, and destabilize and reorganize, utilizing the resulting "new normal" conditions as the basis for new livelihoods and strategies. Probably, if they are able to make their own decisions, they will continue to successfully navigate future disturbances.

This case study was presented in order to illustrate the utility of such approaches. Explaining the resilience of the uplanders requires a look at more than two millennia of time. It is only with this longer and closer examination that we can understand the difference between the marginality of Småland and the marginality of other "deprived" parts of Europe. It involves a distinctly socionatural perspective with expertise on a number of fronts that together feed into the true picture of why things happen as they do.

Collaborations between natural and social scientists, when they occur, have often been only moderately successful at integrating views into a socionatural perspective on short- and long-term human-environment relationships. We already have a large number of specialists with different bodies of knowledge, and further efforts must occur. Resilience Theory predicts that people do not act until they are on the cusp of serious change but need only to make the right decisions at that crucial point in order to avoid total release and reorganization. The need for collaboration is urgent, and there is not a lot of time to create revolutionary paradigmatic change. Hopefully, the decision for more effective partnerships will come soon.

Notes

1. G. Judkins, M. Smith, and E. Keys, "Determinism within Human-Environment Research and the Rediscovery of Environmental Causation," *Geographical Journal* 174, no. 1 (2008): 17–29; B. Peiser, "From Genocide to Ecocide: The Rape of Rapa Nui," *Energy & Environment* 16, no. 3–4 (2005): 513–39; A. Sluyter, "Neo-Environmental Determinism, Intellectual Damage Control, and Nature/Society Science," *Antipode* 35, no. 4 (2005): 813–17; D. Tedlock, Review of *Guns, Germs, and Steel: A Short History of Everybody for The Last 13,000 Years*, by Jared Diamond, *The Times Higher Education Supplement* (May 9, 1997): 23.

2. V. Strang, "Integrating the Social and Natural Sciences in Environmental Research: A Discussion Paper," *Environment, Development and Sustainability* 11, no. 1 (2009): 1–18.

3. T. Jahn, M. Bergmann, and F. Keil, "Transdisciplinarity: Between Mainstreaming and Marginalization," *Ecological Economics* 79 (2012): 1–10.

4. J. Apgar, A. Argumedo, and W. Allen, "Building Transdisciplinarity for Managing Complexity: Lessons from Indigenous Practice," *International Journal of Interdisciplinary Social Sciences* 4, no. 5 (2009): 255–70.

5. R. Niesenbaumand T. Lewis, "Ghettoization in Conservation Biology: How Interdisciplinary Is Our Teaching?" *Conservation Biology* 17 (2003): 6–10.

6. H. Newing, "Interdisciplinary Training in Environmental Conservation: Definitions, Progress and Future Directions," *Environmental Conservation* 37, no. 4 (2010): 410–18.

7. G. Feinman, "Science and Public Debate: A Role for Archaeology in Today's News Media," *Anthropology News* 51 (2010): 12–13; A. Fischer, H. Tobi, and A. Ronteltap, "When Natural Met Social: A Review of Collaboration between the Natural and Social Sciences," *Interdisciplinary Science Reviews* 36, no. 4 (2011): 341–58; F. Hassan, "Human Agency, Climate Change, and Culture: An Archaeological Perspective," in *Anthropology and Climate Change: From Encounters to Actions*, ed., S. Crate and M. Nuttall (Walnut Creek, CA: Left Coast Press, 2009), 39–69; F. Hayashida, "Archaeology, Ecological History, and Conservation," *Annual Review of Anthropology* 34 (2005): 43–65; M. Hudson et al., "Prospects and Challenges for an Archaeology of Global Climate Change," *Wiley Interdisciplinary Reviews: Climate Change* 3, no. 4 (2012): 313–28; P. McAnany and N. Yoffee, eds., *Questioning Collapse: Human Resilience, Ecological Vulnerability, and the Aftermath of Empire* (Cambridge: University of Cambridge Press, 2009); C. Redman, and A. Kinzig, "Resilience of Past Landscapes: Resilience Theory, Society, and the Longue Durée," *Conservation Ecology* 7, no. 1 (2003): 14 http://www.consecol.org/vol7/iss1/art14; C. Redman, *Human Impact on Ancient Environments* (Tucson: University of Arizona Press, 1999); S. van der Leeuw and C. Redman, "Placing Archaeology at the Center of Socio-Natural Studies," *American Antiquity* 67, no. 4 (2002): 597–605.

8. F. Berkes and C. Folke, eds., *Linking Social and Ecological Systems: Management Practices and Social Mechanism for Building Resilience* (Cambridge: Cambridge University Press, 1998); R. Costanza, "The Need for a Transdisciplinary Understanding of Development in a Hot and Crowded World," in *Interdisciplinarity and Climate Change: Transforming Knowledge and Practice for Our Global Future*, ed., R. Bhaskar et al. (London: Routledge, 2010), 135–48; R. Costanza, L. Graumlich, and W. Steffen, eds., *Sustainability or Collapse? An Integrated History and Future of People on Earth* (Cambridge: MIT Press, 2007), 3–17; L. Gunderson and C. Holling, eds., *Panarchy: Understanding Transformations in Human and Natural Systems* (Washington, DC: Island Press, 2002); C. Holling, "Understanding the Complexity of Economic, Ecological, and Social Systems," *Ecosystems* 4, no. 5 (2001): 390–405; C. Holling and L. Gunderson, "Resilience and Adaptive Cycles," in *Panarchy*, ed. Gunderson and Holling, 25–62; A. Kinzig et al., "Nature and Society: An Imperative for Integrated Environmental Research" (2000); http://lsweb.la.asu.edu/akinzig/report.htm; E. Moran, *Environmental Social Science: Human-Environment Interactions and Sustainability* (Malden, MA: Wiley-Blackwell, 2010); E. Ostrom, "Linking Social and Ecological Systems: Management Practices and Social Mechanisms for Building Resilience," *Ecological Economics* 28, no. 1 (1999): 151–53; N. Sayre, "The Politics of the Anthropogenic," *Annual Review of Anthropology* 41 (2012): 57–70; B. Walker et al., "Resilience, Adaptability, and Transformability in Social-Ecological Systems," *Ecology and Society* 9, no. 2 (2004); http://www.ecologyandsociety.org/vol9/iss2/art5.

9. Gunderson and Holling, *Panarchy.*

10. Gunderson and Holling. "Resilience and Adaptive Cycles," in *Panarchy*, 25–62.

11. Berkes and Folke, eds., *Linking Social and Ecological Systems.*

12. Redman, *Human Impact on Ancient Environments.*

13. Redman and Kinzig, "Resilience of Past Landscapes."

14. P. Lagerås, K. Jansson, and A. Vestbo, "Land-Use History of the Axlarp Area in the Småland Uplands, Southern Sweden: Palaeoecological and Archaeological Investigations," *Vegetation History and Archaeobotany* 4 (1995): 223–34.

15. P. Cooke and C. De Laurentis, *The Index of Knowledge Economies in the European Union: Performance Rankings of Cities and Regions* (Regional Industrial Research Report 41 Centre for Advanced Studies Cardiff University, 2002).

16. Y. Moon, *IKEA Invades America.* Harvard Business School Case No. 9-504-094 (Boston: Harvard Business School, 2004).

17. S. Fridjonsson and E. Mersmann, *Associating Brands to Nations: Why and How? A Case Study of Orrefors Kosta Boda* (BS Thesis, Uppsala University, Department of Business Studies, Uppsala, Sweden, 2010).

18. B. Gerdes and J. Hayshida, "No More Strike Anywhere," *Rethinking Marxism* 20, no. 2 (2010): 217–37.

19. H. Fredriksson, *Husqvarna AB: A Study on Pricing and Quality* (MA Thesis, Jönköping International Business School, Dept. of Economics, Jönköping, Sweden, 2006); J. Svensson, K. Blomberg, and J. Eriksson, *Mapping of Relations and Dependencies Using DSM/DMM-Analysis: Casting Mold Manufacturing at Husqvarna* (Jönköping University, Jönköping, Sweden, 2005).

20. Cooke and De Laurentis, *The Index of Knowledge Economies in the European Union.*

21. V. Moberg. *Utvandrarna [The Emigrants]* (Stockholm: Albert Bonniers Forlag AB, 1949).

22. N. Linder, J. Rosén, T. Westrin, B. F. Olsson, and B. Meijer, eds. *Nordisk familjebok: konversationslexikon och realencyklopedi, innehållande upplysningar och förklaringar om märkvärdiga namn, föremål och begrepp* (Nordisk Familjeboks Forlags Aktiebolag, Stockholm, 1890), 1479.

23. Ibid.

24. V. Ceccato and L. Persson, "Dynamics of Rural Areas: An Assessment of Clusters of Employment in Sweden," *Journal of Rural Studies* 18, no. 1 (2002): 49–63; "Differential Economic Performance (DEP) in the Periphery: Evidence from Swedish Rural Areas," *European Journal of Spatial Development* 7 (2002): 2–28.

25. V. Ceccato and L. Persson, "Dynamics of Rural Areas," 49–63.

26. Ibid., 15.

27. Ibid.

28. L. Trägårdh, "Swedish Model or Swedish Culture?" *Critical Review* 4, no. 4 (1990): 569–90; S. Valocchi, "The Origins of the Swedish Welfare State: A Class Analysis of the State and Welfare Politics," *Social Problems* 39, no. 2 (1992): 189–200.

29. G. Brulin, "Faktor X–en fråga om lokal och regional kultur? [Factor X—A Matter of Local and Regional Culture]," *Plats, drivkraft, Samhällsprocess. Vad gör kulturarvet till en resurs för hållbar regional utveckling? [Location, Momentum, Social Process. How Do You Make Heritage A Resource for Sustainable Regional Development?]*, *Riksantikvarieämbetet Rapport* (2003): 41–46; B. Johannisson, "A Cultural Perspective on Small Business–Local Business Climate," 32–41; B. Johannisson and C. Wigren, "The Dynamics of Community Identity Making in an Industrial District: The Spirit of Gnosjö Revisited," in *Entrepreneurship as Social Change*, ed. C. Steyaert and D. Hjorth (Northampton, MA: Edward Elgar, 2003), 188–209; C. Wigren, *The Spirit of Gnosjö—The Grand Narrative and Beyond* (Dissertation Series No. 017, Jönköping International Business School, Jönköping, Sweden, 2003).

30. C. Nuur, *Cluster Dynamics and Industrial Policy in Peripheral Regions: A Study of Cluster Formation as a Local Development Process* (PhD dissertation, Royal Institute of Technology, Department of industrial Economics and Management, Stockholm, Sweden, 2005).

31. Ibid., 41.

32. J. Scott, *The Art of Not Being Governed: An Anarchist History of Upland Southeast Asia* (New Haven: Yale University Press, 2009).

33. F. Hervik, "The Nordic Countries in Isakhan," in *The Edinburgh Companion to the History of Democracy*, ed., B. Isakhan and S. Stockwell (Edinburgh: Edinburgh University Press, 2012), 143–53.

34. M. Korpiola, " 'Not without the Consent and Goodwill of the Common People': The Community as a Legal Authority in Medieval Sweden," *The Journal of Legal History* 35, no. 2 (2014): 95–119.

35. Ibid.

36. T. L. Thurston, "Bitter Arrows and Generous Gifts: What Was a King in the European Iron Age?" in *Pathways to Power New Perspectives on the Emergence of Social Inequality*, ed., T. Price and G. Feinman (New York: Springer, 2010), 193–254.

37. R. Drews, *The End of the Bronze Age: Changes in Warfare and the Catastrophe ca. 1200 BC* (Princeton: Princeton University Press, 1993); K. Kristiansen, "The Emergence of the European World System in the Bronze Age: Divergence, Convergence, and Social Evolution during the First and Second Millennia B.C. in Europe," in *Europe in the First Millennium BC*, ed. J. Collis (Sheffield, UK: JR Collis Publications, 1994), 7–30; K. Kristiansen, "The Emergence of Warrior Aristocracies in Later European Prehistory and Their Long-Term History," in *Ancient Warfare*, ed., J. Carman and A. Harding (Sutton: Stroud, 1999), 175–89;

K. Kristiansen and T. Larsson, *The Rise of Bronze Age Society: Travels, Transmissions, and Transformations* (Cambridge: Cambridge University Press, 2005).

38. M. Giles, "Making Metal and Forging Relations: Ironworking in the British Iron Age," *Oxford Journal of Archaeology* 26, no. 4 (2006): 395–413; T. Hodos, *Local Responses to Colonization in the Iron Age Mediterranean* (New York: Routledge, 2006); Kristiansen, "The Emergence of the European World System in the Bronze Age," 7–30; I. Morris, "Negotiated Peripherality in Iron Age Greece: Accepting and Resisting the East," in *World-Systems Theory in Practice: Leadership, Production, and Exchange*, ed. N. Kardulias (Lanham, MD: Rowman and Littlefield 1999), 63–84; C. Oubiña, "Looking Forward in Anger: Social and Political Transformations in the Iron Age of the North-Western Iberian Peninsula," *European Journal of Archaeology* 6, no. 3: 267–99; T. L. Thurston, "Bitter Arrows and Generous Gifts," 193–254; T. L. Thurston, "Unity and Diversity in the European Iron Age: Out of the Mists, Some Clarity?" *Journal of Archaeological Research* 17, no. 4: 347–423.

39. Kristiansen, "The Emergence of Warrior Aristocracies in Later European Prehistory and Their Long-Term History," 175–89.

40. A. Christophersen, "Drengs, Thegns, Landmen and Kings: Some Aspects on the Forms of Social Relations in Viking Society during the Transition to Historic Times," (Meddelanden från Lunds Universitets Historiska Museum, 1981–1982):115–34; J. Lindow, *Comitatus, Individual and Honor: Studies in Northern Germanic Institutional Vocabulary* (Berkeley: University of California Publications in Linguistics); Å Ström, "Personal Piety in Nordic Heathenism," in *Old Norse and Finnish Religions and Cultic Place-Names*, ed. T. Ahlbäck (Åbo: Donner Institute, 1990), 374–80; T. Vestergaard, "Class and State Development In Scandinavia: Necessary and Voluntary Relations," *Kontaktstencil* 16: 25–52.

41. C. R. Bowlus, "Ethnogenesis: The Tyranny of a Concept," in *On Barbarian Identity. Critical Approaches to Ethnicity in the Early Middle Ages*, ed. A. Gillett (Brepols: Turnhout, 2002), 241–56.

42. H. Steuer, "Warrior Bands, War Lords and the Birth of Tribes and States in the First Millennium AD in Middle Europe," in *Warfare and Society: Archaeological and Social Anthropological Perspectives*, ed. Ton Otto (Aarhus: Aarhus University Press, 2006), 227–36.

43. S. Burmeister, "Fighting Wars, Gaining Status: On the Rise of Germanic Elites," in *Mortuary Practices and Social Identities in the Middle Ages*, ed. D. Sayer and H. Williams (Liverpool: Liverpool University Press, 2012), 46–63; D. Skre, *Herredømmet. Bosetning og besittelse på Romerike 200–1350 e.Kr. [Domination. Settlement, and Possession in Romerike 200–1350 AD]* (Oslo: Scandinavian University Press, 1998); O. Sundqvist, *Freyr's Offspring: Rulers and Religion in Ancient Svea Society* (Uppsala: Acta Universitatis Upsaliensis, 2000).

44. C. Crumley, "Remember How to Organize: Heterarchy across Disciplines," in *Nonlinear Models for Archaeology and Anthropology: Continuing the*

Revolution, ed. C. Beekman and W. Baden (Abington, Oxon.: Ashgate Publishing, 2005), 35–50; *Alternativity in Cultural History: Heterarchy and Homoarchy as Evolutionary Trajectories. Hierarchy and Power in the History of Civilizations*, ed. D. Bondarenko and A. Nemirovskiy (Moscow: Center for Civilizational and Regional Studies Press, 2007); A. Gonzalez-Ruibal, "House Societies vs. Kinship-Based Societies: An Archaeological Case from Iron Age Europe," *Journal of Anthropological Archaeology* 25, no. 1 (2006):144–73; S. James, *The Atlantic Celts: Ancient People or Modern Invention?* (Madison: University of Wisconsin Press, 1999); Morris, "Negotiated Peripherality in Iron Age Greece," 63–84; T. L.Thurston, "Unity and Diversity in the European Iron Age," 347–423.

45. C. Crumley, "Heterarchy and the Analysis of Complex Societies," in *Heterarchy and the Analysis of Complex Societies*, ed. R. Ehrenreich, C. Crumley, and J. Levy (Washington, DC: Archeological Papers of the American Anthropological Association, 1995): 1–6; P. Wells, *The Barbarians Speak: How the Conquered Peoples Shaped Roman Europe* (Princeton: Princeton University Press, 1999).

46. R. Blanton, G. Feinman, S. Kowalewski, and P. Peregrine, "A Dual-Processual Theory for the Evolution of Mesoamerican Civilization." *Current Anthropology* 37, no. 1 (1996): 1–14.

47. M. Axboe, "Towards the Kingdom of Denmark," *Anglosaxon Studies in Archaeology and History* 10: 109–18; J. Barrett et al., "What Was the Viking Age and When Did It Happen? A View from Orkne," *Norwegian Archaeological Review* 33: 1–38; T. Earle and K. Kristiansen, *Organizing Bronze Age Societies* (Cambridge: Cambridge University Press, 2010); K. Smith, "Patterns in Time and the Tempo of Change: A North Atlantic Perspective on the Evolution of Complex Societies," in *Exploring the Role of Analytical Scale in Archaeological Interpretation.* ed. J. Mathiew and R. Scott (BAR International Series 1261, Archaeopress, Oxford), 83–99.

48. Smith, "Patterns in Time and the Tempo of Change," 83–89; A. Sanmark and S. Semple, "Places of Assembly: New Discoveries in Sweden and England," *Fornvännen* 103: 245–59; S. Semple and A. Sanmark, "Assembly in North West Europe: Collective Concerns for Early Societies?" *European Journal of Archaeology* 16: 518–42.

49. F. Iversen, "Concilium and Pagus—Revisiting the Early Germanic Thing System of Northern Europe," *Journal of the North Atlantic* 5 (2013): 5–17.

50. S. Oosthuizen, "Beyond Hierarchy: The Archaeology of Collective Governance." *World Archaeology* 45 (2013): 714–29.

51. M. H. Smith, "Thorir's Bargain: Gender, Vaðmál, and the Law," *World Archaeology* 45 (2013): 730–46.

52. *Danmarks historie. 1. Tiden indtil 1340*, ed. A. Christensen (Copenhagen: Gyldendal, 1977).

53. Korpiola, "Not without the Consent and Goodwill of the Common People," 95–119.

54. Ibid.

55. Ibid.

56. C. Mierow, Jordanes. The Origin and Deeds of the Goths (Princeton: Princeton University Press, 1908); P. Skoglund, "A Traveller's View of Migration Period Scandinavia. Jordanes' Scandza and the Material Evidence," in On The Road. Studies in Honour of Lars Larsson, ed. B. Hårdh, K. Jennbert, and D. Olausson, Acta Archaeologica Lundensia in 4o, no. 26: 276–81.

57. M. Burström, "Reconstructing the Spatial Extension of Ancient Societies: A Scandinavian Viking Age Example," Archaeologia Polona 34 (1996): 165–81.

58. R. Blanton and L. Fargher, "Collective Action in the Formation of Pre-Modern States," Social Evolution & History: Studies in the Evolution of Human Societies 8, no. 2 (2008):133–66; L. Fargher and R. Blanton, "Revenue, Voice, and Public Goods in Three Pre-Modern States," Comparative Studies in Society and History 49, no. 4 (2007):1–35.

59. M. Cederholm, "De värjde sin rätt. Senmedeltida Bondemotstånd i Skåne och Småland [They Defended Their Rights: Late Medieval Peasant Resistance in Scania and Småland]," (PhD Dissertation, Department of History, Lunds Universitet, Lund).

60. Ibid.

61. Swedish Meteorological and Hydrological Institute, "Dataserier med normalvärden för perioden 1961–1990 [Data series with the normal values for the period 1961–1990]," last modified 2009. http://www.smhi.se/klimatdata/meteorologi/temperatur/dataserier-med-normalvarden-1.7354.

62. L. Gren, "Fossil åkermark: äldre tiders jordbruk—spåren I landskapet och de historiska sammanhangen [Fossil Fields: Ancient Agriculture—Traces in the Landscape and Their Historical Context]," (Fornlämningar i Sverige 1. Riksantikvarieämbetet, Stockholm); P. Lagerås and M. Regnell, "Agrar förändring under sydsvensk bronsålder [Agrarian Change during the Bronze Age in Southern Sweden]"; Spiralens öga—tjugo artiklar kring aktuell bronsåldersforskning [The Eye of the Spiral: Twenty Papers on Current Bronze Age Research] (Skrifter 25, Riksantikvarieämbetet, Lund), 263–76; P. Lagerås, "Järnålderns odlingssystem och landskapets långsiktiga förändring. Hamnedas röjningsröseområden i ett paleoekologiskt perspektiv [Iron Age Farming Systems and Landscape's Long-Term Change, Clearance Cairns in Paleoecological Perspective]," in Arkeologi och paleoekologi i sydvästra Småland, Tio artiklar från Hamneda-projektet, ed. P. Lagerås (Skrifter 34, Riksantikvarieämbetet Lund), 167–229; M. Widgren, Fossila landskap—en forskningsöversikt over odlingslandskapets utveckling från yngre bronsålder till tidig medeltid [Fossil Landscape—A Research Overview of Agricultural Landscape Development from the Late Bronze Age to the Early Medieval], Kulturgeografiskt seminarium 97, no. 1 (Kulturgeografiska Institutionen, Stockholms universitet).

63. The Cultural Landscape during 6000 Years in Southern Sweden. The Ystad Project, ed. B. Berglund (Copenhagen: Munksgaard International).

64. L. Björkman, "The Role of Human Disturbance in the Local Late Holocene Establishment of Fagus and Picea Forests at Flahult, Western Småland, Southern Sweden," *Vegetation History and Archaeobotany* 6: 79–90; K. Jansson, and A. Kristensson, *Knutpunkt Bredestad Undersökningar av järnåldershärdar och ett vikingatida hus, fornlämningarna 76 och 78* [*Crossroads Bredestad: Investigation of Iron Age Hearths and a Viking Age House*] (Jönköpings Läns Museum, Jönköping, 2004), 36.

65. Lagerås, "Järnålderns odlingssystem och landskapets långsiktiga förändring. Hamnedas röjningsröseområden i ett paleoekologiskt perspektiv." 167–229.

66. Lagerås, Jansson, and Vestbo, "Land-Use History of the Axlarp Area in the Småland Uplands, Southern Sweden," 223–34.

67. H. Marks, "Bereft of Property: Change and Continuity in Family Organization in Härjedalen, Sweden, 1850 to 1930," in *Distinct Inheritances: Property, Family and Community in a Changing Europe*, ed. H. Grandits and P. Heady (New Brunswick, NJ: Transaction Publishers, 2003), 245–61.

68. L. McCann, "Seasons of Labor: Family, Work, and Land in a Nineteenth-Century Nova Scotia Shipbuilding Community," *The History of the Family: An International Quarterly* 4, no. 4 (1999): 485–527.

69. L. Häggström, "Att datera agrara lämningar med OSL. Om OSL-metoden och dess tillämpning i Öggestorp, norra Småland," in *Aktuella metodfrågor*, ed. M. Lönn (Riksantikvarieämbetet UV, Skrifter 58. Stockholm), 132–41.

70. H. Slotte, "Harvesting of Leaf-Hay Shaped the Swedish Landscape," *Landscape Ecology* 16, no. 8: 691–702.

71. H. Göransson, *Neolithic Man and the Forest Environment around Alvastra Pile Dwelling* (Lund: Lund University Press, 1988); H. Göransson, "Man and the Forests of Nemoral Broad-Leafed Trees during the Stone Age," *Striae* 24 (1986): 143–52.

72. M. Regnell, "Charcoals from Uppåkra as indicators of leaf fodder," *Centrality-Regionality: The Social Structure of Southern Sweden during the Iron Age*, in Acta Archaeologica Lundensia, series in 8 40, ed. L. Larsson, and B. Hårdh (Lund: Lund University Press, 2003): 105–15.

73. Björkman, "The Role of Human Disturbance in the Local Late Holocene Establishment of Fagus and Picea Forests at Flahult, Western Småland, Southern Sweden," 79–90.

74. A. Florén et al., "The Social Organisation of Work at Mines, Furnaces, and Forges," in *Iron-Making Societies: Early Industrial Development in Sweden and Russia, 1600–1900*, ed. M. Ågren (New York: Berghahn Books, 1998), 61–140.

75. R. Gordon and T. Reynolds, "Medieval Iron in Society-Norberg, Sweden, May 6–10, 1985," *Technology and Culture* 27, no. 1: 110–17; G. Magnusson, "Om Järnets Roll [On Iron's Role]," in *Järnets roll Skånelands och södra Smålands järnframställning under förhistorisk och historisk tid* [*Iron's Role. Scania and*

Southern Småland's Iron Industry in Prehistoric and Historic Times], ed. B. Helgesson (Kristianstad, Sweden: Regionsmuseet).

76. M. Lorentzon, *Historisk kolning och förhistorisk odling* [*Historic Charcoaling and Prehistoric Farming*], Jönköpings Läns Museum, *Arkeologisk rapport* (2005): 27.

77. K. Olsson, "Walakäringa: Tjärtallar och tjärframställning i landskap och samhälle [Walakäringa: Tar Pines and Tar Production of Landscape and Society]," (Bachelor of Science thesis, Landscape Science, Högskolan Kristianstad, Sweden).

78. Lagerås, Jansson, and Vestbo, "Land-Use History of the Axlarp Area in the Småland Uplands, Southern Sweden," 223–34; J. Agertz, "Ortnamn och bebyggelsehistoria i Gränna-Visingsöbygden [Place Names and Settlement History in the Gränna-Visingsö District]," in *Visingsöartiklar. tolv artiklar om Visingsö från bronsålder till medeltid*, ed. P. Nicklasson (Jönköpings läns museum, Jönköping, Sweden).

79. L. Kardell, R. Dehlén, and B. Andersson, *Svedjebruk forr och nu* [*Slash-and-Burn Cultivation Then and Now*], Environmental Forestry Section Reports No. 20 (Swedish University of Agricultural Sciences, Stockholm); P. Lagerås, "Den svenska skogens historia och hur den formats av människan och hennes husdjur [The Swedish Forest's History and How It Was Shaped by People and Their Animals]," in *Människan Och Skogen*, ed. L. Östlund (Nordiska Museet, Stockholm), 116–34.

80. A. Vestbö-Franzén, *Råg och rön: Om mat, människor och landskaps-förändringar i norra Småland, ca 1550–1700* [*Research on Rye: On Food, Humans and Structural Changes in the Agrarian Landscape of Northern Småland 1550–1700*] (Jönköpings läns museum, Jönköping, Sweden).

81. A. Andrén, "Against War! Regional Identity across a National Border in Late Medieval and Early Modern Scandinavia," *International Journal of Historical Archaeology* 4, no. 4: 315–34.

82. Ibid.; Cederholm, "De värjde sin rätt. Senmedeltida Bondemotstånd i Skåne och Småland."

83. H. Hallenberg, J. Holm, and D. Johansson, "Organization, Legitimation, Participation: State Formation as a Dynamic Process—the Swedish Example c 1523–1680," *Scandinavian Journal of History* 33, no. 3: 247–68; K. Katajala, "Against Tithes and Taxes, for King and Province. Peasant Unrest and Medieval Scandinavian Political Culture," in *Northern Revolts: Medieval and Early Modern Unrest in the Nordic Countries*, ed. K. Katajala (Finnish Literature Society, Helsinki), 32–52.

84. Hallenberg, Holm, and Johansson, "Organization, Legitimation, Participation," 247–68.

85. Brulin, "Faktor X, Arbete och Kapital i en lokal värld"; Cooke and De Laurentis, *The Index of Knowledge Economies in the European Union*; Ceccato and Persson, "Dynamics of Rural Areas," 49–63; O. Gummesson, *Därför lyckas Gnosjö bygden som har blivit ett begrepp* [*Why Gnosjö Succeeded—The District That*

Has Become a Concept] (Ekerlids Förlag, Stockholm, 1997); Johannisson, "A Cultural Perspective on Small Business," 32–41; Johannisson and Wigren, "The Dynamics of Community Identity Making in an Industrial District," 188–209; C. Nuur, *Cluster Dynamics and Industrial Policy in Peripheral Regions*; Wigren, *The Spirit of Gnosjö—The Grand Narrative and Beyond*.

86. Ibid., note 46.

87. L. Jörberg, "Structural Change and Economic Growth in Nineteenth Century Sweden," in *Sweden's Development from Poverty to Affluence, 1750–1970*, ed. S. Koblik (Minneapolis: University of Minnesota Press), 92–135.

88. J. Gjerde, "The Scandinavian Migrants," in *The Cambridge Survey of World Migration*, ed. R. Cohen (Cambridge: Cambridge University Press, 1995), 85–90; H. Norman and H. Runblom, *Transatlantic Connections: Nordic Migration to the New World after 1800* (London: Norwegian University Press, 1987); H. Runblom and H. Norman, *From Sweden to America: A History of the Migration: A Collective Work of the Uppsala Migration Research Project*, Studia Historica Upsaliensia, vol. 74 (1976), Acta Universitatis Upsaliensis, Uppsala.

16

The Holocene Catastrophe

ANDRÉ COSTOPOULOS

Introduction

Our modern, politically centralized, largely coastal, sedentary, and agro-industrial societies have evolved over the past eight millennia under conditions of unusual climate stability. As a result, our institutions—from our land tenure regimes to our laws and kinship organization—are adapted to life in a stable environment. We have densely populated the areas of our globe that are hospitable to our subsistence strategy, which is based on increasingly intensive sedentary agriculture. For the past 8,000 years, this strategy, as it has spread around the world and been adopted by nearly the entire human population, has faced no serious environmental challenge.

There are now strong indications that these climatically and environmentally stable conditions are ending, and that we will be facing even greater climatic and environmental variability in the near future. How will we react to this increasing rate and magnitude of environmental change? Our ancestors have gone through these kinds of changes before and have successfully adapted. What can the small amount of relevant archaeology available tell us about their experience?

Before this chapter discusses these questions, it must deal with the cause of the current episode of climate change. In this discussion, the chapter deliberately stays away from this emotional and divisive question, not because it is unimportant, but because, in the final analysis, it does not change the chapter's message. If the increasing rate and magnitude of climate change we are experiencing is anthropogenic, we should do something about it, because we have to. Even if it is not, there are plenty of other good reasons to treat our environment with respect, to avoid polluting it as much as we can, and to be acutely aware at all times of the environmental consequences of our actions.

Regardless of the cause, however, and whether humans are a primary driver of contemporary climate change, we will have to deal with its consequences, and we will have to adapt to them. This means that many parts of our adaptive system that served us very well under stable conditions of the mid- and recent Holocene will not work in the near future. In fact, they will probably become deeply harmful to us as a species, as local communities, and as individuals.

A History of Stability

The first feature of our cultural systems this chapter examines is their emphasis on tradition, cultural conservatism, and history. This may seem strange for an archaeologist to argue, especially in light of this paper's opening paragraphs, but we may have to, at least temporarily, abandon our cherished Holocene conviction that the past is our best guide to the future. Under conditions of environmental stability, both cultural conservatism and a concern for tradition are highly adaptive. What worked yesterday will probably work tomorrow. What our grandparents did got us this far, and we should be hesitant to change it. We have adapted to this reality. Our social systems, starting with their legal components, are fundamentally conservative.[1] They are usually based on legal precedent or on some other kind of tradition. As the links between the American and British legal systems show, this conservatism often survives even violent revolution.[2] Our land tenure regimes are based on intergenerational inheritance and are therefore inherently conservative.[3] All human societies respect and value elders and their knowledge.

Yet this may not have been the case in most of the world between about 18,000 and 10,000 years ago. The archaeological evidence is extremely scant, of course, but this is a period during which humans went from living in full glacial conditions to living in a full interglacial environment.[4] Not only did average temperatures and precipitation change radically, but also global sea levels went up 125 meters (about 400 feet).[5] Shorelines moved, and plant and animal communities changed very rapidly.[6] The human populations that were making a living off these communities also changed very rapidly from a very sparsely spread out, loosely connected network of highly mobile hunter-gatherers 12,000 years ago to an almost universally dense, highly politically centralized, constantly warring collection of sedentary agricultural communities by 5,000 years ago.[7] The process was faster in some places than others, but it happened almost everywhere, and especially in environments where this new strategy was best adapted.

The early Holocene, the period right after the last deglaciation, was not a time of cultural conservatism. It was a time for rapid environmental and social change.[8] If tradition was valued in the early Holocene, it was not the same kind of tradition that characterizes our later Holocene communities. Tradition, at the end of the last ice age and in the period of intense change immediately following, would have meant a respect for the capacity of elders to rapidly adapt to changing circumstances. It would not have been the kind of essentialist tradition that values the way things have been done in the past and advocates stability of practices. It would have been the kind of tradition that values successful algorithms for deciding how things should be done in a particular, often unique, and never before encountered context.

Once climatic and environmental conditions stabilized in the mid-Holocene, by about 7,000 years ago, there would have been increasing pressure to continue to do specific things that were done in the past and worked well.[9] As the sedentary agricultural adaptation spread, this pressure would have rapidly extended to nearly all communities it touched. It is much easier and cheaper, both energetically and cognitively, to learn a practice and repeat it than to learn a problem-solving strategy that must be applied in any context to generate a unique solution each time. Later Holocene communities literally and justifiably hate reinventing the wheel. We much prefer to learn how to make it, and we do not generally worry too much about whether it is needed or how it should be used. We just make it, and it continues to work because the natural and social environments in which we are making and using it have not significantly changed since our grandparents made and used it.

And here is one of the core lessons we have to learn in the post-Holocene world, whether it should be called Anthropocene, or

Neocene, or something else: in a time of rapid and significant change, adaptive algorithms rule and essentialist tradition or stability of practices is a recipe for disaster.

A Sense of Place

As human communities settled down and became less mobile in the early and middle Holocene, they tied themselves to spatially discrete resource bases, such as the large and predictable cereal plant concentrations that eventually evolved into agricultural fields or the very favorable estuarine fishing areas of the coast.[10] This means that they tied themselves, their subsistence, and their very destiny to specific (and sometimes very limited) places. Place became tied not only to subsistence and survival, but overwhelmingly to identity as well. Place of origin is such a fundamental component of identity for many Holocene communities that in our industrial cities, migrants from different places have sometimes remained spatially and socially segregated for generations.[11]

Place has also become important in another way. For mobile hunter-gatherers, the main method of conflict resolution is to walk away. This is possible because mobile hunter-gatherers tend to think of a place in terms of the resources that can be found there and of the role it plays in a subsistence strategy. In any given landscape, there are usually a range of accessible places that can provide similar resources and play the same role in a subsistence strategy. People can use one place or another—and some are better than others—but generally speaking, the cost of moving to a slightly less favorable location that serves the same purpose is substantially less than the cost of interpersonal or intergroup conflict. This is because while mobile hunter-gatherers spend some energy managing their environment and their resources, sedentary agriculturalist social networks invest massive resources into the intensive management of plant and animal populations (e.g., domestication) and in modifying the landscape to make it suitable for these resources (e.g., irrigation), sometimes over generations.[12]

Communities that rely on agricultural fields and domesticated herds that require very specific environmental conditions found in a very limited range of places tend to conclude that intergroup conflict is less costly than simply walking away from their investment. They are attached to the places where they live, and they tend to think of places in terms of who lives there, rather than in terms of what resources can be found there. Mobile hunter-gatherers use a range of locations to assemble a subsistence strategy, whereas sedentary agriculturalists survive by assembling a few key resources in one place and work at making it viable for those resources.[13] The first strategy is spatially flexible. The second is not.

Because mobile hunter-gatherers move around a great deal, their populations tend to be less dense. High mobility imposes constraints on the frequency of births per woman. A local group simply cannot physically carry a large number of toddlers over the distances required for a mobile adaptation. Settled populations are released from this constraint, and birth spacing is free to decrease, leading to larger and denser populations. This in turn puts pressure on the landscape. Mobile hunter-gatherers can afford to move away from familiar places to less optimal locations because their population densities never approach the carrying capacity of their environment. If you need to capture 10 large animals per season to survive as a community, it is not such a horrible prospect to move from an area that can provide 20 to an area that can provide 15. It may, in fact, be a much better prospect than risking life and limb in an intergroup conflict to stay in the more favorable location. Settled agriculturalists, however, quickly increase their population to the carrying capacity of their local area. A physical move to an even slightly worse area could mean disaster for the entire community.

This combination of heavy investment of energy into the management of local resources and the local landscape—and of life on the edge of carrying capacity—results in a uniquely Holocene calculus of the value of place. Place is highly valuable physically and symbolically, and that value is expressed as ownership. Loss of place is unimaginable and the worst trauma that can be visited upon a community.

In a pre- or post-Holocene world, this combination of extreme attachment to place, reliance on immobile resources, and populations on the edge of carrying capacity creates massive problems. When global sea levels went up 125 meters at the end of the last ice age, entire regions that had been available to human occupation disappeared.[14] Within a very short time, the North Sea went from being a fertile plain inhabited by large herds of social herbivores to being what we now know. People moved. They were able to move because there were other similar places nearby where they could practice their adaptive strategy and where they could replicate the solutions to environmental problems that they had faced in a different context, not long ago, not far away.

Today, a rise in global sea levels of 50 centimeters will have catastrophic consequences for large swaths of our species. Entire communities will vanish as a result of environmental disaster or as a result of the great social disruptions that will result from an absolutely minor adjustment of sea levels. Many people will have to move. But where? And who will let them? Will they even want to? And if someone lets them, and if they accept moving, they will try to follow tradition in a new place to which it is not adapted.

A World of Adaptability

Because our sedentary agricultural Holocene adaptation has been so successful for so long under such stable conditions, even very minor changes in climate and environment will have dire consequences for us and will lead to species-level disruption. Unless, that is, we manage to learn something from a more remote past than our cherished Holocene tradition currently allows. Key to our adaptation to these newly variable conditions will be the mobility and adaptability that made our ancestors so successful in a period of intense change at the end of the last glaciation. After all, despite the very rapid changes taking place at that time, it is the period during which humans very rapidly and for the first time expanded their range to the entirety of the New World and reoccupied the northern third of the globe.

We will have to learn how to let each other move without war, and we will have to learn to love to reinvent "the wheel" again, because the wheel we build in one context at one time will not work a little later and a little farther on. But the principles that allowed us to build one that works in one context will allow us to build one that works in another. We will have to value problem-solving algorithms rather than specific solutions, and we will have to be attached to a way of life rather than to the place where we exercise it. And we will have to do this at Holocene population sizes and densities, something our late glacial ancestors did not have to do.

Notes

1. E. Bodenheimer, "The Inherent Conservatism of the Legal Profession," *Indiana Law Journal* 23 (1948): 221.

2. Ibid., 222.

3. E. Cooper, "Inheritance Practices and the Intergenerational Transmission of Poverty in Africa," Working Paper no. 116, Chronic Poverty Research Centre (Dec. 2008).

4. L. Straus et al., eds., *Humans at the End of the Ice Age* (New York: Plenum Press, 1996), 3.

5. R. Poore, R. Williams Jr., and C. Tracey, "Sea Level and Climate," U.S. Geological Survey, https://www.usgs.gov.

6. Ibid.

7. "Hunter-Gatherers and Immigrant Farmers Lived Together for 2,000 Years in Central Europe," *Science Daily*, Oct. 10, 2013; https://www.sciencedaily.com/releases/2013/10/131010142704.htm.

8. Nn.

9. "The Holocene," Smithsonian National Museum of Natural History; http://paleobiology.si.edu/geotime/main/htmlversion/holocene1.html.

10. T. Denham, "Archaeological Evidence for Mid-Holocene Agriculture in the Interior of Papua New Guinea: A Critical Review," *Archaeology in Oceania* 38 (2003): 159–76.

11. B. Ray, "The Role of Cities in Immigrant Integration," Migration Policy Institute, October 1, 2003; http://www.migrationpolicy.org/article/role-cities-immigrant-integration.

12. M. Gallivan, *James River Chiefdoms: The Rise of Social Inequality in the Chesapeake* (Lincoln: University of Nebraska Press, 2003): 51.

13. Ibid.

14. Ibid., note 6.

17

Effects of Natural and Social Stressors on Human Biology

Northern Sweden in the Little Ice Age

THEODORE STEEGMANN

Introduction

By the late twenty-first century, environmental change will be massive, regardless of our counterefforts. This chapter considers agents of change-related stressors and how those may impact human biological well-being. Rather than a forecast,[1] this is a proposed historical case study to explore causes, effects, and adaptations during change. The assumption is that human response will be instructive whether the climate gets hotter or cooler.

Onset of the Little Ice Age was a dramatic environmental shift. Its climatic effects and other natural events such as plague combined with human mismanagement to produce "the late medieval crisis" in fourteenth- and fifteenth-century Europe. Those were the worst of times, a well-recognized rough passage, especially since "its disorders cannot be traced to any one cause; they were the hoof prints of more than the four horsemen of St. John's vision, which now had become seven—plague, war, taxes, brigandage, bad government, insurrection, and schism in the church."[2] Famine and weather extremes also played their roles.

Yet historical accounts are frustratingly inexact. As Barbara Tuchman pointed out in *A Distant Mirror*, dire events may have been exaggerated retrospectively through multiple reports of single events and were perhaps enhanced due to fascination with disorder. As an example, she directed readers to any contemporary television newscast.

While her cautions are well founded, stressors embedded in the late medieval crisis are believable. One example will suffice. In northern Europe, the Catholic Church expanded steadily as it grew into a dominant social institution. Sweden—the venue for this study—saw church construction increase at a rising pace, starting around AD 1000. Human and material capital needed to build social constructions are efficient indicators of a community's general strength and social discipline. Consequently, it is telling that building faltered about AD 1300 (Figure 17.1), fell precipitously when the Plague hit Sweden in 1350, and had

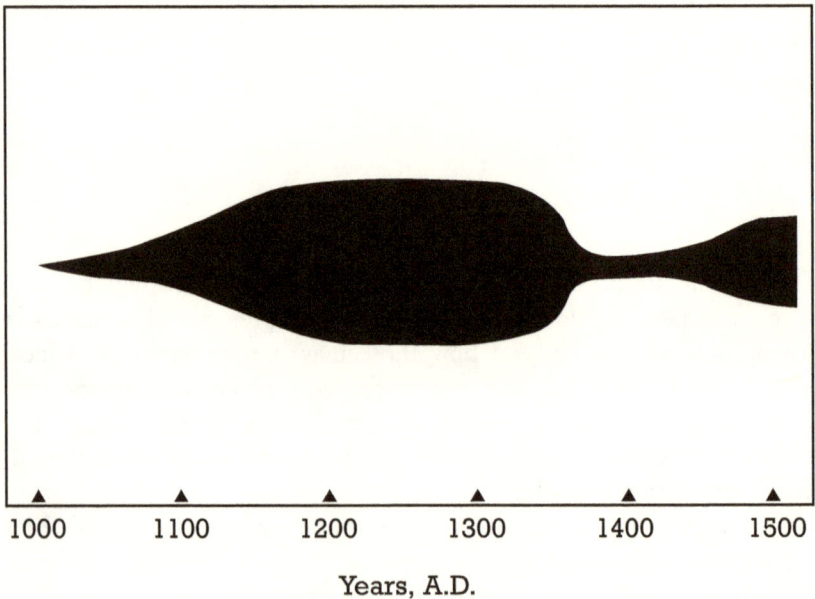

Years, A.D.

Figure 17.1. Christianity was established in Sweden about AD 1000. This figure shows growing parish church construction, an index of community resources and social will, during the medieval warming period. Construction declined sharply with Little Ice Age onset and the black death in 1350. Redrawn after Myrdal, 2011.

not yet recovered by 1500. Here is graphic evidence of hard times and stressed populations of the late medieval crisis. Janken Myrdal discusses conditions specific to Sweden.[3] See Figure 17.2 for a general model at stressors on the population.

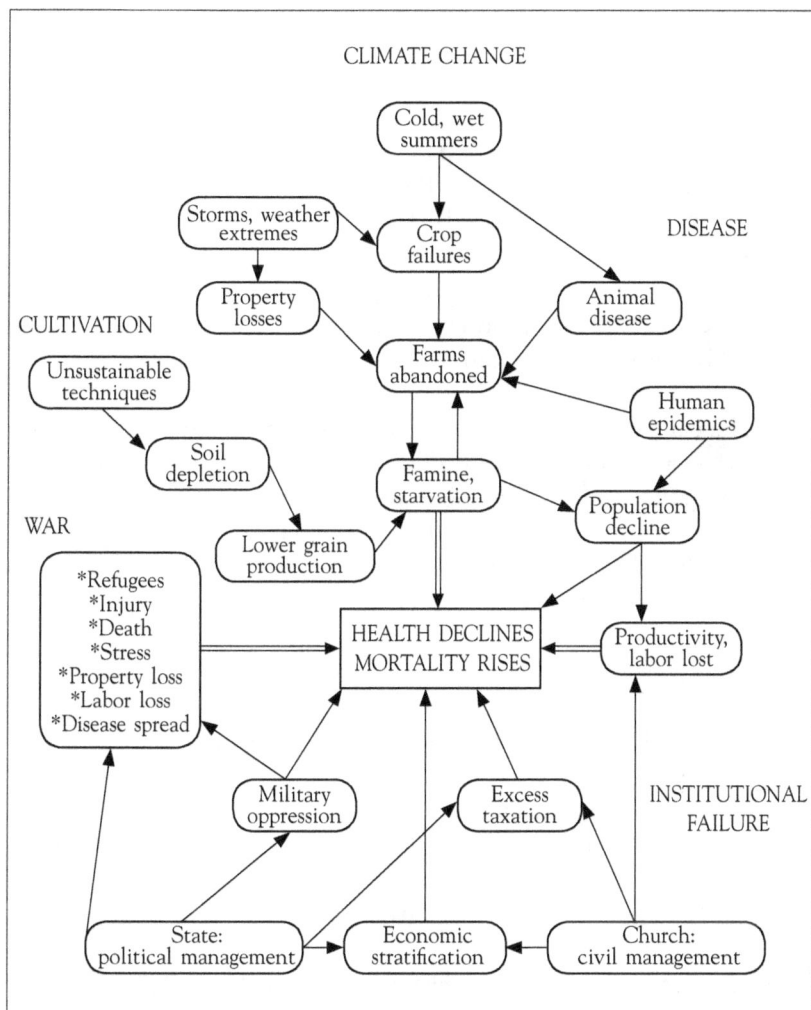

CLIMATE CHANGE

Cold, wet summers

Storms, weather extremes

Crop failures

DISEASE

Property losses

Animal disease

CULTIVATION

Unsustainable techniques

Farms abandoned

Human epidemics

Soil depletion

Famine, starvation

Population decline

WAR

Lower grain production

*Refugees
*Injury
*Death
*Stress
*Property loss
*Labor loss
*Disease spread

HEALTH DECLINES
MORTALITY RISES

Productivity, labor lost

Military oppression

Excess taxation

INSTITUTIONAL FAILURE

State: political management

Economic stratification

Church: civil management

Figure 17.2. This model illustrates the action of natural and social independent variables on human health and mortality. These factors led to declines in population, availability of labor, and general well-being in late medieval Sweden.

Specific Stressors of Medieval Populations

In the present research scenario, factors that influenced medieval Swedish health and survival are seen as independent variables. As shown in Figure 17.2, they were extrinsic pressures assumed to have caused human well-being to improve or decline, typically acting in pairs or multiples rather than alone.[4]

Climate Change

Starting about AD 1000, the northern European climate grew benign. The "Medieval Warming Period" describes conditions of temperature, precipitation, and stability favorable to dependable harvests and agricultural expansion into previously marginal areas.[5] Although there is no exact estimate of European population size in the high Middle Ages, it probably grew to more than 100 million people by 1300, based on land-use estimates.[6]

The early 1300s saw an end of good times as weather deterioration made for poor harvests. Not only did temperatures decline, but there was also heavy, erratic rainfall and more weather extremes.[7] These harbingers marked the beginnings of the Little Ice Age. However, there is consensus that other developments in the fourteenth and fifteenth centuries exacerbated the stresses of climate change.

Famines

Brought on by bad weather, the Great Famine struck northern Europe in AD 1315, lasted several years, and affected more than 30 million people.[8] Beyond starvation, undernutrition may leave its survivors with lifetime health and fertility problems, as judged through modern case studies.[9]

Epidemic Disease of Humans and Livestock

Stressful weather has been associated with past "murrains"—livestock epidemics that induced high animal mortality and intensified human food shortages.[10] In the 1340s, the Plague also descended. By the time it ran its course in 1350, northern Europe and lost 30–50 percent of its population. Though death rates were not uniform,[11] Scandinavia was heavily impacted.[12] It must have seemed like the end of times, a psychological disaster, compounded by the loss of food producers.

Marginal Lands, Unsustainable Agriculture, and Farm Abandonment

Medieval warming conditions drew farmers into marginal lands, sustainable only with good weather and proper soil care.[13] A combination of plague-driven mortality and unsustainable practices produced widespread farm abandonment and brought on the late medieval crisis.[14] Food production dwindled, possibly in disproportion even to the population of plague survivors.

Social Management Failures: Church and State

Despite population declines, nobles and church leaders increased taxation and plunder of landholders, as shown by increases in castle construction after 1350.[15] This was often accompanied by war between competing factions and raids by uncontrolled bands of soldiers. Eventually, peasants rebelled and further disorder ensued.[16]

War

Destruction of crops and property were major objectives of medieval warfare.[17] Refugees from the fighting fled to other areas to then become a further burden on already disrupted societies. Based on studies of communities caught in twentieth-century wars, people suffered more deaths, injuries, grief, undernutrition, impaired immune response, disease, and reduced fertility.[18]

Multiple Stressors

As shown above, the fourteenth and fifteenth centuries offered abundant hazards to human health and survival. Since effects were doubtless configured in a patchy fashion, detailed archival and archaeological records are required to estimate effects in any specific parish. Further, local conditions in those areas during the preceding twelfth and thirteenth centuries must also be examined to estimate local impact and to determine whether conditions actually grew worse during subsequent centuries.

Study Location

It is reasonable to assume that the foregoing conditions would have been exacerbated in an area already marginal for medieval farmers. We selected Jamtland County, in north-central Sweden, as an ideal test case site for the impact of social and natural factors on human well-being. At AD 1100, it was the northernmost inland area settled by medieval European farmers. Its high latitude supported Norse farming ecology only because milder temperatures, induced by the North Atlantic Current, flowed over the mountains and down into this lake basin area. Our assumption is that climate change of the early Little Ice Age would have been especially taxing in such a marginal location, well above 62° north. Specific changes at both abandoned and sustained farmsteads can be determined empirically through use of environmental archaeology.

Biological Markers of Stress, Poor Health, and Mortality

"Skeletal health" is a somewhat ironic term subsuming an array of biological markers used to estimate physical well-being during life.[19] While assessments are used for individual forensic analysis, the present application as demonstrated in this chapter is to define biological status of entire skeletal populations. Not all of the following markers should be weighted evenly. For instance, being relatively short in height is not necessarily a disadvantage in economic productivity or fertility. In contrast, enamel hypoplasias or fluctuating bilateral asymmetry, discussed below, indicate stress early in life and carry higher risk of lifetime poor health or longevity outcomes.

Height (Stature)

A range of environmental conditions, including those reviewed earlier, influence human adult height.[20] Primary height-limiting factors are undernutrition and disease, of sufficient persistence so that either growth is stunted or normal height is not reached at maturity. Stunting is well understood and predictable enough so that short populations are assumed to have had poor growth conditions. As an eighteenth-century illustration, Steegmann and Haseley (1988) reported a sample of low socioeconomic status British men with a mean height of 163.1 cm (64.25 in) compared to a sample of equivalent but better nourished Americans at 172.5 cm (68 in).[21] Living stature can be estimated accurately from skeletons.[22]

Fluctuating Bilateral Asymmetry

Tissues on both sides of the body are developed under direction by identical genes. If growth is disturbed by stressors, genetic instructions are disrupted and mirror image body areas are less identical. The degree of asymmetry is taken as a measure of the amount of stress during growth.[23]

Dental Enamel Hypoplasias

Before teeth move into their final positions, they form within the facial skeleton and gums, developing from the crown toward the roots. If growth is interrupted by undernutrition or disease, the crown enamel stops growing and, consequently, pits or grooves form on the enamel surface. Since we know the age at which each type of tooth forms, these lineal enamel hypoplasias are markers of when specific growth disruption occurred in the child's life.[24]

Other Skeletal Information

Biological markers described above are only three out of dozens available for analysis. For example, average age at death in a group, injury prevalence and type, arthritis, and other inflammations all tell their tales. Simply put, it is better to be alive than dead, better to be healthy than ill, and preferable to be well nourished in lieu of starved. These views have strong validity.

Multiple Stressor Indices

Using skeletal stress markers alone, or as elements in composite indices, a population can be ranked for its "health" relative to other groups—especially its own ancestors or descendants. Steckel et al. (2002) explain how multiple variable indices are constructed, although their prototype model did not weight each factor.[25] How accurately such indices actually reflect biological status is the topic of discussion. Wood et al. (1992)[26] and Byers (1994)[27] illustrate the origins of this question.

Were Jamtland Populations During the Late Medieval Crisis in Poorer Biological Condition than Their Ancestors?

The answer to the question as to whether Jamtland populations during the late medieval crisis were in poorer biological condition than their ancestors requires comparison for biological status of two skeletal populations. One population from Jamtland's earlier medieval warming period (Westerhus) has been extensively analyzed.[28] There is no matching local group from late medieval crisis times. It will have to be excavated, and several parish cemeteries of the proper period are available.

Comparisons must be age standardized, since we would not want to compare an older and younger group for age-related conditions such as arthritis. Some of the measures such as stature and the composite health index should be normally distributed. Consequently, simple t-tests can be used to establish presence or absence of statistically significant differences.

If People During the Late Medieval Crisis Had Poorer Health or Higher Mortality than Their Ancestors, How Do We Assess Factors That May Have Been Responsible?

Staying with the same pattern used for the skeletal health index, a natural/social environmental stress index for use as a primary independent variable can be developed. However, some individual measures will be subjective, coded as categorical (nominal) variables. Consequently, the environmental stress index will convert all scores, nominal or otherwise, into present/absent or high/low values, standardized so as to be additive. Then, conditions can be compared between the earlier and later periods. Significance of association can be run using chi-squared tests between environmental and skeletal indices. Further, relationships between nominal variables can be sorted out by log linear statistics. This allows estimation of relative predictive strengths of each variable area.

Realistically, the actual shape of the analysis will develop as data materialize. One example rests in historical interpretation. Knowledge gained from letters, maps, laws, and other archival sources is powerful and will be complementary to statistical insights.[29] The project has an advantage in its capacity to integrate information from history, historical geography, environmental archaeology, osteology, and human biology.

What If People During the Late Medieval Crisis Were No Better or Worse Off Biologically than Their Medieval Warming Period Ancestors?

Human biologists concur that bad conditions lead to biological damage. This is the general theory that guides contemporary research on stressed human populations.[30] However, that doesn't always happen, and the exceptions are of great interest. Sometimes populations resist stressors well enough to protect themselves from biological compromise. This is referred to as resilience or, more generally, as adaptive response.

Exactly what behaviors, economic strategies, and technologies past populations have deployed in self-protection would be useful to know. Given the magnitude of oncoming twenty-first-century climate change and its potential impact on our near descendants, it is quite a practical challenge to determine what has worked and what has not.

How do we identify resilience? Everett Rogers's classic analysis considered innovation and its diffusion as a product of culturally determined receptiveness and social networks.[31] These are intrinsic patterns but ones that show great variation within our species.[32]

In addition to studies of contemporary cultural process, anthropological archaeology analyzes the grand sweep of past cultural change. Productive examples[33] have focused on the ebb and flow of empires or archaic states where patterns have been cyclical. There has been particular attention to formation and collapse of strong central authority and the key roles of trade and warfare.

Studies of highly integrated, centralized states offer their insights, but northern Sweden was a marginal occupation zone in the medieval period and, to some extent, still is. Nevertheless, if the Little Ice Age brought grain cultivation to an end—or possibly just doomed marginal operations—then we must look for major subsistence shifts. Environmental archaeology, conducted as part of the proposed project, will focus on both abandoned and sustained farms in central Jamtland. Local investigations have already revealed an upsurge in iron production for trade, possibly intensification of cattle raising, and forest exploitation.[34]

If northern Norsemen weathered the medieval crisis well and were able to protect their health and longevity, then we can be confident we will eventually develop a full picture of what resilience behaviors and technologies they brought to bear. Several useful case studies, opposed to the "collapse" scenarios promoted by Jared Diamond,[35] offer rich insights and paths for investigation.[36]

Conclusion

This chapter outlines a work in progress. Our long-range goal is to understand both effective and ineffective human responses to climate change. Specifically, how did a medieval Norse society, in a marginal, far-northern setting, adjust to the oncoming Little Ice Age and to a complex of other exacerbations? How did they weather the late medieval crisis? At the core of the study are three propositions.

First, climate change was not simple in the past and will not be simple in the future. It will be accompanied by other natural factors as well as by human behaviors that will intensify its effects or interfere with attempted solutions. Consequently, our understandings of the past and strategies for the future will be complex and multidisciplinary.

A second element will be identification of resilience and resourcefulness and how they can offset both human-made and environmental stressors. Their effectiveness can be gauged by the biological protections they offer. Although the biological measures of well-being as presented here are straightforward, resilience-marker identifications are far from a simple task. Even with archival and archaeological data, we lose a lot of rich detail of exactly how adaptations worked. Ultimately, this dimension of the project will search well beyond the bounds of history. As an example, ethnographic study of how contemporary farmers and traders cope with change in the subarctic will help fill in fine-grained details.[37]

The cognitive structure of anthropology itself forms a third dimension. While anthropology is far from the only discipline concerned with consequences of climate change, it has some unique advantages. Specifically, we maintain pervasive interests in how an enormous range of preindustrial and industrial cultures adapt to stressors or falter under pressure.[38]

That is, we can use the full spectrum of human adaptive inventiveness as guides for our own future responses to change. In parallel, environmental archaeology offers lessons from past crises. These perspectives offer hope that we can identify optimum solutions to recurrent problems. If this project succeeds, that is precisely what it intends to do.

Notes

1. A. McMichael et al., eds., "Climate Change and Human Health" (Geneva: World Health Organization, 1996); T. McMichael, H. Montgomery, and A. Costello, "Health Risks, Present and Future, From Global Climate Change," *BMJ* (2012); J. Randers, *2052: A Global Forecast for the Next Forty Years* (White River Junction, VT: Chelsea Green, 2012).

2. B. Tuchman, *A Distant Mirror: The Calamitous 14th Century* (New York: Ballantine Books, 1978), xiii.

3. J. Myrdal, "Farming and Feudalism 1000–1200," in *The Agrarian History of Sweden 4000 BC to 2000 AD*, ed. J. Myrdal and Morell (Lund: Nordic Academic Press, 2011), 72–116.

4. J. Alberth, *From the Brink of Apocalypse: Confronting Famine, War, Plague and Death in the Later Middle Ages* (New York: Routledge, 2002), 6.

5. B. Fagan, *The Great Warming: Climate Change and the Rise and Fall of Civilizations* (New York: Bloomsbury Press, 2008), 25; O. Lageras, *The Ecology of Expansion and Abandonment: Medieval and Post Medieval Settlement Dynamics in a Landscape Perspective* (Oxford: Oxbow Books, 2007), 26.

6. J. Kaplan, K. Krumhardt, and N. Zimmermann, "The Prehistoric and Preindustrial Deforestation of Europe," *Quaternary Science Reviews* 28 (2009): 3016–34; U. Buntgen et al., "2,500 Years of European Climate Variability and Human Susceptibility," *Science* 331(2012): 578–82.

7. H. Lamb, *Climate, History and the Modern World*, 2nd ed. (New York: Routledge Books, 1995); B. Fagan, *The Little Ice Age: How Climate Made History 1300–1850* (New York: Basic Books, 2000).

8. W. C. Jordan, *The Great Famine: Northern Europe in the Early Fourteenth Century* (Princeton: Princeton University Press, 1996), 8.

9. Z. Stein et al., *Famine and Human Development: The Dutch Hunger Winter of 1944/1945* (New York: Oxford University Press, 1975); T. Gage, S. Dewitte, and J. Wood, "Demography Part I: Mortality and Migration," in *Human Biology: An Evolutionary and Biocultural Perspective*, 2nd ed., ed. S. Stinson, B. Bogin, and D. O'Rourke (New York: Wiley-Blackwell, 2012), 695–755, 734.

10. Ibid., 7, 95.

11. S. Scott and C. Duncan, *The Biology of Plagues: Evidence from Historical Populations* (Cambridge: Cambridge University Press, 2001), 103.

12. W. Adderley, I. Simpson, and O. Vesteinsson, "Local Scale Adaptations: A Modeled Assessment of Soil, Landscape, Microclimatic and Management Factors in Norse Home-Field Productivities," *Geoarchaeology* 23 (2008): 500–27, 159.

13. Ibid.

14. H. Antonson, "The Extent of Farm Desertion in Central Sweden During the Late Medieval Crisis: Landscape as a Source," *Journal of Historical Geography* 35 (2009): 619–41.

15. J. Myrdal, "Farming and Feudalism 1000–1700," in *The Agrarian History of Sweden 4000 BC to AD 2000*, ed. J. Myrdal and M. Morell (Lund: Nordic Academic Press, 2011), 72–117, 97–101.

16. K. Katajala, ed., "Northern Revolts: Medieval and Modern Peasant Unrest in the Nordic Countries," *Studia Fennica Historica v. 8* (Helsinki: Finnish Literary Society, 2004).

17. D. Nicolle, *The Great Chevauchee: John of Gaunt's Raid on France, 1373* (Oxford: Osprey Publishing, 2011).

18. I. Pike et al., "Documenting the Health Consequences of Endemic Warfare in Three Pastoral Communities of Northern Kenya: A Conceptual Framework," *Social Science & Medicine* 70 (2010): 45–52.

19. M. Katzenberg and S. Saunders, eds., *Biological Anthropology of the Human Skeleton*, 2nd ed. (Hoboken, NJ: Wiley, 2008).

20. S. Stinson, "Growth Variation: Biological and Cultural Factors," in *Human Biology: An Evolutionary and Biocultural Perspective*, 2nd ed., ed. S. Stinson, B. Bogin, and D. O'Rourke (New York: Wiley-Blackwell, 2012), 586–637.

21. A. Steegmann Jr. and P. Haseley, "Stature Variation in the British American Colonies: French and Indian War Records, 1755–1763," *American Journal of Physical Anthropology* 75 (1988): 413–21.

22. H. Maijanen and Niskanen, "New Regression Equations for Stature Estimation for Medieval Scandinavians," *International Journal of Osteoarchaeology* 20 (2010): 472–80.

23. S. Dongen, "Fluctuating Asymmetry and Developmental Instability in Evolutionary Biology: Past, Present and Future," *Journal of Evolutionary Biology* 19 (2006): 1727–43.

24. C. Larsen, *Bioarchaeology: Interpreting Behavior for the Human Skeleton* (Cambridge: Cambridge University Press, 1997): 44.

25. R. Steckel, P. Sciulli, and J. Rose, "A Health Index from Skeletal Remains," in *The Backbone of History: Health and Nutrition in the Western Hemisphere*, ed. R.H. Steckel and J. Rose (Cambridge: Cambridge Univ. Press, 2002), 61–93.

26. J. Wood et al., "The Osteological Paradox: Problems of Inferring Prehistoric Health from Skeletal Samples," *Current Anthropology* 33 (1992): 343–70 (includes reviewers' critiques).

27. S. Byers, "On Stress and Stature in the 'Osteological Paradox,'" *Current Anthropology* 35 (1994): 282–84.

28. E. Iregren, V. Alexandersen, and L. Redin, eds., *Vasterhus: Kapell, Kyrkogard och Befolkning* (Stockholm: Royal Academy of Letters, 2009).

29. H. Bernard, *Research Methods in Anthropology*, 4th ed. (Lanham, MD: AltaMira Press, 2006), 463.

30. Stinson, "Growth Variation: Biological and Cultural Factors."

31. E. Rogers, *Diffusion of Innovations*, 5th ed. (New York: Free Press, 2003).

32. M. Gelfand [and 44 other authors], "Differences Between Tight and Loose Cultures: A 33 Nation Study," *Science* 332 (2011): 1100–04.

33. C. Redman, "Resilience Theory and Archaeology," *American Anthropologist* 107 (2005): 70–77; J. Tainter, "Archaeology of Overshoot and Collapse," *Annual Review of Anthropology* 35 (2006), 59–74.

34. Jamtland archaeologist Anders Hansson, personal communication.

35. J. Diamond, *Collapse: How Societies Choose to Fail or Succeed* (New York: Viking Penguin Press, 2005).

36. P. McAnany and N. Yoffee, eds., *Questioning Collapse: Human Resilience, Ecological Vulnerability, and the Aftermath of Empire* (New York: Cambridge University Press., 2010).

37. S. Crate, *Cows, Kin, and Globalization: An Ethnography of Sustainability* (Walnut Creek, CA: AltaMira Press, 2006).

38. S. Crate and M. Nuttall, eds., *Anthropology and Climate Change: From Encounters to Actions* (Walnut Creek, CA: Left Creek Press, 2009).

18

Surviving Climate Change

Yup'ik Indigenous Environmental Knowledge, a Film Project

SARAH ELDER

Because of polar amplification, the impacts of climate change on human populations in the Arctic are currently greater than anywhere else on Earth. Over the past 60 years, the average winter temperature in Western Alaska has increased by 3.3°C (6°F).[1] These climatic changes have resulted in rising sea levels, increasing coastal storm surges, loss of ancestral salmon fisheries, invasive new species, and a warming tundra.[2] Alaska Native peoples are suffering from a cascading chain of environmental collapse.[3]

While research and mitigation of these environmental impacts are vital, equally important is the recognition that rapid warming simultaneously threatens some 10,000 years of Indigenous knowledge and the ancestral subsistence practices of the aboriginal peoples in the circumpolar North. Loss of indigenous environmental knowledge, with its embedded cultural dimension, is comparable to the loss of species variety or to DNA loss; this loss reduces our world irrevocably. There is a critical need to publicly communicate and to archive the voices and lived experiences of those who are on the front line of global warming, and to communicate as well the worldviews of aboriginal cultures that have been navigating survival, environmental uncertainty, and the capacity to adapt to extreme change since prehistory.

The film *Surviving Climate Change* (Sarah Elder, 2011) presents personal narratives and empirical observations by Yup'ik elders about their changing environment.[4] The film was shot in the Yup'ik Eskimo village of Emmonak, Alaska (62.7772° N, 164.5450° W), two meters above sea level on Kwiguk Pass in the middle mouth of the Yukon River. Emmonak is surrounded by the vast lower Yukon River delta and sits 10 miles from the coast of the Bering Sea. The delta is one of the largest river deltas in the world and comprises an area greater than the state of Pennsylvania. It is a landscape of lakes, tundra, estuaries, and small sloughs and is federally protected as part of the Yukon Delta National Wildlife Refuge, the second-largest wildlife refuge in the United States. Residents live on a mixed economy of subsistence (hunting/fishing/gathering) and employment in local commercial fishing, seasonal construction, service jobs, and public assistance income. The Yupiit are the largest Native group in Alaska and the second-largest Native language speakers in the United States after the Diné (Navajo).

I filmed *Surviving Climate Change* with the express purpose of documenting the sociocultural and environmental consequences of climate change in one remote Alaska Native community. The film is intended to stimulate and engage viewers from all demographics—Alaska Native communities, scholars, policymakers, the general public, and aboriginal peoples around the world. The film reveals a shift in cultural consciousness as the natural environment no longer nurtures and sustains but rather threatens the practices of daily living. In the Arctic, land, sea, and weather have always presented a precarious balance between being the source of great food abundance and the source of extinction for both humans and animals. Recognizing the perspectives of Indigenous voices in the larger climate change dialogue is essential to navigating the challenges of a steadily warming planet in the twenty-first century.

Collaborative Methods

In 1978, Leonard Kamerling and I filmed the ethnographic documentary feature film *Uksuum Cauyai: The Drums of Winter* (1988) in collaboration with Emmonak dancers and elders.[5] The film explores traditional Yup'ik dance, music, and spirituality. We employed community collaborative methods of shared filmmaking where both filmmakers and community members decide what issues, events, and people will be filmed. In *Drums*, Emmonak elders encouraged residents to participate, gave permission to set up movie lights in the *qasiaq* (dance house), translated when necessary, initiated situations to film (such as taking us to fishing sites), and cautioned us on certain topics to avoid.[6] We filmed more than 40 hours of film footage that is currently stored in the Alaska Film Archives, University of Alaska Fairbanks. *Drums of Winter* was well received by the village and continues to be a favorite in Emmonak households, in non-Native and Alaska Native communities, and is still screened nationally and internationally. In 2006, it was selected to the United States National Film Registry of the Library of Congress, and in 2015 was digitally remastered with the support of the National Film Preservation Board.

In April 2010, I returned to Emmonak to make a film about the impacts of local climate change. I found a population that had nearly doubled to 760 people since I first began working there in 1972. Predictably, I also found many infrastructure improvements that included a new airstrip (with an access road susceptible to dangerous seasonal flooding), a health clinic, an updated school, a washeteria, and a water treatment plant. Astronomically high gasoline and heating costs as well as television were now a part of daily life. I did not anticipate and was very surprised by the extreme weather changes and the increased poverty that I found. Like many other Alaska Native communities, Emmonak now suffered from food insecurity—due to loss of salmon and wild game and to unsafe local traveling conditions, and also premature death rates, high rates of diabetes, high youth suicide rates, and a large increase in public assistance services. Residents were eager to talk with me about the changes.

I used the same ethnographic methods of shared participatory filmmaking that I had employed in 1978.[7] Again, I invited residents to determine research questions and to select interviewees and filming locations. I met with the Emmonak Tribal Council, the Emmonak Corporation Board, the mayor and city manager, tribal elders, Kwik'pak Fisheries, Sacred Heart Catholic Church leaders, and Emmonak High School Native teachers and staff. I obtained permission to work, ascertained village filming priorities, and began visiting house-to-house, inviting open conversations and collecting individuals' concerns. Between April and July of 2010, I shot 90 hours of video recordings. As of 2019, the film is still in production, and I am currently seeking funds to finish the project.

The Film Interviews

In general, Yup'ik speakers, particularly elders, formally avoid making broad conceptual claims and regularly characterize their narratives by saying, "I can only tell you what I know; I only know a part." They are hesitant to generalize about global phenomena. In 2010, residents were quick to tell me they were unfamiliar with the terms *global warming* or *climate change*, but were keen to offer climate observations from their lived experiences—stating only what they knew to be fact for the film's record. Our conversations were in English. They spoke of the early return of swallows, houses falling into the slough, new varieties of insects, increased shrubs, lack of snowfall, and the deadly dangers of traveling on thin river ice.

In an attempt to respect the Yup'ik narrator's style—as well as the observational style of this particular film—I have chosen here to present straightforward transcriptions of these oral histories rather than offer interpretation. The speaker's chosen words, poetics of thought, turn of phrase all contribute to the speaker's rich meaning. It is these details that trigger the imagination of the reader or film viewer: the Alaska Native, the stranger, the general public. I have grouped the excerpts into four recurring themes: (1) The observed environment; (2) Impacts of a changing environment on food security and human health; (3) Intimacy with land and place; and (4) Reciprocity between human actions and the natural world.[8] All interview excerpts are from the film project, *Surviving Climate Change*, Sarah Elder ©2011.

The Observed Environment

In April 2010, Emmonak Tribal Council employee Ted Hamilton toured me around the village to see the changes since the 1970s: new housing, a water processing plant, the eroded river bank, and the still-standing but condemned (due to lead paint contamination) Bureau of Indian Affairs elementary school building. Standing on frozen river ice, we looked back at the snow-covered village. Ted spoke of "invading" songbirds, of wolves and moose, and treacherous traveling:

> I like the sound of these spring birds. We're seeing a whole bunch of these different birds compared to the seventies and eighties. . . . We now have blue colored ones, orange colored ones. Yellow ones that are about the size of robins. We never

had those before. These guys only come during the summer. You won't find them on any major river, but you will quite definitely in the smaller sloughs especially when you stop and look and listen. We're also seeing spruce grouse that we never had before. Even rose hips in certain areas. Most of the upriver species are steadily moving down as everything warms up . . .

Predator species come here too like coyotes and wolves that we never had before. The wolves were here definitely long time ago, when we had caribou, but they moved out. And now they are back again because of the new large moose population. It's different. It's definitely different.

Knowing how to travel amongst the land during these dangerous times, it becomes even more unforgiving to go out there. You make one tiny little mistake, and you get wet and that might mean your life. It's now harder to gauge those types of things right now as compared when I was younger when everything was a little bit colder and a little bit more stable. Now, it seems right now that Mother Nature is making sure that we're going to wind up in the grave quicker than might be normal. That's what it seems like, and it almost seems there's too many people in the world now. Now, this doggone pollution going on.

On a rainy July day, respected hunter and elder Gordon Westlock talked with me inside his house about global warming, saying that he does not know much about global things, but he spoke passionately about warming on the delta:

I don't know who to believe. Animals . . . sometimes there's lots, sometimes they're not too many. Sometimes we have lots of snow, sometimes we have no snow . . . we don't have [spring] break-up like we used to have. The ice don't roll anymore. It just floats by. Long time ago, ice used to really roll and jam and flood. But today it just takes its good old time. It's different from when I was a young feller.

High school advisor Tillie Oktoyuk welcomed me back after many years. We reminisced about old times when I was a schoolteacher in 1972 and there were no roads, only paths and ditches around town. She spoke sadly of ice:

Here I think the winters are warmer. Our ice is not as thick.
I remember when they used to get huge chunks of ice from
the Yukon just to service the teachers that come out here
so they could have running water. Those guys used to haul
those big blocks of ice. I mean a block of ice is nothing now.

Raymond Waska is a successful hunter and family provider, deacon of
Emmonak's Catholic Church, Yup'ik dance leader, and an influential
elder. He is considered a significant knowledge bearer of the lower Yukon
delta. Sitting at his kitchen table late in the evening after his evening
fire bath and after his household had gone to bed, Ray spoke of the
cold winters in his youth:

The weather is unpredictable. It's not cold like it used to be.
Wintertime was like almost 60° below, crystal clear, blue sky.
The Yukon would be five, six, seven feet deep. Right now it's
four feet thick compared to seven eight feet thick. . . . Our
summers are longer than usually. Winters are getting mild not
like many years ago . . . I know that too.
    Now when it's supposed to be warm, it's cold, it's chang-
ing. I don't know; it must have to do with our world.

*Impacts of a Changing Environment on Food Security and
Human Health*

Gordon Westlock talked with me about low salmon counts and the hordes
of invasive beaver in the delta's once-plentiful shellfish and blackfish
habitat. Because of rapid shrubification, particularly new willow growth,
beaver from upriver are colonizing the delta and not only pushing out
fish, but also causing significant permafrost degradation. Just 25 years ago
beavers were rare in the area. Unlike interior Athabascans, coastal Yupiit
do not particularly like to eat beaver meat. Gordon actively leaned forward to me and my camera lens energetically driving his points forward,
clearly aware that he was speaking to film viewers beyond our intimate
space. With intense focus Gordon danced between conversation with
me and the wider world:

Something is wrong with our fish [salmon]. There's hardly
any more fish. It's just like a young child taking candy.
It's gone . . . we never talk about that. But these beavers!

They're blocking the sloughs; it's a disaster. There are so many everywhere. You see maybe twenty a day. There are so many beavers. Too many of them. There used to be none of them. There were absolutely no beavers when I was a boy. I sure wish that we could get rid of them some way because they are closing the spawning area for blackfish, some sheefish; some sloughs are closed.

We used to drink water from the sloughs and lakes, but today there's too many beavers. There's beaver bugs [*Giardia lamblia*] that will hurt humans' stomach, and it stays alive like that. I've heard about it. I never did have that beaver bugs, but I've heard about it. So we don't drink water from out there where the beavers are.

With his children and wife listening, Ted Hamilton lamented the fate of once-plentiful sea mammals in the region (from the Bering Sea), when wild game gave themselves to a hunter if he lived a compassionate and proper life. Now they show up diseased and damaged:

We're also finding more animals with diseases than we used to in the past. Blisters out on the skin, meat, cysts on the inside of the meat; foul odors coming from the insides once you open them. It's like when we find animals like that we bring 'em back to the sea, and we don't eat those ones.

For many generations Yup'ik elders heard oral predictions of unpredictability—of a future massive warming. In conversations with Nelson Island elders in 2007, anthropologist Ann Fienup-Riordan documented elder Peter John from the village of Newtok speaking about the "first ones" giving dire warnings of a future warming world. He stated, "I'm not surprised that it doesn't get as cold as it did in the past as I used to listen to sayings and predictions. Those first ones said that our land will no longer have a winter season in the future."[9] In 2010, Emmonak elder Maryann Andrews echoed this knowledge, telling me that for centuries Yup'ik elders predicted a warming world. She spoke of her food concerns as she gutted and chopped up a snow goose for soup, ending her thoughts with an affirmation of Yup'ik survival and resilience:

The MELTING! How we going to live? Last year the fish were dying too from warm water. Everything is getting changed right now. It's getting fewer right now, even those fish they getting fewer every year. Even the animals like birds, jack rabbits, even those seal sometimes we hardly get them. It's getting hard to get. But Eskimos NOT going to starve. They could eat anything.

Intimacy with Land and Place

Film participants often spoke eloquently of their love and attachment to their wilderness place of tundra, lakes, and sloughs on the middle mouth of the Yukon River 10 miles from the Bering Sea. The film documents remote scenes of seal hunting, checking winter fish traps, setting up camp, berry picking on the tundra, and traveling down Yukon River sloughs. Local leader Robert Moore told me, "People from the Outside will never understand. If they moved here, they'd never survive. We'll survive. It's paradise." We hear similar thoughts from Lala Charles Hunt about her comfort in wilderness:

> I really enjoy being out on the tundra. You can just hear everything around you. There is no noise. I always have a sense of feeling like I belong. I'm secure where I am, and I cannot imagine myself in any other place in the world.
>
> When we're traveling on the Yukon or sloughs, I always have this sense of belonging. This is my place and no one's going to take it away from me. When I was growing up I used to talk to plants and bushes and the big tall trees. I would say, "Oh it's nice to see you. You've grown, and you say I've grown too." This was when I was a little girl. That was when there was sand bars, and now in those places there's no sand bars. There's grass growing, tall bushes growing, willows. Our surroundings are changing. . . . It's just peaceful out there. The smell of the plants, the tea, the Labrador tea. It's a sweet smell . . . and the breeze. It's just peaceful.

Tillie Oktoyuk:

> All I know is I live on the land; that I've lived off the land all my life. It's part of who I am. It's part of whoever out there maybe grows potatoes or has a farm or all the Natives

of the world that have been in touch with nature—they are noticing the changes that are going on.

Ray Waska:

> I like to take my grandchildren out and let them see how peaceful it is out there. And yet it could be mean. The weather and wilderness could turn mean. If we don't pay attention to it, if you don't know how to survive it, it could take your life. Like the river. . . . Sometimes I get mad at the mosquitoes; they're pests, but I start realizing they are out there for a purpose to feed the birds, feed the little birds. I get mad at them all right, but I start thinking why not—they try to live like me.

Reciprocity between Human Actions and the Natural World

Yup'ik Elders believe that over the last century the Yupiit (as well as all humans) have not lived with the "right actions" of compassion and restraint; they have not followed ancestral oral instructions or traditional words of wisdom (qanruyutet) and are out of balance with weather, land, sea, and other humans.[10] Emmonak Elders suggested to me that this Yup'ik understanding of the reciprocity and interrelatedness between human actions and the natural world could be a fruitful educational framework for Native and non-Native leaders to address the human causes of climate change—a successful approach to capture the public's attention and imagination in taking greater personal responsibility for the reduction of fossil fuel burning.[11]

Reflecting this human-world interconnectedness, Raymond Waska spoke to the old Yup'ik adage "the world is changing following its people."[12] He draws the connection here between the reciprocity of people's actions and the weather as well as between people's actions and other people. Ray sees change happening in two directions: from people to weather, and from weather to people, and he sees the overall trajectory of both humans and weather going from good to worse to bad:

> I think there is global warming somewhere because the ice is not thick like it used to be. . . . It's changing. I don't know it must have something to do with our world. Too much

smog in the air. I don't know what it is. Science say that
we're having plastic over our earth, because of smog, I don't
know, something . . . changing a lot, along with the people
too. People are changing as well. People are changing, the
weather is changing. It's going both ways. It's going from
good to worse, to bad.

When her husband Ted finished talking about climate instability, Joann
Hamilton spoke quietly about her parents' treatment of animals and
the land. She alluded to the Yup'ik belief in the inherent personhood
of animals and their need for respect and dignity:

> My dad he respected the land because that was where he got
> food for us. So he was like, "You treat the land right, the
> land will take care of you." Like the first spring seals that he
> went out to the coast to get [gesturing in the direction of the
> ocean], if he brought that in [to the house] . . . for my mom
> to work on it, before anybody said anything or did anything
> to the seal, he'd let my mom go pour water [in the mouth]
> to welcome the animal. Let it drink water. That's how my
> mom described it when I asked her "why are you giving the
> dead seal water for?" She said, "Because it's a spirit that just
> came to visit. They're thirsty."
>
> I remember the otter was the greatest, the strongest spirit
> that ever walked in our house. My dad caught my mom a
> whole bunch of otters. And every time he brought an otter
> home, we had to be quiet all night until the next day. We
> couldn't make no loud bangs. No loud noises. We had to be
> quiet. Quiet, quiet, quiet. Respect it. That spirit will not feel
> welcome if we are loud, and my dad won't catch no more.

Ray Waska told me of his foolishness when he was a young man and
he did not follow the *qanruyutet* (oral instructions) or the *inerquutet*
(admonishments)—the respectful and proper rules for living taught to
him by the elders and passed down for thousands of years. The *qanruyutet*
teach that there is clear reciprocity between right human behavior and
the natural world as well as reciprocity between right (or wrong) human
behavior and other humans. The environment (*ella*) has awareness and
is responsive to all human thought. If you mistreat nature, your wrong
actions eventually come back to you. Ray was gently eldering here,

advising film viewers that human action affects the natural world in not so obvious ways:

> I had one experience with the whale [beluga]. Many years ago, I used to hear about not to play with game. Well, anyway, I saw a whale down there [on the coast]; the kids were with us and were small. I brought him to shallow water. I was hitting him with my oar just playing with it. Because that poor whale was going really slow, not going fast just getting tired. I was having fun. Well, I thought I was having fun. Finally, I let it go. . . . It took me thirty years to catch a whale. Every time we see a bunch of whale, even in shallow water, we get there and they just disappear. They sneak away. Finally, last year I caught a whale. When I finally caught that whale, I told him, "I'm sorry I play with you before, and I want to kill you right now." There were about twenty or thirty whales all around us.
>
> After that experience I tell my kids; I tell young people not to play with games. Take what you can, and if you cannot take it, leave it. I let it suffer, and I couldn't get one for a long, long time. Took me thirty years to finally catch a whale. Every fall I tried to catch a whale. Can't catch. None of my family. Finally, we catch a whale. It took us a long time.
>
> So we have to respect [everything]. Even little mouse. Got to respect it. We don't eat the mouse, but we can eat the mouse food [anlleq, mouse caches of plant tubers]. They are the best.

In the community hall at a First Dance ceremony for young new dancers, family members give away vast amounts of food to the whole community. Gifts include hundreds of pounds of frozen moose meat and ducks, cases of ramen and Sailor Boy Pilot Bread crackers, and useful and decorative handmade items. Darleen Johnson-Edwards spoke for the film about the practice of giving away food and sharing in general, and the unknowable consequences of our actions:

> I do know that a long time ago those gifts were directed toward the elderly, or the people that couldn't provide for themselves, or the widows that would lose their husbands and have no hunter at that time. There may be somebody that

doesn't have any luck hunting or fishing and when you give that food they're going to be extremely appreciative for it. In our culture if you have more than what you need, share so that you can help someone else because that will come back to you one and two and three and four times fold.

It can come back to you in ways that you wouldn't even realize. When I say that—you could have good luck in fishing after sharing a food that you had too much of. It could be looked at in that way. It could come back to you in the way that people treat you. It could come back to you in material things. The different degrees of what comes back to you I guess would be left up to you to decide if this is something that is a result of what you've done. And, that all comes through the values that you learn and you're taught through the Yup'ik culture.

Looking Forward

The Film Project

Our previous Emmonak film project, *Uksuum Cauyai: The Drums of Winter* (40 hours of total film footage), documented an older way of living with now-deceased elders. Similarly, the 90 hours of video recordings in the *Surviving Climate Change* project serve as a historical heritage archive that documents the transitory period of time when residents publicly began to articulate their climate perspectives. Upon completion of the project, I will store this digital film ethnography in the Alaska Film Archives at the University of Alaska Fairbanks, where it will be available to Native communities and researchers. The documentation of local observations, subsistence practices, and oral histories of Indigenous knowledge is an essential perspective to contribute to the human archive. We will only understand its full significance years from now when the world looks backward to the early history of the thaw.

The Community: Resilience and Adaptability

Alaska Natives do not show any desire to leave their ancestral lands. They reject the idea of becoming urban climate change refugees and are rapidly taking initiatives to adapt to the changes around them. In 2010, when I started filming in Emmonak, most people were not familiar with the term *climate change*—although they were certainly experiencing the local effects of warming. Now they are planning for a resilient future. In 2012, Emmonak retrofitted eight large public buildings saving $90,000 per year in fuel costs and significantly reducing the community's carbon energy footprint.[13] In a predictable adaptive response, the community-based regional Kwik'pak Fisheries started buying and selling newly plentiful beaver pelts. By 2015, Emmonak erected four 100kW wind turbines with an electrical intertie to the neighboring village Alakanuk. The *Renewable Energy Alaska Project* subsequently invited the school to participate in their "Wind for Schools" curriculum to educate kids in renewable energy studies and the STEM fields.[14] In his 2017 article, "What Rural Alaska Can Teach the World about Renewable Energy," David Shaw points out, "What is remarkable is that these small, remote, economically challenged communities have successfully integrated renewable energy into their existing, diesel-based power grids with more success than just about anywhere else in the world."[15] Emmonak continues to develop adaptation, risk reduction, and local mitigation plans[16] while it also explores prohibitively expensive relocation plans to move their village to a site less vulnerable to the impacts of riverbank erosion, coastal storm surges, and extreme flooding.

Residents, meanwhile, talk with humor of learning to grow potatoes and learning to like the taste of moose and beaver when they cannot put their favorite fish and seal meat on the table. Everyone in Emmonak speaks of climate change now. My sense is that they understand more of the enormity of future warming than do most residents in temperate and tropical zones.

On a cultural, spiritual, and social dimension, Yup'ik elders for more than a decade have been formally gathering to record and document "for those yet born" the *qanruyutet*, the extensive oral instructions that teach the rules and proper behavior essential to live in the environment with integrity.[17] Elders are also revisiting their traditional worldview *yuuyaraq*—the Yup'ik ways of being a human being, and initiating *yuuyaraq* discussion groups to give guidance and teach young people traditional knowledge practices to help them navigate the accelerating rate of change in the Arctic. Elders, residents, and youth are actively documenting their culture through powerful initiatives such as the Calista Education and Culture programs[18] and online resources like the Yup'ik Atlas, a part of the Yup'ik Environmental Knowledge Project.[19]

They look to the term *ella,* which in the Yup'ik language is a compound concept "that includes both natural and social phenomena."[20] The word *ella* translates as weather, environment, climate, consciousness, awareness or world, and it conveys the perception that the human mind and the natural world are one interrelated system. *Ella,* in fact, speaks to the core challenges we face as a global community in a steadily warming world: Where does human mind end and weather begin; where does weather end and human society begin?

Our Future Warming World

Throughout our filming, participants consistently positioned their own climate change observations and understanding as fundamentally a moral relational issue stemming directly from the reciprocity and interrelatedness between human action and the natural world, and between human behavior and the treatment of one another on an individual, community, and corporate basis.[21] As our world struggles to survive warming, this moral ecological framework in conjunction with its ancestral legacy of a strong adaptive capacity provides a new lens—from a very old lens—to contextualize and advocate today's sustainable initiatives.

Our film, *Surviving Climate Change,* presents the personal narratives and voices of one small subarctic community. By communicating the daily lived realities of warming, the film collaborators and I hope to contribute to the increasing voices of tribal peoples who insist that the perspectives of Indigenous knowledge move from the margins of climate change discourse to a more central position. Local knowledge, like most knowledge, is not static or fixed but responsive to changing landscape.[22] If we are to develop effective sustainable strategies, our vulnerable environment needs all of us on all fronts to work for solutions. Multidisciplinary research models with shared knowledge systems that contain both Western sciences and Indigenous knowledge systems provide effective tools for sustainable climate change investigation and adaptive solutions.

Acknowledgments

My great thanks and gratitude to the many Emmonak residents who generously collaborated with me. Quyana. Film interviews and issues discussed here were conducted with Benedict Tucker, Mike Andrews Sr.

and Maryann Andrews, Raymond Waska Sr. and Laurentia Waska, Gordon Westlock, Lala Charles Hunt, Martin B. Moore Sr., Robert Moore, Matilda Oktoyuk, Nick Tucker, Stella Kameroff, Darleen Johnson-Edwards, Ted Hamilton, Joann Hamilton, Robert Andrews, and Lenora Hootch. My thanks also go to the many others in Emmonak who supported and participated in the film project. Special thanks to the Raymond Waska Sr. family with prayers of thanks for Stanley Waska who eldered me in the 1970s and 1980s. The film project, *Surviving Climate Change*, was supported by the University at Buffalo Civic Engagement Research Fellowship, UB Humanities Institute Faculty Research Fellowship and The Baldy Center for Law and Social Policy Research Grants.

Notes

1. "Temperature Changes in Alaska," Alaska Climate Research Center, accessed March 7, 2016; http://akclimate.org/ClimTrends/Change/TempChange.html.

2. "Climate Impacts in Alaska," United States Environmental Protection Agency, accessed March 3, 2016; https://19january2017snapshot.epa.gov/climate-impacts/climate-impacts-alaska_.html; Stuart Chapin III and Sarah F. Trainor, "Alaska Climate Report," *National Climate Assessment* (2014).

3. Larry Hinzman et al., "Evidence and Implications of Recent Climate Change in Northern Alaska and Other Arctic Regions," *Climatic Change* 72, no. 3 (Oct. 2005): 251–98; Igor Krupnik and Dyanna Jolly, eds., *The Earth Is Faster Now: Indigenous Observations of Arctic Environmental Change* (Fairbanks: ARCUS, 2002); Robin Bronen, "Climate-Induced Displacement of Alaska Native Communities," *Alaskan Immigration Justice Project, Brookings Institute* (Jan. 2013).

4. The film was screened at the conference, "The Big Thaw: Policy, Governance and Climate Change in the Circumpolar North," University at Buffalo, State University of New York, Buffalo, NY, April 2013.

5. Sarah Elder and Leonard Kamerling, *Uksuum Cauyai: The Drums of Winter*, Film (1988); http://www.der.org/films/drums-of-winter.html.

6. Sarah Elder, "Collaborative Filmmaking: An Open Space for Making Meaning, A Moral Ground for Ethnographic Film," *Visual Anthropology Review* 11, no. 2 (Sept. 1995): 94–101.

7. Ibid.

8. Excerpts of interviews with Raymond Waska Sr., Gordon Westlock, Maryann Andrews, Ted Hamilton, Joann Hamilton, Matilda Oktoyuk, Lala Charles Hunt, Darleen Johnson-Edwards, and Robert Moore are taken from the film *Surviving Climate Change*, Sarah Elder ©2011.

9. Peter John, 2007, Newtok, 59 (in Fienup-Riordan 2010), A. Fienup-Riordan, "Yup'ik Perspectives on Climate Change: The World Is Following Its People," *Études/Inuit/Studies* 34, no. 1 (2010): 55–70, 69.

10. Ann Fienup-Riordan and Alice Rearden, *Ellavut: Our Yup'ik World and Weather: Continuity and Change on the Bering Sea coast* (Seattle: University of Washington Press with Calista Elders Council. 2012), 354.

11. Ann Fienup-Riordan, "Yup'ik Perspectives on Climate Change: The World Is Following Its People," *Études/Inuit/Studies* 34, no. 1 (2010): 55–70, 68, 69.

12. Ann Fienup-Riordan, ed., *Nunamta Ellamta-llu Ayuqucia/What Our Land and World Are Like: Lower Yukon History and Oral Traditions* (Fairbanks: Calista Elders Council and Alaska Native Language Center, 2014).

13. Alaska Energy Authority, City of Emmonak, Alaska, "Energy Audit Final Post Installation Report," Ameresco, Inc. (July 2012); http://www.akenergyauthority.org/Content/Efficiency/EEC/Documents/Ameresco%20-%20Emmonak%20Final%20Post%20Install%20Report%2023%20July%202012.pdf.

14. "Renewable Energy Alaska Project (REAP)," U.S. Department of Energy, accessed March 7, 2016; http://alaskarenewableenergy.org.

15. David W. Shaw, "What Rural Alaska Can Teach the World About Renewable Energy," *Ensia* (March 2017); https://ensia.com/features/alaska-renewable-energy/.

16. See Yukon-Kuskokwim Delta Community Sustainability Model Lower Yukon—Emmonak, Alakanuk, & Nunam Iqua (May 2017); http://nuvistacoop.org/wp-content/uploads/2017/07/YK-Delta-Community-Sustainability-Model-2017-0627-web.pdf; Discovery Report FEMA Region X, City of Emmonak, Yukon Delta Watershed, Alaska Discovery Meeting: June 16, 2015; https://www.commerce.alaska.gov/web/Portals/4/pub/Discovery_Report-Emmonak_City_of-Yukon_Delta_Watershed.pdf.

17. A. Fienup-Riordan, *Ellavut*, 2012.

18. "Calista Education and Culture, Inc." Calista Corporation; http://www.calistaeducation.org/.

19. Yup'ik Environmental Knowledge Project, "What our Land and World are Like," Exchange for Local Observations and Knowledge of the Arctic; http://eloka-arctic.org/communities/Yup'ik/; http://eloka-arctic.org/communities/yupik/maps.html; Ann Fienup-Riordan, *"Ella-gguq allamek yuituq/They say the world contains no others, only persons," Hau: Journal of Ethnographic Theory* 7, no. 2: 133–37.

20. Ann Fienup-Riordan, "Yup'ik Perspectives on Climate Change: 'The World Is Following Its People,'" *Études/Inuit/Studies* 34, no. 1 (2010): 55–70; http://www.jstor.org/stable/42870073.

21. Ann Fienup-Riordan, *"Ella-gguq allamek yuituq/They Say the World Contains No Others, Only Persons," Hau: Journal of Ethnographic Theory* 7, no.

2 (Nov. 2017): 133–37; https://www.haujournal.org/index.php/hau/article/view/hau7.2.016.

22. Julie Cruikshank, *Do Glaciers Listen?: Local Knowledge, Colonial Encounters, and Social Imagination.* Vancouver: University of British Columbia Press, 2006.

19

Resilience, Reindeer, Oil, and Climate Change

Challenges Facing the Nenets Indigenous People in the Russian Arctic

Maria S. Tysiachniouk, Laura A. Henry, Svetlana A. Tulaeva

Introduction

Indigenous reindeer herders in the Russian Arctic face many challenges in the contemporary period, including dislocation due to changing economic and political governance, significant hydrocarbon development on their territory, and new threats related to climate change. In the past, scholars have analyzed adaptation to large-scale petroleum development and climate change through the lens of the broader economic post-Soviet economic transition.[1] In this chapter, we analyze these challenges to indigenous groups' traditional ways of life by employing the concepts of adaptation and resilience and focusing on the political-institutional and economic resources available to these communities. We ask: How do these communities understand and manage the vulnerability that is engendered by these challenges? Are they resilient and able to adapt to changing conditions? If so, what is the source of their resilience?

337

In order to investigate resilience and adaptation to change in the Russian Arctic, we examined four reindeer herding communities in the Nenets Autonomous Okrug (NAO). We conducted 44 interviews and three focus groups in May and June 2012, six additional interviews in April 2013, 14 interviews in April and May 2014, and nine interviews in February and March 2015. In addition, to better understand the general challenges climate change poses on Russian indigenous communities, we held participant observation and five interviews at COP-21 in Paris in December 2015.

The four NAO villages differ in the economic organization of their traditional livelihoods, ranging from private brigades of reindeer herders to collective farms that have survived from the Soviet period. The villagers also have experienced varied consequences from the expansion of the hydrocarbon industry. Our research indicates that communities are more or less effective in seeking compensation for the disruptions of oil and gas development and managing their relations to the local and regional authorities based on their ability to document damage to the tundra and familiarity with their rights under different models of corporate social responsibility and Russian law. However, even those communities most capable of seeking redress for damage are at risk of dependency on financial support from the oil and gas sector and have little control over how the resources transferred to communities are used in practice. The effects of climate change loom as an imminent challenge that local residents and the state authorities are just beginning to confront. Russian indigenous peoples' active participation in COP-21 in Paris represented their growing concern as they joined indigenous communities from around the world to argue that the indigenous in the Arctic have the "right to cold weather" in order to continue their traditional economic and cultural activities.

Nenets Autonomous Okrug: The Impact of Soviet and Post-Soviet Regimes on Local Communities

Located in the northwestern part of Russia, NAO borders the Barents Sea. It is an autonomous region of the Arkhangelsk oblast, and the administrative center of the territory is the city of Naryan-Mar. Most of the NAO territory is located above the Arctic Circle and comprises tundra and forest tundra ecosystems; as a result, the NAO experiences severe climatic conditions, reaching minus 20 degrees Celsius in the winter. The total population of NAO is just over 42,000 and includes members of the Russian (26,648, 63.3 percent), Nenets (7,504, 17.8 percent), and Komi (3,623, 8.6 percent) ethnic groups. Under Russian law, the Nenets are designated among the "indigenous small-numbered populations of the North" (korennye malochislennye narody Severa). Traditionally, the Nenets people pursued reindeer herding as one of their primary economic activities.

In this study, we examined four villages that differ in how the practice of reindeer herding is organized and how they are affected by oil and gas development. In addition, we acknowledged that all Nenets villages are affected to some degree by climate change, although these shifts are just starting to be felt—notably during the winter of 2014–2015 when freezing and melting snow created an ice cover that prevented reindeer from foraging.

The study locations are near one another but have some important differences. The village of Krasnoe is located near Naryan-Mar. It was founded in 1956 in conjunction with Harp, a collective farm focused on reindeer herding. Currently, the village is home to about 1,600 people. Due to Krasnoe's proximity to Naryan-Mar, the village has more social infrastructure as compared to other NAO villages. The settlement of Khorey-Ver, on the banks of Kolva River, is 200 kilometers from the city of Naryan-Mar and is accessible only by plane or helicopter. It was founded in the early 1920s and has a population of approximately 800. Nelmin-Nos is situated on the Pechora River, 60 kilometers from Naryan-Mar and is home to about 1,000 residents. It was established after World War II—in the early 1950s. Finally, the village of Bugrino is situated on Kolguev Island, located 70 kilometers offshore in the southeast shelf zone of the Barents Sea and is accessible only by helicopter. Bugrino has approximately 400 residents, mostly Nenets.

In carrying out this study, we investigated how residents of these villages manage their vulnerability to externally initiated shifts in political and economic institutions and the natural environment. Are they able to adapt, yet still continue their traditional way of life despite these deep structural changes? This research allows us to begin to evaluate the resilience of Nenets reindeer herding communities—in other words, the level of change they can accommodate while pursuing their livelihoods and maintaining their culture, even as they find new survival strategies.[2] Available sources of resilience may include the resources and skills of specific actors, access to institutions, new relationships, and learning by community members.[3]

The Cultural and Economic Survival of the Nenets

The life of modern Nenets reindeer herders is a blend of centuries-old traditions, practices developed in the Soviet period, and responses to the economic disruptions of the post-Soviet period. Reindeer herding is pursued by more than 7,500 of the region's inhabitants from the Nenets ethnic group, as well as some people from the Komi ethnic group or of mixed heritage.[4] As they have for decades, the herders traverse the tundra with their reindeer, continuing to use some customary tools and clothing and still practicing traditional Nenets rituals.

During the Soviet period, with encouragement from state officials, the Nenets people shifted from a nomadic way of life to a partially settled lifestyle in which herders lived in settlements for a portion of the year and engaged in herding seasonally. Under the Soviets, reindeer herding generally was not perceived as a "way of life" but merely as a job. After World War II, traditional reindeer herding communities were transformed by collective farms, and the methods of herding and processing were "modernized" to some degree.

In addition, under the Soviets, the leaders of Nenets communities and Nenets shamans were sent to state labor camps, disrupting traditional Nenets practices; under pressure to assimilate, many local residents no longer used or never learned the Nenets language.[5] Families were separated as herders' children were sent to boarding schools in the villages during the academic year and rejoined their families in the tundra only in summer. Lacking the experience of year-round life on the tundra, fewer children were interested in reindeer herding following high school graduation, and the number of herders began to decline. A greater number of Nenets youth pursued higher education and settled in urban areas.

This trend of education and urbanization contributed to the emergence of a Nenets intellectual elite, further separating urban Nenets from herding and the Nenets language and customs. As a Nenets journalist dwelling in Naryan-Mar commented, "Previously, all the professions we acquired [in addition to herding] were secondary. Unfortunately, today everything is the wrong way around. We have mastered this society and its space, and reindeer herding has become secondary, even though it is our traditional way of life, through which we can preserve language and culture."

The end of the Soviet regime prompted more dramatic changes to the herders' way of life. In the 1990s, many Soviet collective farms based on reindeer, fishing, and fur production collapsed; only a few farms that raise and process reindeer meat for sale are still operating. These remaining farms have developed a near monopoly in reindeer processing in NAO, and they are able to set the price for meat. In rural areas, local residents still support themselves through reindeer herding, fishing, and hunting, but they face many obstacles to selling what they produce—including low prices and long distances to markets. Villagers also experience an array of problems related to alcoholism and unemployment. Unemployment is exacerbated by state policies; when the state funds local infrastructure projects, they often do not employ local residents but instead put the contract out to tender and award it to the lowest bidder, generally an outside construction firm.

Thus, due to the intervention of starkly different political and economic regimes in the past half-century, life in NAO encompasses a juxtaposition of the traditional and the modern, presenting the visitor with many contrasting images. Herders may drive traditional sleighs pulled by reindeer or cross the tundra on snowmobiles and all-terrain vehicles. Nenets homes boast traditional deerskin cloaks (*malitsa*) as well as globally recognized brand-name products. Nenets who for part of the year still live in the tundra in a *chum*—a deerskin tent similar to a North American teepee—often equip these dwellings with modern appliances, such as washing machines, and technology, including televisions and satellite phones. The majority of *chum* dwellers also possess a modern house in a village; others spend part of the year in the village living in a trailer or the *chum* itself. Finally, the trend of young Nenets choosing professions other than reindeer herding and relocating to the city continues and even accelerates.

The Nenets culture is interdependent with reindeer herding, and the profound transformation of the Nenets' traditional way of life creates significant challenges for cultural survival. For example, the Nenets language evolved in close conjunction with the daily life of herders, so using it in a modern urban setting can be difficult. This challenge contributes to its gradual extinction of spoken Nenets and the use of the Russian language. A similar pattern applies to Nenets traditional rituals and customs. The head of a reindeer herding cooperative in Krasnoe commented, "Civilization has had a big influence [on the Nenets] in recent years: mobile phones, TV, satellite dishes—each with one hundred channels. It's very distracting." Thus, a gradual decline in traditional reindeer herding has contributed to the erosion of Nenets traditional culture.

Representatives of the NAO state administration and local communities recognize the negative effect that "modernization" has on herding communities, culturally and economically. An official from a state agency in Naryan-Mar expressed concern that new sources of financial support for herders—whether from the state or from oil companies—could further disrupt traditional practices: "Reindeer herding—it is not a job, it is a way of life. For herders, their houses in the village are like vacation homes. If this situation changes, then the children will no longer live in the tundra. It is not necessary to 'impose' all these benefits on herders." However, in interviews, reindeer herders do not express a sense of tension between the modern and the traditional aspects of their lives. Placing washing machines and satellite phones in traditional tents is seen as simply a way to make life in the tundra more comfortable—a natural evolution of nomadic reindeer husbandry.

Variation across Villages

The impact of the economic transformation varies depending on the organization of reindeer herding in communities across the region. In the Soviet era, the village of Nelmin-Nos was the site of the Vyucherski collective farm (*kolkhoz*). The farm collapsed in a long and difficult process in the 1990s and early 2000s, during which nearly all of the livestock was destroyed. Widespread alcoholism among the residents and reindeer poaching contributed to the problem. Since Nelmin-Nos is located relatively close to Naryan-Mar, city dwellers traveled to the village, offering to illegally exchange reindeer for alcohol and other scarce products. A resident of Nelmin-Nos remembers, "At night the whole poaching brigade went and slaughtered deer. So the herd was gone. Well, alcoholism crippled many. People exchanged deer and fish for alcohol."

The collective farm was eventually replaced by eight family- and tribal-based reindeer brigades—Ilebts, Tabseda, Neruta, Opseda, Wark, Seng, Vynder, and Malozemelets—that became the main producers of reindeer in the village. However, it was difficult for the brigades to entirely substitute for the kolkhoz, with challenges ranging from the need to reestablish the herd and obtain veterinary certificates to making meat production economically viable. The member of one Nelmin-Nos brigade stated, "We are earning almost nothing. And people live only on what they produce themselves and they produce almost nothing." Generally, reindeer herders are not familiar with navigating the state bureaucracy in Naryan-Mar. "It is so difficult to get the reindeer for a medical examination," stated one resident. "And the city is not a place I often go. It seems better just to take my axe to hunt a bear." To survive, residents also manufacture souvenirs, fish, and hunt for their own needs. These subsistence activities are complicated by the political-legal context, such as the need to obtain documents including fishing licenses or permits for hunting rifles. In general, the standard of living in Nelmin-Nos is lower than in other communities in this study due to the severe consequences of the economic reorganization. In the current period, residents rely on state subsidies and state support for village infrastructure to survive.

In Khorey-Ver, the community has experienced more continuity with the Soviet period. The local collective farm, Put' Ilyicha, has continued to operate.[6] The farm is considered one of the most prosperous in the region. Overall, there is a lower level of alcoholism among the reindeer herders, and residents complain less about economic hardship. However, as described below, reindeer herders in Khorey-Ver are more likely to be negatively affected by oil development and in some cases have had to alter their herding practices.

In Krasnoe, the Soviet reindeer collective farm Harp persists. In the Soviet period, Harp possessed more than 20,000 reindeer and also managed diverse activities such as breeding horses, fishing, and raising animals for fur. As part of the post-Soviet reorganization, some herders left the farm and formed a reindeer cooperative named Erv. These two institutions have different management structures. Harp generally continues the Soviet practice of decision making by the farm administrators and collective ownership of the reindeer, although the herders are allowed to keep some private stock among the herd. Herders working in Harp have retained their pensions and social benefits such as paid sick leave. In contrast, the cooperative Erv represents a collective group of private deer herders. Decisions within the cooperative are taken by vote at a general meeting of the group. Reindeer herders in Erv initially did not have access to public pensions, although this has changed recently.

Reindeer herding began on Kolguev Island in the mid-nineteenth century when the tsarist government settled several Nenets families there.

By 1910, reindeer herding was the dominant local economic activity, with herds reaching 15,000–20,000. In 1956, the Kolguev state farm and Red October collective farm were established, and then both were privatized in the post-Soviet period. The island is remote and lacks infrastructure; its economy is characterized by few jobs and low incomes. Subsistence activities, such as collecting driftwood, fishing, and picking cloudberries, are essential activities.

The Kolguev reindeer enterprise is the main employer for the village of Bugrino. From the start, reindeer herding in Bugrino differed from that of the mainland. Due to natural geographic limits and the absence of large predators, there was no need to guard the herds. A semi-free herding regime allowed residents to adopt more settled practices, in contrast to traditional nomadic lifestyles. A Kolguev reindeer herder states, "In recent years, seasonal pasturing has been almost entirely abandoned." The oil industry occupies part of the island distant from Nenets settlements and generally does not affect reindeer herding. In addition, to the herds of the Kolguev reindeer enterprise, individuals may possess 25–200 reindeer that are interspersed with those from the enterprise. The growth in the reindeer population set the stage for later population collapse.

Drilling and Herding: Coexistence or Confrontation?

Many indigenous Nenets people attempt to continue the traditional, seminomadic practice of reindeer herding, even as national and transnational companies explore the region for hydrocarbons and exploit the vast oil and gas reserves. For the state administration of the NAO, the challenge is to strike a balance between the interests of local communities, whose way of life is based on a close relationship with nature, and companies involved in the oil industry.

Oil exploration in the NAO region began in the Soviet era, but oil extraction started in earnest only in the early 1990s. In the 1970s, a Soviet geological survey expedition discovered multiple oil reserves and initiated commercial oil production in the area in the late 1980s and early 1990s. Today, Russian and multinational oil companies—Lukoil, Rosneft, Total, and Conoco Phillips among others—are drilling in the area. According to a government brochure, 98 percent of all companies active in NAO are involved in the oil and gas sector. Reserves estimated for the region encompass 1.2 billion tons of oil and 525 billion cubic meters of gas. Experts estimate that by 2027, the annual oil production will be 37 million tons.[7] Taxes from the oil industry are divided in favor the federal government, with 95 percent going to the federal budget and only 5 percent to the regional budget. One exception is income from Kharyaga oil deposit, which according to a special agreement requires that 10 percent of income be paid to the NAO.[8] As a result of this revenue, the NAO budget has among the highest surpluses of Russia's regional budgets.[9]

Challenges of Oil and Gas Development

The perception of oil companies in local communities varies considerably. The oil industry is seen as very important to Russia's national economic development. Residents also recognize the opportunity to obtain financial support from oil companies at the local level. However, villagers perceive the arrival of oil companies as a threat to their traditional way of life due to the loss of grazing land and damage to the tundra ecosystem caused by development and pollution.

Villagers articulate a variety of complaints toward the oil and gas industry. First, the NAO lacks oil and gas refining facilities; instead, oil and gas are transported outside the region for processing. Thus, gasoline prices for local residents remain high. Second, although many oil companies have active drilling operations in the region, they employ few local people. In part, this is because local residents may not have the relevant skills. However, local residents also see the practice of hiring outsiders as a way of cutting costs. A village official from Krasnoe states, "It is more profitable to recruit people from central Russia—pay them thirty thousand and they are happy. In the North, we need different salaries."[10] Over time, the oil and gas industry has introduced an influx of workers, some competing for resources such as freshwater fish and some becoming involved in poaching.[11]

Land use—and the decreasing availability of grazing land for the reindeer herds—is a more central issue for communities. Grazing land has been lost to drilling, pipeline construction, and the development of other infrastructure. Reindeer herders lament the loss of land that they have traditionally used for their seasonal migrations. A resident of Krasnoe stated, "If they [the Nenets people] no longer walk across their land, it is as if they have lost their home. Here we have a very respectful attitude toward the land. . . . If a matter concerns an oil company, it means that it has grabbed a plot of land. It is the seizure of pasture." At the same time, the companies have a legal right to drill because the state is the owner of the land, not the reindeer herders, and the companies have obtained a license from the state. An oil company manager emphasized the legal situation: "We need two licenses to begin our work: one for production and another for land. The lands were already rented to the reindeer herders. And they say: it is our land. But it is not their land, it is state land." Land use issues are exacerbated by the fact that Nenets families generally have three or more children and land for grazing and home construction may be in short supply.

Infrastructure, such as pipelines, also disrupts the migratory routes of reindeer. Companies take different approaches to constructing crossing points and bridges for reindeer traversing the tundra. For example, in the region near Khorey-Ver, Conoco-Phillips has built passageways over and under the pipeline; residents say that these bridges are well planned and are used by the animals. However, some companies construct crossing points that are too far apart—up to eight kilometers—and it is hard for the reindeer to find them, while others build arches in the pipeline that are too low to the ground for the deer to use. "Companies make calculations as they try to make [reindeer crossings] as cheaply as possible," stated an NGO representative in Naryan-Mar. Referring to a particular case, the representative continued, "It was important to raise the bridge above the pipeline, but [the company] did not do it. They said it was impossible. Then it turned out that it was possible, just more expensive." An aggravating factor is that oil companies in the NAO do not share pipeline infrastructure; initially, some firms made an effort to negotiate shared pipeline arrangements, but they failed to agree. Each company has built its own pipeline, leading to irrational situations. The vice governor of the NAO acknowledged, "Near Karataika, there are eight pipes all going parallel to one another. Each pipeline has crossings for reindeer in different places. For the deer, passage is impossible. A large territory for reindeer is lost because of that situation."

Oil spills occasionally contaminate grazing land and bodies of water. In the 1990s, during the early years of drilling in the region, the negative environmental impact of the industry was significant and very visible, leading to conflict between communities and companies. A resident of Krasnoe remembers, "It was terrible what was happening! The entire territory of grazing land was destroyed. Iron, metal, and garbage—all of it was left behind." Another member of the village states, "These spills occur everywhere—and how do they combat the spill? They just detonate an explosion and soil from the explosion covers the oil that was spilled. That way nobody can see it."

The companies' compliance with environmental laws and regulations is monitored by representatives of the federal Natural Resources Oversight Service (*Rosprirodnadzor*), but in practice the agency has limited ability to carry out its work. Because of the distances involved and the expense of traveling by helicopter, the agency has insufficient funds to check each company—compliance is inspected only once every three years. The reindeer herders are usually the first see an oil spill and to report it to the company and the state agency. By law, these violations should be documented by the agency, yet Rosprirodnadzor is often not capable of investigating due to budgetary constraints. When they do investigate, they must rely on the company itself to provide a helicopter for transportation to the spill. This practice is subject to manipulation. A leader of the Erv cooperative complains, "The company arranges the flight in a such a way that the spill is invisible, or for a time when they have already covered it with soil."

Negotiating with Oil Companies

A source of contention among state authorities, oil companies, and local communities in NAO is how much social support the companies should provide for the region's population. Generally, the oil companies conclude agreements referred to as "socioeconomic partnerships" with the NAO governor to determine the level and type of social support that they will provide to the region. Under these agreements, companies voluntarily bestow a significant—albeit variable—amount of funding for the NAO budget and/or donate infrastructure to the region. For example, oil companies have constructed a cultural center and museum, health care facilities, schools, sports halls, and slaughterhouses for reindeer herders. Private sector funding has been used to subsidize transportation from villages to the administrative center. These socioeconomic partnerships have helped to improve the quality of life in Naryan-Mar and some villages, enhancing health care in the region, and creating educational opportunities for some NAO residents. Financial contributions from oil companies have become a vital support for the widely scattered population.

These socioeconomic partnerships are determined through a largely informal process, however. NAO regional laws guide these partnerships, but the agreements result from closed-door meetings between oil company representatives and the governor's office. The level and type of support depend entirely on the outcome of these negotiations. Factors such as the number of years that a company has been active in the region, the stage of development of its oil production, and the quantity of oil produced all influence the agreement. The substance of the agreement is influenced by the preferences of oil company officials and the company's internal corporate social responsibility policies, which may be more robust in multinational firms and more rooted in Soviet-era practices in Russian state-owned companies. Personal ties and connections to the federal government in Moscow also may play a role. As one industry representative commented, "the state does not control the process [of determining social partnerships]." Ultimately, the level of funding is negotiable and discussions occur without public input.

In addition to agreements at the gubernatorial level, oil companies provide support to the administration of the Polar district, a subregional administrative unit, and sometimes make agreements directly with specific villages or groups of reindeer herders. In discussions with oil companies, reindeer herders tend to frame their demands by appealing to norms of social support from the Soviet period, while company representatives tend to justify their response based on economic necessity. Usually companies' support for villages is relatively low, and is typically not financial, but in-kind. Oil companies may provide assistance by purchasing specific items for villages, providing scholarships to university students, offering transportation to villagers, or building winter roads. Even more informally, individuals at oil company installations in the tundra may engage in barter with reindeer herders, provide herders medicine and food, or allow them to store equipment at the installation site.[12]

In theory, conflicts between companies and local residents and efforts to determine compensation for the disruption of traditional practices such as reindeer herding should have been mediated by the state authorities. However, in practice, the parties have relied on informal negotiations.[13] Before 2012, neither the company officials nor the reindeer herders used formal methodologies for calculating the damage to reindeer herders' income and livestock. As a result, differences in information, knowledge of the law, and relative political influence between industry officials and herders inevitably shaped the outcome of negotiations. Since 2012, reindeer herding brigades have started to request formal compensation for damage from oil companies. By 2015, almost all reindeer herding enterprises had begun to receive compensation, except those of the Kolguev Island, where socioeconomic agreements remained the dominant form of support.

The effects of this kind of social support are ambiguous. Funding from oil companies helps to maintain and enhance the infrastructure of the NAO, which prior to the "oil era" was eroding due to the post-Soviet economic crisis. The current process of determining how much and what kind of support is provided does not contribute to the sustainable development of the territory, the implementation of existing laws and regulations, or public participation in long-term planning. Instead, it either leads to the construction of high profile but less essential amenities, such as an "ice palace" hockey arena in Naryan-Mar, or it contributes to the general dependence of the territory and its residents on the largesse of oil companies.

Oil company representatives remark that there does not appear to be a long-term plan for the development of the NAO. They suggest that this type of plan would allow companies to invest in social programs more strategically. An oil company manager comments, "We participate in okrug development programs, but we cannot assess the region's needs to choose where to contribute." A representative of the Naryan-Mar administration acknowledges, "When the oil ends, this level of well-being will end. People here are not accustomed to entrepreneurship. If the law changes again, this money will disappear from okrug. Right now, people take everything for granted—the subsidies, benefits, and support from oil companies. The strategy for developing the Arctic is in the hands of the oil industry." Some villagers have even more pessimistic predictions. A resident of Krasnoe stated, "They will exhaust all the oil and abandon us with our problems. The tundra will take many years to restore itself."

Case Studies

The type of interaction between reindeer herders and companies varies across our cases because the impact of oil development in each village is different, and the socioeconomic conditions of village life vary as well. In Nelmin-Nos, reindeer grazing land is located far from oil industry development. For that reason, the herders do not receive direct compensation from oil companies, although they do benefit from funds provided by industry to the NAO budget. In recent years, oil companies have provided funds for reindeer herders to build houses and a modern gymnasium in Nelmin-Nos. The lack of oil infrastructure near Nelmin-Nos is seen as an advantage rather than a disadvantage by many residents, who expressed the opinion that oil drilling leads to irreversible damage to the natural environment. A villager stated, "Once, in an area with oil development, I saw reindeer there walking as though in a bad dream. Large machines were all around, immediately in the reindeer's path, and the land all plowed under. We had the same oil companies working here in the nineteen-seventies, and the land healed only ten years ago." Another villager remarked, "Pumping oil damages rivers. They all become shallow. There is no flowing, no fish. The fish move down to places where the water is constant. This happened a couple of years ago." In the coming years, however, the lands around Nelmin-Nos are also expected to be a site of oil production, creating new challenges for herders in the village.

Several large oil companies conduct operations in the grazing land around the village of Khorey-Ver. As a result, since the early 2000s, the reindeer herding enterprise Put' Iliicha has been able to negotiate several socioeconomic agreements with representatives of different companies, and the village administration has received occasional informal support. The head of one brigade within the Put' Iliicha enterprise describes their agreement, stating: "We are negotiating by ourselves so these are symbolic prices. To ask a big company to buy one tractor in two years, it is almost nothing—half a tractor per year! So for them it is funny money. And we are not asking for much." This person also acknowledges, "Through state's social program, lots of homes have been built." In the shift from informal socioeconomic agreements to formal compensation for damage, reindeer herders may now be able to receive 10 times the amount of funding as in the past, according to one industry representative. Oil companies sometimes voluntarily provide additional assistance to the village. For example, a multinational consortium of oil companies built a new school building in Khorey-Ver.

Living in proximity to oil development creates opportunities for socioeconomic agreements and compensation, but it also negatively affects village life, including poor air quality and increased pressure on grazing land. A local resident commented, "There is strong smog from the burning. We are concerned about it. We cannot let our children go outside because there has been such a cloud over the village." The development of oil fields and the construction of pipelines make it impossible to herd reindeer on traditional migratory routes. A reindeer herder in Khorey-Ver stated, "We have only certain amount of biological resources. We are limited. That is, our current conditions do not allow us to increase the deer population for the simple reason that we do not have enough pasture land." The reindeer herding enterprise may be able to negotiate formal compensation from companies, but the Khorey-Ver village administration and residents who are not ethnically Nenets are not entitled to compensation, although they experience adverse effects of the activities of oil drilling. "They [the companies] sent us to the okrug administration for support. All large contributions go to the okrug and we are not able to ask the companies directly," remarked a resident of the village. Despite some ongoing challenges, however, Khorey-Ver offers an example of negotiated coexistence between a local community and the oil industry through informal, short-term social agreements.

In Krasnoe, reindeer herders from both the Harp reindeer farm and Erv reindeer cooperative interact frequently with oil companies that operate on their grazing territory. The leader of Erv, in particular, has become very experienced in negotiating with oil companies, using diverse mechanisms and different types of leverage. The Erv leader first learned to pursue the community's interests—in this case, their right to sell fur products—through the courts in the 1980s, during Soviet era, when he was still a member of the collective farm. He recalled, "Then I realized that in fact some laws exist that can be used on our behalf. Then my attitude to the law was that if there is a law, we must implement it." His exceptional experience with the legal system shapes the cooperative's interactions with the oil companies today. The Erv leader remembers advice he was given by early oil survey teams: "When we were working with geologists, they told us, 'Guys, we would help you, but we have no money. But when the oil companies come, they have a lot of money and they will help you more.'" When the oil industry began to develop near the village, the Erv leadership was eager to negotiate for compensation. Initially, the herders' negotiations with oil companies were difficult, in part because of the high expectations of the local community and the oil companies' unwillingness to interact directly with the herders' cooperative instead of the regional administration.

Ultimately, the herders have used the federal Land Code and the Russian Law on the Rights of Indigenous Peoples as the main tools to defend their interests in their disputes with oil companies. In order for the laws to work, however, the herders had to use a formal methodology to calculate the damage to their traditional grazing land. With the financial support of the district administration, the reindeer cooperative conducted the geological and botanical survey of their territory necessary to calculate of the impact of oil infrastructure development. The Erv leader appealed to a Moscow expert who estimated compensation for damages from land taken for oil infrastructure. With this estimate in hand, the leader appealed directly to companies operating on the herders' territory. "Well, I came, saying, 'Here is what we think you owe us. If you reckon it as less, give us an estimate as proof.' And they had already prepared to build the pipeline." Since the company is legally required to obtain written consent from herders, it was forced to agree to the estimate or the reindeer cooperative could go to court. The Erv cooperative first signed a formal agreement for compensation with an oil company in 2001.

The case of the Erv cooperative in Krasnoe was a rare instance in which an active leader successfully used the law to protect the rights of reindeer herders. Instead, until 2012 the amount paid by oil companies to reindeer herders in most NAO villages was determined by the ability of herders to negotiate rather than the damage sustained to their territory. Since 2012, most reindeer herding enterprises work with expert organizations from Moscow that have geological and botanical data on all NAO territories and can assist in calculating damage; oil companies cover the costs of this work. Occasionally, oil companies will hire their own experts if they deem the proposed compensation to be too high.

The economy of Kolguev Island, as in the rest of the NAO region, is dependent on the oil and gas industry and reindeer herding by the Nenets indigenous community. However, the territories of reindeer herding and oil drilling do not overlap on the island. The Nenets people mainly live in the village of Bugrino on southern part of the island, while oil drilling and companies' temporary settlements are on the northern and eastern sections—in Peshchanka, where 250 oil company personnel reside in shifts. Drilling is done in a relatively small part of the island, and reindeer herders report that the drilling does not disturb them. Companies operating on the island conclude annual socioeconomic agreements with the Kolguev reindeer herding enterprise and have maintained friendly and informal relationships with the reindeer herders.

The companies are struggling with significant debts, however. When one company was unable to fulfill the agreement, its management provided gasoline to herders, repaired their machinery and snowmobiles, and allowed some herders to stay in the oil workers' dormitory. Occasionally, when the reindeer are doing well, herders barter meat for other goods. Snowmobiles were introduced to compensate for the lack of road infrastructure on the island, gradually becoming an indispensable part of herding.

Yet these changes may prove less resilient under conditions of climate change. Generally, on the island, the relationship between the reindeer herders and oil companies is peaceful and even mutually beneficial. However, changes to traditional herding practices—including the lack of annual migration across the tundra—have made the reindeer more vulnerable. Since the reindeer do not change pastures, the tundra has become degraded and their diet has changed. Increases in the reindeer population exacerbated these problems.

Challenges of Climate Change

Scientists predict that reindeer husbandry in the NAO could be adversely affected by climate change as the distribution of vegetation, the amount and duration of snow cover, and the timing of freezing temperatures shift. Reindeer herders perceive numerous changes to the natural environment in recent years. They report that the direction of the wind has become unpredictable throughout the year. In the summer, herders rely on cold winds from the north to blow away clouds of mosquitoes. They also point out that lakes on their territory are shallower and now freeze to the bottom in winter, killing fish. Some lakes have dried up completely and herders have been forced to change their migratory routes to find the water that they need for the herd. Due to the changing climate, over the past few decades, shrubs and brush have grown noticeably taller. The deer often get lost in them, increasing the labor of herders; the growth of these shrubs also leads to loss of grazing land.[14] Herders have begun to avoid these areas.

On Kolguev Island in particular, reindeer herders blame climate change for higher reindeer mortality. During the 2013–2014 winter slaughter, thousands of reindeer died as a perfect storm of factors came together to precipitate a near collapse of reindeer herding in the area. Of the initial population of approximately 8,000 animals, 4,000 were slaughtered, and only about 200 reindeer survived the winter. Factors contributing to this catastrophe included the deterioration of pasture land, poor enterprise management, and reindeer herders' changing husbandry practices. Furthermore, unpredictable fluctuations in the weather, including unusual freezing and melting, created an ice cover that prevented reindeer from foraging. Herders attempted to feed the animals commercial food, but they could not adapt to it. A director of the Kolguev enterprise states, "Reindeer mortality is connected exclusively with the ice. What else can it be? Half-wild animals are not used to feedstuff."

In other communities, most reindeer herders do not label shifts in the weather as part of global climate change. Herders are preoccupied with the day-to-day tasks of managing their livestock. Many of them have never heard that the climate is matter of a global concern, but they notice changing weather patterns and they are especially sensitive to precipitation (whether it is rain or snow) and the timing of freezing temperatures. A herder in Krasnoe stated, "It is not good for the deer when the snow melts and then freezes again; several deer broke their legs last spring." Another resident of Krasnoe remarked, "We needed to move the slaughtering period several years ago. We used to do it in December, but now it is at the end of January. And the deer are still here [in the village] because of the weather."

In recent years, reindeer herders have become more aware of global climate change, primarily from scientists conducting research in the region. Several projects have been undertaken in the area, including two European Union projects, "Barents Sea Impact Study" and "Global Change Vulnerabilities in the Barents Region: Linking Arctic Natural Resources, Climate Change and Economies" (BALANCE). Both projects focus on reindeer herders' perceptions of the climate and its effect on human-animal relations in the tundra[15] and both concluded that the indigenous people of the tundra have a high level of adaptability to changing weather. Due to their partially nomadic lifestyle, herders and their reindeer have been able to travel to avoid damaged areas and exploit alternative territories. In fact, in the recent past, industrial development has caused a greater impact on the tundra ecosystem's topography and hydrology than climate change has.[16] Tundra ecosystems have proven to be vulnerable to disturbances related to oil infrastructure development—such as damage from heavy machinery and erosion leading to sand and dust storms—as well as contamination by petrochemicals. Thus far, however, oil and gas development and nomadic pastoralism have been able to coexist despite new pressures of climate change.[17] The research shows a fairly high level of resilience in the ecosystem. However, increasing industrialization and climate disturbances will likely contribute to a cumulative adverse effect on reindeer grazing land over time.

Analysis

There are three major challenges to the way of life of indigenous reindeer herders in the NAO: the post-Soviet economic transition, the increasing development of the oil and gas industry, and climate change. Over the past two decades, reindeer herders have had to grapple with the manifestations of these deep structural changes: the collapse of collective farms, the loss of grazing land to oil and gas development, the rapid migration of young people to the cities, the availability of modern technology, and the increased variability of the climate. Nenets reindeer herders have attempted to adapt to all of these large-scale changes simultaneously. In addition to other disruptions to their way of life, the herders confront starkly contemporary climate contradictions more than any other population.

For now, Nenets communities are preoccupied with improving their current economic situation and facilitating the coexistence of reindeer herding and oil and gas development. Revenue from the oil industry, both from formal and informal channels, plays a significant role in the economic recovery of the NAO. However, in the long term, climate change represents a real threat to the viability of the Nenets traditional nomadic way of life.[19] And, of course, the exploitation of carbon-based fuels also contributes to the variability in climate. Actors in the NAO must strike a balance between encouraging oil development and safeguarding the interests of local residents, whose livelihood is closely linked to the state of the environment—a difficult challenge.

Research carried out in Naryan-Mar and four villages reveals that these communities are still recovering from the severe economic downturn caused by the shift from a planned economy to a market economy and the growing influence of the oil industry, even as they confront climate change. Communities have been forced to find new ways to adapt to the changing conditions. Despite overall similar trends, the process of adaptation proceeds differently in the villages studied. There are several factors that influence the resilience and adaptability of reindeer herding communities, including:

- The geographic location of the settlement (proximity to an urban center and availability transportation)

- The institutional upheaval of post-Soviet economic reform (existing social infrastructure) and the organization of rein-deer herding (ranging from the continuation of collective farms to the emergence private herds)

- The impact of industrial oil development around the village and on grazing lands

- The willingness and ability of herding communities to effec-tively self-organize and negotiate with oil companies (related to the experience and resources of local leaders)

All of these factors will influence the sustainability of traditional ways of life in indigenous Arctic communities, which are dependent on surrounding natural environment. The four case studies illustrate four different scenarios in regard to resilience and adaption.

Of the communities studied, Nelmin-Nos was the most signifi-cantly affected by post-Soviet economic restructuring, which led to the mismanagement of the village's collective farm and the almost complete disappearance of the community's reindeer herd. The village's grazing land has not yet been affected by oil development. At present, the village receives support from state subsidies, and the maintenance of village infrastructure is funded by the social agreements concluded by the NAO governor. Oil companies have also provided limited funds for the construction of new houses for herders. Nelmin-Nos lacks a meat processing and refrigeration facility; instead, reindeer are slaughtered in the fields and butchering is heavily dependent on freezing temperatures. However, due to the slow recovery of the herd, villagers have not yet faced some of these issues surrounding developing revenue from reindeer harvesting. If and when the herd returns to full size, these issues related to sustainable adaptation will loom large.

Khorey-Ver is relatively far from Naryan-Mar and can be reached only by airplane or helicopter. The lack of roads has made it harder to maintain local infrastructure. Reindeer herding around Khorey-Ver was less affected by economic restructuring, however. The collective farm survived the Soviet collapse; it was prosperous in the Soviet era and continues to be economically viable under a market economy. Although herders' grazing land is severely affected by oil companies, Khorey-Ver provides an example of negotiated coexistence of deer herders with the oil companies. Herders receive compensation from oil companies as well as funds from the NAO administration.

The village of Krasnoe has a significant advantage due to its proximity to and easy access by road to Naryan-Mar. Although economic restructuring seriously impacted the collective farm, the reindeer herd has recovered, and both Harp—the collective farm—and Erv—the reindeer cooperative—appear to be economically viable. These institutions have negotiated several socioeconomic agreements with oil companies and pursued compensation for damage. The reindeer cooperative was the first entity that attempted to use formal methods of land valuation and damage estimates in its interactions with oil companies. These methods became a model for other herders. Reindeer herders from Harp and Erv have an advantage because they have a meat processing facility and can easily transport their product to Naryan-Mar. Nevertheless, the yearly rhythm—including harvesting—will have to adjust to climate change.

Kolguev Island represents the most remote settlement, lacking roads and reachable only by helicopter. The Kolguev reindeer enterprise successfully concluded socioeconomic agreements with oil companies and has not pursued compensation, given the distance between pasturelands and oil drilling. After perestroika, the Kolguev reindeer herding enterprise survived the economic transition even more successfully than herding enterprises in other NAO communities. Herders also shifted to new technology, such as snowmobiles, and moved away from traditional lifestyles more rapidly than other Nenets communities. However, success was dampened when herders initially allowed the number of reindeer to exceed the carrying capacity of the island's habitat, and the pasture land deteriorated. After the mass reindeer mortality of 2014–2015, the herders had to rely on state support from the NAO administration in order to save reindeer husbandry on the island. Kolguev also experiences more severe weather fluctuations than mainland settlements. The combination of these factors creates doubt about the overall resilience of Kolguev communities.

Conclusion

The coincidence of post-Soviet economic disruption, oil development, and climate change has presented NAO villagers with an unprecedented challenge and highlights their vulnerabilities. However, we see that Nenets reindeer herding villages thus far exhibit several strategies of adaptation. These varying capacities to adapt—or to undertake actions to preserve their traditional ways of life—are based in part on the economic and political institutional resources that they have at their disposal. A key source of resilience resides in the traditional practices and skills of the reindeer herding communities. Direct and indirect funding from oil companies has become a substitute for support provided by the state and state-owned enterprises in the Soviet era. These benefits, which may be valuable in the short term, create dependencies and reproduce paternalistic relationships in the long term. Further, oil development leads to increasing tensions between industry and reindeer herding.

So far, adaptive strategies used by the reindeer herders are largely informal and generally are not based on existing legal frameworks or public participation, possibly limiting their future utility. However, the reindeer herders of the NAO, with the possible exception of Kolguev Island, have demonstrated a high level of adaptive capacity. For this reason, as the reindeer herds recover to their earlier numbers and oil and gas development continues, the herders are likely to pursue a negotiated coexistence, at least in the short term.

The challenges faced by the Nenets people are occurring beyond their region of Russia's Arctic as well. Indigenous peoples across the Russian Arctic have begun to recognize climate change and are mobilizing to address it. Russian indigenous leaders are actively involved in climate research and development of strategies of adaptation in other regions. For example, in Kamchatka, the indigenous NGO Lach established a network for monitoring climate change. The Russian indigenous peoples' delegation, including leaders from Primorski Krai, the Republic of Sakha/Yakutia, and other places in Siberia and Kamchatka, was very active at COP-21. The delegation reported on unpredictable weather fluctuations and how they impact traditional ways of life.

Traditional knowledge once helped people from the Arctic regions predict and manage extreme weather; however, new weather patterns have undermined this knowledge, putting people in danger. According to COP-21 participants from the Russian indigenous community, people living in wetland areas, which make up the majority of Arctic and sub-Arctic territory, face the greatest challenge because they rely on freezing temperatures to create winter roads for travel. In the past several years, mild weather has created dangerous weakness in the ice, prevented travel, and in some cases led to incidents of drowning. The effects of variable and milder weather create a variety of problems: obstacles to hunting; lack of necessities in villages, including medicines; unpredictable wildlife behavior, including bears that do not hibernate; parasitic animal illnesses; severe flooding; and melting permafrost. As one participant states, "Nature does not trust us any longer; it does not communicate with us. It is angry at our behavior." Residents of the Russian Arctic will continue to be among the first to face the need to adapt to climate change in the years ahead.

Notes

Acknowledgements: This research was supported by the Finnish Academy Arctic Program ("Oil Production Networks in the Russian Arctic," No. 286791), the National Council for Eurasian and East European Research ("National Interests and Transnational Governance: Russia's Changing Environmental Policy," No. 827-06), the NWO, and the Netherlands Organization for Scientific Research, Arctic Program ("Developing benefit sharing standards in the Arctic," No. 866.15.203). This chapter draws on the authors' research previously published in Laura A. Henry, Soili Nysten-Haarala, Svetlana A. Tulaeva, and Maria S. Tysiachniouk, "Corporate Social Responsibility and the Oil Industry in the Russian Arctic: Global Norms and Neo-Paternalism," *Europe-Asia Studies* 68, no. 8 (2016): 1340–68.

1. B. Forbes and F. Stammler, "Arctic Climate Change Discourse: The Contrasting Politics of Research Agendas in the West and Russia," *Polar Research* 28 (March 5, 2009): 28–42.

2. D. Nelson, W. Adger, and K. Brown, "Adaptation to Environmental Change: Contributions of a Resilience Framework," *Annual Review of Environment and Resources* 32 (Nov. 2007): 395–419.

3. C. Folke et al., "Adaptive Governance of Social-Ecological System," *Annual Review of Environment and Resources* 30 (Nov. 2005): 441–73.

4. A. Sukhanovski, "Pomoskaya Stolitsa," NAO-2012: Numbers, Facts, Achievements, Special Issue 01 (2013).

5. A. Golovnev and G. Osherenko, *Siberian Survival: The Nenets and Their Story* (Ithaca: Cornell University Press, 1999).

6. Put' Ilycha can be translated as "the way directed by Ilyich [Vladimir Ilyich Lenin]."

7. Sukhanovski, "Pomoskaya Stolitsa."

8. F. Stammler and V. Peskov, "Building a 'Cuture of Dialogue' among Stakeholders in North-West Russian Oil Extraction," *Europe-Asia Studies* 60, no. 5 (2008): 835.

9. Sukhanovski, "Pomoskaya Stolitsa."

10. At the time of interviewing, 30,000 rubles equaled approximately $1,000 per month.

11. T. Kumpula et al., "Land Use and Land Cover Change in Arctic Russia: Ecological and Social Implications of Industrial Development," *Global Environmental Change* 21 (2011): 550–62.

12. Participant observation, Ardalin; see also Kumpula, "Land Use," 2011: 559.

13. Representative of the administration of the Polar region, June 2012.

14. W. Rees et al., "Vulnerability of European Reindeer Husbandry to Global Change," *Climatic Change* 87 (March 2008): 199–217.

15. Forbes and Stammler, "Arctic Climate Change," 28–42.

16. B. Forbes et al., eds., "High Resilience in the Yamal-Nenets Social-Ecological System, West Siberian Arctic, Russia," *Proceedings of the National Academy of Sciences of the United States of America* 106 (Dec. 29, 2009): 22041–48.

17. B. Forbes, "Equity, Vulnerability, and Resilience in Social-Ecological Systems: Contemporary Example from the Russian Arctic," *Research in Social Problems and Public Policy* 15 (2008): 203–36; O. Lavrinenko, I. Lavrinenko, and B. Gruzdev, "Response of Plant Cover of Tundra Ecosystems to Oil-and-Gas Extraction Development," in *Social and Environmental Impacts in the North: Methods in Evaluation of Socio-Economic and Environmental Consequences of Mining and Energy Production in the Arctic and Sub-Arctic*, ed. R. Rasmussen and N. Koroleva (Dordrecht: Kluwer, 2003), 257–72.

18. Forbes, "Arctic Climate Change," 28–42.

20

Representations of Environmental Problems and Climate Change

The Case of the Young Inhabitants of the City of Buenos Aires

ENRIQUE DEL ACEBO IBÁÑEZ

Editors' Note

All of the articles in *The Big Thaw* with the exception of this chapter consider the impact of the Big Thaw in the far northern areas of the Northern Hemisphere. Of course, the impacts are similar in the far southern areas of the Southern Hemisphere. In recent times, precipitation in Argentina has increased between 10 and 40 percent and the temperature by 0.5 degree Celsius.

The changes in Argentina are not only impacting supplies of Malbec. The editors felt it would be inappropriate to consider the Big Thaw without at least tipping our collective hats to the Southern Hemisphere. We wish to acknowledge, even if only as a token, the scientific importance and cultural similarity of the Southern issues.

Acebo Ibáñez's chapter is particularly apt to this task. It focuses on environmental perceptions of the youth of Buenos Aires. There are many findings that correspond to Northern perceptions. For example, the importance of the environmental issues is considered to be far greater than the actual performance by governments or other civic groups. In some cases, what the author found was far more unexpected. For Buenos Aires youth, the immediate environmental problems—such as deforestation and toxic waste—are twice as important as the broader and long-term environmental issues such as climate change.

Zubrow's previous chapter emphasizes the scientific connectedness of climate change, which is linked through the worldwide atmospheric and marine systems. In contrast, Acebo Ibáñez's surveys show that culturally, the perception of worldwide interconnection does not exist in Buenos Aires. He finds that 40 percent of Buenos Aires youth believe that there is no link between the Southern Hemisphere and the Northern Hemisphere; 36.3 percent said that there was some link and only 17.7 percent said that there was a significant link.

Perhaps what is most disheartening is that Acebo Ibáñez finds a high degree of pessimism regarding not only the socioeconomic future but also the environmental future of the Southern Cone. Inasmuch as the youth are the future, clearly the Big Thaw as it plays out across the planet will have major impacts in the Far South.

The Sociocultural World as a Total Phenomenon

The atmosphere and oceans connect the entire world and its inhabitants into a global system. Environmental change in one area of the world impacts other areas of the world. I was asked to provide a Southern counterweight for this book. The problems of the Big Thaw are not just problems for the Northern Hemisphere, but they also are problems for the Southern Hemisphere.

The reality of the Big Thaw is as urgent in the southern part of the Southern Hemisphere as it is in the northern part of the Northern Hemisphere. The research in this piece is focused on the relation the individual has with the community and how the individual and the community jointly and disjointly perceive the role of climate change in environmental problems. Furthermore, I focus on the young, not the old. There are more of the young and even more importantly, they are the future.

Social sciences and anthropology have stressed the sociocultural components as inextricably united as well as integrated to any concept dealing with the environment. In fact, the environment and the sociocultural world are total phenomena: multidimensional and interdependent, it is both a natural realm and a built-up realm; hence, both interdisciplinary and transdisciplinary approaches are required.

Culture, society, the subject, and environment are dimensions of the sociocultural world with manifest (evident, clearly perceived) and nonmanifest aspects (not evident, implicit, not immediately perceived), all being so interdependent that every change in one impacts the others, explicitly or implicitly, in the short or long term. This can be seen in Figure 20.1, where time and territory are the coordinates where this

SOCIOCULTURAL WORLD AND CLIMATE CHANGE

SOCIOCULTURAL WORLD		
DIMENSIONS	MANIFEST ASPECTS	NON MANIFEST ASPECTS
CULTURAL SUBSYSTEM	Built Environment Technology Language	Social uses Customs Norms/ Anomie Values Beliefs Knowledge Social Representations Social Institutions
SOCIAL SUBSYSTEM	Population Social Actors Migratory processes Primary & Secondary Groups Organizations, NGO's Group Adaptive Strategies Agents of Socialization Social Interaction Social Structure	Socialization Processes (primary, secondary and resocialization) Power relations
PERSONALITY SUBSYSTEM	Social Action Behavior (toward the Environment) Adaptive strategies Status-Role Social networks	Attitudes Expectations Socio-psychological & existential needs Individual Adaptive Strategies
BIOLOGICAL & ENVIRONMENTAL SUBSYSTEM	Climate change Environmental disasters Satisfaction/dissatisfaction of Human biological needs	Natural Environment Human biological needs Social representations on Environmental disasters Social representations on Climate Change

(Left axis label: TERRITORY)

(Bottom axis label: TIME)

Figure 20.1. Sociocultural world and climate change.

world occurs. This also deals with the "sociological imagination," many times highlighted by C. Wright Mills.[1]

Hawley considers "community" to be a collective response to the habitat involved, an adaptation of the human organism to the milieu it lives in: While *culture* is an "ecosystem considered from an analytic outlook," an ecosystem is "culture considered from a synthetic outlook."[2] A self-criticism of ecological-human thinking is very valuable when they introduce *self-consciousness*; consequently, the environment can be seen as an *interiorized milieu*.[3]

This self-criticism allows links to be established with an existential sociology as a fresh sociological reading of the existentialist thinking.[4] Because the human being not only develops strategies aimed at the biological survival during his/her stay on board the planet Earth, but also the human being *founds* space or territories that represent "realms for meaning." So, the subject *inhabits* in the existentialistic meaning Heidegger gives to this concept.[5] Precisely, the fact of inhabiting is a *proprium*, that is, a characteristic that defines the human being as such. Every ecological crisis is not free from strong ethic and existential connotations with reference to either its causes or its consequences and the possible ways for the solution and prevention thereof. But those connotations belong to specific and concrete local communities and sociocultural worlds.

On the one side is the internalization of the "exteriority," and on the other the exteriorization of the "interiority," according to the public/private and local global dynamics (see Figure 20.2).

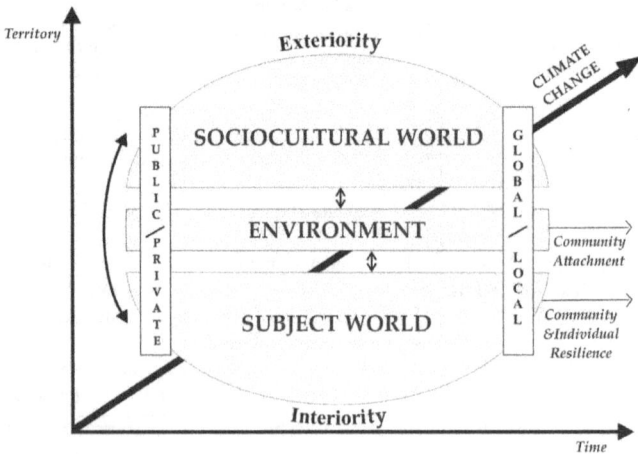

Figure 20.2. Climate change and sociocultural world as total phenomena. Source: E. del Acebo Ibáñez (2010).

Rootedness Approach

The attachment of humans to territory tends to emerge as rootedness, understood as a complete spatial-sociocultural phenomenon. Since individual, society, and culture—together with the space and time coordinates—constitute factors that are inextricably joined and interdependent, rootedness offers a pluri-dimensionality that emerges from such components as:[6] (1) *spatial rootedness*, understood as the identification of a human with a place, the "territorial imperative" that exists already in animals (as modern ethology has analyzed); (2) *social rootedness*, the extent to which the individual attaches or feels that sense of belonging to different groups and organizations, but this social rootedness also depends on the existence of participating structures and attitudes; and (3) *cultural rootedness*, which implies the normative-axiological background that specifies such historical society in which one lives. In the antipodes of *anomie* (cultural rootlessness), a human—a free, responsible, and symbolic creature—critically identifies with such background that conforms that human and which that human helps to conform, thus nurturing a *Weltanschauung* that shelters and strengthens that human, a realm that is full of shared senses, the background and ways of human living that tend to—and facilitate—a nourishing rootedness.

Rootedness appears, then, as vocation and fulfillment: the human being lives (must live) on the planet by means of forms of rootedness; otherwise, the human excludes himself or herself, leaves solidarity aside, and becomes depredatory.

The community attachment is continuously reproduced in terms of everyday life processes and social imaginaries, a fact that must be taken into account by every policy on climate change and the consequent and necessary resocialization processes (see Figure 20.3 on page 342).

The Environmental and Climate Change Issue: A Case Study

Different climate change impacts were reported in Argentina during the last decade: (1) unusual extreme weather events, such as flooding in the Pampas (2000–2002) and a hailstorm in the Buenos Aires metropolitan area (2006), and (2) an increase in rainfall in the southeast Argentine Pampas and the impact on land use, crop yields, and the frequency and intensity of floods. Future sea level rise, weather and climatic variability,

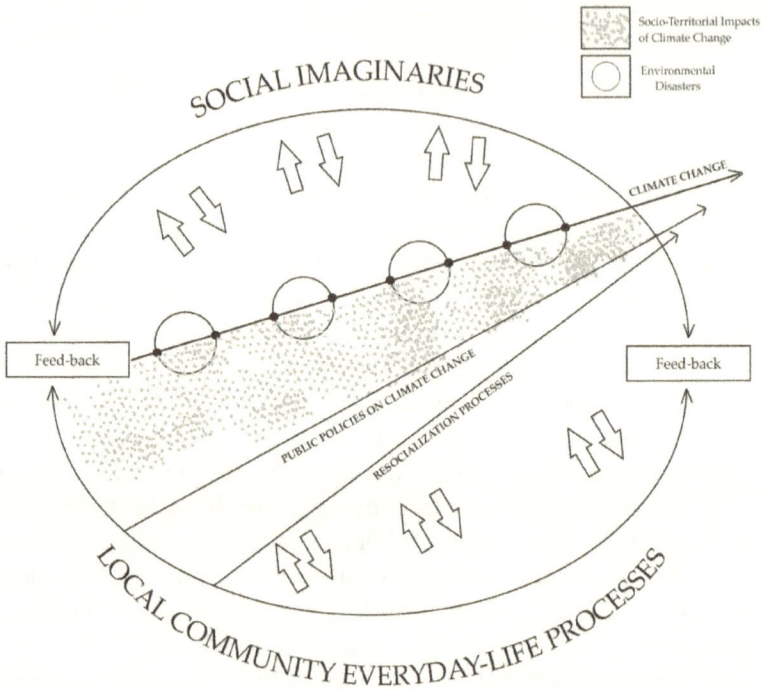

Figure 20.3. Climate change as a multidimensional complex phenomenon.

and extremes modified by global warming are variables that must be taken into account because of the impacts on low-lying areas, such as the province of Buenos Aires coast.[7] There has been a general increase in spring and winter average temperatures over the country, making the occurrence of warm seasonal temperatures more frequent and cold seasonal temperatures less frequent.

At the same time, there are some climate change impact projections for Argentina, such as: (1) southwest and northern areas being vulnerable to a moderate increase in water stress; (2) an increase in precipitation extremes; and (3) a tendency for increasing flood risk. The country was ranked fifth highest (out of 84 developing countries) with respect to the amount of agricultural land that could be submerged due to a one-meter sea level rise and, according to a subnational-scale study, the city of Buenos Aires could be affected significantly by sea level rise.[8]

These are data located at the *objective level* of reality, surely indispensable for better planning and forecast. Nevertheless, there is a *subjective level* of reality that emerges as indispensable, too. In fact, environmental problems, natural disasters, and climate change are phenomena that deal with attitudes, social and individual representations, local communities and contexts, *Weltanschauungen*, beliefs, and values. This means that the connections among local perceptions, behaviors, and discourses on climate change at local contexts, on one side, must be realized, and at global concepts, on the other. As Karjalainen, Järvikosky, and Luoma[9] state, although the study can speak about globalization of the environment, at the local level it has only partly homogenized public perceptions, opinions, and behaviors because "an individual's engagement with the surrounding environment, local conditions, and socio-political contexts shape perceptions of climate change."[10] As the authors point out in relation to the Komi Republic (but this also applies to different developing countries and regions), climate change can be more a personal concern related to daily life and survival strategies than an environmental, societal, or global issue. Once again, the dialectic between local/global emerges as indispensable to better understanding reality, avoiding ethnocentrism and chronocentrism as points of departure.

As we usually speak in terms of globalization as a necessary process, perhaps we can also investigate how explanatory it would be to refer to both globalizing and globalized countries. Nature is not only nature; it impacts the different sociocultural worlds all over the planet and, vice versa, it also implies social and power relationships that impact in nature itself.

On the basis of such considerations and theoretical discussions, an empirical study to check the representations was designed, concerning *urban dwelling* and *environmental problems* (including *climate change*) in Buenos Aires and in the South Cone of Latin America with people between 15 and 25 years old. A questionnaire with both open and closed questions was administered to a non-probabilistic sample (N = 450) considering adequate quotas in terms of age, gender, and socioeconomic level (SEL), to measure perceptions, attitudes, and behaviors with respect to their urban habitat and the environmental problems thereof. The study also measured spatial, social, and cultural rootedness and grades of consumerism life, creating the respective indexes and looking for explanatory variables.

Self-Criticism among Inhabitants
of the City of Buenos Aires

The city is territory, buildings, open and closed areas, streets, and avenues, but mainly its inhabitants and their everyday life and social interactions. In this sense, it is important to investigate how the young citizens perceive themselves as inhabitants. The answers were classified as follows:

1. *Lack of respect for norms* ("I don't respect rules," "I'm not considerate," "I don't respect order," "soiling the city," "throwing garbage on the street"): 30.8 percent (significant percentage differences when introducing gender, age, and SEL variables were impossible to determine).

2. *Being individualistic* ("my individualism," "I'm not committed," "I don't participate," "lack of solidarity," "lack of love for my city," "I only do what I please"): 29.8 percent.

3. Introducing gender and age variables, percentages increase for females (37.7 percent versus 23.1 percent among males) as well as among young people within the 20–25 age group (38.6 percent versus 20.1 percent among the 15–19 age group). The percentage is significantly reduced when introducing the SEL variable: those dealing with lower SELs, especially the lowest level (10.0 percent versus 39.8 percent at the highest SEL). Regarding young people in lowest social stratum, the lower ratio of individualism could be explained by their strong need for the solidarity networks they have a tendency to set up, insofar as those networks operate as adaptive and survival strategies when facing situations very close to marginalization and abject poverty.

4. *I have nothing to criticize myself about*: 21.0 percent.

5. *Lack of tolerance* ("overreacting badly," "being violent," "being in a bad mood"): 2.5 percent. Percentages double and even triple when dealing with those in the lower SELs and young people ages 20–25.

6. Do not know or did not answer (DK/DA): 15.6 percent.

Individual Representations on the Environment

This study investigated how the "environment" is perceived and valued by the young inhabitants of Buenos Aires. The results are shown in Figure 20.4.

1. A *holistic vision* conceives habitat as a spatial-sociocultural phenomenon ("that's the space where we live," "anything surrounding us," "physical space and architectural space," "a relationship among the environment, people, and living creatures inhabiting it," "society, rootedness, interaction," "our habitat"): 47.0 percent.

2. A *proactive, belligerent attitude* with regard to the environment: ("that's the place we have to take care of so that we can live," "all that is disappearing," "all that is neglected," "contamination, pollution," "a thing most valuable"): 27.4 percent.

3. A *bucolic vision* of the environment ("it's the plants," "it's nature," "beaches, the sea," "air, oxygen," "green areas," "animals"): 15.3 percent.

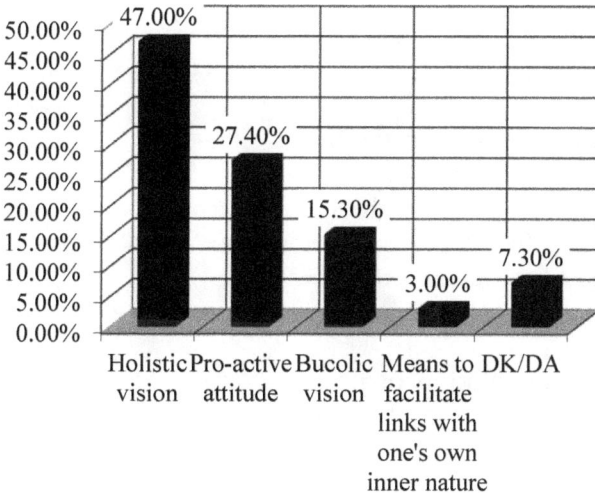

Figure 20.4. What does the term *environment* mean to young people? (inhabitants of Buenos Aires City, ages 15–25). Source: E. del Acebo Ibánez & A. Mendez Diz (2010).

4. *Habitat as a facilitator for innerness* ("it's your possibility for contemplation," "it's feeling well with everything," "peace," "purity," "something that gives you joy," "something that allows me to live fully"): 3.0 percent.

5. *DK/DA:* 7.3 percent

The *holistic* vision of habitat as a spatial-sociocultural phenomenon is more present among male (51.2 percent) than female (41.5 percent) subjects and people in the 20–25 age group (52.4 percent) versus ages 15–19 (40.1 percent). Percentages drop dramatically when it comes to individuals with a lower SEL: among D-level people, 39.3 percent of their answers were registered, and among E-level people, the percentage dropped even more—to 15.0 percent.

The *belligerent* vision increases percentagewise among sample subjects with an SEL D level up to 35.7 percent and diminishes among subjects with an SEL E level to 15 percent. Maybe these people are much more concerned with their day-in, day-out survival and the related satisfaction of their primary needs. The percentage is somewhat higher among male subjects accepting the belligerent vision (30.0 percent) compared to females (23.3 percent).

The *bucolic* vision appears to a greater percentage among females (19.7 percent) than males (11.6 percent), for 15–19 year-olds (19.7 percent), and for 20–25 year-olds (11.6 percent). The bucolic vision is also on the increase among individuals pertaining to both extremes of the socioeconomic scale: 20.7 percent for higher SELs, 20.0 percent for lower SELs, and lowest for the E.

What might be considered ignorance (resulting from the choice of DK/DA) is markedly on the increase among young people with the lower SELs: Either 45 percent do not answer or they acknowledge that do not know how to answer the question.

Perception of Environmental Pollution and Climate Change

Once the environment was defined, the study focused on the perception of *environmental pollution* and *climate change*, as can be seen in the Figure 20.5.

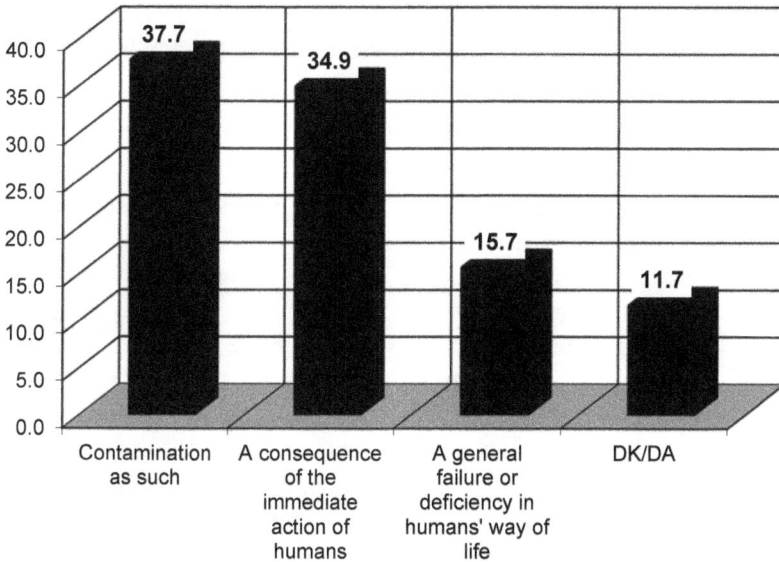

Figure 20.5. Perception of *environmental pollution* and *climate change* (inhabitants of Buenos Aires City, ages 15–25). Source: E. del Acebo Ibánez and A. Mendes Diz (2010).

1. *Contamination as such* ("something that is not natural," "something that is not pure," "something altered, debased," "something deteriorated," "a lack of environmental-ecological equilibrium," "air pollution"): 37.7 percent. There is a somewhat higher rate of answers among young people 15–19 (40.4 percent versus 32.9 percent among 20–25-year-olds). Among subjects in the E SEL, the percentage drops to 27.3 percent.

2. *A consequence of the immediate action of humans* ("refuse," "filth," "maltreating, destroying, or marring the environment," "people just don't care"): 34.9 percent.

3. *A general failure or deficiency in humans' way of life* ("a wrongdoing," "unhealthiness," "lack of green areas," "excessive advertising," "an existing evil," "a problem requiring urgent solutions"): 15.7 percent. This answer is mostly found among males (20.4 percent versus 14.3

percent among females) and young people 20–25 years
old (22 percent) versus 15–19-year-olds (12.1 percent).
Percentage, however, diminishes markedly among subjects with the lower SEL (9.1 percent versus 21.6 percent
among those with the higher SEL.

4. *DK/DA:* 11.7 percent. This lack of information is on the
increase among subjects within the 15–19 age group (16.3
percent) versus those 20–25 years old (6.9 percent). It also
increases gradually as the SEL decreases, down to 22.7
percent among the subjects in the SEL E group.

When subjects were asked about *the grade of environmental pollution
in the city of Buenos Aires*, a great majority evidenced a high degree of
environmental consciousness: Indeed, 50 percent of young people state
that contamination is "very high" and another 40.3 percent consider it
to be "high," which sums up to a significant 90.3 percent.

Measures against the Contamination and the Consequences of Climate Change: Grade of Effectiveness

In terms of how effective different measures are against contamination
and the consequences of climate change, the study discovered the following percentages:

Table 20.1. Measures against the contamination and the consequences
of climate change: grade of effectiveness (inhabitants of Buenos Aires
City, ages 15–25)

Measures	Higher effectiveness	Medium effectiveness	Lower effectiveness	Neither
Penalties for whoever pollutes	72.7%	12.0%	14.7%	0.6%
More information and environmental campaigns	70.6%	16.0%	13.4%	0.0%
Increase the participation of the Buenos Aires inhabitants	67.0%	19.7%	12.4%	1.0%
Other measures	8.0%	0.7%	4.4%	7.0%

Increases in information and/or environmental campaigns are measures of the effectiveness of what is considered to be at the higher level. The percentage increases markedly for subjects with the lower SELs: As many as 60.5 percent of subjects with the higher SEL are concerned that this measure would be endowed with the higher effectiveness, while among subjects with the lower SELs, the ratio increases to 80 percent.

In that sense too, the participation of Buenos Aires residents is deemed to be an alternative of maximum effectiveness, the percentage of which increases as the SEL of our interviewees decreases, namely: 62.3 percent, 67.6 percent, 74.1 percent, and 80.0 percent (from the highest SEL to the lowest, respectively).

With respect to *the need for penalties to polluters*, the study observed that the percentage of subjects that are agreeable is somewhat higher among males and people within the 20–25 age group.

Socialization Agents with Regard to Environmental Problems and Climate Change

It could be observed from the results of this study that to keep informed, two-thirds of our sample subjects resort to audiovisual media. In turn, use of graphic media (read by 21.6 percent) increases as the subjects' SEL increases (23.7 percent of subjects with higher SELs versus 10.0 percent of with lower SELs).

The importance of mass media increases as sample subjects' SEL decreases. While 71.2 percent of young people with a higher SEL mention mass media as a source for information, the ratio of young people with the lowest SEL resorting to the mass media climbs to 90 percent.

Our study shows that 54 percent resort to television as an information medium. Females, subjects within the 15–19 age group, and individuals in the lower SELs have a higher tendency to use television. Twenty percent listen to radio, with females and those with lower SELs preferring broadcasting. Newspapers are preferred by 19.3 percent (mainly males, 20–25-year-olds, and subjects with higher SELs). Only 2.3 percent mentioned magazines.

Self-obtained information occurs mainly among sample subjects within the 20–25 age group (12.7 percent versus 6.8 percent within the 15–19 age group).

Either *high school or university college* is mentioned among subjects within the 15–19 age group (9.9 percent versus 1.7 percent of subjects

within the 20–25 age group). Neither high school nor college are mentioned among sample subjects with the lowest SELs.

Ecologist organizations are mentioned only by sample subjects pertaining to the high strata of society (no subject with a lower SEL mentions
ecologists' organizations).

Socialization Agents Regarding Environmental/ Climate Change Problems: Importance Level Assigned and Degree of Dissatisfaction with Their Performance Thereof

While different levels of importance were assigned to the "socialization
agents," the inhabitants showed their degree of dissatisfaction in relation
to the "expected performance" of those agents. Figure 20.6 shows the
high degrees of that dissatisfaction:

1. The *worst institutional qualification*, in terms of "what they
   really do" and "what they would have to do," are the
   following socialization agents, including political parties,
   the federal administration, and the Government of the
   Autonomous City of Buenos Aires.

2. Nonetheless, the dissatisfaction is also present in a high
   percentage when the inhabitant refers to the school—primary and secondary (61 percent), neighborhood associations (58 percent), and the university (54 percent).

Rootedness, Participation, and Consumerism

Social rootedness occurs whenever: (1) the subject leads an active life in
the groups where he/she belongs and (2) pertains to any organization
endowed with a clear participative attitude and/or evidence of a service
attitude toward the community involved.

To participate in organizations is "slightly important" for 42 percent
of the sample. This answer was mainly found among males (48.1 percent
versus 35 percent among females) and subjects from the 15–19 age group
(51 percent) versus the 20–25 age group (34.2 percent).

While only 17.7 percent say that they rather frequently attend
meetings organized by some district, environmental, political, or student

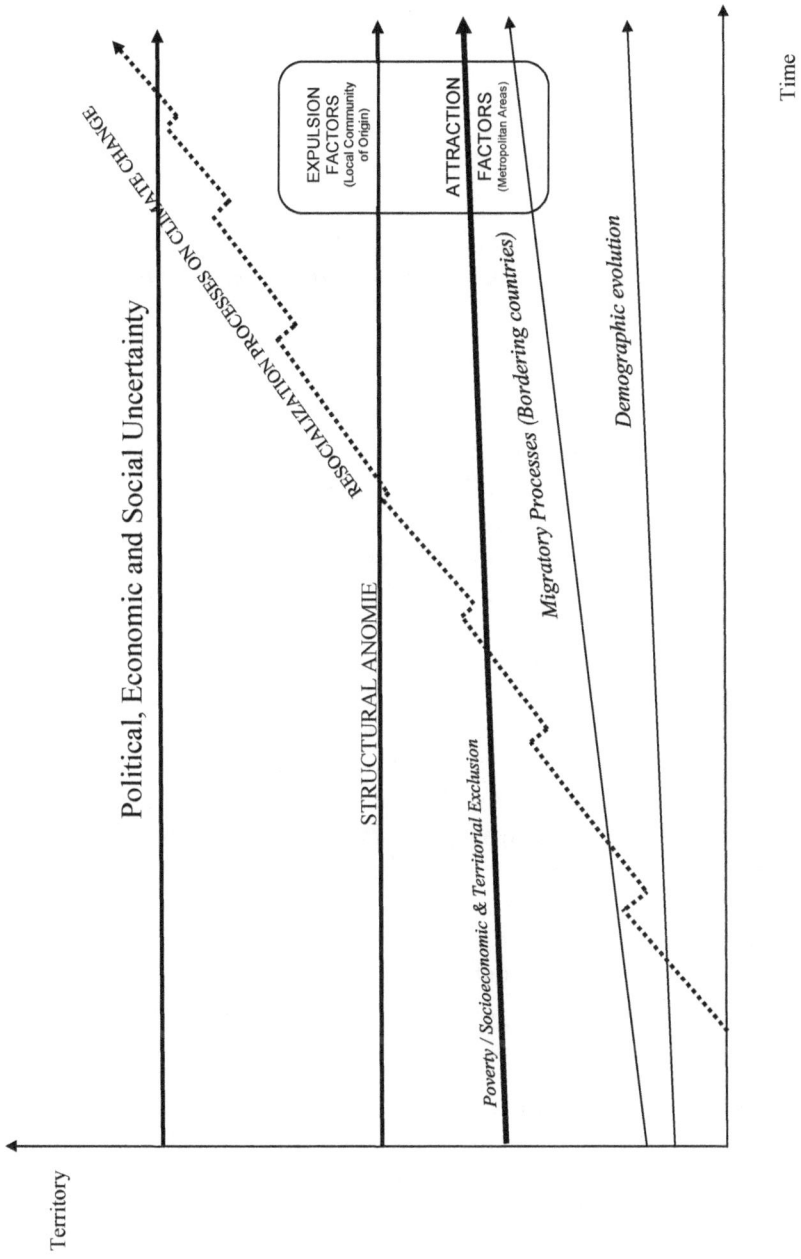

Figure 20.6. Climate change as a multidimensional complex phenomenon (variable influencing every policy on climate change in Latin America).

organization, a significant 70.3 percent state plainly that they "never attend" meetings organized by these types of institutions, mainly due to motives linked to "lack of interest" and "no time to go there."

In that sense, the study classified the reasons for not participating as follows:

1. *Motives linked to the personality subsystem* ("lack of interest," "participating just didn't occur to me," and "unawareness," in addition to especially negative attitudes such as "just no good" or "it isn't worth my time"): 47.8 percent.

2. *Motives linked to the social and cultural subsystem* ("no time to go there," "personal problems," "lack of opportunities," "I'll go when I'm a grown-up"): 36.6 percent.

The study found that young people are not given (and they themselves do not find) genuine participation possibilities, so they kept being "pushed on the backburner," that is, to a massive participation in the consumption market. When our interviewees were asked, *"What is the organization you would like to participate in?"* again the study observed that sample subjects with the lowest SELs evidenced the higher percentages for a *potential participation*. So, it could be considered that if they do not participate, this is due to the time they input in achieving adaptation strategies aimed at overcoming marginalization situations.

Regarding the *actual participation* of young people, our index shows that a third actually participate while an important percentage (66.6 percent) do not. A higher percentage of males do participate: 37.5 percent versus 28.6 percent of females. While a higher percent of young people in the 15–19 age group participate, the percentage decreased to 29.2 percent for the 20–25 age group.

It is important to see that the lower the consumerism life, the greater the actual participation, as can be seen in Table 20.2.

Table 20.2. Relation between actual participation and consumerism life (inhabitants of Buenos Aires City, ages 15–25)

Actual participation	Consumerism life		
	Intense	Moderate	Low
Yes	30.6	33.7	40.7
No	69.4	66.3	59.3
Total	100.0	100.0	100.0

This demonstrates the tendency to compensate a less "active" participation with a greater "passive" participation, that is, a participation limited to the overconsumption of goods and service.

At the same time, the survey showed that the higher the total rootedness, the lower the consumerism life, while the more intense consumerism life is mainly present in those inhabitants with low or medium total rootedness.

Table 20.3. Relation between total rootedness and consumerism life (inhabitants of Buenos Aires City, ages 15–25)

Total rootedness	Consumerism life		
	Intense	Medium	Low
High	18.4	21.1	33.3
Medium/Low	81.6	78.9	66.7

As shown in this table, the higher the total rootedness (cultural, social, and spatial), the lower the consumerism life and the lesser the total rootedness, the more intense the consumerism.

Representations from the South Cone of Latin America

The South Cone of Latin America was included in the study. This region includes Argentina, Brazil, Bolivia, Paraguay, Uruguay, and Chile.

Common Environmental Problems: An Identification Process

Consulted with regard to the common environmental problems in the South Cone, more than one-third (37 percent) of the sample did not answer/did not know the topic. This percentage increased whenever a given subject's *individual anomie level* is greater and his/her *rootedness grade* is reduced. The answers from the remaining 67 percent have been grouped as follows:

1. *Problems caused by immediate, obviously predatory, human actions* (deforestation, tree cutting, nondiscriminate animal hunting, lack of cleanliness, filth, toxic waste, contamination, "couldn't-care-less" attitude of industrialists, drainage system to rivers directly): 53.8 percent.

2. *Environmental problems themselves caused by mediate human actions* (reduction of the ozone layer, greenhouse effect, El Niño current, climate changes): 25 percent.

3. *Problems derived from life in the great cities* (noisy cities, overcrowding, air pollution, smog): 16.8 percent.

4. *Problems caused by disasters and/or accidents* (floods, fires, oil spillage, nuclear power plants): 2.9 percent.

5. *Lack of environmental consciousness* (lack of awareness, insufficient environmental education, unaware that recycling is a need and a must): 1.4 percent.

The awareness of human beings' immediate responsibility as far as environmental problems are concerned increases: (1) as subject's individual anomie grade decreases and (2) as subject's rootedness grade/inner life grade increases. Precisely, interviewees evidencing a "lesser" inner life tend, in a greater ratio, to place the cause of problems "out of the subject."

As can be seen, a great majority (78.8 percent) acknowledge the human being's "capacity for neglect" as the first cause for the South Cone environmental problems—that is, problems caused by either the immediate or mediate human action, even though such percentages decrease as interviewees' SEL are also on the decrease. The study detected an interesting fact: subjects with the lower SELs mention problems caused by catastrophes and/or accidents in a greater percentage; this may be because their marginality conditions cause them to be more vulnerable or exposed to such situations.

Possible Solutions to South Cone's Environmental Problems

Regarding the possible solutions to the above-mentioned environmental problems, more than one-half of interviewees (57.4 percent) are "unaware of" or "do not know." This is most especially noted among subjects evidencing a *lesser participation level*. From the subpopulation who did answer this question, the study assessed the following categories:

1. *Information/socialization* (people should be made aware of these problems, more information, there is a need for a

worldwide campaign aimed at taking care of the environment, educating people): 37.5 percent.

2. *Control/punishment* (stronger controls, regulations, there is
   a need for punishment, fines, disciplinary measures, creation of an international police corps): 25.0 percent.

3. *Prevention* (refraining from using aerosols, refraining from
   using leaded gas, recycling waste and refuse, creating more
   green areas, creating more national parks): 19.2 percent.

4. *Administration action proper* (government must act, there
   must be a political will for action, a greater economic
   development must be generated): 14.0 percent.

5. *International cooperation* (interdisciplinary tasks performed
   among countries, cooperation among nations): 2.2 percent.

6. *No solution at hand* (there exist no solutions at all, any
   solution is Utopian): 1.5 percent.

As can be seen, actions arising from the *education subsystem* (information, socialization) and the *political subsystem* as well (prevention, administration action proper) are privileged. One-quarter of the interviewees,
however, say that any solution for environmental problems should arise
from the *normative subsystem* (control, punishment).

Looking for a Possible Link between Southern and Northern Environmental Problems

When subjects have been asked whether they considered that there
existed any link between the environmental problems the countries of
the Southern Hemisphere and the Northern Hemisphere were facing,
40.0 percent replied that there was *no link whatsoever* (this was particularly true among *females*: 45.7 percent versus 35.0 percent of males). At
the same time, the percentage is markedly on the increase as an interviewee's SEL decreases. Now, 36.3 percent said that there was *some link*,
and only 17.7 percent said that there was a *high link* (this percentage
increases as subject's SEL increases, a fact easily understood when taking
into account a probable higher education level and a greater access to
information).

The subject population members who observed that "there exists a link among the environmental problems both hemispheres are facing" were asked for their opinion about such a link (e.g., what was exactly the matter). Replies varied.

Among subjects answering that "*there was some type of link*," 81.4 percent said that there were *either common or similar problems* (in many cases, reference was made to the globalization process, namely: "these are global phenomena," "the world is an only world," "this is a worldwide phenomenon"). The percentage decreased significantly when dealing with subjects whose SEL is at the *lower level*. The remaining 18.6 percent resorted to the *power the North exerts on the South* ("Southern countries depend on the North," "both prevention and the economic resources are greater in the North," "the problems the North is facing have an impact on the South," "the North throws more waste on us") and, most especially, that was the case for subjects with the lower *SELs*, the number of which is twofold or even threefold the percentage of subjects pertaining to the other SELs.

Representations about the Future in the Southern Cone Countries

IN CONNECTION WITH THE ENVIRONMENT

Young people from Buenos Aires have been asked about the future of the Southern Cone countries as far as the environment is concerned, 10 years from now. More than two-thirds (68.3 percent) were *evidently pessimistic* (it will be much worse: 22.3 percent; it will be worse: 46.0 percent), a percentage that increases significantly in the case of subjects with a *low anomie level*, and decreases in the case of subjects with a *lower SEL*.

As far as 19.2 percent of subjects are concerned, the situation of these countries will be *the same in the future* (a percentage that increases significantly to 33 percent within subjects with the *lower SELs*).

Only 12.4 percent of subjects evince *optimism* (it will be better: 9.7 percent; it will be much better: 2.7 percent). However, the optimistic subjects are young people with a higher grade of *individual anomie* and are within the 20–25 *age range* (17.4 percent versus 6.5 percent of subjects in the 15–19 age range).

IN CONNECTION WITH THE SOCIOECONOMIC CONDITIONS

Regarding the socioeconomic future of the Southern Cone countries 10 years from now, subjects evidenced a *marked pessimism*, the percentage of which, however, is lower than the percentage that referred to the environment: 48.3 percent (more significantly among young people with a *higher grade of individual anomie*, and *a lesser grade of rootedness*. As far as 24.3 percent of subjects are concerned, the socioeconomic situation of those countries will remain the same.

Optimism with regard to the socioeconomic situation increases if compared to the environmental situation: 24.6 percent of subjects say that the socioeconomic future of the region will be better, and 2.7 percent of subjects say that it will be "much better." In the 20–25 age group, optimism earns a higher optimistic percentage: 32.3 percent versus 20.9 percent of subjects in the 15–19 age group.

Toward Some Conclusions

Regarding solutions to environmental and climate change problems, the sample population results indicate that solutions can come from the *Education Subsystem* (information/socialization) and the *Political Subsystem* (prevention/government action proper). One-fourth of our interviewees, however, find some solutions to the environmental problems within the *Normative Subsystem*(control/penalties).

1. The importance of *information/socialization* (Education Subsystem) is especially believed by female subjects and those who evidence a *low grade of anomie*. The percentage reduces as an interviewee's SEL decreases.

2. The importance of *control/penalty* (Normative Subsystem) increases markedly as, also, the subject's SEL increases. This aspect is present in a greater ratio among people evidencing *low levels of individual anomie, high rootedness level*, and also with a greater relationship intensity in their primary groups.

3. The importance of *prevention/government action* (Political Subsystem) is found in a greater percentage among male subjects than female subjects (39.3 percent versus 23.5 percent).

In fact, resocialization processes are indispensable, not only because of the changing climate conditions, but also to overcome some important structural conditions, such as anomie, disadvantaged socioeconomic conditions, documented and nondocumented migration, and, consequently, to diminish political, economic, and social uncertainties, as shown in Figure 20.7. In relation to a rooted inhabitant, that tends to identify the city from the *spatial* point of view, and the city is a *value*. The anonymity that urban life is likely to "offer" is not appreciated. Consequently, they give the "highest value" to social urban relationships at both the private and the public levels. They are less individualistic than the rootless residents, and they mix with a majority of their neighbors, whose "respect" is their most valued quality. They are happy with what they do, most of their time, so they do not tend to suffer from tedium or boredom—because they feel involved with the realm they live in, into a kind of *affective adaptation* with it.

- "Loving the city" is something they give the highest value, as well as urban participation and all aspects dealing with supporting the normative structure of the urban community.

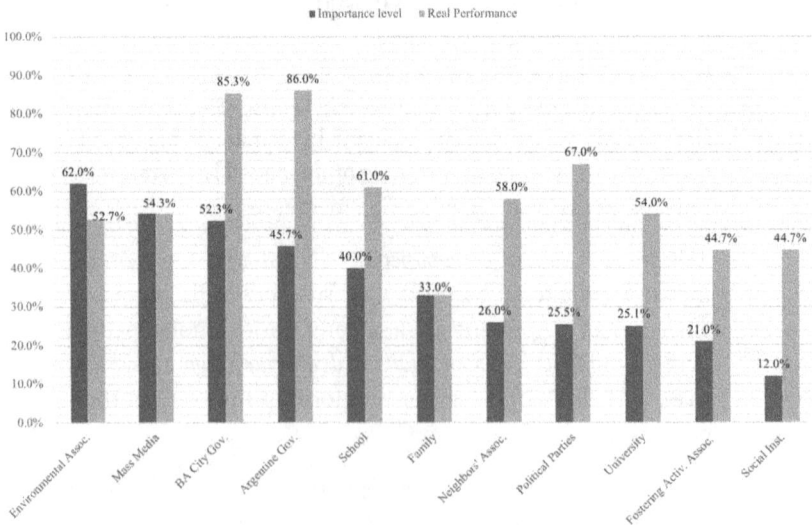

Figure 20.7. Agents of socialization about environmental issues and climate change (how they are perceived by the inhabitants of the city of BA in terms of "objective importance" and "real performance") (%).

- They have a clear participation attitude and vocation: With regard to environment, they can be classified as "active" or "belligerent" individuals in connection with both the natural environment and the sociocultural aspect. Precisely, they consider that the maximum responsibility for environmental problems not only falls on the authorities of the City of Buenos Aires, but also on its residents. At the same time, they deem contamination/pollution as a problem that also falls on the responsibilities of citizens—this is why they trust the effectiveness of environment-related information and campaigns.

The rootless person gives "slight importance" to aspects linked to participation (be it actual or potential), to spatial rootedness (i.e., affective adaptation to the realm), to cultural rootedness, and to existential achievement. They value the anonymity the city is able to offer, as well as their individualism.

As far as responsibility for urban and environmental problems are concerned, the rootless are likely to favor a not-thinking attitude in terms of "near" social actors. Instead, the idea is locating responsibilities further, or the furthest—that is, make the federal administration responsible. Regarding contamination/pollution, their criticism is much more aimed at causes that are predominantly structural.

The anomic person is, in a way, a subtype of rootless person. They have not been living in the city for long (less than five years). They give value to their *home* as "a place where they can do what pleases them most" and where they spend more than 13 hours a day.

- They value "to have friends" but not so much "genuineness." What do they prefer in their district? Friends and family. That has been precisely the place where they have met their best friends. What anomie generates—confusion and mistrust in terms of "the others"—finds a palliative among one's closest people.

- They like the city, and they think they will still live there 10 years from now—maybe a realm wherein they envision the possibility to find alternative means and adaptive strategies so that they can face survival in a social world they perceive as a blurred, changing normative structure. They identify the city as physical place or district or as a place to meet friends and relatives. Again, it seems that what they feel the cultural-normative structure fails to give them, they look for within the social structure at an interaction level with a basically affective orientation, that is, face to face, one on one.

- They do not feel happy with what they do most their time, but they do not feel either tedium or boredom.

- They acknowledge that nobody cares for the environment, but their actual participation is scarce (that is, they only participate at a level of "fans' group"), and they refrain from committing themselves to the problems the city endures. The higher the degree of anomie, the lesser active and potential participation.

- They seldom indulge in self-criticism with regard to their behavior in society, a fact that would be linked to the "drowsiness" of their urban consciousness.

- "Loving the city" and serving the community is losing importance for the anomic, a fact that is intensified when they face the question of "not soiling the city." They just couldn't care less. They neither value the historical knowledge nor the urban heritage, and they simply give no value to the fact that the city is likely to make their personal achievement easier.

- It could be noted that there exists a great number of young subjects from the city of Buenos Aires that lack any knowledge about the environmental problems the South Cone of Latin America is facing. And this lack of knowledge is also important when it comes to asking them about Antarctica. Percentages climbed to higher figures when subjects were asked about the possible problem-solving process. This is likely to mean that the environmental problems are a topic referred to in general terms instead of being a problem of magnitude and consequences that people should be keenly aware of.

The study observed that individuals with a high rootedness level and a low anomie level tend to identify environmental problems of the

South Cone with problems dealing with the *immediate human action* in terms of *depredation and/or direct pollution*. This can be envisioned as an explicit acknowledgment of the individual's responsibility as far as the etiology of the contemporary environmental problems is concerned. At the same time, this type of social actor (rooted and not anomic) tends to give priority as a solution to the *socialization and information processes*. In this case, too, subjects are resorting to the capacity and responsibility of individuals in the sense that individuals are likely to modify their behaviors through an adequate information and formation process. This also implies a certain hope with respect to the possibility of modifying human behavior and, hence, solving environmental problems.

Perhaps a clear visualization, coupled with a clear experience, of the normative-axiological web of a given society could anchor individuals and they could be in a better position to identify the environmental problems and their possible causes and solutions.

A *high grade of anomie* causes people *to envision the future in a most pessimistic way*. Representation is both immediate and mediate with respect to the environmental problems affecting both the city of Buenos Aires and the South Cone of Latin America.

The study also observed that, as peoples' SEL decreases, their pessimism increases with regard to the environmental problems the South Cone is suffering from. They tend to identify the main environmental problem in the South Cone as "*the immediate, predatory human action*" while looking for a solution in the *socialization and information processes*. Conversely, as someone's SEL increases, a solution to the environmental problems of the South Cone tends to be found in the *control/punishment* procedure.

Control and punishment as a way to put a remedy to the environmental problems tends to be emphasized predominantly for 20–25-year-olds, with a higher percentage of female subjects. The same solution is also suggested by people suffering from a low actual as well as potential participation level.

Young people 20–25years old tend to be more optimistic than those 15–19 regarding *the future of the South Cone*, both from an environmental and a socioeconomic approach.

Finally, the study frames the sociological research on climate change attitudes and behaviors in a total phenomenon that clearly states the differences—but also the convergences—between local and global in terms of a "global" approach. As shown in Figure 20.5, although it is necessary to look for the "resolution of problems," it is even more necessary to "question reality" with its uncertainties in everyday life, where a person's world is continuously linked to the sociocultural world.

Local communities emerge and develop as an "assemblage" because, as Deleuze and Guattari state,[11] the assemblage implies that bodies and signs are present and related in terms of problems and problematizations—assemblage that becomes territorial on account of a mixture of chaos, organization, and change.[12]

The results of this study thus suggest that policies on climate change will be successful if (and only if) all these apparently contradictory dimensions are taken into account: (1) local interests and objectives, but also human needs and motivations; (2) environmental global problems, but at the same time, local territory and local everyday life; and (3) social representations, social imaginary, and cognitive processes. All this represents a sort of articulating interface between global and local: the "*glocal.*"

As Karjalainen et al. state,[13] "*glocal* perception means that an individual's perception of the environment is embedded in his/her everyday life engagement with the surroundings—this is why it is *glocal*, but the framework for interpretation of perceptions is influenced by global concepts and discourses (e.g., 'global warming'), and thus it is also global. Consequently, climate change may also have regional and national 'shapes' of interpretations or meanings."

In sum, the necessary relationship between "local perception" and "local representation" of environmental changes and the global environmental discourses creates a need to be alert because, as Karjalainen et al. explain,[14] some scholars "argue at least that the global discourse takes its shape in each country and in different locations on the basis of local conditions and socio-political contexts."[15]

These contexts may prioritize other social problems, such as poverty, unemployment, lack of education, internal and external migratory processes, and so on, creating different levels of uncertainties. But it does not mean that the global environmental discourse is not relevant, rather that the climate change discourse is not only scientifically based, it is also closely linked to social change, to the relationship between North and South, and between the sociocultural world and nature.

Notes

1. C. Wright Mills, *The Sociological Imagination* (New York: Oxford University Press, 1959).

2. A. H. Hawley, *Human Ecology: A Theory of Community Structure* (New York: Ronald Press, 1950).

3. D. Erpicum, "Individuo y Reordenamiento Ecológico," in *Perspectivas en Ecología Humana*, Institute of National Public Administration, ed. G. E. Bourgoignie (Madrid: Instituto de Estudios de Administración Local, 1976).

4. M. Heidegger, *Caminos de Bosque* (Madrid: Alianza, 1995).

5. Heidegger, "Bauen, Whonen, Denken," in *Vorträge und Aufsätze* (Pfullingen: Neske, 1954), 139.

6. E. del Acebo Ibáñez, *Homo Sociologicus. Mundo Sociocultural, Organizaciones y Mundo del sujeto* (Buenos Aires, 2010); E. del Acebo Ibáñez, "Bordering Immigrants in Argentina. The Case of the Chilean Immigration to Patagonia and Tierra del Fuego," *Arctic and Antarctic International Journal on Circumpolar Sociocultural Issues* 4 (2010): 47–65; E. del Acebo Ibáñez and A. M. Mendes Diz, "Rootedness and the City: Representations on the Urban Dwelling Among Young People From the City of Buenos Aires," in *Urban Social Problems*; E. del Acebo Ibáñez and Universidad del Salvador (Buenos Aires, 2010), 229–309; E. del Acebo Ibáñez, "The Mountain and the Sea as Mirrors of the Soul. An Approach from Georg Simmel's Aesthetics and Gaston Bachelard's Poetics," *Arctic and Antarctic International Journal on Circumpolar Sociocultural Issues* 2 (2008): 137–56; E. del Acebo Ibáñez, *Sociología del Arraigo. Una Lectura Crítica de la Teoría de la Ciudad* (Buenos Aires: Claridad, 1996); E. del Acebo Ibáñez, *Sociología de la Ciudad Occidental. Un Análisis Histórico del Arraigo* (Buenos Aires: Claridad, 1993).

7. Intergovernmental Panel on Climate Change, *Climate Change 2007: Synthesis Report. Contribution of Working Groups I, II and III to the Fourth Assessment Report of the Intergovernmental Panel on Climate Change*, The Core Writing Team, R. K. Pachauri, and A. Reisinger, eds. (Geneva: Intergovernmental Panel on Climate Change, 2007).

8. "Climate: Observations, Projections and Impacts. Argentina," Met Office United Kingdom; http://www.metoffice.gov.uk/media/pdf/1/l/Argentina.pdf.

9. T. P. Karjalainen, T. Järvikoski,and P. Luoma, "Local Perceptions of Global Climate Change in the Komi Republic in Russia," *Arctic and Antarctic International Journal on Circumpolar Sociocultural Issues* 2 (Jan. 2008): 75–109.

10. Ibid., 75.

11. G. Deleuze and F. Guattari, *Qu'est-ce que la Philosophie?* (Paris: Editions de Minuit, 1991).

12. B. M.Sörensen, "Immaculate Defecation: Gilles Deleuze and Felix Guattari in Organization Theory," *The Sociological Review* 53 (Oct. 2005): 122.

13. Karjalainen et al., "Local Perceptions," supra note 9, 76.

14. Ibid.

15. The same can be said in relation to the conceptualization of "vulnerability." K. Burningham and M. O'Brien, "Global Environmental Values and Local Contexts of Action," *Sociology* 28 (Nov. 1994): 913–32; H-M. Füssel,"Vulnerability: A Generally Applicable Conceptual Framework for Climate Change Research," *Global Environmental Change* 17 (May 2007): 155–67.

21

Future?

TORILL CHRISTINE LINDSTRØM

Introduction

This chapter will, hopefully, amuse you. It will also hopefully surprise
and challenge you with direct unfolding of, display of, description of,
and promotion of certain Norwegian/nordic/Arctic[1] ideas regarding a
possible future for life on this planet.

The Agony of Saint Paul

"The good that I want to do, I don't do, and the evil that I don't want
to do, I do!" complained Paul the apostle.[2] Indeed, his words are mine,
yours, ours—desperate exclamations of a humanity that knows things are
going wrong on planet Earth, primarily due to our collective behaviors.

Simply expressed: Many are already highly motivated to do something about it, and want to make *others* do something about it—politicians, professionals, lawyers, and laypeople alike—and not only here
and now. We want no less than the human race to change its attitudes,
ethics, morality, habits, and behaviors toward this planet and its finely
attuned life forms—changes on macro and micro levels, globally and
locally, and politically and personally, that are desperately needed. To
attain this modest goal, this chapter is dedicated to suggest but one tiny,

contributing element.

I will suggest some minor changes in behaviors and in legislations that may alter people's attitudes toward nature and environmental problems and thereby, at least, contribute to and motivate people toward changes and actions on both personal and political levels.

As St. Paul noted, behaviors are not easily changed. Even when desperately wanting to change, people resist changes in intricate ways, as Freud registered and documented.[3] Freud coined the term *resistance*, which has become one of the most important concepts in psychology and relevant to all forms of therapy. A lot of effort is directed at overcoming resistance, as change is the goal of all psychotherapy.

Meanwhile, a completely different branch of psychology, behaviorism, based on the experimental studies of learning developed by Pavlov, Watson, Thorndike, Skinner, Tolman, Bandura, and others,[4] identified the processes involved in creating behavior change. This knowledge led to the development of new psychotherapies with a focus on behavior modification. These therapies are documented to be effective.[5] The reason they manage to change people's behaviors and habits is that they focus directly on the *conditions* that create and sustain behaviors.

Learning theories tell us that punishment or threats do not work very well as behavior modifiers. They can prevent the performance of behaviors by making people hold them back, but they do not erase the impetus toward those behaviors. Reinforcement, on the other hand—in everyday language usually called rewards—works. A reinforcement is, physiologically speaking, something that excites the reward centers in the brain (primarily through the *nucleus accumbens*, which is part of the limbic system, though the *hypothalamus* is also involved). Simply put, the result of a reinforcement is experienced as pleasure, well-being, joy, and happiness.

"The Pursuit of Happiness"

Environmental psychology is dedicated to exploring people's perception of environmental problems, risks, and threats—how these perceptions influence what policies they will vote for, governance they will support, and political actions they are willing to take part in. Environmental psychology also studies people's view of their private individual behaviors, decision making, and choices regarding issues such as commuting, consumption, recycling, energy sources, tourism, and lifestyle. Furthermore, environmental psychology studies people's motivation to change their behaviors and habits in accordance with their threat perception and insight into global environmental problems.

Without trying to cover all the intricate details of this large field of research, I will mention some important findings: Cross-cultural investigations show that people from various cultures, with small variations, are concerned about anthropogenetic environmental changes and further risk perception.[6] People express two types of considerations connected to environmental risk perception: consequences for people and consequences for nature.[7] These differences are related to general principles regarding morality and ethics—consequentialism and deontology. The contrast between consequentialist and deontological principles is that consequentialism is connected to evaluation of *consequences* as being good or bad, while deontology is connected to *general principles* about good or bad and right or wrong.[8] The deontological principle makes people more immune to manipulations regarding standpoints, attitudes, and behaviors; meaning that if someone regards something as absolutely right and tremendously important, he or she will be less likely to give it up (for money, convenience, etc.) and more likely to make sacrifices for it.

I am a member of, and have worked for, *Norges Naturvernforbund* (Friends of the Earth, Norway), an organization with considerable influence in Norway. It is included in official hearings regarding environmental issues and is involved in a wide range of national and international research projects. Norges Naturvernforbund represents an important source of information to the public regarding environmental problems. Although people in Norway often seem to take their country's abundance of nature and wilderness for granted, they (as do other peoples around the world) increasingly acknowledge the fact that the world's environmental problems require changes in human behaviors on global and local—collective and individual—scales. Some of the needed behavior changes include reduced luxury consumption (and reduced consumption in general); less traveling, car driving, and more collective commuting; more recycling; having to pay more for fuels, foods, and other products (as ecological and fair trade foods usually cost more); reducing population growth; more expensive but also more sustainable and renewable energy sources; and so on.

Many, if not most people who acknowledge environmental problems claim that they are quite motivated and willing to change their individual lifestyles and behaviors if—and the "if" is important—everybody else does, particularly the wealthy, and large corporations, and if the world's governments take concrete action on a global scale (beyond signing conventions).[9] In short, the attitude is "I'll join in, if everybody else does, but I'm waiting for the others to start." This position often results in nobody doing anything. This way of reasoning and reacting reflects a well-known concept within social psychology: diffusion of responsibility.[10]

Admittedly, this is not a uniform attitude, as many people worldwide seem to be deeply aware of environmental problems and many do take action. But the delays caused by diffusion of responsibility on individual and governmental levels present an extremely sad state of affairs when we know both that taking action is pertinent and that time is running out. Governments can impose laws and regulations that can promote and enforce changes globally, locally, and individually. But the problem is: Will people vote for parties and politicians that put restrictions on people's consumption and freedom? Are we really willing to make sacrifices?

The ancient Romans voted for politicians that promised people *panem et circenses* (bread and circuses) or, put in modern terms: income and entertainment. I am afraid that we have not changed much since Roman times. Humans are hedonists. We want that which stimulates the reward center in the brain and is experienced as "good," that which gives us pleasure, joy, health, and happiness. And we want to have the freedom to seek these good goals—as well as freedom from anything that can jeopardize or destroy them—once we have found whatever it is that gives us pleasure, joy, health, and happiness.

Against this background, is it possible to motivate people for global, local, and individual changes of behavior in order to counteract the environmental problems of the world and preserve the planet's nature and innumerable life forms? What are possible immediate and long-term benefits that could act as reinforcers for such motivational and behavioral changes? As stated above, a reinforcer is that which is experienced as good and that which gives pleasure, joy, happiness, and health—and the freedom to seek these good goals (in short, the pursuit of happiness).

What Is Good?

In this section, I offer an answer (among other possible ones) about what is "good" and what gives "happiness." I do that by first presenting a somewhat exaggerated (although some would say: exact) picture of my tribe, the Norwegians. I will start with Norwegians' perceptions of nature and how that is mirrored in Norwegian culture, and I will present some peculiarities from the Norwegian language, lifestyle, and legislation.

The philosopher Bruno Latour claims that in Western scientific ontology, conceptions, and ways of thinking, there is a "Big Divide" between nature and things on one side and culture and humans on the other side.[11] He claims that this Big Divide runs through Western philosophical thinking.[12] But I believe that many, if not most, Norwegians would not recognize this divide. If there is any divide for Norwegians, it is between culture and things on one side and nature and humans on the other. The reasoning is simply that the categories of culture and things belong together because both are human-made, whereas the categories nature and humans belong together because both are "God-given." Indeed, human-made objects (artifacts) are the very indices of culture in archaeology and in some forms of cultural anthropology. Within this perspective, humans are seen as belonging primarily in nature and only secondarily in culture. In principle, culture is a human creation and therefore secondary to nature—in time, at least (for many, also in importance). Although human culture is (as Latour also advocates) intractably interwoven with and enmeshed with nature, to the Norwegian mind, nature sets the premises and therefore has primacy.

To take this argument to the extreme: to the Norwegian mind, culture and its things are the alien stuff, the apart, the potentially unreliable and dangerous—the alien "It."[13] Nature is the trustworthy and safe—the well-known "Us." To put it bluntly: Norwegians trust nature and distrust culture: culture is multiverse but very potentially "bad," whereas nature is intrinsically "good."[14]

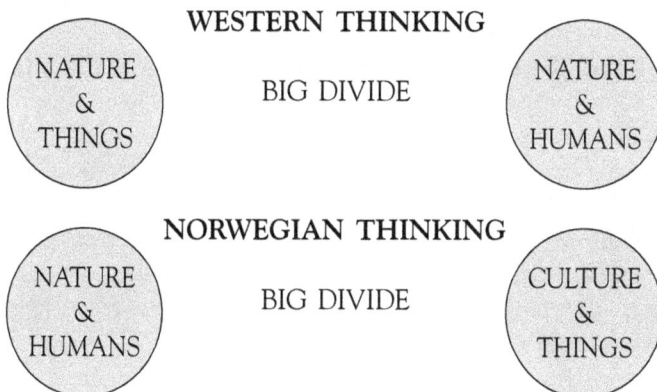

Figure 21.1. Western ways of thinking regarding "The Big Divide" (according to Latour 1993, and others), contrasted to a Norwegian way of thinking about "a Divide." Western philosophy tends to cluster "nature" and "things" together, and "culture" and "humans" together; whereas Norwegians tend to cluster "culture" and "things" together, and "nature" and "humans" together.

Inside: Chaos. Outside: Cosmos.

According to the philosopher and cultural historian Nina Witoszek, a deep attachment to nature characterizes Norwegian mentality and culture, and runs as "a red thread" throughout our history—political as well as ideological and cultural. She explains this well in a book called *Norske naturmytologier. Fra Edda til økofilosofi* (*Norwegian Nature-Mythologies. From Edda to Ecophilosophy*). Its original title was *Nature's Mythologies* (1998). Norwegian ideas about the sacred are connected to nature. Our ancient Norse mythology is as connected to nature as is any indigenous people's mythology, and it is common to hear Norwegians say that they meet God more profoundly in nature than in churches, which is actually regarded as a more okay statement than to admit (yes, we would say: "admit") to attending church regularly.

When Norwegians need to seek clarity of mind and find solutions to difficult questions, including existential ones, they commonly seek solutions when taking walks in nature—preferably long ones: this is captured in *Solvitur ambulando* [Diogenes of Sinope], "you solve (problems) when walking." In other words, Norwegians regard as an axiomatic truth that spending time in nature brings clarity in mind, a healthy psyche and body, and is "the right thing to do" in most of life's circumstances.

This attitude is also deeply pervaded with ideas such as rationalism, egalitarianism, and anti-urbanism (city dwelling being regarded as inferior to living close to, or in, nature). Beliefs in democratic values, education, freedom, and equal rights are key concepts, as is a focus on health and the need to be surrounded by beauty. Natural beauty is nature's beauty, an aesthetic idea of beauty that is so fresh, complete, detailed, and overwhelmingly impressive that culture's products—cities, buildings, works of art—are regarded as artificial and inadequate surrogates, pale and weak attempts to copy the grandeur of Nature, "the Real Thing." "Art" connects to "artificial," and the term *artificial* in Norwegian (*kunstig*) has far more negative, derogatory denotations of unnatural, false, feigned, treacherous, and not trustworthy, than in the English term *artificial*.

Despite this connection between art and the artificial, the most famous works of art in Norwegian culture are indeed pervaded with this attitude toward nature's perfection: Grieg's music describes a solemn tonal nature just as the paintings of Tiedemand, Gude, and Astrup describe nature's magnificent forms, lights, and colors. Vigeland's sculptures show human bodies in their natural, liberated states. Hamsun's novels and Munch's pictures both display the liberating, life-giving nature outside, in contrast to the grotesque choking, cramped, and claustrophobic culture inside—inside cities, houses, and families. "Inside," in other words, is seen culturally as oppressing: damp, dusty, and dirty (literally and symbolically). Inside, people become anxiety-ridden, grief-struck, and desperate.[15] Family life is full of demands, manipulations, and conflicts.[16] *Ute* (outdoors), by contrast, one is free from these burdens and dangers of culture. Henrik Ibsen repeats this theme over and over: People are troubled, oppressed, depressed, and destroyed in culture. Contrastingly, people become authentic, liberated, and purified in nature: *"Mitt lavlandsliv har jeg levet ut, her oppe på fjellet er frihet og Gud—der nede kravler de andre!"* ("My lowland-life I have lived to its end, up here, on the mountain, is freedom and God—down there crawl the others!").[17] Also, modern Norwegians find such statements quite "natural." When E.T. points to the stars and says "Home!" a Norwegian would say "Home!" when pointing to mountains and moors. Inside is chaos; outside is Cosmos.

According to Nina Witoszek, this attitude is an essential part of the Norwegian *meme* (culturally conveyed mental *schemata*: ways of thinking). Nature is a constant in Norwegian culture, penetrating everything. Witoszek argues that as a consequence, it was out of this cultural background that the Norwegian philosopher and professor Arne Næss developed his "deep ecology" and "ecosophy," viewed by many as possibly the most comprehensive philosophical position with regard to the global environmental problems.[18] The Norwegian cultural backdrop, but in particular the outdoor activities of his childhood (being *ute*), impressed him for life. Later, Næss spent the best times of his life at Tvergastein, a *hytte* (hut) that he built high up on a foothill of Hallingskarvet Mountain.[19] A deep unity with and belongingness within nature penetrates his arguments for a better life for the individual, a sustainable human culture, and for preservation of life's multiple forms and diversity on Earth. In many respects, his holistic ideas resemble those of Hildegard von Bingen.[20] Humans are part of nature. Instead of the materialistic "standard of living," he identified "quality of life" as *the* appropriate measure of human happiness.

Figure 21.2. Professor Arne Næss, ecophilosopher.

Norwegian Peculiarities in Language, Lifestyle, and Legislation

There is no Norwegian word for "nature" or "environment." We regard nature as ever present and take it for given and granted. We have borrowed the French words *nature* and *milieu* and spell them *natur* and *miljø*. We could say *omgivelser* (the same as the German *Umgebungen*) for surroundings, but that can refer equally to inside and outside. So, regarding ecological issues, *miljø* is the word we use. We do have a word for landscape: *landskap*. But that is a word with an urban touch to it. *Landskap* sounds a bit strange in the mouth of Norwegian farmers. For them there is no "scape," only "land." And the expression "out in the countryside" is *på landet* (literally on the land) in Norwegian.

English has its "outdoors." Norwegians can say *utendørs*, but that means primarily to be "just outside the doors," in a courtyard or a garden. English also has its "outside," to which Norwegian has no exact equivalent. It sounds strange: "Outside what?" as if one were locked out (literally: excluded) from something, left out, as if the "in-side" would be a better place. But inside (*inne* or *innendørs*, literally: inside the doors) is for many Norwegians almost synonymous to "locked up" (*innestengt*).

The Norwegian word *utside* (outside) means outer surface and *innside* means inner surface. When wanting to say outdoors/outside, Norwegians simply say *ute*, with no -doors or -side to it. One can say *ute i naturen* (out in nature), but that is a pleonasm. *Ute* is an absolute locational adverb, a place that rests in its own definition and existence without having to refer to culture's -doors or -sides.

This Norwegian linguistic peculiarity reflects a lifestyle parallel. *Ute* is a better place. Whereas *innendørs* (indoors) for many Norwegians is associated with being locked up, *ute* for most Norwegians is laden with positive, joyful associations, meanings, and memories.[21] To have a party *ute*, eat *ute*, share drinks *ute*, sleep *ute*, and so forth, is regarded as much better than doing the same things *inne* (inside). To be *ute* is luxurious! Norwegians complain that their weekend or holiday is ruined if the weather is so bad that they cannot be *ute* to do the things they want to do. Holidays (and going to foreign and exotic countries) are supposed to be spent *ute*, preferably walking, hiking, biking, skiing, kayaking, wild camping, and so forth. *Ute* means being in nature, that is. To be *ute* on a balcony, terrace, garden, or park is inferior. Only nature counts as a proper *ute* location.

Norwegians thus react with shock, contempt, disbelief, and disgust when television shows that kindergartens (some, hopefully not all) in the United Kingdom and the United States take away natural grass and trees and install artificial grass and constructed climbing apparatuses. Those artificial surroundings are designed to keep the children confined and surveyed by custodians that make sure that the children do not do anything that might give them the slightest bruises or pain. To Norwegians, that kindergarten concept comes close to child abuse.

Norwegian children are supposed to be *ute* in *natural* surroundings as much as possible. To keep children indoors a lot is regarded as child neglect—almost child abuse—and at least bad parenting. Babies should have an outdoor nap during the day, every day, all through the year. In Norway, older children, in kindergartens, often sleep outdoors. My cousin's husband, who works in a kindergarten, says that the children sleep much better when it is cold, preferably below freezing. The reason is evident: there is more oxygen in the air in colder weather, giving deeper and more restorative sleep. He works in a *Naturbarnehage* (Nature Kindergarten), now the most popular kind of kindergarten in Norway, where the children are *ute* almost all the time.[22]

In some nature kindergartens, the children are received in the morning around an open fire in a *lavvo* (*sami* tent). The children take walks in nature almost every day—they play in natural surroundings where branches may break, stones tilt, and ants bite. They learn to

Figure 21.3. *Lavvo* (*sami* tent) in an urban kindergarten.

prepare food on open fires outdoors—they are taught to make such fires, even in rain—and they learn to use knives and axes from the age of three to four years. They learn activities that are essential in life. And they love it! The children are permitted, actually encouraged, to climb, bump, slide, fall, tumble—to test out their bodies—and they sledge whenever there is snow, or just frost, on the ground. In fact, children usually learn to sledge, ski, and skate as soon as they can walk, and some learn swimming first. Having some bruises, falls, scrapes, and hurts is regarded as natural and necessary elements in a natural and healthy child development, because then the children learn how to behave in nature, how to move about quickly and adequately with little falling and stumbling, and how to take proper care of themselves and help others when being *ute*. Through practice, they learn what to wear in different kinds of weather, what conditions to be prepared for, what surfaces are slippery versus solid, what rocks will move versus be stable, and they are instructed to know what berries, herbs, and mushrooms are edible. All this becomes implicit parts of their upbringing. People are quite safe in nature when they have the adequate experience and competence. In this way, we believe that we prepare our children for enjoying a really good life, with a lot of time spent *ute*—in nature.

One of the largest and most popular organizations in Norway is *Den Norske Turistforening* (*The Norwegian Trekking Association*). Enigmatically, its journal name is the imperative *UT!* (Get out!). A lifestyle of outdoor activities is usually maintained throughout life. One example will suffice: Bergen, the city where I live, is surrounded by mountains. The mountains

Figure 21.4. Children playing in an urban kindergarten, among trees on a steep snow-clad hill.

have individual names, but as a group are referred to as Byfjellene (the city mountains). Now, since the city has expanded, the mountains are within the city and therefore more accessible than ever. And they are used! Every day of the year, regardless of weather or temperature, you will find hundreds, often thousands, of people of all ages and physical abilities, who *går tur* (walks tour) (or hike, ski, sledge, bike, jog) on the narrow roads (few) and paths and trails (many) of Byfjellene. The

Figure 21.5. The author walking in "Byfjellene" surrounding the city of Bergen, Norway.

søndagstur (Sunday walk) has been essentially mandatory for generations of Bergensers, regarded by some (sulky teenagers, in particular) as a compulsory moral obligation, but for most as a joyful "must."

At this point you may wonder: Are people allowed to roam freely about, everywhere in nature? Are there no legal restrictions? What about private property? Yes, there are restrictions . . . but they primarily restrict the proprietors.

In the United Kingdom, I have seen many places in the countryside where signposts say "Public Footpath." That is irresistibly amusing to a Norwegian! First, the signpost is practically void of content, because it gives you no important information. In contrast, Norwegian signposts connected to paths and trails tell you where you will end up if you follow them, the distances to those places, sometimes how strenuous the routes are, and whether the paths/trails are meant for walking or for skiing. Second, "footpath" is amusing because it is a pleonasm: How can a path *not* be for feet? But the most amusing part is the word *public*, because how can a path possibly be private? Philosophically, the Norwegian mirth is related to the content of the quote: "Who owns the cleanness of the air and the glittering of the waves?"[23]—conceptually, nature cannot be owned. A path in nature is created by thousands of feet, often through thousands of years. To claim a path in nature to be private is therefore ludicrous.

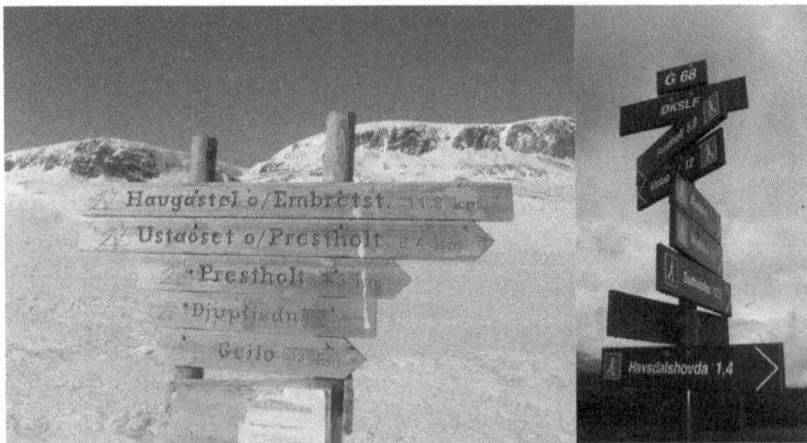

Figure 21.6. Signposts in Norway. Telling directions, distances, and whether the paths (trails, tracks) are for summer/autumn/spring or for winter (ski trails).

There is no word for "trespassing" in the Norwegian language.[24] We regard it as a human right to be in nature. This conviction and conception is the legal principle called *Allemannsretten*, literally "everybody's right" or "The Common Right" (to be in nature), which is expressed in *Friluftsloven* within the Norwegian Constitution (*Norges Lover*). Its content is regarded as part of our cultural heritage and as a characteristic expression of the Norwegian mentality. And, because the idea of *Allemannsrett* already was taken for granted, there was no need to confirm it as a law only until 1957. That law (*"Friluftsloven av 1957"*) declares:

> The purpose of this law is to protect people's outdoor activities in nature, and its fundament in nature, and to ensure the general public's right to walk, stay, etc. in nature; so that the possibility to enjoy outdoor activities in nature as a health-promoting, well-being creating, and environmentally friendly (eco-friendly) leisure-time activity is protected and promoted.[25]

The main aspects of this law are: everybody has the right to move about in nature (walk, ski, skate, swim, dive, use boats). "Nature" includes almost everywhere outdoors, including farmers' fields. Regarding farm-

Figure 21.7. My daughter Amira Christine camping and cooking, with an open fire.

ers' fields, there is a distinction between the farm's *innmark* (tilled and planted fields) and *utmark* (pastures and wilderness). There are restrictions regarding *innmark* in the growing and harvesting seasons, but the *utmark* is free for everybody. However, one must take care not to destroy anything, litter, or cause fires. One is permitted to use wood and pick berries, herbs, and mushrooms. It is, in fact, illegal for owners to try to prevent people from moving about in nature. When moving about, one is expected to leave only perishable traces (such as ski tracks, footprints, and remnants of fires). This means that motorized vehicles, except boats as a general rule, are not allowed in nature. Everybody is allowed to land a boat, to sit on land for the day, or to camp overnight, anywhere along the coastlines and also on private property, relatively close to houses. Camping outdoors (in nature) is also permitted for everybody for three nights in one place. After that, a landowner may ask the campers to leave if their camping is inconvenient. It is forbidden to fence people out or tell people to leave using "private property" as a cause. One may put up signs saying private property, but that does not make it illegal to walk or ski on the premises. In order to protect the waterfronts (of both seas and lakes), houses are not allowed to be built closer than 100

Figure 21.8. The author and the dog "Stella," after a bath in spring.

meters from the waterline of lakes or the sea. There are a few restrictions, such as on the use of fire in summertime in order to prevent forest fires, and on hunting and fishing in lakes and rivers. Fishing licenses may usually be bought, and some lakes are truly private regarding fishing, but swimming and the use of kayaks are allowed in them. Regardless of license, all children under 16 years are allowed to fish freely. There are no restrictions regarding being naked on land or when swimming.[26]

In short, the Norwegian *Friluftsloven* is the legal expression of and protection of ancient attitudes toward nature, the conviction of a basic human need to be in nature, and therefore a human right to be in close and constant contact with nature. It reflects the close connection between "the peculiarities" of Norwegian language, lifestyle, and legislation.

Solvitur Ambulando

These peculiarities in language, lifestyle, and legislation are deeply embedded in the Norwegian culture. Yet there are, of course, exceptions. Not all Norwegians are equally fascinated by these values and lifestyles. Some proprietors try to circumvent *Friluftsloven* by putting up private property signs and fences. But they meet with little success, as they are generally regarded as grumpy and pompous people who obviously make fools of themselves. Norway also has "sofa sitters," people who feel uncomfortable and clumsy *ute*, for whom parks, gardens, terraces, and balconies are *ute*-places and who regard those as sufficient substitutes for nature. But even the most resistant sofa sitters regard nature as having an extraordinary value and usually feel the need to excuse and defend their indoor and city life style.

The tribal Norwegian values presented here, although definitely Norwegian, are clearly not exclusively so. Many other tribes—peoples as well as people (groups as well as individuals)—hold similar attitudes, value nature as an indispensable part of life, and value activities in nature as necessary for keeping body and mind healthy—in short, to have a good life quality. Organizations in the United States, such as the Children in Nature Network and People in Nature (and I am convinced that there are many more), also promote such ideas and values. But for native Norwegians, it is a bit outlandish that organizations are needed to promote values and behaviors that are taken for granted, and regarded as basic in life.

Be that as it may, it is nevertheless generally viewed as good that "green values" and "closeness to nature values" are being promoted in order to enhance people's health and life quality. But . . . is that really so? Are activities in nature really so good for you? Were Diogenes of Sinope, Hildegard of Bingen, and Henrik Ibsen and Arne Næss of Norway really right?

In 1984, biologist Edward Wilson proposed a theory he called *Biophilia.*[27] He claims, like Hildegard von Bingen and Arne Næss before him, that human beings have a naturally given love for, longing for, and deep connectedness with nature and other living creatures. Although regarded as untested, speculative, and sentimental—with little concrete evidence at the time when the Biophilia Theory was presented—evidence has piled up. Only a few will be mentioned here, but there are numerous investigations that testify that seeing nature, being in nature, and moving about in nature have profound positive effects on people's life quality—including somatic, social, cognitive, and mental health—for healthy people as well as for those who face bodily, mental, or social

Figure 21.9. My mother, Sigrid Askeland, aged 84, mountain hiking.

afflictions.[28] Activities in nature also have considerable positive effects on children's intelligence and on their bodily, motoric, cognitive, and personal development and capacities; on their resilience against stress, reduction of stress and of hyperactive behaviors; and more.[29] Yes, Diogenes, Hildegard, Henrik, and Arne were right.

Conclusion: Suggestions for a "Public Footpath"

Public means common and for everybody. Path is, in a double sense, the most natural guideline that exists. It is natural because it adapts to the natural landscape (instead of forcing its way), and it is natural also as the product of a multitude of feet finding and following the best way (both literally and symbolically). I have in this chapter implicitly suggested a path—a public one—for everybody, a path toward making people more willing, both individually and collectively, to change their behaviors regarding environmental issues.

Based on the premises of behavioral psychology: positive reinforcers work to change behaviors, meaning that when behaviors are followed by rewards—consequences that are perceived as good—those behaviors are likely to be resumed, repeated, and perpetuated. And, people will also be deeply interested in keeping the contextual premises for those behaviors to be actualized (so, for example, those who love to play football will not let their football ground be destroyed). Accordingly, I propose the following connection: People who experience the rewarding, positive consequences of nature, of activities in nature, and of simply being in nature—the well-being, the life quality, the health and happiness—will not accept the ongoing destruction of nature (global warming, pollution, extinction of species, cutting down of rain forests, etc.).

There is an underlying premise, though, that has to be fulfilled: people must have had the opportunity to experience these positive consequences themselves. And this depends on a series of contingent conditions. Let me describe them as a series of "ifs" and "thens."

If legislation is such that everybody is free to be in nature (approximately as described in *Friluftsloven*) and *if* children are brought up in the family, kindergarten, and school, to enjoy being as much as possible in nature and learning the skills required for outdoor activities and living, *then* it is highly likely that those people growing up will continue to treasure nature as an irreplaceable and absolute value; and *then* the next

Figure 21.10. T-shirt texted with a subtle double meaning: Either: "Why sit in(side), when all hope is gone?" Or: "Why sit in(side), when all (good) hopes are out(side)?"

generations will be more willing, on individual as well as on collective, political levels, to change their behaviors toward (what in English is called) "the environment." And finally, *then* we may all have a FUTURE.

Notes

1. In this chapter, I will not use the term "Norwegian/nordic/Arctic," but just "Norwegian." It is more precise in relation to the content of this chapter.

2. A. Næss, *Økologi, samfunn og livsstil: utkast til en økosofi* (*Ecology, Society and Lifestyle: A Proposition for an Ecosophy*) (Oslo: Bokklubben Dagens Bøker, 1999); Paul. Letters to the Romans, 7.19), in: *Bibelen* ("The Bible") (Oslo: Bibelselskapet, 2011).

3. S. Freud, *Analysis Terminable and Interminable*, ed. E. Jones and trans. J. Riviere, *Collected Papers*, vol. 1 (New York: Basic Books, 1959 [1896]), 155–82.

4. M. Olson and B. Hergenhahn, *An Introduction to Theories of Learning* (Boston: Pearson, 2005).

5. W. Serketich and J. Dumas, "The Effectiveness of Behavioral Parent Training to Modify Antisocial Behavior in Children: A Meta-Analysis," *Behavior Therapy* 27 (2006): 171–86; S. Morley, C. Eccleston, and A. Williams, "Systematic Review and Meta-Analysis of Randomized Controlled Trials of Cognitive Behaviour Therapy and Behaviour Therapy for Chronic Pain in Adults, Excluding Headache," *Pain* 80 (1999): 1–13.

6. A. Bostrom et al., "Causal Thinking and Support for Climate Change Policies: International Survey Findings," *Global Environmental Change* 22 (2012): 210–22.

7. G. Böhm and H. Pfizer, "Consequences, Morality and Time in Environmental Risk Perception," *Journal of Risk Research* 8 (2005): 461–79.

8. Examples: A consequentialist viewpoint: to regard the extinction of wolves as "good" because it would benefit grazing flocks of sheep, and therefore the farmers. A deontological viewpoint: to regard the human-caused extinction of any wild species as "bad" regardless of beneficial consequences for other species, or for humans. A consequentialist might regard global warming as "good" if it would give nicer weather during people's summer holidays. A deontologist would regard global warming as principally "bad" regardless of "positive" short-term consequences. G. Böhm and C. Tanner, "Environmental Risk Perception," in *Environmental Psychology: An Introduction*, ed. L. Steg, A. van den Berg, and J. de Groot (New York: Wiley, 2013); M. Leary and D. Forsyth, "Attributions of Responsibility for Collective Endeavors," *Review of Personality and Social Psychology* 8 (1968), 167–88.

9. The governments seem to have a similar attitude, considering their delays in CO_2-reducing action.

10. J. Darley and B. Latané, "Bystander Intervention in Emergencies: Diffusion of Responsibility," *Journal of Personality and Social Psychology* 8 (1968): 377–83; Leary and Forsyth, "Attributions of Responsibility for Collective Endeavors," 167–88.

11. B. Latour, *We Have Never Been Modern* (London: Harvard University Press, 1993). Here, I boldly use the term *culture* instead of Latours's "society," as I think that "culture" is a better contrast to "nature" than "society" is, but without altering the meaning of Latour's "Great Divide" idea.

12. Scientifically, that means that phenomena in nature and things (material objects) are seen as belonging together and in science studied by certain methodologies and theories, whereas culture and humans are classed together and studies by other methodologies and theories. Clearly, this division was preceded by Plato's division between mind and body, and by Descartes's division (dualism) between subject-object, physical-mental, body-mind, etc. Descartes regarded a dog's screams of pain as noise from a machinery (*machina animata*), giving no grounds for compassion; and he was interested in warfare, not studying the reasons *why* people killed each other, but *how* they did it (Rasmussen 2018: 50–53,

59). I therefore find it most disturbing that he has had a strong influence in Western thought and science and still is regarded as an important philosopher.

13. It resembles the horrors of "The Thing" of fiction and philosophy alike (Botting 2012).

14. Norwegians are not ignorant of the potential dangers of nature, but we regard them as small when you have adequate experience and competence.

15. Edvard Munch's most famous painting, "The Scream," being one (of several) exceptions in his art, though.

16. To some extent, this is objectively right, as one of my friends, a lawyer, informed me: most murders and harassments happen within the closest family.

17. H. Ibsen, The Collected Works of Henrik Ibsen, Vol. III (New York: Charles Scribner's Sons, 1908).

18. A. Næss, Deep Ecology for the Twenty-Second Century, in Deep Ecology for the Twenty-First Century, ed. G. Sessions (Boston: Shambhala, 1995). One of Arne Næss's goals was to create a philosophy and lifestyle of attaining "maximum happiness with a minimum of material means," thereby also promoting sustainability and preservation of nature.

19. He called this mountain "father of the long, good life" (Næss 1995), an epithet that Norwegians find quite "natural." Hallingskarvet is loved by many and experienced somewhat like a "person" in its own right, slightly reminiscent of "animism" as defined by Descola (2006).

20. H. von Bingen with H. Schipperges, Das Buch der Lebensverdiens (The Book of the Rewards of Life) (Salzburg: Otto Müeller Verlag, 1986 [1158–1163]).

21. You cannot punish a Norwegian by saying, "Get out!" because "ute" is where the Norwegian wants to be.

22. There are many different types, degrees, and variations of the Naturbarnehage concept. What they all share is a focus on outdoor life, few constructed playthings and toys, and a focus on children's immediate experiences in nature and their use of their own fantasy to create "toys" and use of natural objects as structures to play with and in. Children in Naturbarnehager get a superior motoric development, and motoric development in children is connected to improved intelligence development, coping, resilience, and positive self-perception.

Personally, I have never slept better since I started to sleep outdoors (on my balcony) most nights, all year round. In addition, I enjoy the relaxing meditative experience of watching the trees, mountains, rain, snow, clouds, sunsets, stars, moon, and occasional Northern Lights.

23. Seathl of Duwanishtam, 1855, Letter to U.S. President Franklin Pierce. From a letter written by American Indian chief Seathl of Duwanishtam (now within the state of Washington) to U.S. President Franklin Pierce, in 1855.

24. The idea of "trespassing" would have to be expressed approximately like this: Å gå inn på et område hvor det er forbudt å gå ("to go/walk in on an area where it is forbidden to go," but a Norwegian would immediately question

the right to "forbid walking in" if the area looks like nature (and would probably ignore the sign, and "trespass").

25. Author's translation.

26. However, most people are bashful enough to skinny dip and take naked sunbaths in privacy.

27. E. Wilson, *Biophilia* (Cambridge: Harvard University Press, 1984).

28. S. Kaplan, "The Restorative Benefits of Nature: Toward an Integrative Framework," *Journal of Environmental Psychology* 15 (1995): 169–82; B. Giles-Corti and R. Donovan, "Relative Influences of Individual, Social Environmental, and Physical Environmental Correlates of Walking," *American Journal of Public Health* 93 (2002): 1583–89; J. Davis, *Psychological Benefits of Nature Experiences: An Outline of Research and Theory—with Special Reference to Transpersonal Psychology*, Napata University and School of Lost Borders, 2004; A. Van Den Berg, T. Hartig, and H. Staats, "Preference for Nature in Urbanized Societies: Stress, Restoration, and the Pursuit of Sustainability," *Journal of Social Issues* 63 (2007): 79–96; S. Bell et al., *Greenspace and Quality of Life: A Critical Review*, Greenspace, Scotland, 20080; M. Berman, J. Jonides, and S. Kaplan, "The Cognitive Benefits of Interacting with Nature," *Psychological Science* 19 (2008): 1207–12; A. Novotney, "Getting Back to the Great Outdoors," *Monitor* 39 (2008): 52, American Psychological Association; T. Sugiyama et al., "Associations of Neighbourhood Greenness with Physical and Mental Health: Do Walking, Social Coherence, and Local Interaction Explain the Relationships?" *Journal of Epidemiology and Community Health* 62 (2008): e9; J. Barton and J. Pretty, "What Is the Best Dose of Nature and Green Exercise for Improving Mental Health? A Multi-Study Analysis," *Environmental Science & Technology* (2010): 3947–55.

29. But admittedly, most of these, and similar, investigations have been done in Western and/or technologically advanced countries. I. Fjortoft, "Landscape and Playscape: The Effects of Natural Environments on Children's Play and Motor Development," *Children, Youth and Environments* 14 (2004): 21–44; P. Kahn Jr. and S. Kellert, *Children and Nature: Psychological, Sociocultural, and Evolutionary Investigations* (Cambridge: MIT Press, 2002); S. Kellert, "Nature and Childhood Development," in S. Kellert, *Building for Life: Designing and Understanding the Human-Nature Connection* (Washington, DC: Island Press, 2005): 63–89; S. Muñoz, *Children in the Outdoors: A Literature Review*, Sustainable Development Research Centre, 2009; V. Vedul-Kjelsås et al., "The Relationship between Motor Competence, Physical Fitness and Self-perception in Children," *Child, Care, Health and Development* 38 (2011): 394–402; R. Louv, "Every Child Need Nature: 12 Questions about Equity and Capacity," *Psychology Today* (May 9, 2012); N. Wells, "At Home with Nature: Effects of 'Greenness' on Children's Cognitive Functioning," *Environment and Behavior* 32 (2000): 775–95; N. Wells and G. Evans, "Nearby Nature: A Buffer of Life Stress among Rural Children," *Environment and Behavior* 35 (2003): 311–30.

22

Conclusion

Elegy for the Arctic?

Errol Meidinger, Ezra B. W. Zubrow,
and Kim Diana Connolly

As we were working on this volume, the NGO Greenpeace published a video of composer-pianist Ludovico Einaudi performing his original piece, "Elegy for the Arctic," on a raft floating in front of a glacier amid drift ice in the Arctic.[1] The spare, haunting notes of the piano are accompanied by ice periodically peeling off the glacier and crashing into the sea. After the final notes, the pianist very slowly removes his hands from the keyboard and listens, as do we. We hear the eternal sound of the sea, and of the performance raft bobbing slightly, but no people. We must conjure people into the soundscape. We all are there of course. Together we live the life patterns that drive the climate change that leads to the calving ice, and indeed the performance.

In this book, we offer a multilayered composition featuring many of the voices engaged in Arctic life and governance. It has no single melody. It is not synthetically orchestrated. Instead, it is a collage of perspectives and analyses. It presents at once harmony and cacophony, hope and despair, emerging climate commitment and frighteningly inadequate climate governance institutions.

The chapters in Part 1 describe multiple efforts to better document and understand the intricate and manifold dynamics of climate change:

411

its causal patterns, its physical and social effects, its "reality." We learn of numerous efforts to gather better data on the labyrinthine ways in which climate change expresses itself, including research by Cree hunters, many varieties of scientists, transnational NGOs, local community members, and others. We learn how climate change reverberates through bird populations, short-lived chemicals, food sources, Northern peoples, and other phenomena, and how the Arctic climate is connected to that in other regions, including the tropics. While the Arctic is sometimes described as "the canary in the coal mine" of climate change, it is an immense "canary," one deeply interconnected with and inseparable from the earth system of which it is part. We now have growing evidence that the Arctic's melting permafrost could release huge amounts greenhouse gases as the atmosphere warms, thereby accelerating its own destruction through a perverse feedback loop.[2] Both in the Arctic and worldwide, 2016 was the hottest year on record;[3] 2017 was the third hottest.[4] The atmosphere now has 400 parts per million of carbon dioxide, a level never before experienced in human history and just 50 ppm from a threshold widely understood to be perilous.[5] Thus, the knowledge mosaic reflected in Part 1 grows ever more garish and more urgent.

Part 2 provides a sampling of the many policy and governance initiatives being mounted to address the multifarious challenges of climate change. These include what some see as a cacophony of actions by national and international institutions—all with their severe limitations and contradictions.[6] They reach from local indigenous peoples struggling to deploy human rights principles to defend their lifeways to the grand stage of geopolitics, where the once-quiescent Arctic may be triggering new moves by powerful players pursuing empire, treasure, and security on a rapidly changing stage. The authors struggle mightily to envision scenarios in which sufficient globally coordinated actions can be taken to effectively mitigate and adapt to climate change in the Circumpolar North—but none with much confidence. The policy initiatives discussed are sluggish, partial, tentative, fragmented, internally and externally conflicted, and highly fragile. It seems apparent that to help bring together and focus these initiatives, a growing degree of globally shared understanding of the challenges and appropriate responses to climate change will be required.

Part 3 adds to this complex picture by sampling a variety of cultural understandings regarding climate change. Expectations and institutions relevant to climate change vary greatly across societies and over time. We see examples of ancient societies that managed to respond effectively—if perhaps turbulently—to climate change during their eras. We also see examples of modern societies with very different attitudes toward nature, economy, and climate. There are profound disagreements about how to conserve nature and maintain economic vitality. Whereas a great many societies have traditionally assumed climate and cultural stability, both now wobble with instability. Under the circumstances, can we find and foster sufficient shared understanding to carry out concerted action to respond effectively to climate change? Can we do it at all?

Looking at this book as whole, it is difficult to answer this question optimistically. And yet we also see some grounds for hope, including both resilience in past cultures and rapidly growing concern and capacity for innovation in modern ones. While we know that many of our cultures and institutions—for example, fixed property and territorial nation-states—tend to assume protective stasis in nature and destructive dynamism in the economy, we also know that these assumptions are undergoing challenge and transformation as connections between the two become apparent.

One of the most striking examples of change is the movement of many large businesses and business associations from indifference or opposition to engagement in climate action and public support for active climate governance, including change in their own operations. While the reasons for this movement are variable and often murky, they seem generally to include a desire to protect brand reputations and to minimize business risks, including potential legal liability, from climate change.[7] Recently, "We Mean Business," one of several global networks of corporations and investors advocating for policies to cut carbon emissions, publicly celebrated its 1,000th commitment to climate action, a pledge by an Indian information technology company.[8] In the run-up to the Conference of the Parties to the UN Framework on Climate Convention (UNFCCC) in Paris (COP 21 or "Paris process"), more than 150 large companies doing business in the United States signed on to the "American Business Act on Climate Pledge," in which they promised both to voice support for a strong outcome in Paris and to demonstrate an ongoing commitment to climate action in their own operations—for example, by reducing their emissions or increasing their investments in low carbon activities.[9] These processes complemented the larger UN "Lima to Paris Action Agenda," in which cities, subnational regions, companies, investors, and civil society organizations register commitments to climate action.[10]

Business organizations making commitments under the above programs are generally free to define their own pledges. Not surprisingly, those pledges show great variety in both substance and stringency, giving rise to widespread concern about their seriousness and adequacy to achieve effective climate action. At the same time, there is evidence that standards and rules for managing carbon are slowly being developed by extensive, loosely coupled networks of businesses, NGOs, government agencies, research organizations, and others.[11] This kind of process is extremely important in climate governance as well as other transnational problem areas,[12] offering the possibility of creating a system of shared expectations and standards for the many different types of actors who affect the nature of and responses to climate change.

While the large and growing multitude of climate-related initiatives and standards cannot and need not be detailed here, it is important to note that they include a diverse array of market reshaping actions, including creation of carbon markets,[13] travel offsets,[14] climate bonds,[15] internal carbon pricing,[16] corporate social responsibility programs,[17] and a broad range of transparency initiatives.[18] Moreover, insurers are increasingly pricing coverage for flooding, hurricanes, drought, and wildfires based on climate change projections, thus turning market forces slowly toward climate change mitigation and adaptation.[19]

Taken together, this conglomeration of nonstate-centered initiatives is impressive and important—indeed essential, given the multifaceted and complex nature of the problem.[20] Nonetheless, private initiatives remain slow, partial, fragmented, inconsistent, and even contradictory. For example, many of the firms that have made climate pledges also support or even undertake anti–climate protection lobbying.[21] Many of the banks that have made climate pledges still provide capital to carbon-intensive industries (although they appear to have reduced their support of coal burning energy sources).[22] Moreover, without a strong governance framework, businesses continue to have strong incentives to enhance profits by pursuing climate-damaging short-term cost reductions. Hence, prudent analysts generally espouse the need for effective governmental regulation and international cooperation in climate governance.[23]

National regulation and international cooperation for climate protection have been painfully slow to develop. Even ambitious governmental statements of commitment have rarely been matched by effective action—often out of fear that difficult and expensive emissions reductions in one country would quickly be obliterated by opportunistic increases in others. After more than three decades of ponderously slow, clearly inadequate progress, the "Paris Agreement" negotiated in December 2015 seemed to have stepped up the pace, ambition, and level of participation in the intergovernmental system.

It seems important to note for readers that the Arctic was not prominent in the Paris process. Our research uncovered only three official events (of more than 200) focused on the Arctic—two side events and a symposium. There was also an 80 metric ton display of arctic ice hauled in from a Norwegian fjord that was allowed to melt over the course of the meetings.[24] The official documents resulting from the conference, the "Decision" and the "Agreement," do not mention the Arctic.[25] Nor could we find mention of it in the subsequent COP 22 Marrakech outcome documents.[26] Many of the most influential countries in the UNFCCC negotiations have no direct interest in the Arctic—the United States and Russia being important exceptions. Yet when it comes to international collaborations, to a considerable degree the fate of the Arctic is left in the hands of other actors with broader or different interests.

Nonetheless, the Paris Agreement may offer some cause for hope for the Arctic—or at least for restraining despair. Agreed to by virtually every country in the world, it commits signatories to the goal of "holding the increase in global average temperature to well below 2° Celsius above pre-industrial levels and to pursue efforts to limit the temperature increase to 1.5° Celsius."[27] Yet the editors acknowledge that achieving even the 2° Celsius goal will be exceedingly difficult, requiring commitments well beyond those made to date.[28] If it is not achieved, the consequences for the Earth will be dire, and those for the Arctic catastrophic.

Prospects for meeting the 2° Celsius goal are highly uncertain. While every country in the world has now acknowledged the goal's importance and committed to it to some degree, limiting temperature increases to 2° Celsius will require an unprecedented level of sustained implementation and cooperation. Under the climate governance regime taking shape through the Agreement, each country determines its own level of greenhouse gas reduction (its "nationally determined contribution" or NDC) and then records it in an international registry. While the overall target may be formally legally binding, the NDCs are not. And even though the target is "binding," it is difficult to imagine how any individual party could be held responsible for the collective failure to achieve the goal.

The only formally binding requirements are that every party submit an NDC, communicate it, produce information on implementation, and periodically update it. The drivers for the system, then, are the "new governance"[29] ones of transparency, clear accounting requirements, and a five-yearly "stock taking" process—all conducted under the shadow of manifestly intensifying climate change problems.[30] An underlying assumption, as in other new governance strategies, is that the transparency, monitoring, reporting, and regular review—all subject to public criticism and comparison to other actors—will lead to a "ratcheting up" of protections.

The primary focus of the Paris Agreement is on climate change "mitigation"—the reduction and control of greenhouse gases in the atmosphere. An equally or more pressing concern of the Arctic regions is "adaptation"—that is, how to respond to climate change impacts that are already in evidence, as discussed in Part 1 of this book. Those adaptations are dealt with much less effectively in the Paris Agreement. It mainly recommends increased cooperation and communication among the states. It encourages them to enhance adaptive capacity, strengthen resilience, and reduce vulnerability to climate change.[31] It recognizes the importance of funding to assist adaptation but includes no financial commitment to provide such funds. Moreover, although the Agreement notes the importance of "averting, minimizing and addressing loss and damage associated with the adverse effects of climate change,"[32] a provision in the Conference of the Parties (COP) Decision document provides that "Article 8 of the Agreement does not involve or provide a basis for any liability or compensation"—at least conceptually, therefore precluding liability of industrialized countries for damages resulting from climate change.[33]

Almost every country in the world agreed on the terms of the Paris Agreement. It became formally binding in October 2016, when 55 countries representing 55 percent of global emissions signed and ratified the agreement.[34] Momentum toward ratification accelerated when the United States and China (together, responsible for about 38 percent of global emissions) jointly announced their ratification on the eve of a G20 summit in early September 2016.[35] As this book went to press, the Agreement had 196 signatories and 166 countries had ratified, accounting for more than 87 percent of global greenhouse gas emissions.[36]

The United States played an important role in the negotiation and adoption of the Agreement. Climate change action was a major part of the Obama administration's agenda. In ratifying the Agreement, the United States submitted an NDC promising to cut emissions by 26–28 percent by 2025 as compared to 2005 levels.[37] The United States also officially made climate change a top priority in the first three-quarters of its two-year (2015–2017) position as chair of the Arctic Council under then-president Obama.[38] The Arctic Council is a high-level organization of eight countries with Arctic territories and six native groups that inhabit the region.[39] In related developments, negotiations with Canada and Mexico yielded a joint commitment to produce half of the continent's electricity from non-emitting sources, including hydropower, wind, solar, and energy efficiency by 2025.[40]

With the Trump presidency, however, the United States commitment has been thrown into serious doubt. In June 2017, President Trump announced his intention to withdraw from the Agreement (legally permissible on November 4, 2020, three years after the Agreement came into force) or to negotiate more advantageous terms (although it is unclear what such terms might entail). United States public support for action on climate change remains contested and fragile. Recent opinion research finds Americans increasingly polarized regarding the environment; indeed, there appears to have been an upsurge in organized denial responding to the Paris Agreement and other international treaties.[41] A large number of U.S. politicians openly and vociferously question the scientific basis and desirability of climate action. There has been a significant increase in the recurrent efforts in Congress to withdraw funding from climate change–related initiatives. A major element of the Obama administration's effort to achieve climate change goals through executive action, the Clean Power Plan, was first delayed by a lawsuit challenging its legality[42] and now seems likely to be replaced by much weaker regulations by the Trump administration. U.S. withdrawal from the Paris Agreement is a very real possibility—and perhaps a likelihood. U.S. actions at COP24 in Poland in 2018 continue to reflect the retreating direction away from climate action that the Trump administration and U.S. leadership are taking.[43]

These developments in the United States have fostered doubt, hesitation, and distress around the world. Nonetheless, the primary reaction of most other countries has been a reaffirmation of their commitment to the Agreement.[44] Similarly, 14 U.S. states and one territory, representing 40 percent of the U.S. economy, have jointly vowed to meet their portion of the U.S. commitment on their own, regardless of the activities of the federal government. They claim that they are successfully doing so while also achieving economic growth.[45] This "U.S.

Climate Alliance" was also represented at the November 2017 COP23 in Germany. Additionally, considerable movement toward climate change mitigation is occurring through market processes, as many businesses move away from high-carbon fuels. How damaging the U.S. retreat from climate action leadership will be remains to be seen, as other countries see geopolitical opportunities in taking greater leadership roles. But there can be no doubt it is damaging.

Meanwhile, Arctic temperatures continue to increase, with 2015 temperatures as much as 3° Celsius above long-term averages and 2017 temperatures reflecting a continuing warming trend.[46] Arctic glaciers continue to retreat. Arctic sea ice continues to disappear, now lasting three to nine weeks less than it did in 1979.[47] Taking advantage, luxury cruise ships have passed through the Northwest Passage two summers in a row.[48] A Russian tanker has carried a cargo of liquefied natural gas from Norway through the northern sea route above Russia to South Korea.[49] Arctic shorelines erode more quickly every year. Arctic permafrost continues to melt. The list goes on.

We close with a question: Is this book an elegy to the Arctic? The answer depends in part on what we mean by "elegy." If it means "a song or poem of lamentation for the dead,"[50] then no, this is not an elegy because the Arctic is not (yet) dead. It is changing rapidly, however, and in many ways irreversibly. On the other hand, if by elegy we mean "a piece of writing . . . imbued with a sense of mourning or melancholy affection for something,"[51] then yes, this book is a very much an elegy. Whether it becomes an elegy by the first definition depends critically on whether enough of the many potential governance responses outlined above can be activated quickly, cooperatively, fully, and comprehensively enough to prevent catastrophic climate change, thereby allowing life in the Arctic to adapt and take on new, sustainable forms. Unfortunately, we cannot really know at publication time whether this book will turn out to be an elegy of the first kind. The Arctic can be described as mortally wounded and dying . . . but it is not dead yet.

Elegy

1. A song or poem of lamentation, esp. for the dead; a memorial poem. Also as a mass noun.

2. *Music.* A piece of instrumental music created as a lament or having a melancholic or mournful style.

3. A piece of writing, drama, art, etc., imbued with a sense of mourning or melancholy affection for something. Chiefly with *for, to.*

Notes

1. L. Ludovicoeinaudi, "Ludovico Einaudi—'Elegy for the Arctic,' Official Live (Greenpeace)," YouTube, Jan. 20, 2016; https://www.youtube.com/watch?v=2DLnhdnSUVs.

2. K. Anthony et al., "Methane Emissions Proportional to Permafrost Carbon Thawed in Arctic Lakes since the 1950s." *Nature Geoscience* 9 (Aug. 22, 2016): 679–82, http://www.nature.com/ngeo/journal/v9/n9/full/ngeo2795.html.

3. J. Blunden and D. S. Arndt, eds., "State of the Climate in 2016," *Bulletin of the American Meteorological Society* 98, no. 8 (2017): S93–S128, Doi :10.1175/2017BAMStatementoftheClimate.I.

4. U.S. Dept. of Commerce, National Oceanic and Atmospheric Administration, D. Nuccitelli, "NOAA: 2017 Was 3rd Warmest Year on Record for the Globe: NOAA, NASA Scientists Confirm Earth's Long-Term Warming Trend Continues," Jan. 18, 2018; https://www.noaa.gov/news/noaa-2017-was-3rd-warmest-year-on-record-for-globe.

5. G. Vaidyanathan, "Earth Shattered a Lot of Climate Records in 2015," *ClimateWire,* Aug. 3, 2016; http://www.eenews.net/stories/1060041122.

6. For a helpful recent review of implementation efforts, see J. F. C. Dimento, "Environmental Governance of the Arctic: Law, Effect, Now Implementation," *University of California at Irvine Law Review,* 6 (2017): 23–60.

7. B. Hulac, "As Green Group Marks Milestone, Firms Struggle to Say Why Climate Matters," *ClimateWire,* Aug. 18, 2016; http://www.eenews.net/climatewire/stories/1060041774.

8. Ibid.

9. The White House, "White House Announces Additional Commitments to The American Business Act on Climate Pledge," Dec. 1, 2015; https://www.whitehouse.gov/the-press-office/2015/12/01/white-house-announces-additional-commitments-american-business-act.

10. Global Climate Action, "NAZCA, Tracking Climate Action" (Oct. 10, 2016), http://climateaction.unfccc.int/.

11. J. Green, "Order Out of Chaos: Public and Private Rules for Managing Carbon," *Global Environmental Politics* 13, no. 2 (May 2013): 1–25.

12. B. Cashore, G. Auld, and D. Newsom, *Governing through Markets: Forest Certification and the Emergence of Non-State Authority* (New Haven: Yale University Press, 2004); S. Wood et al., "The Interactive Dynamics of Transnational Business Governance: A Challenge for Transnational Legal Theory," *Transnational Legal Theory* 6, no. 2 (Sept. 14, 2015): 333–69.

13. R. Stavins, "Carbon Markets: US Experience and International Linkage, Paper Prepared for Track II Dialogue to Strengthen China-U.S. Collaboration on Energy, Climate Change, and Sustainable Development, Beijing, China, June 12–13, 2016" (May 27, 2016).

14. J. Higham et al., "Climate Change, Tourist Air Travel, and Radical Emissions Reduction," *Journal of Cleaner Production* B, no. 16 (Jan. 16, 2016): 336–47.

15. Climate Bonds, "Climate Bonds Initiative," n.d.; http://www.climate-bonds.net/.

16. D. Cusick, "Ranks of Companies Setting an Internal Price on CO2 Emissions Almost Triple in a Year," *ClimateWire*, Sept. 21, 2015; http://www.eenews.net/stories/1060025003.

17. I. Rosen-Zvi, "You Are Too Soft!: What Can Corporate Social Responsibility Do for Climate Change?" *Minnesota Journal of Law, Science & Technology* 12, no. 2 (6) (2011): 527–72.

18. CDP, "Carbon Disclosure Project," n.d.; https://www.cdp.net/en.

19. C. Spreng and B. K. Sovacool, "All Hands on Deck: Polycentric Governance for Climate Change Insurance," *Climatic Change*, Aug. 26, 2016; http://link.springer.com/article/10.1007/s10584-016-1777-z.

20. Note also the growing reliance on private initiatives by individual governments as well as the Paris COP's invitation to nonparty stakeholders to contribute and increase their efforts. Paris Decision paragraphs 133–34; https://unfccc.int/resource/docs/2015/cop21/eng/l09.pdf.

21. P. Frumhoff and N. Oreskes, "Fossil Fuel Firms Are Still Bankrolling Climate Denial Lobby Groups," *The Guardian*, March 25, 2015; https://www.theguardian.com/environment/2015/mar/25/fossil-fuel-firms-are-still-bankrolling-climate-denial-lobby-groups.

22. Rainforest Action Network, Sierra Club, Banktrack, and Oilchange International, "Shorting the Climate: Fossil Fuel Finance Report Card 2016," Oil Change International; http://priceofoil.org/content/uploads/2016/06/Shorting_the_Climate_2016.pdf.

23. Green, "Order out of Chaos."

24. O. Eliasson and M. Rosing, "Ice Watch," Dec. 3–12, 2015; http://icewatchparis.com/.

25. United Nations Framework Convention on Climate Change, "Adoption of the Paris Agreement." The Paris Outcome included, first, a "Decision" of the COP and second, an "Agreement" framed as an annex to the Decision.

The Agreement is relatively short, including 29 articles on approximately 11 pages, while the Decision includes 140 paragraphs on approximately 19 pages. The Decision discusses a number of procedural matters and, importantly, the importance of nonparty actors, including businesses, financial institutions, NGOs, cities, and other subnational authorities (Paris: Nov. 30–Dec. 11, 2015); https://unfccc.int/resource/docs/2015/cop21/eng/l09.pdf.

26. United Nations Climate Change Conference (Paris 2015 and Marrakech 2016), *The Marrakech Partnership for Global Climate Action*; http://unfccc.int/files/paris_agreement/application/pdf/marrakech_partnership_for_global_climate_action.pdf.

27. United Nations Framework Convention on Climate Change, 2015, Article 2.1.a. While the 2° goal may be achievable with extraordinary effort, the 1.5°, insisted upon most urgently by low-lying island countries, seems nearly impossible. The COP Decision includes a request that the IPCC undertake assessment of possible 1.5° pathways. COP21 Decision paragraph 21; https://unfccc.int/resource/docs/2015/cop21/eng/l09.pdf.

28. R. Cleetus, "US Must Do More to Meet Paris Climate Change Commitments," Union of Concerned Scientists, May 10, 2016; http://blog.ucsusa.org/rachel-cleetus/us-paris-agreement-climate-change-commitments; J. Rogelj et al., "Paris Agreement Climate Proposals Need a Boost to Keep Warming Well Below 2° C," *Nature: International Weekly Journal of Science* 534 (June 30, 2016): 631–39; http://www.nature.com/nature/journal/v534/n7609/full/nature18307.html?WT.feed_name=subjects_climate-change-mitigation.

29. "New governance" is a term that has been used over the past two decades to refer to mechanisms that do not rely primarily on hierarchical rules to achieve public goals. For an overview see, e.g., T. J. Melish and E. Meidinger, "Protect, Respect, Remedy, *and Participate*: 'New Governance' Lessons for the Ruggie Framework," in *The UN Guiding Principles on Business and Human Rights: Foundations and Implementation*, ed. Radu Mares (Leiden and Boston: Martinus Nijhoff, 2012).

30. D. Bodansky, "The Paris Climate Change Agreement: A New Hope?" *American Journal of International Law* 110 (May 17, 2016).

31. United Nations Framework Convention on Climate Change, "The Paris Agreement," Article 7.1; http://unfccc.int/paris_agreement/items/9485.php.

32. Ibid., Article 8.1; http://unfccc.int/paris_agreement/items/9485.php.

33. Ibid., Paragraph 52; http://unfccc.int/paris_agreement/items/9485.php.

34. Ibid., Article 21.1; http://unfccc.int/paris_agreement/items/9485.php.

35. T. Phillips, F. Harvey, and A. Yuhas, "Breakthrough as US and China Agree to Ratify Paris Climate Deal," *The Guardian*, Sept. 3, 2016; https://www.theguardian.com/environment/2016/sep/03/breakthrough-us-china-agree-ratify-paris-climate-change-deal.

36. United Nations Framework Convention on Climate Change, Paris Agreement—Status of Ratification, "From the UN System"; http://unfccc.int/2860.php.

37. J. Chemnick, "U.S. and China Formally Commit to Paris Climate Accord," *Scientific American*, Sept. 6, 2016; https://www.scientificamerican.com/article/u-s-and-china-formally-commit-to-paris-climate-accord/.

38. It is worth noting that climate change is the third of three priorities, the first two being economic development and safety and security; U.S. Department of State, "U.S. Chairmanship of the Arctic Council," n.d.; http://www.state.gov/e/oes/ocns/opa/arc/uschair/.

39. Ibid.

40. J. Eilperin and B. Dennis, "U.S., Canada and Mexico Vow to Get Half Their Electricity from Clean Power by 2025," *Washington Post*, June 27, 2016; https://www.washingtonpost.com/news/energy-environment/wp/2016/06/27/u-s-canada-and-mexico-to-pledge-to-source-half-their-overall-electricity-with-clean-power-by-2025/?utm_term=.c20c2aef734f.

41. R. Dunlap, A. McCright, and J. Yarosh, "The Political Divide on Climate Change: Partisan Polarization Widens in the U.S.," *Environment: Science and Policy for Sustainable Development* 58, no. 5 (Aug. 25, 2016): 4–23; http://www.tandfonline.com/doi/full/10.1080/00139157.2016.1208995.

42. West Virginia v. EPA, 136 S.Ct. 1000 (2016) (mem).

43. M. McGrath, "Climate Change: Five Things We've Learnt from COP24," *BBC News*, Dec. 16, 2018; https://www.bbc.com/news/science-environment-46582265.

44. S. Sengupta et al., "As Trump Exits Paris Agreement, Other Nations Are Defiant," *New York Times*, June 1, 2017.

45. A. Skibell, "Governors Denounce Trump, Announce Progress to Paris Targets," *E&E NewsPM*, Sept. 20, 2017, https://www.eenews.net/eenewspm/stories/1060061245/search?keyword=governors+denounce+trump.

46. National Oceanic and Atmospheric Administration, "Unprecedented Arctic Warmth in 2016 Triggers Massive Decline in Sea Ice, Snow," Dece. 13, 2016; http://www.noaa.gov/media-release/unprecedented-arctic-warmth-in-2016-triggers-massive-decline-in-sea-ice-snow. R. Lindsey, "2017 Arctic Report Card: Extreme Fall Warmth Drove Near-Record Annual Temperatures," NOAA Climate.gov, Dec. 12, 2017; https://www.climate.gov/news-features/featured-images/2017-arctic-report-card-extreme-fall-warmth-drove-near-record-annual.

47. C. Harvey, "Every Single Part of the Arctic Is Becoming Worse for Polar Bears," *Washington Post*, Sept. 4, 2016; https://www.washingtonpost.com/news/energy-environment/wp/2016/09/14/every-single-part-of-the-arctic-is-becoming-worse-for-polar-bears/?utm_term=.fb7723b82a25.

48. C. Beeler, "Climate Change Brings Melting Ice, and Cruise Passengers, to Canada," *USA Today*, Sept. 20, 2017; https://www.usatoday.com/story/

news/world/2017/09/20/climate-change-brings-melting-ice-and-cruise-passengers-canadas-north/684090001/.

49. P. Barkham, "Russian Tanker Sails through Arctic with Icebreaker for First Time," *The Guardian*, Aug. 24, 2017.

50. J. A. Simpson and E. S. C. Weiner, *The Oxford English Dictionary*. 3rd ed. (Oxford: Clarendon Press, 2014).

51. Ibid.

Acknowledgments

The editors of *The Big Thaw* wish to express their deep appreciation to the many individuals and organizations who helped make this book a reality.

Anna Kertulla, Director for Social Sciences in the National Science Foundation's Polar Program, recognized the value of such a conference early on and strongly advocated for this work to further understanding of the human impacts on and of climate change in the Arctic and Antarctic. Key financial support was provided by the Social Science Division of the National Science Foundation's Polar Program (Grants 1139711, 1045099) and by the Baldy Center for Law & Social Policy at the University at Buffalo, State University of New York. Staff from the Baldy Center, University at Buffalo School of Law's Clinical Legal Education Department, and University at Buffalo's Department of Anthropology and Archaeological Survey provided logistical support for the conference and additional assistance along the route to publication.

Numerous postdoctoral, graduate and law students contributed to this project, including: Andrea DiNatale (law), Devin Franklin (law), Hans Harmsen (anthropology), Dr. Priyantha Karunaratne (anthropology), Heidi Lee, Amanda LeGasse (law), Matthew McClesky (sociology), Dannielle O'Toole (law), Erika Ruhl (anthropology), Bridget Steele (law), and Yaqi Yuan (sociology). Some are pursuing professional careers addressing issues raised in this book.

Finally, and most importantly, organizational wizard Elisa Lackey kept the whole enterprise moving forward while the three editors went off in too many directions to count. We could not have done this without her.

Contributors

Enrique del Acebo Ibáñez holds a licenciate in sociology from the University of Buenos Aires, Argentina. He received his Master's and Doctorate degrees in sociology from Complutensis University of Madrid, Spain, and completed postgraduate studies in educational management in Brussels, Belgium. He also holds a degree in film studies from Argentina's Union of the Cinematographic Industry (SICA). He has served as a visiting professor at various universities in the United States (U.C.L.A., Bergen College (where he was a Fulbright Professor), University of Southern California, University of San Diego, University of Notre Dame) and in Europe (Paris, France; Oslo, Norway; Reykjavík, Iceland; Akureyri, Iceland; Siena, Italy; Prague, Czech Republic; La Coruña, Spain; Jyväskylä, Finland; Oulu, Lapland-Finland; Niš, Serbia). He served as Fulbright Professor at the Bergen Community College (1993–1994). Currently del Acebo Ibáñez serves as a full professor at the University of Buenos Aires, principal researcher at the Argentine National Council for Scientific Research, director of the Center for Research on Local Community & Participation, president of the International Association of Circumpolar Sociocultural Issues (IACSI), and editor-in-chief of three peer-reviewed scientific journals: *Arctic & Antarctic—International Journal on Circumpolar Sociocultural Issues*, *Realidad—Latin American Journal on Social Psychology*, and *Organizational Analysis—Latin American Journal on Social Sciences*. del Acebo Ibáñez is the author of 25 books, some translated to Finnish, Icelandic, and English, and numerous scientific articles published in national and international journals. He has directed widely submitted and viewed experimental and documentary films.

Cinnamon Piñon Carlarne is a professor of law at the Michael E. Moritz College of Law at the Ohio State University. She teaches in the areas of environmental, energy, and tort law. Carlarne's scholarship focuses on the evolution of systems of international environmental law, with an emphasis on climate change. She has written numerous articles exploring questions of international environmental law as well as a book on comparative climate change law and policy with Oxford University Press, and an edited textbook on oceans and human health. She is also one of the editors for Oxford University Press's forthcoming *Handbook of International Climate Change Law* as well as being on the editorial board for *Transnational Environmental Law* (Cambridge University Press) and *Climate Law* (IOS Press). Prior to joining the Moritz faculty, she was the Harold Woods Research Fellow in Environmental Law at Wadham College, Oxford, and an assistant professor at the University of South Carolina's School of Law. Professor Carlarne received her J.D. from the University of California, Berkeley, and her B.C.L. and M.Sc. in environmental change and management from the University of Oxford, where she was a Marshall Scholar.

Kim Diana Connolly, a professor of law at the University at Buffalo School of Law, serves as the vice dean for advocacy and experiential education, director of clinical legal education, and director of the Environmental Advocacy Clinic. Her areas of scholarly interest include natural resources and environmental law, particularly wetlands law and policy and other Clean Water Act matters as well as climate change and resiliency. Her scholarly works have appeared in various journals and books, and she has spoken frequently nationally and internationally on wetlands and other matters. Professor Connolly was part of the U.S. Delegation to the 2012 Ramsar Conference of the Parties and has been admitted as a wetlands expert at other Ramsar conferences, served as chair of the U.S. National Ramsar Committee, writes on international wetlands matters, and serves clients with her clinic students seeking legal support for Ramsar nominations. Before joining the law faculty at University at Buffalo School of Law, Professor Connolly taught at the University of South Carolina School of Law. Prior to her teaching career, she practiced law with a number of Washington, D.C., law firms, and for a number of years represented various Alaska Native and governmental units in the Arctic region of the United States. She received her J.D., magna cum laude, from Georgetown University Law Center and her LL.M. with highest honors from George Washington University Law School.

André Costopoulos is vice-provost, dean of students, and professor of anthropology at the University of Alberta. Previously he served as professor of anthropology and dean of students at McGill University. Born and raised in Montreal, Costopoulos holds a BA (Hons) in anthropology from McGill, an MSc in anthropology from the Université de Montréal, and a PhD in archaeology from the University of Oulu, Finland. His research interests include survival strategies of prehistoric and modern hunters and gathers (including the homeless), the evolution of social complexity, human adaptation to environmental change, quantitative and computational methods in archeology, agent-based simulation in anthropology, and prehistoric exchange networks. He has had numerous grants from Canadian and U.S. granting agencies and has numerous publications. He has done considerable anthropological and archaeological field work in Northern Finland and Northern Canada, particularly in Northern Quebec near James Bay.

Duncan Depledge is the Politics & International Studies Fellow at Loughborough University and senior advisor to the British All-Party Parliamentary Group for the Polar Regions. His research interests include critical geopolitics, geopolitics, global politics, international security, international relations, assemblages, materialism, climate change, and the polar regions. Over the past decade, Depledge has explored the changing geopolitics of the Arctic, with a specific focus on Britain's response. Depledge's work has been funded by the UK Economic and Social Research Council and the Royal United Services Institute, an internationally renowned defense and security think tank based in London. Depledge is a member of the United Kingdom's Arctic and Antarctic Partnership Steering Committee. He received his PhD from Royal Holloway (University of London) in the United Kingdom, and also holds an MPhil in geographical research (University of Cambridge), an MA in political theory (University of Sheffield), and a BA (Hons) in history (University of Sheffield).

Sarah Elder serves as professor of film in the Department of Media Study at the University at Buffalo and adjunct professor in the Department of Anthropology. She is also research associate at the Alaska Center for Documentary Film at the University of Alaska, Fairbanks. Elder is an international award–winning documentary filmmaker whose work focuses on collaborative media practices and the ethics of filming across cultural and social boundaries. She teaches courses in documentary film, ethnographic media, nonfiction studies, media ethics, visual anthropology, and media exhibitions. Her research focuses on documentary practice, Alaska Native cultures, Indigenous knowledge, interviewing practices and climate change. Her current project, *Surviving Arctic Climate Change*, looks at the consequences of warming on the Yup'ik Eskimo village of Emmonak, Alaska. Working in Alaska since 1973, Elder filmed with Alaska Native communities pioneering a community collaborative approach to making documentary. She co-founded and co-directed the Alaska Native Heritage Film Project at the University of Alaska from 1973–1993. Elder's films have won numerous awards and distinctions: In 2006, her documentary *Uksuum Cauyai: The Drums of Winter* (produced and directed by Elder and Kamerling) was selected to the prestigious National Film Registry (Library of Congress). Her films have exhibited at MOMA, Cinémathèque Française, Musée de L'Homme, Royal Anthropological Institute, International Center for Photography, Flaherty, Aperture, and ARTE TV. In 2006 she received the SUNY Buffalo Chancellor's Award for excellence in teaching.

Michael B. Gerrard is Andrew Sabin Professor of Professional Practice at Columbia Law School, where he teaches courses on environmental and energy law and directs the Center for Climate Change Law. He is also associate chair of the faculty of Columbia's Earth Institute. Before joining the Columbia faculty in January 2009, he was partner in charge of the 110-lawyer New York office of Arnold & Porter LLP; he now serves as senior counsel to the firm. He practiced environmental law in New York City full time from 1979 to 2008 and tried numerous cases and argued many appeals in federal and state courts and administrative tribunals. He was the 2004–2005 chair of the American Bar Association's 10,000-member Section of Environment, Energy and Resources. He has also chaired the executive committee of the New York City Bar Association, and the Environmental Law Section of the New York State Bar Association. He is currently a member of the executive committees of the boards of the Environmental Law Institute and the American College of Environmental Lawyers. Gerrard is author or editor of eleven books, two of which were named Best Law Book of the Year by the Association of American Publishers: *Environmental Law Practice Guide* (twelve volumes, 1992) and *Brownfields Law and Practice: The Cleanup* and *Redevelopment of Contaminated Land* (four volumes, 1998). He is also the editor of *Global Climate Change and U.S. Law; The Law of Adaptation to Climate Change: U.S. and International Aspects* (with Katrina F. Kuh) (2012); and *Threatened Island Nations: Legal Implications of Rising Seas and a Changing Climate* (with Gregory E. Wannier) (2013). Gerrard received his BA from Columbia University and his JD from New York University Law School, where he was a Root Tilden Scholar.

Laura A. Henry has a PhD in political science from the University of California, Berkeley, and is an associate professor of government at Bowdoin College. Her research investigates Russia's post-Soviet transformation, focusing on state society relations, environmental politics, and the interaction of transnational and local nonstate actors. Henry is the author of *Red to Green: Environmental Activism in Post-Soviet Russia* (Cornell University Press, 2010) and the co-editor of *Russian Civil Society: A Critical Assessment* (M. E. Sharpe, 2006). Her work has appeared in *Post-Soviet Affairs, Environmental Politics, Global Environmental Politics,* and *Europe-Asia Studies,* among other journals.

Elizabeth Ann Kronk Warner joined the University of Kansas law faculty in June 2012. Professor Kronk Warner teaches property, federal Indian law, Native American natural resources and tribal law. In addition to teaching, Professor Kronk Warner also directs the KU Tribal Law and Government Center. Prior to her arrival at KU, Kronk Warner served on the law faculties at Texas Tech University and the University of Montana. In 2010, Kronk Warner was selected to serve as an Environmental Justice Young Fellow through the Woodrow Wilson International Center for Scholars and U.S.-China Partnership for Environmental Law at Vermont Law School. Professor Kronk Warner's scholarship examines the intersection of environmental and natural resources law and Indian law, most recently focusing on the impacts of climate change on indigenous peoples and energy development in Indian country. In 2013, she served as a co-editor and author for *Climate Change and Indigenous Peoples: The Search for Legal Remedies* (Randall S. Abate and Elizabeth Ann Kronk eds, Edward Elgar, 2013). She also is an author of *Native American Natural Resources* (3rd ed., Carolina Academic Press 2013). In addition to teaching, Kronk Warner serves as an appellate judge for the Sault Ste. Marie Tribe of Chippewa Indians Court of Appeals in Michigan. Before entering academia, Kronk Warner practiced environmental, Indian, and energy law as an associate in the Washington, D.C., offices of Latham & Watkins LLP and Troutman Sanders LLP. Kronk Warner previously served as chair of the Federal Bar Association Indian Law Section and was elected to the association's national board of directors in 2011. She received her JD from the University of Michigan Law School and a BS from Cornell University. Kronk Warner is a citizen of the Sault Ste. Marie Tribe of Chippewa Indians.

Torill Christine Lindstrøm, Dr. Philos., is professor of psychology at the Department of Psychosocial Science, Faculty of Psychology, University of Bergen (UiB), Norway, and SapienCE, Centre for Early Sapiens Behaviour, CoE, Faculty of Humanities, University of Bergen, Norway. Her present research-group affiliations are: DICE (Decision, Intuition, Cognition, Emotion), Faculty of Psychology, UiB; CLASSICAL STUDIES, Dept of Archaeology, History, Culture, and Religion (AHKR), Faculty of Humanities, UiB; and she is associated with Causation in Science (CauSci) Dept of Philosophy, University of Oslo, Norway. She holds memberships in: Norsk Adferdsmedisinsk Forening (NAMF), European Association of Archaeologists (EAA), and Associazione Internazionale di Archeologia Classica (AIAC). Her research is transdisciplinary and multi-methodological. Her main fields of research in psychology are: reactions to and, coping with, stress, crisis, and demanding life situations (grief, cancer, old age, chronic pain). Her main fields of research in archaeology are: facial expressions in Minoan Bronze Age painting (Akrotiri, Santorini); gendered and status-related facial expressions in Roman classical art; Roman sexual gender categories and sexual behaviors; Dionysianism as a religion and cult, and its psychological mechanisms; the Great Fresco in Villa dei Misteri (Pompeii, Italy); human-animal relations in Roman contexts; human-animal relations in various contexts and across periods (from Paleolithicum to modern times); and issues regarding methodology and theory of science within archaeology. She has been a leader position in NorgesNaturvernforbund (Earth Norway).

Errol Meidinger is SUNY Distinguished Professor, Margaret W. Wong Professor of Law, and director of the Baldy Center for Law & Social Policy at University at Buffalo School of Law. Much of his current research focuses on efforts to use "supra-governmental" regulatory mechanisms, such as environmental certification and fair labor standards programs, to improve the social and environmental performance of business organizations. He is particularly interested in how these programs coordinate and compete with each other and with state-based programs, and how the larger governance ensembles that are being formed may reshape law globally. Meidinger is also writing on the subjects of "soft law," implementation of corporate social responsibility initiatives, and recent bans by the EU and United States on importation of illegally harvested natural resources. Meidinger serves as director of the Baldy Center for Law and Social Policy, a research institute that advances the university's role in cutting-edge research on law and legal institutions. He previously served as the founding director of the UB Environment & Society Institute. Meidinger also holds an appointment as an honorary professor at the University of Freiburg, Germany, where he served as a Fulbright Professor in 1999–2000. During 2006–2007 he was the Distinguished Environmental Law Scholar at Lewis and Clark Law School in Portland, Ore. He earned his JD and PhD at Northwestern University.

Professor **Milton Núñez** grew up mainly in Cuba and the United States and received his primary and secondary education in both. He studied engineering in Detroit (BSc 1969), quaternary geology in Helsinki, Finland (MSc 1972, FL 1978), and archaeology in Calgary (PhD 1985). Since 1969, he has lived in Finland. He worked as a special researcher in the Museum of the Åland Islands (1984–1994) until called as professor to create an archaeology department at the University of Oulu, Finland, in 1994. He served as the Oulu archaeology chair until October 2012. He has been adjunct professor at the archaeology department of the University of Turku, Finland, since 1991, and at the Faculty of Medicine of the University of Granada, Spain, since 2003. In addition to Finland, he has carried out research and/or taught in Canada, Egypt, France, Italy, Mexico, Russia, Spain, Sweden, Syria, the UK, and the United States. Besides archaeology, his research interests have involved biological and forensic anthropology, paleodiets, paleopathology, paleoclimatology, and shoreline displacement. Throughout his career, Prof. Núñez has obtained numerous research grants. He received several awards including being knighted (First class Knight of the Order of the White Rose of Finland, 2009) and, most recently, an honorary Doctor's degree from Stockholm University, Sweden (2012).

Courtney Price is the communications officer at the Conservation of Arctic Flora and Fauna (CAFF), the biodiversity working group of the Arctic Council, a high-level intergovernmental forum to promote cooperation, coordination, and interaction among the Arctic States, with the involvement of Arctic Indigenous Peoples. Courtney joined the CAFF International Secretariat in Akureyri, Iceland, in 2011 and works to develop a consistent approach to CAFF-wide organizational communications activities and platforms. She has been especially active in the Arctic Biodiversity Assessment and the Circumpolar Biodiversity Monitoring Program. She joined CAFF to specialize in Arctic issues after three years as a science and technology liaison officer at Environment Canada, and two years in communications for the Canadian Wildlife Service, where she worked to promote the findings of the wildlife research community to departmental policy audiences. Before that, she worked at the Centre for Canadian-Australian Studies at the University of Wollongong, Australia, as part of an international internship program of the Canadian government. Ms. Price has a degree in journalism, with a double major in mass communications, from Carleton University, Ottawa, Canada, as well as an MSc in global challenges through the University of Edinburgh, Scotland.

Mark W. Roberts has practiced law for 32 years—specializing in international environmental, energy, and land use law and litigation. He founded ECO Policy Advisors, a consultancy providing support to clients in international fora to find sustainable and collaborative solutions to complex environmental, trade, finance and indigenous land rights issues. He is actively involved in international environmental, climate, deforestation and trade issues. He participates at the Montreal Protocol on Substances that Deplete the Ozone Layer and other international fora to enhance actions to phase out the use of HFCs, to stop deforestation, and to combat illegal trade. Mr. Roberts regularly speaks and writes on legal, technical, and policy issues related to climate change, control of greenhouse gases (particularly HFCs and ozone-depleting substances), availability of HFC-free alternatives and energy efficiency.

Theodore Steegmann received his BA in anthropology from the University of Kansas in 1958 and his PhD in anthropology from the University of Michigan in 1965. Steegmann was on the faculty of the University at Buffalo Department of Anthropology from 1966 to 2004, and now is an emeritus member of the physical anthropology faculty. Honors and positions include the SUNY Chancellor's Award for Teaching Excellence, presidency of the Human Biology Association, UB Anthropology chairmanship, and the HBA Franz Boas Lifetime Achievement Award. Steegmann is widely regarded as one of the world's leading researchers on the biology of cold adaptation among both contemporary and prehistoric human populations. He has done laboratory, archival, and field work centered on specific biological and behavioral human adaptations to stressors, including low temperature, undernutrition, and hard physical work. Several productive field projects included venues in sub-Arctic Canada, Alaska, Northern China, the Philippines, and in Western New York.

David A. Stroud is senior ornithologist with the UK's Joint Nature Conservation Committee, and has been involved in the management of many of the UK's bird monitoring programs including the Breeding Bird Survey, the Wetland Bird Survey, Scottish Raptor Monitoring Scheme, and the Rare Breeding Birds Panel. Stroud has been a member of and now chairs the Ramsar's Scientific and Technical Review Panel (as thematic lead for work on site designation) and has also actively contributed to the work of Wetlands International, the EU Birds Directive's Ornis Committee (and its Scientific Working Group), the African-Eurasian Waterbird Agreement's (AEWA) Technical Committee (currently as chair and representative of NW & C Europe), as well as the International Wader Study Group. Stroud was heavily involved in issues related to the spread of Highly Pathogenic Avian Influenza H5N1 from 2008 and was a member of the Working Group established by the European Food Safety Authority, which undertook a risk assessment of the risk of HPAI H5N1 arriving in Europe, as well as representing the Ramsar Convention on the International Scientific Task Force on Avian Influenza and Wild Birds. Among his ornithological interests is the long-term population study of Greenland White-fronted Geese, having undertaken research through the international range of that population including research on breeding areas in Greenland since 1979. He recently coordinated an international action plan under AEWA to address the causes of long-term population decline of the population. Stroud won the UNEP African-Eurasian Waterbird Agreement Waterbird Conservation Award in the individual category in 2005.

T. L. Thurston studies the late prehistoric, proto-historic, and historic periods in northern and western Europe, roughly 800 BCE to 1650 CE, focusing on the relationships between ordinary people and their leaders, on a continuum from peaceful civic engagement to uprisings and civil war. To study these issues, research is centered on regions where conflicts between communities and their governments have erupted into violent conflict. Fieldwork examines the parallel developments in small rural settlements where stresses are experienced, and the symbolic and practical nodes of government power. This ongoing research currently focuses on case studies on Northern Ireland and Sweden.

Svetlana A. Tulaeva is an assistant professor at the Russian Presidential Academy of National Economy and Public Administration. She holds a PhD in legislative studies from the University of Eastern Finland and PhD (candidat nauk) in sociology from St. Petersburg State University. Her dissertation topics were devoted to the implementation of global standards in Russian forest and oil sectors. She participated in international research projects concerning the role of nonstate actors in the governance of natural resources. Her research interests include legislative studies and economic sociology. She has published numerous articles in a range of journals, including *Europe-Asia Studies*, *Forest Policy and Economics*, *Sustainability*, and others.

Maria S. Tysiachniouk holds a Master of Science in environmental studies from Bard College, NY, a PhD in biology from the Russian Academy of Sciences, and a PhD in sociology from Wageningen University (2012) She has taught at Herzen Pedagogical University in St. Petersburg, St. Petersburg State University, Johns Hopkins University, Dickinson College, Ramapo College of New Jersey, Towson University, Wageningen University, University of Lapland, University of Eastern Finland and Erfurt University. Since 2004 she studied global governance through FSC certification. Since then she has combined her research with practitioners work in the FSC system. Since 2012 she started the extensive research on transnational oil production chains in the Arctic. Maria S. Tysiachniouk has written more than two hundred publications on topics related to transnational environmental governance, edited several books and has had fieldwork experience in several countries and regions. She is currently chair of the environmental sociology group at the Center for Independent Social Research, St. Petersburg, Russia, and a researcher at the Environmental Policy Group at Wageningen University.

Ezra B. W. Zubrow is Distinguished Service Professor of Anthropology at the University at Buffalo, professor of anthropology (SO) at the University of Toronto, and honorary research associate at McDonald Institute of Archaeology, University of Cambridge. He also holds the positions of senior research scientist, National Center for Geographic Information Analysis, as well as president of the Buffalo Center chapter of the United University Professions. He has written or edited more than 10 books and over 100 articles as well as received more than 20 million dollars in grants for his 50 plus expeditions around the world. His research has focused on demographic, ecological, and spatial aspects of extreme environments and climate change.

Index

www.ingramcontent.com/pod-product-compliance
Lightning Source LLC
Chambersburg PA
CBHW030855270326
41929CB00008B/430